European Paintings Before 1500

Catalogue of Paintings : Part One

THE CLEVELAND MUSEUM OF ART

European Paintings Before 1500

Catalogue of Paintings : Part One

Published by The Cleveland Museum of Art : 1974

European Paintings Before 1500 is the first part of The Cleveland Museum of Art
Catalogue of Paintings which will eventually comprise the following:

Part Two   *Illuminated Manuscripts*
Part Three   *European Paintings of the 16th, 17th, and 18th Centuries*
Part Four   *European Paintings of the 19th Century*
Part Five   *American Paintings to 1900*
Part Six   *Modern Painting*

All rights reserved by The Cleveland Museum of Art,
University Circle, Cleveland, Ohio 44106
Library of Congress Catalogue Card Number 72-83626

ISBN: 910386-19-6

Printed in Great Britain at the University Printing House,
Cambridge

Preface

Various rationalizations, some even justified, can be developed to explain the lack of adequate catalogues for the collections of museums in the United States. Isolated early examples can be cited, such as the catalogues of the Indian and Classical collections of the Museum of Fine Arts, Boston, or of the paintings in the Isabella Stewart Gardner Museum in the same city. Other publications were largely confined to highly specialized collections, such as the Buckingham Chinese bronzes and the Sonnenschein Chinese jades in the Art Institute of Chicago. But until recently there were precious few catalogues of whole painting or sculpture collections in public museums. Check lists, picture books, or limited-entry "catalogues" have been our common lot.

The many rationalizations can be reduced to a few with some substance. American collections have been developing rapidly. Not many are as extensive and fixed as the holdings in the Old World inherited from royal, princely, or other aristocratic sources. The demanding task of acquiring works of art does take a major portion of a scholar's energies. American museums have been involved with a wider public and in educational activities foreign to European museums until recent years. This too demands time, energy, and intelligence from the professional staff. Quality publication *is* a complicated and expensive process in this country, and the necessary monies have seemed to be a luxury to the administrations of the museums. American museums are understaffed when compared with their major European counterparts. And, finally, there has been a varying gap between the predominantly scholarly attitude of institutions of higher learning and the often aesthetic and/or popular approach of the art museums.

This general situation has begun to change. Well-documented, scholarly catalogues of their painting and sculpture collections have recently been published by The Metropolitan Museum and The Frick Collection, among others. The need has been obvious for decades. While not books for popular education, such catalogues provide the basic sources for approaching the truth of the works of art committed to the care of our museums.

At the Cleveland Museum we have been – and will probably continue to be – tardy in producing the numerous catalogues we owe to both scholars and public. This is the first part of a series of painting catalogues. The second part, comprising illuminated manuscripts and single leaves before 1500, and the third part, European paintings from 1500 to 1800, are presently in preparation. In addition, a catalogue of the Museum's important collection of early textiles will soon be published. While all of these (and more) have been projected for some time, and have existed in embryonic form for a somewhat lesser time, the generous program of grants from The Ford Foundation has given the needed final impetus for their completion. Museum Trustees have encouraged and supported the now-continuing project; the contributions of staff and colleagues are noted in Henry Sayles Francis' foreword. To all we give deserved praise and thanks.

The perfect catalogue exists in some empyrean realm, desired by all, and sometimes nearly achieved. Most scholars have their own Dantean register of catalogues, populated in increasing density from Paradise to Purgatory to the Inferno. But one cannot be judged without first being published. The very act of bringing a catalogue into existence is a large step forward, and we have now begun to perform the task. We hope the result is a useful addition to the growing number of American art museum catalogues.

Sherman E. Lee, *Director*

Contents

CONTENTS

Foreword

By 1966 – its fiftieth year – The Cleveland Museum of Art had assembled a notable representation of European and American paintings through generous gift, bequest, and purchase. Since the opening of the Museum in 1916, an effort has been made to publish important acquisitions in the CMA *Bulletin* and, occasionally, catalogues of collections which were bequeathed or donated. Ensuing research and scholarship in the art history field made changes in attribution necessary in some cases; more complete information was made possible in other cases – so by the time of the Museum's Golden Anniversary, some of our earlier publications were out of date. That, and the fact that there has never been a definitive catalogue of the primary collection, prompted the decision by the Trustees of the Museum – on recommendation of the Director and staff – to provide a thorough catalogue for the benefit of visitor, student, and scholar.

With the cooperation of The Ford Foundation, a project to publish a comprehensive catalogue of the entire paintings collection officially began at the time of the anniversary year. Fifteen years previous to that time, the beginnings of a systematic catalogue of the painting collection was planned by Louise H. Burchfield (then associate curator) and myself. Since that time, the major effort on this work has been continued by Nancy Coe Wixom, first as assistant curator of the department, and later as research assistant. From 1961 to 1968 Elizabeth de Fernandez-Gimenez helped with research and writing entries, first as assistant, then assistant curator, and later, research assistant. Ann Tzeutschler Lurie, present associate curator of paintings, has helped with the catalogue since she joined the staff in 1956. Wolfgang Stechow, professor emeritus of art history, Oberlin College, completed the German, Dutch, and Flemish entries of this first volume which includes the earliest Western European painting tradition up to the year 1500 – with every painting illustrated, along with details and comparative material.

Special thanks must be given to the many scholars who gave so generously of their time and expert opinions and to the museum staff members and private collectors who responded to our many requests for photographs and information. This catalogue is a cumulative effort of many years and the friendly cooperation of the scholarly community has been invaluable. Names of scholars who have offered opinions are given in the text. Many CMA staff members have cooperated to help in producing this catalogue but particular mention should be made of Georgina Toth, Reference Librarian; Merald E. Wrolstad, Editor of Museum Publications; Hannelore Osborne, Assistant in the Paintings Department; and Jean Cassill, Assistant in the Paintings Department, who edited this book.

A review of the growth of the collection of European paintings follows, although certainly a brief mention cannot begin to pay proper tribute to the enlightened leadership and generosity of the individuals who founded this Museum and these collections. It is no mere coincidence that almost all of the major cultural institutions in the city of Cleveland celebrated their fiftieth anniversaries within a short span of one or two years; many of the same family names appear on their lists of founders and original benefactors. It is our good fortune that our present-day position as an important member of this city's cultural community was given a firm foundation by our original benefactors; and in some cases, their children continue the family tradition of patronage and leadership in the arts.

Interest in art was part of the cultural development in Cleveland during the nineteenth century and resulted in the formation of numerous private collections, which in turn led to several large public exhibitions, including those of 1878, 1894, and 1913. In the late nineteenth century three independent trusts from the Huntington, Kelley, and Hurlbut bequests were designated to be used for a museum. In the early twentieth century they were combined to make The Cleveland Museum of Art a reality. The building was begun in 1914 and completed the winter of 1916. The inaugural exhibition was of considerable size and variety and included the founding gifts (already presented to the Museum for the permanent collection), shown together for the first time on this occasion.

When the Museum was established, the policy with regard to the collections was that all gifts should be unrestricted. Gifts and bequests were to be accepted and purchases made with the understanding that every object in the Museum galleries would be shown in its context of time and place, each properly labeled to credit the donor or fund. When J. H. Wade's initial gift was made, he personally requested that all the objects be exhibited in their respective places in history – not kept together as his collection. Thus began a policy which, with Trustee approval, has been consistently maintained.

The earliest of the donors was Hinman B. Hurlbut, who made his original bequest in 1884, including his own collection comprised primarily of important nineteenth-century American canvases, along with some European pictures. After the death of Mrs. Hurlbut the estate funds were too small to build a museum – his original intention – so the Hurlbut fund was allocated for purchases. Over the years both American and European paintings have come to the Museum through this fund, including two important French works: *Monsieur Boileau at the Café* by Toulouse-Lautrec and *Portrait of Mademoiselle Violette Heymann* by Redon (purchased by William M. Milliken in 1925 and 1926 – a relatively early time – before the great popularity of these artists).

In 1883–1884 Liberty E. Holden purchased for his wife the second collection formed by James Jackson Jarves in Italy; his first collection (with the exception of the Lorenzo di San Severino) had become the property of Yale University in 1864. This second collection was composed of Italian panels of the fifteenth century and later, with a few paintings from other schools. In 1914 Mr. and Mrs. Holden gave fifty-three pictures which were shown in the Cleveland Museum's inaugural exhibition. Subsequently, they both established funds – the L. E. Holden and Delia E. Holden Funds – for future additions to their collection in the field of early Italian painting and drawing. Distinctive items have been acquired through the Holden Funds, including the Andrea del Sarto *Sacrifice of Isaac* in 1937, and the Jacopo Bassano *Lazarus and the Rich Man* in 1939. In 1928, as a future memorial to Mrs. Holden, her family acquired *The Holy Family With the Infant St. John and St. Margaret* by Filippino Lippi – one of the outstanding pictures in the Museum collection.

The John Huntington Art and Polytechnic Trust, which with the Hurlbut Fund and Horace Kelley Art Foundation became the incorporated sources for creating the Museum, included a provision for the acquisition of works of art. The purchases thus made in 1915 became the nucleus of a small but choice group of American portraits. As the Museum grew, so did its purchase funds, and the Huntington Trust rarely appears in later years as the source for purchases except in a few notable instances, such as the acquisition in 1966 of three especially important early Italian panels: one by the earliest of the Lucca painters, Berlinghiero; and two panels by Giovanni di Paolo; all three from the Stoclet Collection, Brussels.

The fourth of the founding gifts to establish the painting collection came at the time of the inaugural exhibition in 1916 from Mr. and Mrs. J. H. Wade. They gave a group of pictures which included the first French Impressionist painting to enter the collection – the superb Monet *Antibes* (purchased from Durand-Ruel in 1893) – and *Ballet Girls* by Edgar Degas (purchased in 1900), both important forerunners of late nineteenth-century French art. Another key picture was the Puvis de Chavannes *Summer*, the finished sketch for the commissioned mural at the Hôtel de Ville, Paris, acquired directly from the artist in 1891. In 1920 these were followed by the Mary Cassatt pastel *After the Bath*, which had been in Mr. Wade's private collection for twenty years. In that same year, Mr. Wade created a trust fund, the income of which was to be used for purchases in every department of the Museum. Over the years this fund has enriched the collection of paintings as diverse as the Museum's first miniature portrait, *Sir Anthony Mildmay*, a water color on vellum by Nicholas Hilliard (purchased in 1926), and an oil painting, *Portrait of a Lady in a Ruff*, by the Dutch master Frans Hals (purchased in 1948).

In the spring of 1926 a group of subscribing patrons was founded – The Friends of the Museum – whose purpose was to aid in the development of the painting collection by providing further purchase funds. Four of their most important contributions were: a memorial to Mr. Wade given in 1926, *The Holy Family* by El Greco; the Franco-Spanish *Bishop Saint with Donor* given in 1928; Strozzi's *Minerva* given in 1929; and the *Coronation of the Virgin* by the Master of the Fröndenberg Altarpiece, a follower of Konrad von Soest, given in 1929. The El Greco eventually became the picture perhaps most closely identified with the Museum. The Strozzi was bought a generation before the great interest in seventeenth-century art made such paintings a rarity on the market.

The initial generosity of the Friends and Trustees in the opening years revealed a pioneer spirit and sense of purpose that evoked a response of further gifts and bequests, permitting even greater growth and expansion in the following decades. Many individual gifts and bequests, as well as the establishment of new purchase funds, widened the department's horizon and increased its depth.

The first of these munificent gifts came from the Museum's third president, John L. Severance, who, with his wife, had given generously at the time of the opening. Working closely with the Museum's director and staff, Mr. Severance continued to build his own collection with an eventual bequest to the Museum in mind. After his death in 1936, his pictures were shown at the Museum in the Great Lakes Exhibition. In 1942 his entire collection came to the Museum. Of considerable diversity and quality, it gave the Museum Italian and Flemish panels, French and British eighteenth-century portraits by Nattier, Drouais, Reynolds, and Gainsborough, as well as the Turner *Burning of the Houses of Parliament, 1834*. *The Death of the Virgin* by the Austrian Master of Heiligenkreuz was given to the Museum as a memorial to Mr. Severance in 1936. In later years the collection was enriched by paintings as varied as the Aved *Portrait of M. Jean-Gabriel de la Porte du Theil* (1964), Monet's *Waterlilies* (1960), and the Courbet *Grand Panorama des Alpes* (1964).

John L. Severance's sister, Mrs. Francis F. Prentiss (Elisabeth Severance), was also a Trustee of the Museum. She and her husband collected works of art for many years with the intent of making the Museum their beneficiary. They made gifts of tapestries at the time of the opening; each left unrestricted funds to the Museum, as well as the contents of their home (after Mrs. Prentiss' death in 1944), which added to the painting collection Del Sarto's *Portrait of a French Lady*, Rembrandt's *Portrait of A Lady*, and Terborch's *Portrait of a Lady Standing*.

Over the years numerous benefactors enlarged the painting collection, and when listed as briefly as they must be in this foreword, such gifts may seem of little consequence – but in each instance a new facet of historical and aesthetic importance was given to the Museum. In 1936 a gift of money from Mrs. James Corrigan as a memorial to her husband permitted the acquisition of Cézanne's *The Pigeon Tower at Montbriand*.

Then in 1938 Commodore Louis D. Beaumont gave Watteau's *La Danse dans un pavillion*, which added an important work to the nucleus of eighteenth-century pictures begun by the Severance bequest. Ten years later, through his foundation, the Museum received the remainder of his collection of French eighteenth-century paintings, including canvases by Boucher, Lancret, and Nattier. In 1940 James Parmelee bequeathed a group of pictures, including the *Crucifixion* by the Sienese Matteo di Giovanni. In 1943 several paintings came from the bequest of Mrs. Grace Rainey Rogers; and in 1961, the great Sir Thomas Lawrence portrait, *Lady Louisa Manners, Later Countess of Dysart, as Juno*, from the bequest of John D. Rockefeller, Jr.

In 1939 an unexpected bequest came from Julia Morgan Marlatt who left a sizeable fund which she specified exclusively for the acquisition of paintings other than Cleveland art. The fund was a memorial to her husband, but was to be designated as the Mr. and Mrs. William H. Marlatt Fund. Their gift has been one of the main purchase funds for the painting collection. The first accession from this fund was made in 1943: the *Portrait of Don Juan Antonio Cuervo* by Francisco Goya, signed and dated 1819 and inscribed to the sitter, a friend of the artist. Since then, many pictures have been acquired through the Marlatt fund, ranging from the early fifteenth-century French primitives – a *Trinity* from Provence(?), an *Annunciation* by possibly a northern artist working in Paris – to Italian paintings as diverse as Sassetta's *St. Francis before the Crucifix* and Titian's *Adoration of the Magi*. Another fine acquisition was a very personal portrait of his first wife, Isabella Brandt, by the Flemish painter, Rubens.

In 1951 yet another facet of painting was added to the collection through the foresighted generosity of Edward B. Greene, with a completeness that made his gift all the more remarkable. A Trustee of the Museum for many years and a son-in-law of J. H. Wade, Mr. Greene had persevered in a lifetime interest, forming his collection of miniature portraits with rigorous attention to the quality of the hundred examples it contained. It covers the full history of the portrait miniaturist's exacting art from the sixteenth through the nineteenth centuries. Commencing with five examples by Nicholas Hilliard and Isaac Oliver, the collection includes Samuel Cooper's unfinished, vigorous portrait of Thomas Hobbes; British and American eighteenth-century works by Engelhart, Plimer, and Cosway; an unusually fine group by Smart, along with a series of his preparatory finished drawings; an exceptional group by the German Füger; and French examples, including Fragonard from the eighteenth century and J. B. Isabey from the nineteenth. In 1961 Mr. Greene's daughter, Mrs. A. Dean Perry, added the important Hilliard *Portrait of an Elizabethan Gallant* to the collection in memory of her parents. In the same year, the Museum was fortunate to receive six English eighteenth-century "eye" miniatures as a gift from Mr. and Mrs. John W. Starr.

Throughout the Museum's history the name of Leonard C. Hanna, Jr. appears frequently and consistently, dating from the time the Museum was first incorporated. His interest in and thoughtful care for the institution's welfare was his chief concern until his death in 1957. In 1914, one year after the Museum was incorporated, he was elected to the Advisory Council, and his first gifts came in 1916 when the Museum was opened. He was elected a Trustee in 1920 and became a member of the Accessions Committee, where his wise advice and discriminating appreciation were reflected in the purchasing policy for all departments.

As early as 1926, when the Friends were organized, Mr. Hanna thought of setting up a fund for acquisitions. This became a reality in 1941 when he established his charitable trust, the Hanna Fund, with the Museum as one of its beneficiaries. From that date on, primarily in the paintings department, but in all other areas of the Museum's collections as well, the Hanna Fund has been the outstanding source for acquisitions. In 1942 the Renoir *Mlle. Romaine Lacaux* was purchased, and the following year, Gauguin's *L'Appel*. Other notable purchases from the Hanna Fund are *The Road Menders at Arles* by Van Gogh, *La Vie* by Picasso, and *Frieze of Dancers* by Degas. In the 1950s the emphasis changed to earlier works: Tintoretto's *Baptism of Christ*, Savoldo's *Dead Christ with Joseph of Arimathea*, Rembrandt's *Portrait of a Young Student*, La Tour's *The Repentant St. Peter*, the Baldung [Grien] *Mass of St. Gregory*, and El Greco's *Christ on the Cross with Landscape*. The latter painting was the discovery and choice of Mr. Hanna himself.

At his death in 1957, one of the most munificent bequests ever made to a museum provided both purchase and operating funds in addition to his personal collection. Mr. Hanna's own particular interests – French Impressionism, Post-Impressionism, and the early twentieth-century School of Paris – provided the basis of his private collection which was shown together

as a unit at the opening of the Museum's new wing in 1958. Afterward, the works were distributed throughout the Museum, adding two notable landscapes by Cézanne, four works by Degas, a Daumier oil, the Manet *Portrait of Berthe Morisot*, Monet's *La Capeline Rouge – Mme. Monet*, three Picassos (an early Blue Period canvas and two of the Rose Period), a fine Redon pastel, and Toulouse-Lautrec's *May Belfort*, to list but a few.

With the monies available from all the aforementioned bequests, the Museum has been able to purchase works with the view of strengthening and filling out the paintings collection as a whole and to emphasize certain areas of European painting when the opportunities for purchase have arisen.

In recent decades important Northern European, French, and Italian paintings of the fourteenth and fifteenth centuries have been purchased, including a polyptych of the *Madonna and Child with Saints* by Ugolino da Siena, in 1961; a pair of panels of *St. Michael* and *St. Anthony Abbot* by Filippo Lippi and a panel of *The Calvary with a Carthusian Monk* from Champmol in Dijon by Jean de Beaumetz, in 1964; a precious fragment with the head of *St. John the Baptist* from a longer panel by Robert Campin and the two previously mentioned predella panels with scenes from the life of St. Catherine by Giovanni di Paolo, in 1966; and a Florentine mid-fourteenth-century panel of the *Virgin and Child Enthroned*, in 1968.

Numerous additions to the seventeenth-century Dutch collection, including several landscapes, were climaxed by the purchase of the Rembrandt portrait, *Old Man Praying*, in 1967, from the Leonard C. Hanna Jr. Bequest. One of the most noteworthy additions to our Flemish collection was *Diana and Her Nymphs Departing for the Chase* by Rubens, also from the Hanna Bequest, in 1959. The Spanish collection has been more than doubled by the addition of such paintings as *The Holy House of Nazareth* by Zurbarán, a 1960 purchase; two paintings by Ribera, *St. Jerome*, purchased in 1961, and *The Death of Adonis*, in 1965; two Murillos, *The Immaculate Conception*, purchased in 1959, and *Laban Searching for His Stolen Household Gods in Jacob's Tent*, in 1965; a Velazquez *Portrait of the Jester Calabazas*, also purchased in 1965; two important Goyas, *Portrait of the Infante Don Luis de Borbón* – an early courtly portrait – purchased in 1966, and, in 1969, a monumental religious portrait of *St. Ambrose*.

In 1959 an important French seventeenth-century

portrait was acquired: *Charles II, King of England* by Philippe de Champaigne; in 1964, the imposing *Cardinal Dubois* by Hyacinthe Rigaud. Among several Italian Baroque paintings bought in recent years are Neapolitan works: *The Apparition of the Virgin to St. Francis of Assisi* by Luca Giordano, purchased in 1966, and *Adoration of the Shepherds* by Cavallino, in 1968; two Bolognese paintings: *The Madonna and Child with St. Joseph and a Music-Making Angel* – a tondo by Guercino – purchased in 1967; and, in 1969, the *Adoration of the Magi* – a late, unfinished, monumental canvas by Guido Reni. As mentioned previously, later nineteenth-century French painting was already well represented in the Museum. Recent accessions have strengthened the collection with representative works from the first half of the nineteenth century, including two paintings by Courbet: *Madame Boreau*, purchased in 1962, and *Grand Panorama des Alpes*, in 1964; *Cupid and Psyche* by David, 1962; *The Roman Campagna* by Corot, 1963; a *Portrait of Comte Jean-Antoine Chaptal* by Baron Gros, 1964; *Antiochus and Stratonice* by Ingres, 1966; and a *Portrait of Madame Henri Lerolle* by Fantin-Latour, purchased in 1969.

During the Museum's comparatively short history, it has received gifts of funds as well as important paintings from private collections, either by bequest or as gifts from the children of collectors in memory of their families. There have also been gifts from individuals, celebrating or commemorating both public and private occasions, which have greatly enriched the Museum. These gifts and funds have combined to form a collection of European paintings of international stature which adds in significant measure to the cultural life of the city of Cleveland.

Henry S. Francis
Curator of Paintings from 1932 to 1967

Abbreviations

EXHIBITIONS

Boston (1883)   Boston, 1883: American Exhibition of Foreign Products, Arts and Manufacturers. Catalogue

Boston (1940)   Boston, Museum of Fine Arts, 1940: Art of the Middle Ages. Catalogue

CMA (1916)   The Cleveland Museum of Art, 1916: The Inaugural Exhibition of the Cleveland Museum of Art. Catalogue

CMA (1931)   The Cleveland Museum of Art, 1931: Art through the Ages. No catalogue

CMA (1936)   The Cleveland Museum of Art, 1936: Twentieth Anniversary Exhibition. Catalogue

CMA (1963)   The Cleveland Museum of Art, 1963: Gothic Art 1360–1440. Catalogue: *The Bulletin of The Cleveland Museum of Art*, L (September 1963)

CMA (1966)   The Cleveland Museum of Art, 1966: Golden Anniversary Acquisitions. Catalogue: *The Bulletin of The Cleveland Museum of Art*, LIII (September 1966)

CMA (1966–1967)   The Cleveland Museum of Art, 1966–1967: Treasures from Medieval France. Catalogue

CMA (1971)   The Cleveland Museum of Art, 1971: Florence and the Arts: Five Centuries of Patronage. Catalogue

MMA (1912)   New York, Metropolitan Museum of Art, 1912: Loan Exhibition of the Holden Collection. Catalogue: *Bulletin of the Metropolitan Museum of Art*, VII (October 1912)

BIBLIOGRAPHY

Berenson, *The Venetian Painters*...   Bernard Berenson, *The Venetian Painters of the Renaissance* (New York and London, 1907)

Berenson, *The Florentine Painters*...   Bernard Berenson, *The Florentine Painters of the Renaissance, with an Index of their Works* (New York, 1899 and 1909)

Berenson, *Central Italian Painters*...   Bernard Berenson, *The Central Italian Painters of the Renaissance* (New York and London, 1908)

Berenson, *North Italian Painters*...   Bernard Berenson, *North Italian Painters of the Renaissance* (New York and London, 1907)

Berenson (1916)   Bernard Berenson, *Venetian Painting in America* (New York, 1916)

Berenson, *Pictures Renaiss.* (1932)   Bernard Berenson, *Italian Pictures of the Renaissance, a List of the Principal Artists and Their Works with an Index of Places* (Oxford, 1932)

Berenson, *Ital. Painters*...   Bernard Berenson, *Italian Painters of the Renaissance* (London, 1952)

Berenson, *Pictures Renaiss., Venetian School*   Bernard Berenson, *Italian Pictures of the Renaissance; a List of the Principal Artists and their Works, with an Index of Places...Venetian School*, I-II (London, 1957)

Berenson, *I Disegni*...   Bernard Berenson, *I Disegni dei pittori Fiorentino*, I–III (Milan, 1961)

Berenson, *Pictures Renaiss., Florentine School*   Bernard Berenson, *Italian Pictures of the Renaissance; a List of the Principal Artists and Their Works with an Index of Places...Florentine School*, I–II (London, 1963)

Berenson, *Pictures Renaiss., Central and North Italian Schools*   Bernard Berenson, *Italian Pictures of the Renaissance; a List of the Artists and their Works with an Index of Places...Central Italian and North Italian Schools...*, I–III (London, 1968)

M. L. Berenson (1907)   Mary Logan Berenson, "Dipinti italiani in Cleveland," *Rassegna d'arte*, VII, no. 1 (January 1907)

Burl. Mag.   *Burlington Magazine*

CMA *Bulletin*   *The Bulletin of The Cleveland Museum of Art*

Crowe and Cavalcaselle, *A New History*...   Sir Joseph Arthur Crowe and Giovanni Battista Cavalcaselle, *A New History of Painting in Italy*, I–III (London, 1864-1866)

Crowe and Cavalcaselle, *History of Painting in Italy*   Sir Joseph Arthur Crowe and Giovanni Battista Cavalcaselle, *A History of Painting in Italy*, I–VI (London, 1903–1914)

Crowe and Cavalcaselle, *History of Paintg. in North Italy*   Sir Joseph Arthur Crowe and Giovanni Battista Cavalcaselle, *A History of Painting in North Italy*, I–III (London, 1871 and 1912)

Francis, *American-German Review*   Henry S. Francis, "Early German Painting in the Cleveland Museum of Art," *American-German Review*, XXI/2 (1954–1955)

Friedländer, *Altniederl. Mal.*   Max J. Friedländer, *Die altniederländische Malerei*, I–XIV (Berlin, etc. 1924-1937)

Friedländer, *Early Netherl. Paintg.*   Max J. Friedländer, *Early Netherlandish Painting*, transl. Heinz Norden, I–VI...(Leyden, 1967–1971...)

Gaz. des B.-A.   *Gazette des Beaux-Arts*

Handbook (1958)   *The Cleveland Museum of Art Handbook* (Cleveland, 1958)

Handbook (1966)   *Handbook of The Cleveland Museum of Art* (Cleveland, 1966)

Jaffé, *Apollo* (1963)   Michael Jaffé, "Cleveland Museum of Art; the Figurative Arts of the West ca. 1400-1800," *Apollo*, LXVIII (December 1963), 457–467

Jarves (1884)   James Jackson Jarves, *Handbook for Visitors to the Hollenden Gallery of Old Masters* (Cleveland, 1884)

Mather (1923)   Frank J. Mather, *A History of Italian Painting* (New York, 1923)

Meiss (1951)   Millard Meiss, *Painting in Florence and Siena after the Black Death* (Princeton, 1951)

MMA *Bulletin*   *Bulletin of the Metropolitan Museum of Art*

Milliken (1932)   William M. Milliken, "The Holden Collection," *The Bulletin of The Cleveland Museum of Art*, XIX (November 1932)

Milliken (1958)   William M. Milliken, *The Cleveland Museum of Art* (New York, 1958)

Offner, *Corpus*   Richard Offner, *A Critical and Historical Corpus of Florentine Painting* (New York University, 1930–   )

Panofsky (1953)   Erwin Panofsky, *Early Netherlandish Painting*, I–II (Cambridge, Mass., 1953)

Prentiss Coll. Cat. (1944)   *Catalogue of the Elisabeth Severance Prentiss Collection, Bequest of Elisabeth Severance Prentiss, 1944* (Cleveland, 1944)

Ring (1949)   Grete Ring, *A Century of French Painting 1400–1500* (London, 1949)

Rubinstein (1917)   Stella Rubinstein, *Catalogue of the Collection of Paintings…Presented by Mrs Liberty E. Holden to the Cleveland Museum of Art, 1917* (Cleveland, 1917)

Selected Works   *Selected Works: The Cleveland Museum of Art* (Cleveland, 1966)

Stange   Alfred Stange, *Deutsche Malerei der Gotik*, I–XI (Berlin, 1934-1961)

Sterling (1938)   Charles Sterling, *La Peinture française, les primitifs* (Paris, 1938)

Sterling (1941)   Charles Sterling, *La Peinture française, les peintres du moyen âge* (Paris, 1941)

Thieme-Becker   Ulrich Thieme and Felix Becker, *Allgemeines Lexikon der Bildenden Künstler* (Leipzig, 1907–1950)

Underhill (1917)   Gertrude Underhill, "The Holden Collection," *The Bulletin of The Cleveland Museum of Art*, IV (February 1917)

Van Marle   Raimond van Marle, *The Development of the Italian Schools of Painting*, I–XVIII (The Hague, 1923–1938)

A. Venturi   Adolfo Venturi, *Storia dell'arte italiana*, I–IX (Milan, 1901–1938)

L. Venturi (1931)   Lionello Venturi, *Pitture italiane in America* (Milan, 1931)

L. Venturi (1933)   Lionello Venturi, *Italian Paintings in America* I–III (New York, Milan, 1933)

Waagen (1854)   Gustav Friedrich Waagen, *Treasures of Art in Great Britain* I-III (London, 1854)

Winkler (1924)   Friedrich Winkler, *Die altniederländische Malerei* (Berlin, 1924)

Wixom (1966)   William D. Wixom, *Treasures from Medieval France* (exh. cat.; The Cleveland Museum of Art, 1966)

Explanations

This is the first of a series of catalogues which in time will include all the collections of The Cleveland Museum of Art. Under a general title of *Catalogue of Paintings: The Cleveland Museum of Art*, this book is *Part I – European Paintings Before 1500*. *Part II – Illuminated Manuscripts* will be published separately at a later date. The manuscript for *Part III – European Paintings of the 16th, 17th, and 18th Centuries* is presently underway. All the catalogues are divided into sections by countries placed in alphabetical order. Within these sections, artists' names appear in alphabetical order with each painting or set of paintings given a catalogue number. Anonymous artists are placed at the end of each section. The Museum accession number is given after the title of each painting.

All measurements are given with height before width. Measurements of the paint surface are listed separately when they differ from the outside measurements of the panel. Dealers' names are placed within parentheses in the listing of collections. Publications in which the CMA painting has been mentioned or reproduced are under Literature at the end of each entry; comparative or related publications are given in the text within parentheses. Publications which appear frequently are abbreviated and their full titles are listed just previously. When a reference is included under Literature, it appears in the text with only the author's last name and the year in parentheses. References to listings under Exhibitions are abbreviated in the text as (Exh: 1936), The Metropolitan Museum of Art is abbreviated as MMA and The Cleveland Museum of Art as CMA.

The initials of the authors are placed at the end of the discussion. They are as follows:

E. F. G.   Elizabeth de Fernandez-Gimenez
A. T. L.   Ann Tzeutschler Lurie
W. S.   Wolfgang Stechow
N. C. W.   Nancy Coe Wixom

The index includes a selection of iconographic references, provenances, collectors' names, comparative works, and artists. The CMA paintings are listed separately in the Appendix. References to comparative illustrations are cross-referenced under the name of the artist, the collection, and the title. References to comparative works mentioned in the text but not reproduced are in parentheses after the name of the owner.

THE CATALOGUE

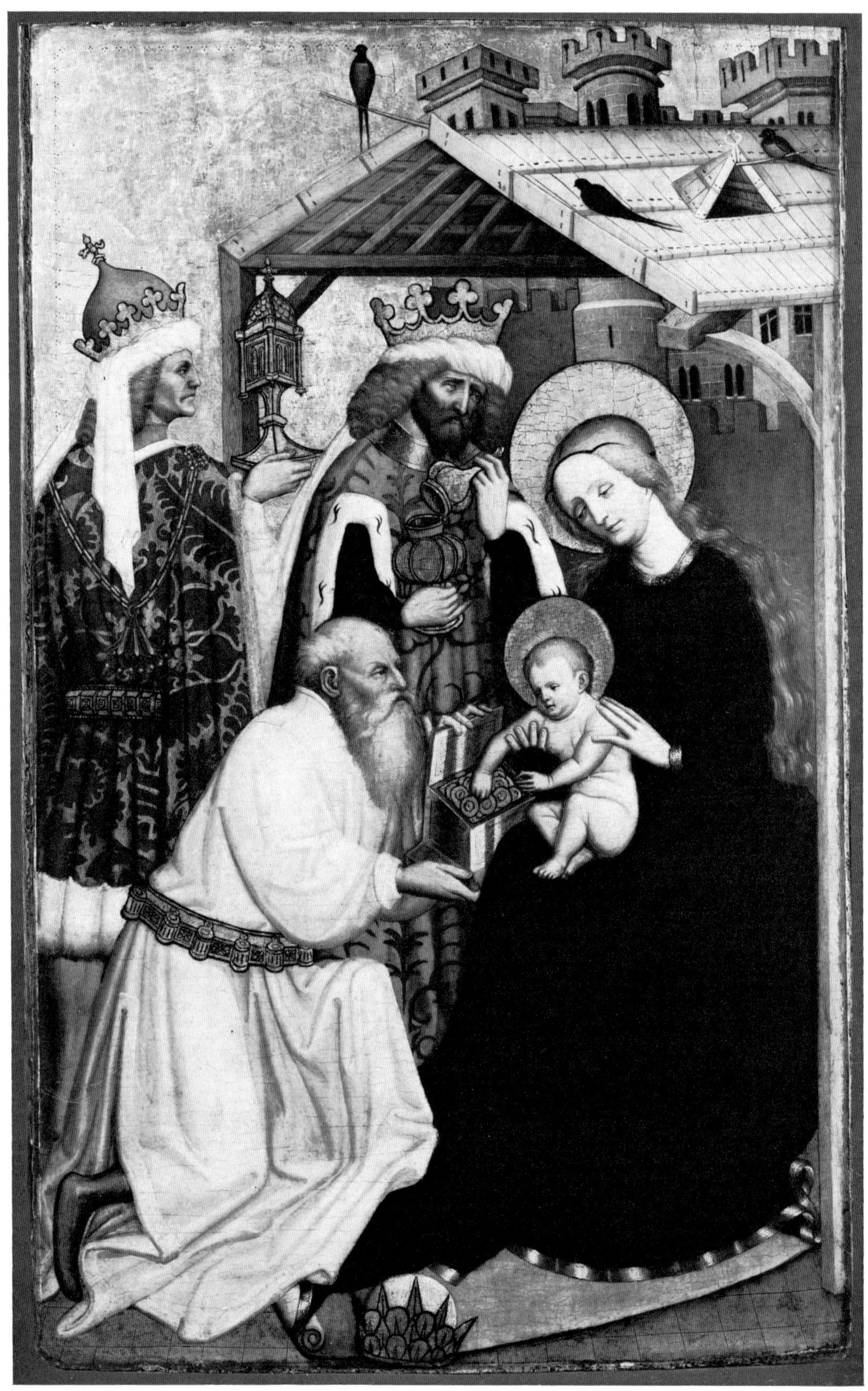

Figure 1. See also Colorplate 1.

KONRAD LAIB, Vienna, active middle of the fifteenth century

Laib was born in "Eyslingen in der von Oting landt" (probably Esslingen near Pappenheim, not far from Nördlingen, South Germany) and presumably is identical with a painter Cunz Laib who is mentioned at Nördlingen in 1431. In 1448 he became a citizen of Salzburg, where a Master Chunradus Pictor is mentioned as early as 1442 and again in 1450; he was still in Salzburg in 1457. Laib had been often called Pfenning on the basis of a misinterpreted inscription on the *Crucifixion* of 1449 in Vienna.

1   *The Adoration of the Magi*   36.18

> Panel (fir), 100 × 63·5 cm (39⅜ × 25 inches). Painted surface: 98 × 61·6 cm (38 9/16 × 24¼ inches).
> COLLECTIONS: E. Proehl, Amsterdam, 1926; (A. S. Drey, Munich and New York).
> Delia E. and L. E. Holden Funds, 1936.

The painting is in very good condition except for Mary's garb and a few strengthened outlines.

The Cleveland panel and a companion piece, the *Nativity* now in the Freising Seminary (Fig. 1 a), are generally accepted as being Laib's earliest known works. They still show the strong influence of the older masters of the Weildorf, Altmühldorf, and Hallstein altarpieces. Oettinger (1942) has suggested that the panel has been cut on its right side and belongs to the same altar as the *Crucifixion* of 1449 in Vienna, but there is no foundation for this assumption on either technical or compositional grounds and the date lies more probably around 1440–1445. The profile of the left king suggests connections with the art of Pisanello, as do the long-tailed birds on the roof (Fischer, 1943). As yet there was little or no contact with Netherlandish art.

W.S.

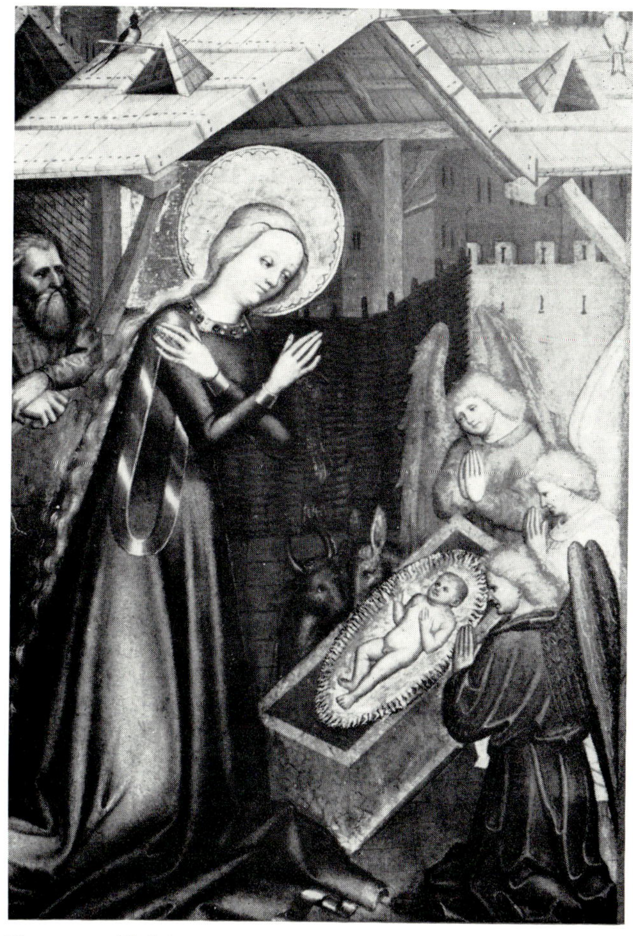

Figure 1 a. *Nativity.* 101·5 × 63 cm (39 15/16 × 24 13/16 inches). Laib. Kunstsammlung, Freising Seminary, Germany, 668.

EXHIBITIONS: Vienna, Österreichisches Museum für Kunst und Industrie, 1926: Gotik in Österreich, cat. no. 188; CMA (1936), cat. no. 199, pl. XL.

LITERATURE: George J. Furlong, "Austrian Gothic Art in Vienna," *Burl. Mag.*, XLIX (1926), 284–285, pl. IIC (with erroneous caption); Otto Pächt, *Österreichische Tafelmalerei der Gotik* (Augsburg, 1929), p. 27; Ludwig Baldass, "Der Meister des Grazer Dombildes und seine kunstgeschichtliche Stellung," *Jahrbuch der kunsthistorischen Sammlungen in Wien*, n.s. IV (1930), 204; Henry S. Francis, "An Austrian Primitive for the Holden Collection," *CMA Bulletin*, XXIII (1936), 135–138, illus. p. 133; Karl Oettinger, *Altdeutsche Malerei der Ostmark* (Vienna, 1942), p. 26; Otto Fischer, "Konrad Laib," *Pantheon*, XXXI (1943), 3; Baldass, *Conrad Laib und die beiden Rueland Frueauf* (Vienna, 1946), pp. 9, 64; Francis, *American-German Review*, p. 6, illus.; *Handbook* (1958), no. 454; Stange, X (1960), 21; *Handbook* (1966), p. 67.

MASTER OF HEILIGENKREUZ, ca. 1400

The artist was named for a diptych now in the Vienna Museum which came from (and was probably painted for) the Cistercian monastery of Heiligenkreuz, Lower Austria. The Austrian origin of the artist has been contested in favor of a French one; in either case he must have worked in or for Austria around 1400.

2   *The Death of the Virgin*   36.496

Panel (fir), 71×54 cm ($26\frac{3}{8} \times 21\frac{1}{4}$ inches). Painted surface: $66 \times 53 \cdot 3$ cm (26×21 inches).

COLLECTIONS: W. Schnakenberg, Munich, 1924; (Jacob Hirsch, New York).

Gift of Friends of the Museum in memory of John Long Severance, 1936.

The painting is particularly well preserved. The back is covered with a layer of gesso on which one can read a few words of a long inscription: Ego Joannes Laurentius Molitor die...Anno Domini 164(?)....

The condition of the backs of the Cleveland picture and its companion piece, now in Washington, D.C. (Fig. 2 a), suggests that they formed a pair of juxtaposed panels rather than a folding diptych. Their original location is unknown. Stange's (1961) assertion that they came from the convent of the Clarisses in Eger cannot be substantiated; other vague reports indicate East Prussia as a possible provenance. As to the painter, several Austrian and German scholars have tended to consider him French while almost all French scholars have refused to do so. There is agreement on his relatively isolated position in Austrian painting of his period; the probability of his having been trained in France has recently been accentuated by reference to stylistic connections with the Parisian illuminator of the Morgan Library's *Roman de la Rose* (MS. 245, *Europäische Kunst um 1400*, exh. cat.; Vienna, Kunsthistorisches Museum, 1962, no. 123), while the identification of the Master of Heiligenkreuz with the Master of the Grandes Heures de Rohan (Ring, 1938) is certainly unacceptable and references to other French centers, including the South (Larsen-Roman, 1943), are hardly more convincing. The ostensible differences of style between the panels from Heiligenkreuz in Vienna and the Cleveland–Washington pair, which have prompted some writers to assume two different hands, are the result of discrepancies of preservation and possibly of date.

W.S.

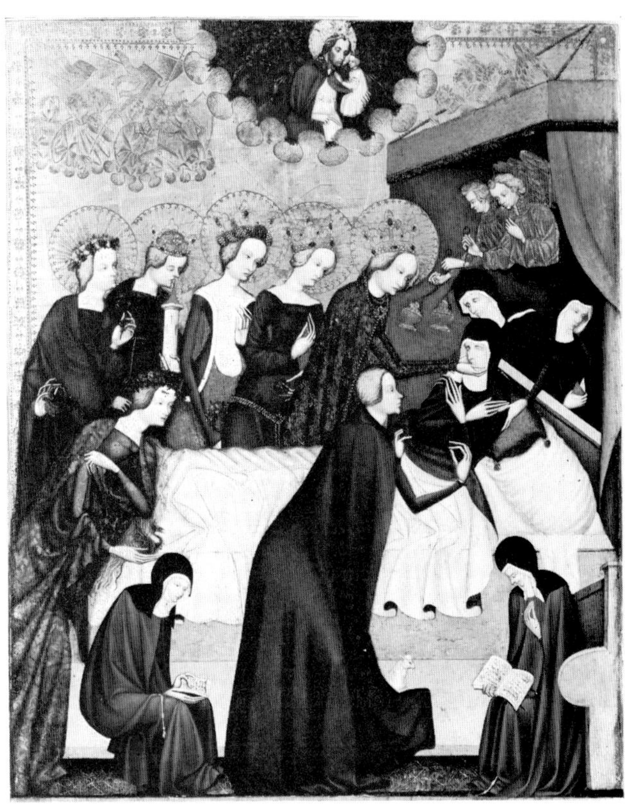

Figure 2 a. *The Death of St. Claire.* $66 \cdot 3 \times 54 \cdot 3$ cm ($26\frac{1}{8} \times 21\frac{3}{8}$ inches). Master of Heiligenkreuz. National Gallery of Art, Washington, Samuel H. Kress Collection, 1162.

EXHIBITIONS: Munich, Alte Pinakothek, 1926; CMA (1936), cat. no. 198, pl. XL; CMA (1963), cat. no. 3, illus. p. 206 (color).

LITERATURE: Ernst Buchner, "Eine Gruppe deutscher Tafelbilder vom Anfang des 15. Jahrhunderts," *Beiträge zur Geschichte der deutschen Kunst*, I (1924), 1, 2, 4, 12, fig. 1; William Suida, *Österreichische Malerei in der Zeit Erzherzogs Ernst des Eisernen und König Albrechts II* (Vienna, 1926), p. 25; Ludwig Baldass, Review of *Beiträge zur Geschichte der deutschen Kunst*, *Belvedere*, X (1926), 133; Baldass, "Die Wiener Tafelmalerei von 1410–1460," *Cicerone*, XXI, Pt. I (1929), 66; Hans Tietze, "Acquisitions nouvelles de la Galerie de Vienne," *L'Amour de l'art*, X (1929), 293; Karl Oettinger, "Zur Malerei um 1400 in Österreich," *Jahrbuch der kunsthistorischen Sammlungen in Wien*, n.s. X (1936), 78; Henry S. Francis, "A Panel by the Master of Heiligenkreuz. A Memorial to John Long Severance," CMA *Bulletin*, XXIV (1937), 153–156, illus. 149, 150; Grete Ring, "Primitifs français," *Gaz. des B.-A.*, I (1938), 158; Sterling (1938), p. 151, n. 31; Sterling (1941), Repertoire B, no. 9, p. 13; Eric and Lucy Larsen-Roman, "Les origines provençales du Maître de Heiligenkreuz," *Apollo – Chronique des Beaux Arts* (Brussels, 1943), no. 18, p. 17; Ring, "An Austrian Triptych," *Art Bulletin*, XXVI (1944), 51; Ring (1949), p. 199; Thieme–Becker, XXXVII (1950), 144; Francis, *American-German Review*, p. 6, fig. 2; *Handbook* (1958), no. 452; Stange, XI (1961), 4; Heinrich Theodor

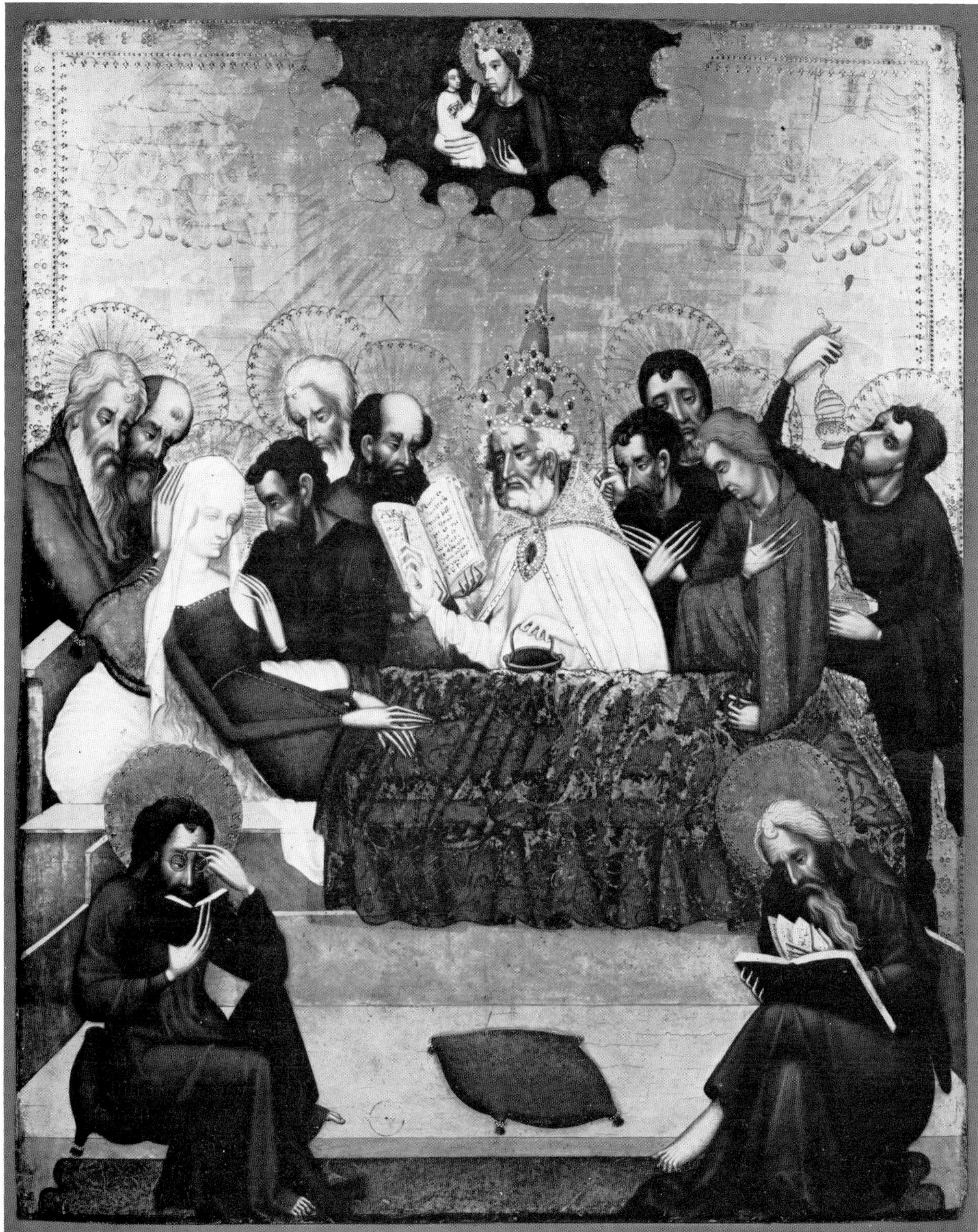

Figure 2. See also Colorplate II.

Musper, *Gotische Malerei nördlich der Alpen* (Cologne, 1961), p. 119 (CMA panel erroneously listed as being in the National Gallery, Washington, D.C.); *Handbook* (1966), p. 66; *Selected Works* (1966), p. 105 (color); Musper, *Altdeutsche Malerei* (Cologne, 1970), pp. 27, 93 (erroneously mentioned as being in collection of National Gallery, Washington, D.C.).

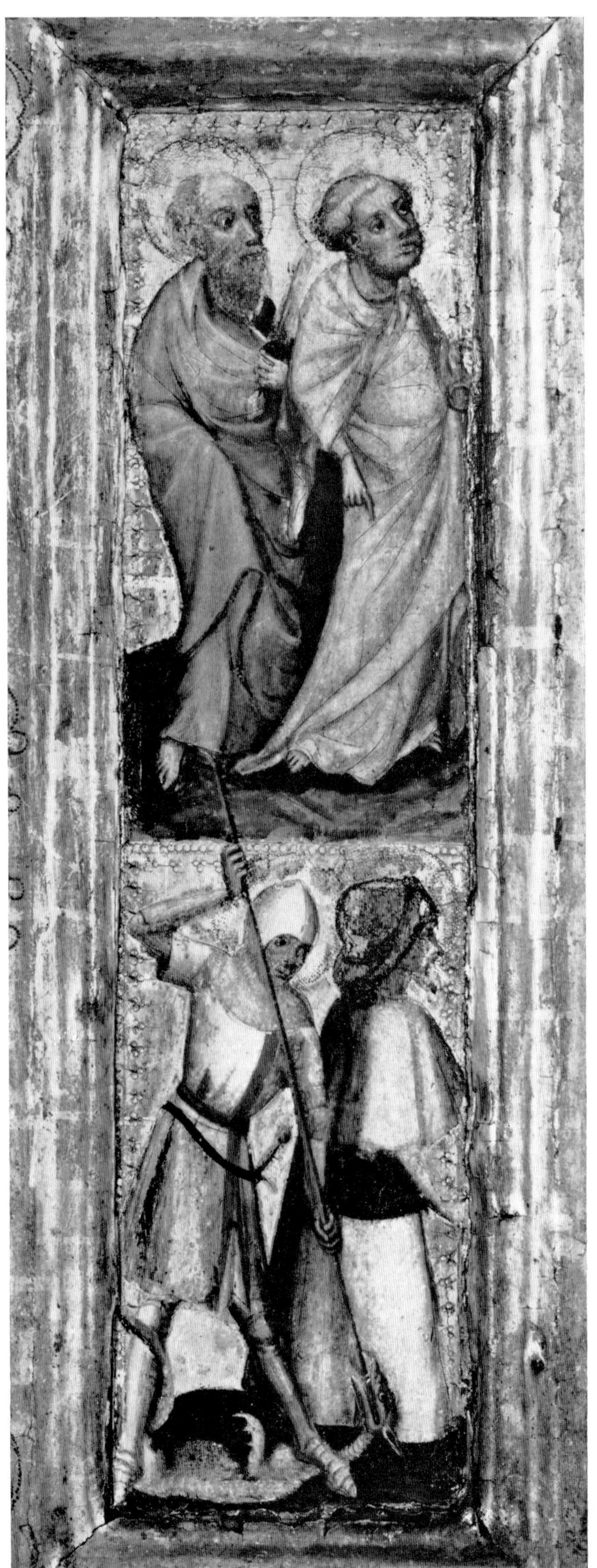

Figure 3 *a*. Dexter wing.

6

ANONYMOUS AUSTRIAN MASTER,
Salzburg, ca. 1425

3 *Adoration of the Magi with Saints*   41.68
   and Donors

Triptych, House Altar

Center above: *Adoration of the Magi*
Center below: *The Donor and His Wife Adoring
   the Group of St. Anne, Mary and the Child*
Dexter wing above: *St. Peter and St. Paul*
Dexter wing below: *St. George and St. James
   Major*
Sinister wing above: *St. Christopher and St.
   Erasmus*
Sinister wing below: *St. Barbara and a Holy
   Nun with a Crucifix*

OUTER WINGS
Dexter above: *Angel of the Annunciation*
Sinister above: *Madonna of the Annunciation*
Dexter below: *St. John the Baptist*
Sinister below: *St. John the Evangelist*

Panel (oak) including original molding, center, 49·7 × 38·1
cm ($19\frac{9}{16}$ × 15 inches). Each wing: 49·7 × 19·5 cm
($19\frac{9}{16}$ × $7\frac{11}{16}$ inches). Inside frames: 39 × 31·7 cm ($15\frac{3}{8}$ × $12\frac{1}{2}$
inches); 39 × 10·1 cm ($15\frac{3}{8}$ × 4 inches).
COLLECTIONS: Baron Kuffner, Castle Diószeg, Hungary
(acquired on the Prague art market in 1905); (Paul Drey,
New York).
Delia E. and L. E. Holden Funds, 1941.

Except for a few abrasions, the triptych is well preserved.
   The origin of this work in Salzburg is highly probable. It shows stylistic connections with Salzburg book
illuminations of the period, including those of Schon-
doch's *Story of the Daughter of the King of France* (Karl
Oettinger, *Hans von Tübingen und seine Schule*, Berlin,
1938, pls. 93 and 94). The second King is strongly reminiscent of that of the (otherwise rather different) Salzburg *Epiphany* in the Berlin Museum, likewise painted
on oak (Oettinger, pl. 90); the genre-like, thin-limbed
women of the *Nativity* in the Lower Belvedere in Vienna
(Heinrich Theodor Musper, *Gotische Malerei nördlich der
Alpen*, Cologne, 1961, p. 132) are also echoed in this
somewhat later work. Several stylistic elements point to
strong western connections as does the iconography of
the outer wings (Fig. 3 *d*) which is similar to that of the
Norfolk triptych of ca. 1415 from the Meuse region in
Rotterdam (no. 2466) and of the Ghent altarpiece. The

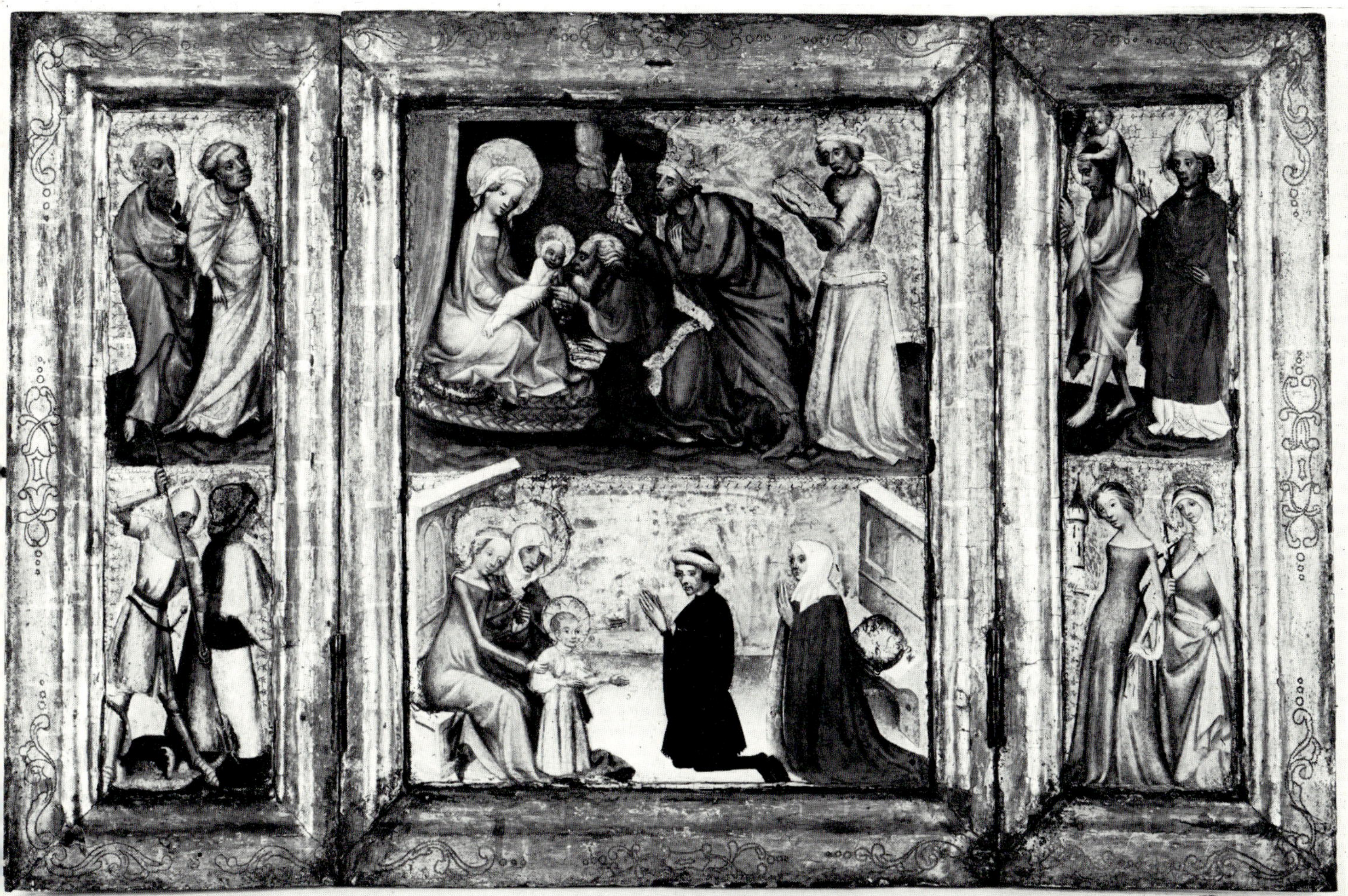

Figure 3.

genre-like group of *Anna Selbdritt* is a remarkably early example of this interpretation. Karl Künstle (*Ikonographie der Heiligen*, II, Freiburg im Breisgau, 1926, p. 213) has pointed out that the Erasmus attribute of spikes under his fingernails is particularly frequent in Austria. Stange's (1960) suggestion of connections with the illuminators of the (much older) Bavarian World Chronicles and the two (Bohemian?) panels of the Waldes collection in Prague is incomprehensible.

W.S.

EXHIBITIONS: CMA (1963), cat. no. 2, illus. p. 178.
LITERATURE: Henry S. Francis, "A Bohemian Primitive," CMA *Bulletin*, XXIX (1942), 102–103, illus. p. 107; Francis, *American-German Review*, pp. 4, 6, fig. 1; *Handbook* (1958), no. 453; Stange, x (1960), 53; *Handbook* (1966), p. 65 (detail).

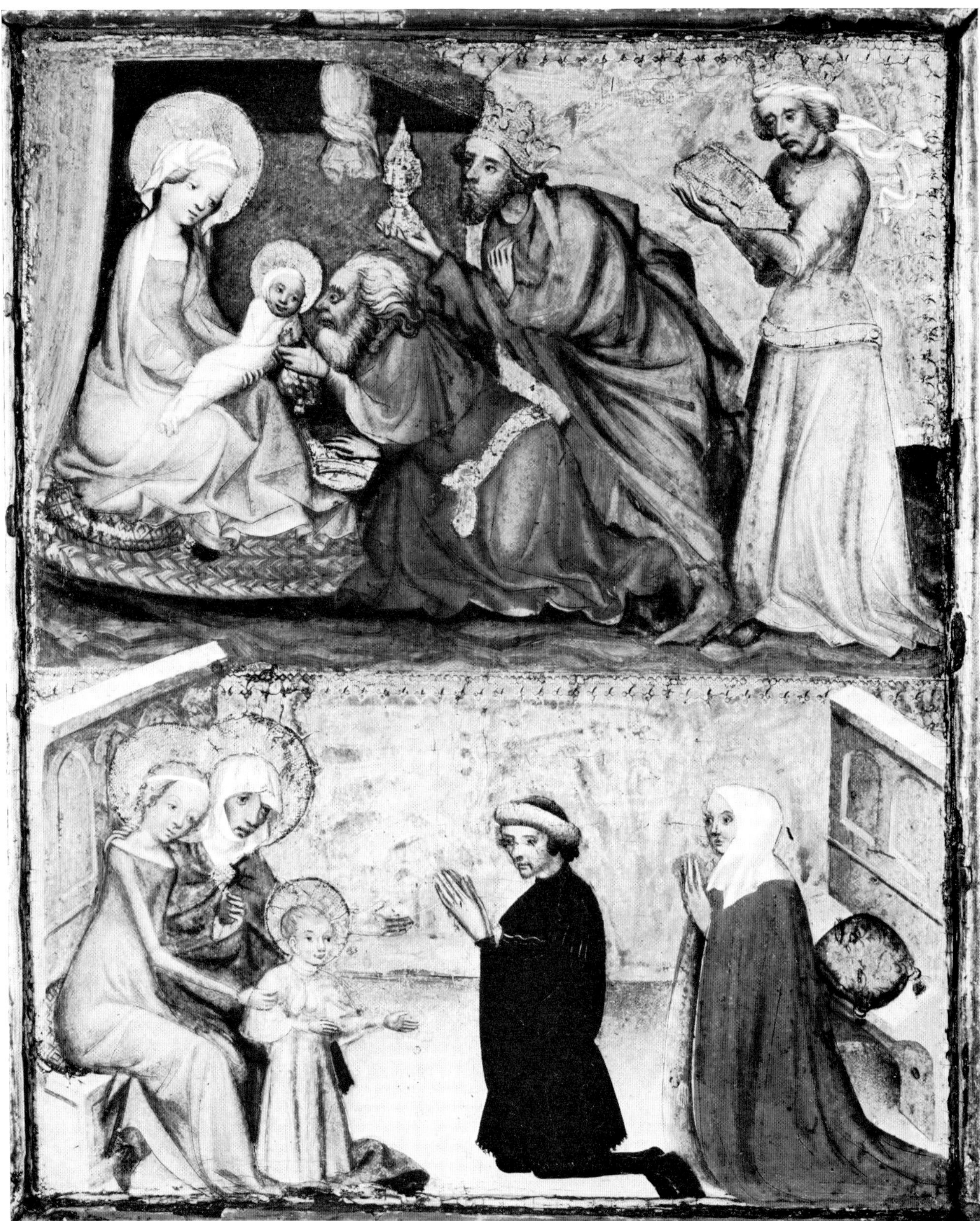

Figure 3 *b*. Center panel.

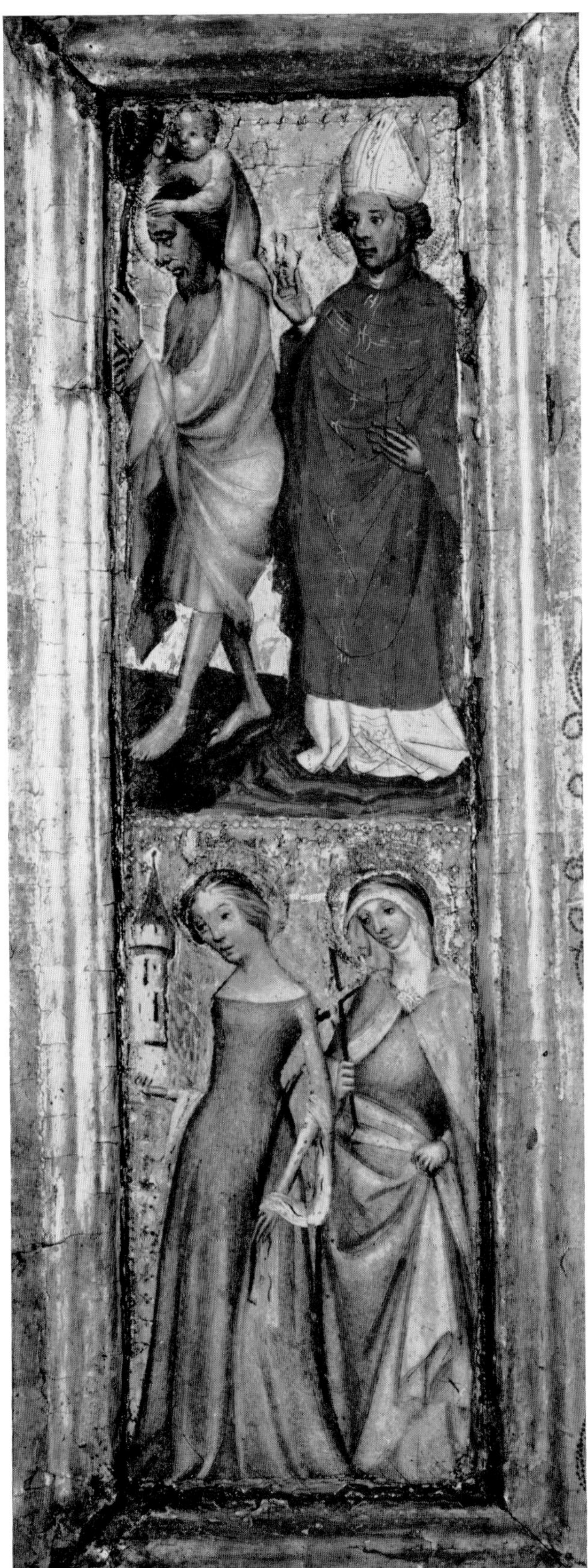

Figure 3 *c*. Sinister wing.

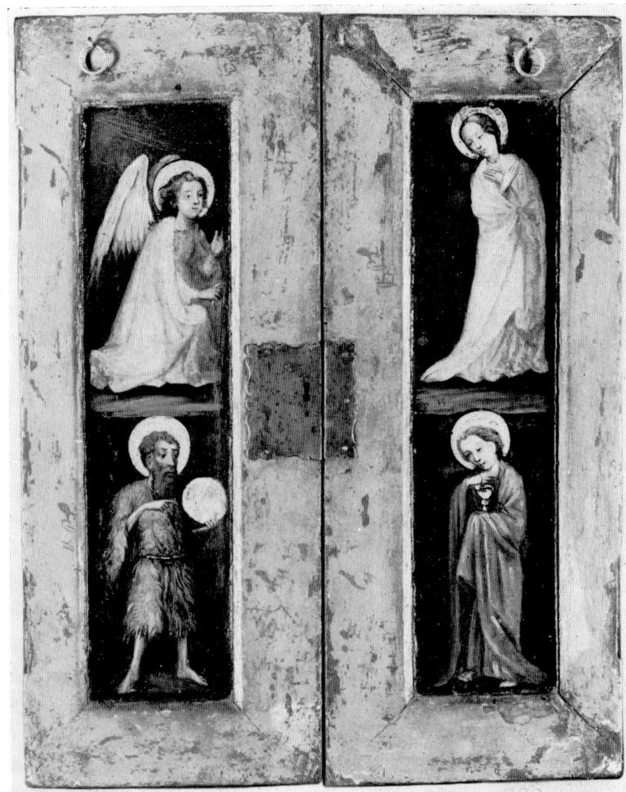

Figure 3 *d*. Outer wings.

ANONYMOUS AUSTRIAN MASTER,
Styria, ca. 1400

4   *Four Scenes from the Passion*   45.115

Diptych

Dexter wing: *Flagellation; Christ before Pilate(?)*
Sinister wing: *Crowning with Thorns; Agony in
   the Garden*
Back of sinister wing: *Man of Sorrows*
Back of dexter wing: painting almost entirely
   destroyed

Panel (linen spread over oak[?]), including original
molding, each wing, $52 \cdot 4 \times 34 \cdot 3$ cm ($20\frac{5}{8} \times 13\frac{1}{2}$ inches).
Inside frames: $45 \cdot 7 \times 27$ cm ($18 \times 10\frac{5}{8}$ inches).
COLLECTIONS: Strossmayer, Zagreb, Yugoslavia (family
seal on the back of the sinister wing, probably referring to
Georg Joseph Strossmayer, 1815–1905; there is also a
clipping from a [sales?] catalogue: Byzantinische Schule);
Frederick B. Pratt, New York; (Arnold Seligmann, Rey &
Co., New York).
Mr. and Mrs. William H. Marlatt Fund, 1945.

Restoration of paint losses and reinforcement in the draperies have been added, especially on the sinister wing.
This was probably not originally a diptych but part of a
larger ensemble.

   While no work with the very distinctive characteristics of the same hand has been made known so far,
stylistic evidence points to an origin in Styria, and thus
to a region not far removed from the location in which
the picture was first recorded. Strong Bohemian bonds
become noticeable by comparing it with the work of
the illuminators of the *Wenceslav Bible*. The sharply
dramatic facial characterization and bold outlines of
the figures against the background occur in works found
in various regions but all are dependent on Bohemian
affiliations such as the Brandenburg altarpiece (considerably older, probably of 1375, Stange, II, fig. 94);
the *Crowning with Thorns*, Thuringia, late fourteenth
century, in Nuremberg (*Die Gemälde des 13. bis 16.
Jahrhunderts*, publ. in Leipzig, Germanisches National-
museum, 1937, p. 179, no. 988, fig. 361); the Marien-
werder altarpiece (similar drapery style, Stange, II, figs.
101–104); the small panels with the martyrdoms of St.
Andrew and St. Dionysius at St. Lambrecht (in Styria,
ca. 1416, Karl Oettinger, *Hans von Tübingen und seine
Schule*, Berlin, 1938, pl. 82); and three panels on a higher
artistic level still in the Strossmayer Gallery at Zagreb

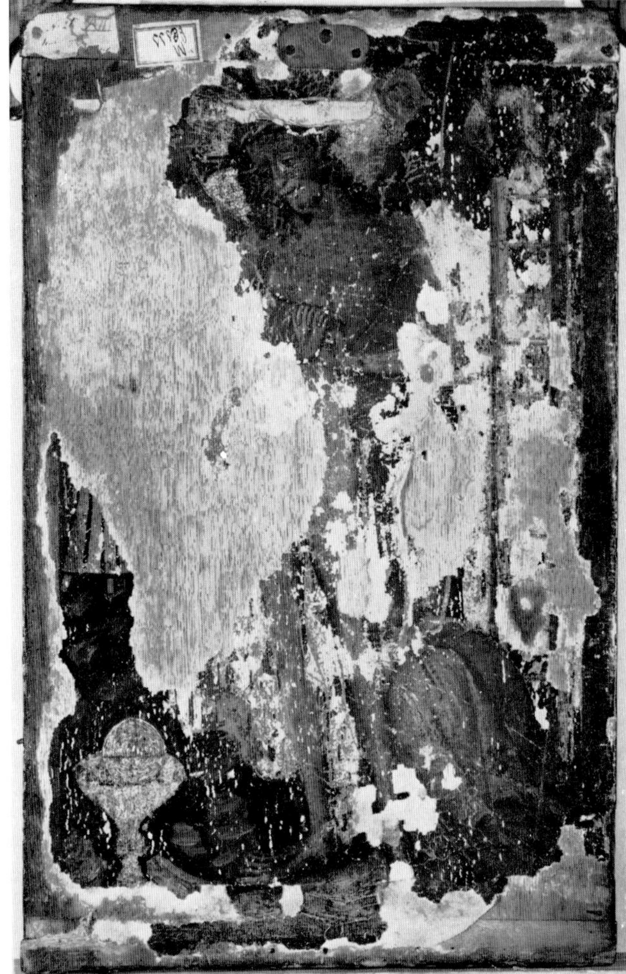

Figure 4*a*. Reverse side of sinister wing.

(Otto Benesch, "Grenzprobleme der österreichischen
Tafelmalerei," *Wallraf-Richartz-Jahrbuch*, n.s. 1, Frankfurt am Main, 1930, 72 ff.). Stange's (1961) reference to
the frescoes in Malmkrog (Almakerek, Malamcrav) in
Transylvania implies no more than a common Bohemian background.

W.S.

EXHIBITIONS: CMA (1963), cat. no. 4, illus. pp. 192–193.
LITERATURE: Henry S. Francis, "A Diptych with Four Scenes
from the Passion," CMA *Bulletin*, XXXIII (1946), 6–8, illus. p. 2;
Francis, *American-German Review*, p. 6; Stange, XI (1961), 159;
Handbook (1966), p. 66.

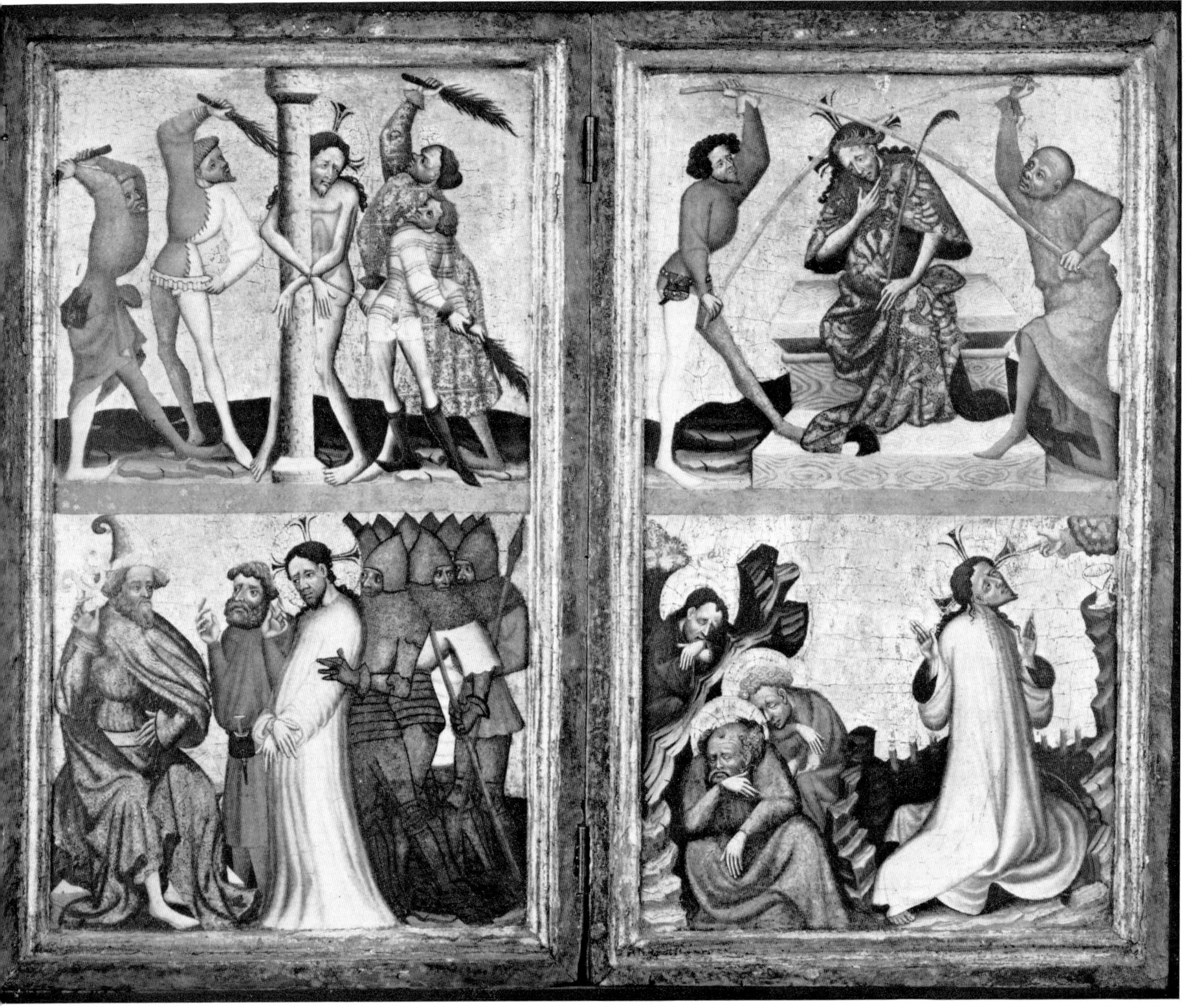

Figure 4.

JEAN DE BEAUMETZ, Burgundy, active 1361, died 1396; and Assistants

The exact birthplace of Jean de Beaumetz is not known, but as he came from Arras, it is probable that he was born in either Beaumetz-les-Loges or Beaumetz-les-Cambrai from which he derived his name. He is recorded in Valenciennes in 1361 where he knew André Beauneveu; he went to Paris where on May 13, 1375, he entered the service of Philip the Bold, Duke of Burgundy, as court painter and was sent to Dijon. He worked on the vaulting of the Carthusian monastery at Champmol from 1384 to 1387. From 1388 to 1391 he executed paintings in Burgundy in the chapel of the Château at Argilly, in several rooms and oratory of the castle of Germolles, and worked on paintings for the Angel's Chapel and church of the Carthusian monastery, but none of these works survive. In 1393 Philip the Bold sent him with Claus Sluter to study the paintings and sculpture which André Beauneveu was working on for the Castle of Mehun-sur-Yèvre for the Duc de Berry. He directed the execution of twenty-six votive pictures for the cells of the Carthusian monks at Champmol and in 1390 one of the several altarpieces for the monks' chapel was erected. After 1377 he is referred to in the records as *valet de chambre* to the Duke.

As court painter to the Duke of Burgundy he had an active workshop with as many as nineteen assistants in 1388; two of the more important of these were Jehan Gentil (who was responsible for grinding pigments) and Girard de la Chapelle (see Prost, II, 1908, 645–646, nos. 3778 and 3779). Many of the invoices for the building of the Chartreuse of Champmol, the original contracts and documents between Jean de Beaumetz and Duke Philip from the Archives of the Court of Burgundy are preserved (see the Archives Départementales de la Côte-d'Or at Dijon, B. 11671, B. 11672, quoted in Prost, 1908, and Dehaisnes, 1886, and C. Monget, *La Chartreuse de Dijon*, Montreuil-sur-Mer, 1898–1905, 3 volumes).

5 *The Calvary with a Carthusian Monk* 64.454

Panel (oak), 56·5 × 45·5 cm (22¼ × 17⅖ inches).
PROVENANCE: La Chartreuse de Champmol, Dijon.
COLLECTIONS: Private collection in the vicinity of Dijon; (Wildenstein & Co., New York).
Purchase, Leonard C. Hanna Jr. Bequest, 1964.

The original panel was thinned down to $\frac{1}{16}$ inch, mounted on a $\frac{1}{4}$-inch oak panel, and cleaned by Suhr in 1964. There was a vertical incomplete crack from the top down along the right edge of the cross. There are losses of paint film in Christ's left eye, the body contour of the right side, the left thigh, and the toes on both feet. Other areas of restoration are in the head and hands of the monk, the face of Mary Magdalen, the lower left arm of Mary, and the cloak of the standing St. John. The gold has been renewed in small areas as has the incised tendril motif.

Until the article by Sterling (1955), no work could be assigned with certainty to Jean de Beaumetz. Sterling published a very convincing theory that the CMA panel and the closely related version of *The Calvary with a Carthusian Monk*, Louvre, formerly Chalandon collection, Lyons (Fig. 5a) (Louis Demonts, *Revue de l'art*, XL, 1936–1937, 248, where it is attributed to Jean Malouel) are two of the twenty-six paintings ordered by Philip, Duke of Burgundy, from Jean de Beaumetz in 1388 for the monks' cells in the Chartreuse de Champmol near Dijon. Although the two panels differ slightly in the modeling and posture of the figures (particularly that of Christ), and in the treatment of the background as well as other details, they are nearly the same in size, color composition, and subject.

None of the documents relating to the twenty-six cell paintings mention their subject. Sterling identifies the panels from the records of a merchant by the name of Thevenin de Sens in Dijon from whom Beaumetz ordered the necessary gilding for the panels in 1389. Another document records the delivery of twenty-six oak panels whose measurements correspond very closely to the Chalandon (60·1 × 48·2 cm) and the Cleveland panels. The measurements as well as the subject matter are exactly appropriate for the little devotional altars for each monk's cell. Although the oak panels were delivered in late 1388, the canvas in the spring of 1389, and the gold leaf bought during the summer of the following year, Sterling points out that the actual painting did not begin before the autumn of 1390 for it was in August of that year that Jean de Beaumetz bought the chalk to pre-

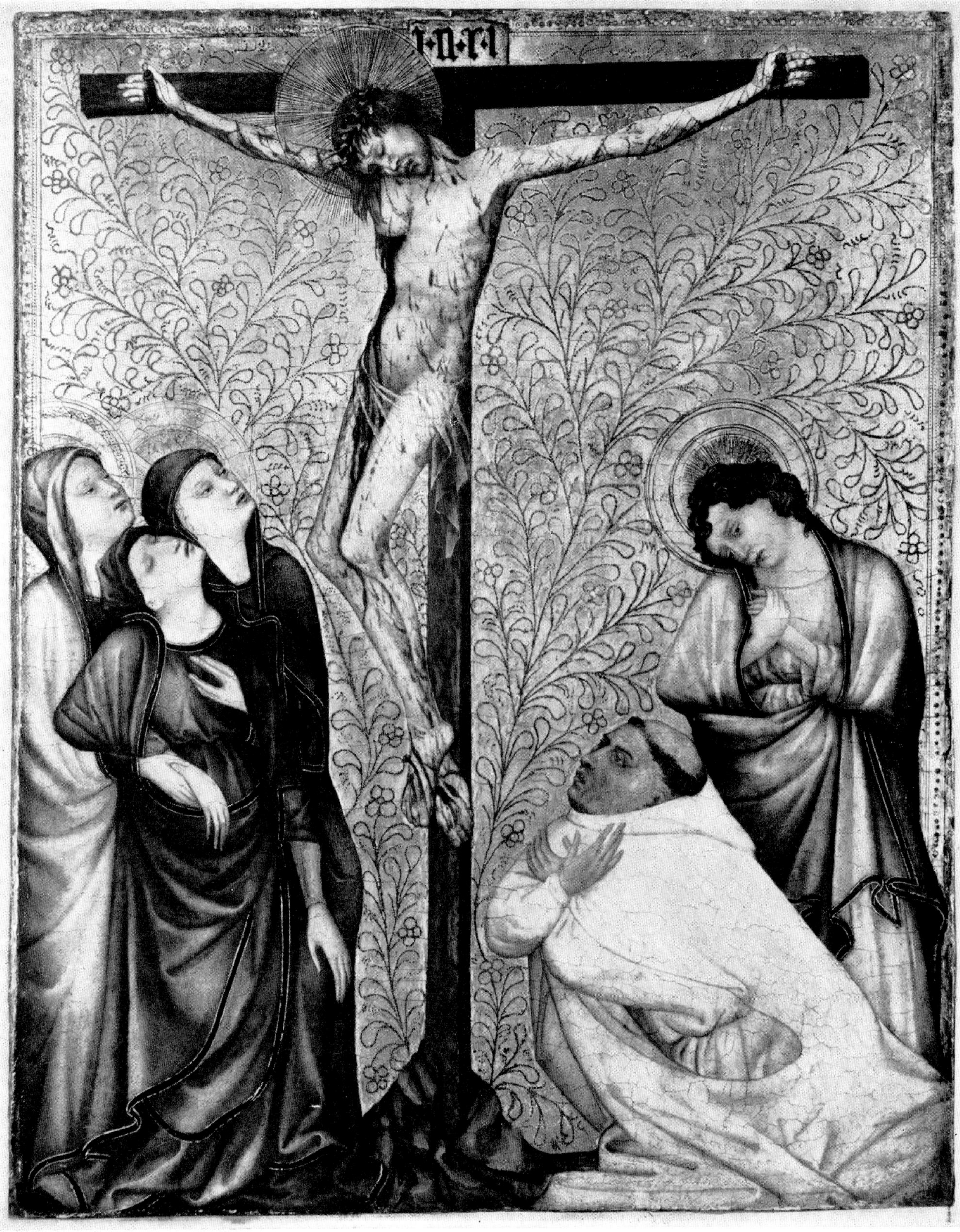

Figure 5. See also Colorplate III.

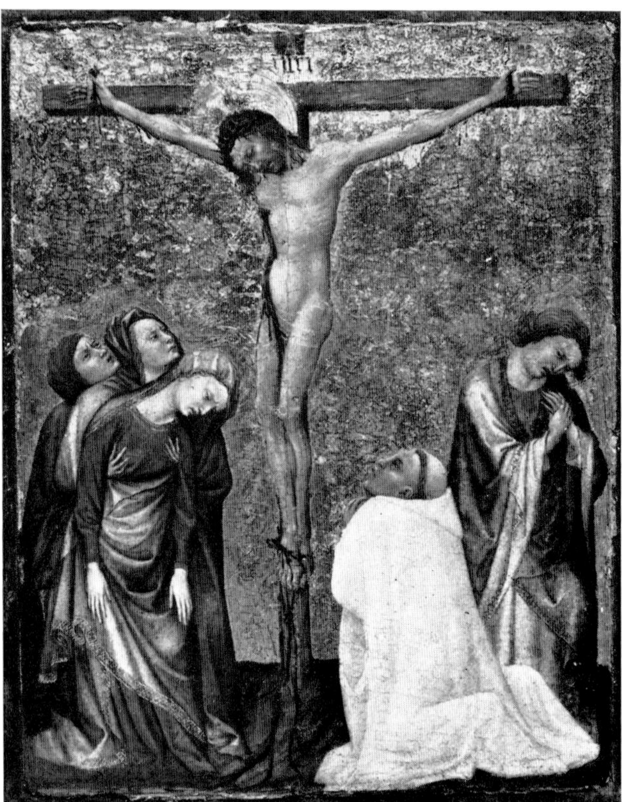

Figure 5a. *The Calvary with a Carthusian Monk.*
60·1 × 48·2 cm (23$\frac{11}{16}$ × 19 inches). Beaumetz.
Louvre, R. F. 1967–3.

pare the plaster ground for the panels. Sterling easily explains this lapse of time by the fact that Jean de Beaumetz was busily engaged by the Duke at Argilly, Germolles, and the Duke's private chapel at Champmol. Girard de la Chapelle played an important role in the preparation of the panels as documented by the time for which he was paid and Jehan Gentil was primarily occupied with grinding the colors; he is recorded elsewhere as having performed the same tasks as Girard for less wages. As Beaumetz was gone from December 1, 1390 until October 31, 1391, Sterling assumes that Girard must have carried out some painting assisted in part by Jehan Gentil. Sterling observes from the records that the cell paintings must have been finished in 1395. Since Jean de Beaumetz was occupied with decorating the main chapel and the Duke's private chapel at Champmol upon his return (where another assistant-collaborator Guillaume le Maire de Francheville was at work), Sterling logically assumes that the two *Calvaries* were ordered from Jean de Beaumetz and executed by him and his assistants under his direction (among these Girard de la Chapelle and Jehan Gentil were the most important), accounting for the stylistic difference in two paintings of such close identity. They were ordered in 1388, begun two years later in 1390, laid aside for three years, and finished in 1395; they can therefore be dated either from 1390–1391 or in 1395.

Various attempts have been made to assign panels to the Chartreuse de Champmol; Jacques Dupont (*Les primitifs français*, Paris, 1935, p. 15) suggested that the *Triptych with the Trinity and the Four Evangelists* (Berlin, Staatliche Museen, no. 1688) was one of the votive panels for the monks' cells and attributed it to Beaumetz. This was reaffirmed by Joan Evans (*Art in Medieval France*, London, New York, 1948, p. 154) who suggested as well that the panels in the Mayer van den Bergh Museum and Walters Art Gallery might also have survived from these cells. On the other hand, Panofsky (1953, p. 112) dismissed the possibility of the Berlin *Triptych* as even having come from the Chartreuse de Champmol, but Sterling proved at least the provenance of the *Triptych* as the Chartreuse before it entered the Baudot collection from a document of 1791 (Monget, *La Chartreuse de Dijon*, III, 1905, 69, n. 25, 78). Sterling (1941, p. 49, n. 32) suggested that because of the Carthusian donor, the *Pietà* in the Berstl collection (Sterling, pl. 30) might have been one of the panels for the monks' cells. It was not until the second *Calvary* panel came to light that he could so logically and convincingly construct the relationship between them and their mutual provenance supported by documentary evidence.

The problem of a regional Dijon school of painting – its sources and influence – is a very complex one. There are several paintings that are stylistically related to the panel by Jean de Beaumetz showing strong influences of Sienese lyricism, Flemish realism, and Parisian opulence. Sterling (1938, fig. 55; 1941, pl. 37) published the Chalandon *Calvary* as the work of a Flemish painter in a Dijon atelier ca. 1395–1400; Ring (1949, no. 50, p. 197) calls it French school, early fifteenth century. Panofsky (1953) groups the Chalandon panel with the *Pietà* and *Martyrdom of St. Denis* attributed to Malouel (later finished by Bellechose), the *Lamentation* and *Entombment* in the Louvre, the *Lamentation* at Troyes, and the *Coronation of the Virgin* in Berlin as more characteristic of the Parisian school of ca. 1400 that Malouel belonged to before going to Dijon. Sterling (1955) compares the *Calvaries* with other scenes, including *Christ on the Cross*, whose Burgundian origins have been definitely established such as: (1) the *Vie de St. Denis* in the Louvre, finished by Henri Bellechose in 1416; (2) *La Grande Pietà ronde* of about 1400 in the Louvre; (3) the miniature of the *Cartulaire de la ville et commune de Dijon* of 1415 in the Bibliothèque Municipale de Dijon, MS. 740; (4) the *Calvaire avec un Chartreux* of about 1440, formerly collection Martin Le Roi; and (5) *Retable de St. Georges*, about 1450 in the Louvre, the latter two carrying on a Burgundian tradition although they are weaker, more conservative interpretations of earlier pictures. Sterling feels the two *Calvaries* are at the beginning in date of this group – the Cleveland panel more French in feeling, the Chalandon panel more Flemish. A similar vine tendril can be found in the following. (1) the Berlin *Triptych* attributed to Jean de Beaumetz by Dupont (*op. cit.*); (2) the *Calvary* in the church of St. Sauveur in Bruges; (3) the Franco-Flemish *Pietà* in the Berstl collection, London; and (4) the *Pietà* in Troyes which Paul André Lemoisne (*Gothic Painting in France, Fourteenth and Fifteenth Centuries*, New York, Florence, 1931, pl. 33) calls Dijon school showing Parisian influence, ca. 1390–1400. See also a group of paintings which Sterling (1941, nos. 27–34) divides into those of more French and those of more Flemish influence, including the Chalandon panel.

N.C.W.

EXHIBITIONS: Musée de Dijon, Palais des Ducs de Bourgogne, 1960: La Chartreuse de Champmol, pl. xx; CMA (1966), cat. no. 55, illus. p. 195; CMA (1966–1967), see Wixom, *Treasures*.

LITERATURE: Chrétien Dehaisnes, *Documents & extraits divers concernant l'histoire de l'art dans la Flandre, l'Artois & le Hainaut avant le XVe siècle*, II (Lille, 1886), 676, fol. 295v (for B. 11671 of Archives départementales de la Côte-d'Or), 728–729, fol. 147 (for B. 11672); Bernard and Henri Prost, *Inventaires mobiliers et extraits des comptes des ducs de Bourgogne de la maison de Valois, 1363–1477*, II (Paris, 1908), 638, no. 3743, 645, no. 3776, and 645–646, nos. 3778 and 3779; Charles Sterling, "Œuvres retrouvées de Jean de Beaumetz, peintre de Philippe le Hardi," *Musées Royaux des Beaux-Arts Bulletin*, IV (Brussels, 1955), 59–62, 68, 71, 72, 74, 78, 80, illus. p. 59; Millard Meiss and Colin Eisler, "A New French Primitive," *Burl. Mag.*, CII (1960), 234, 236; Michel Laclotte, "Peinture en Bourgogne au XVe siècle," *Art de France*, I (1961), 289, no. 4; Albert Châtelet and Jacques Thuillier, *French Painting from Fouquet to Poussin* (Geneva, 1963), p. 15; René Guilly, *Kindlers Malerei-Lexikon*, I (Zürich, 1964), 257, illus. p. 256; William D. Wixom, "The Hours of Charles the Noble," CMA *Bulletin*, LII (1965), 83, n. 58; Henry S. Francis, "Jean de Beaumetz – Calvary with a Carthusian Monk," CMA *Bulletin*, LIII (1966), 329–338, fig. 1; Georg Troescher, *Burgundische Malerei* (Berlin, 1966), I, p. 53, II, pl. 4, fig. 9; H. J. J. Scholtens, "De Chartreuse bij Dijon en haar Kunstenaars 1379–1411," *Oud Holland*, LXXXI (1966), 130, n. 63; *Handbook* (1966), p. 62; Wixom, "Three Gothic Sculptures," CMA *Bulletin*, LIII (1966), 349; *Selected Works* (1966), p. 96; Wixom, *Treasures from Medieval France* (Cleveland, 1967), no. VI 12, p. 238, illus. p. 239; Millard Meiss, *French Painting in the Time of Jean de Berry* (London, 1967), I, 100, 279, 280, 293; II, fig. 831.

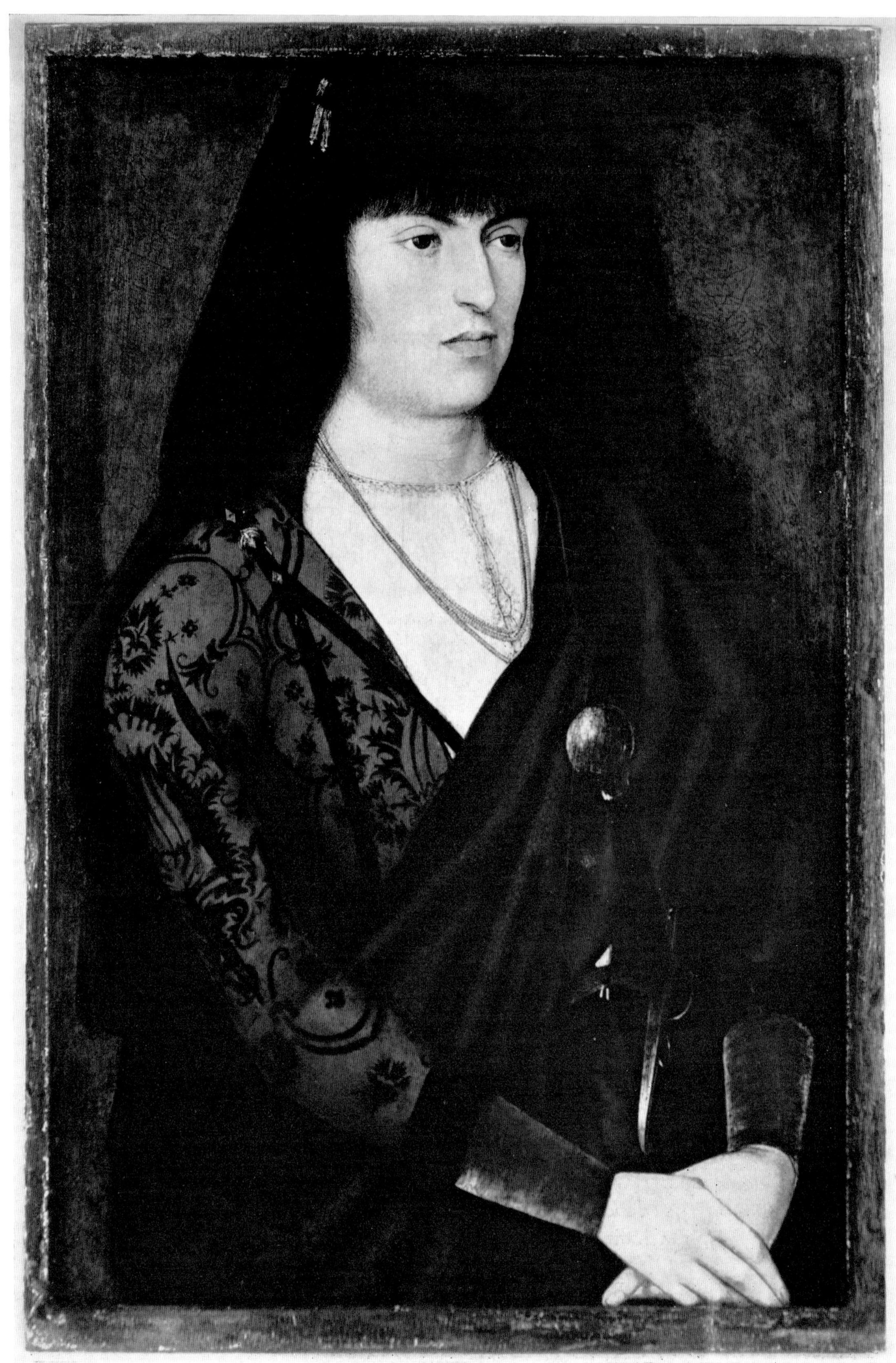

Figure 6. See also Colorplate IV.

ANONYMOUS FRENCH MASTER,
Burgundy(?), ca. 1490–1500

6 *Portrait of a Nobleman*   63.503

Panel (oak), painted surface, 42·5 × 27·6 cm ($16\frac{3}{4}$ × $10\frac{7}{8}$ inches).

COLLECTIONS: (Frederick Mont, New York).

Purchase, Leonard C. Hanna Jr. Bequest, 1963.

The panel is in good condition except for some minor retouches. A slight crack running through the dexter part of the face has been filled in. Some retouching shows on the white shirt, the red velvet of the dexter sleeve, and on the sinister hand. A strip around the four sides of the panel is left unpainted.

The portrait appears to be French, possibly Burgundian. Its color scheme (black and grey over wine-red against dark blue-green), though somewhat reminiscent of Simon Marmion, is very unusual, as is the complicated spatial arrangement of the sword (although its form is typically late fifteenth century) and the position of the hands. The latter may be compared with that of the *Homme à la Canne* in the National Gallery, Washington D.C. (formerly Arthur Sachs collection, Sterling, 1941, pl. 145), which offers a few other comparable features as well (cap, hair style, pronounced contemplative mood). There are also some links with the (surely less impressive) portrait of *Count Engelbert of Nassau*, attributed to the Master of the Princely Portraits who seems to have Burgundian ties (Paul Wescher, "Das Höfische Bildnis von Philipp dem Guten bis zu Karl V," *Pantheon*, XXVIII, 1941, 273).

                                        W.S.

EXHIBITIONS: CMA, December 1963: Year in Review, cat. no. 106, illus. p. 261 (color); CMA (1966–1967), see Wixom, *Treasures*.
LITERATURE: William D. Wixom, *Treasures from Medieval France* (Cleveland, 1967), no. VII 21, p. 334, illus. p. 335 (color); *Handbook* (1966), p. 73.

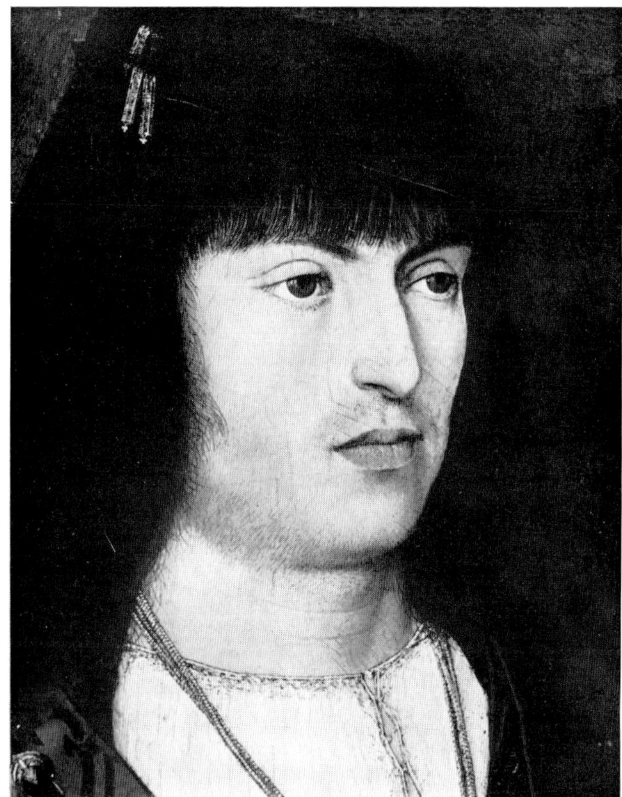

Figure 6a. Detail.

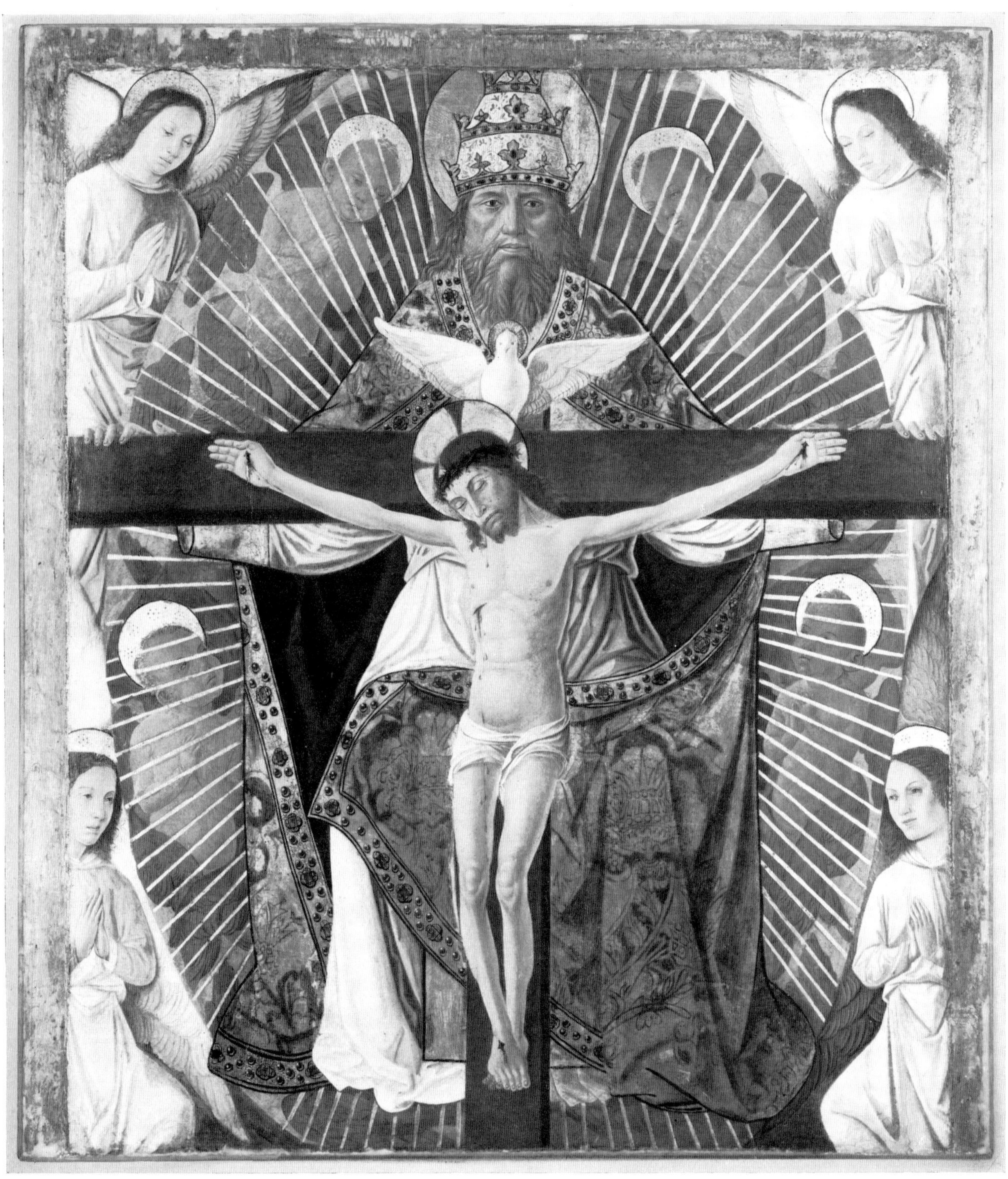

Figure 7. See also Colorplate V.

ANONYMOUS FRENCH MASTER,
Provence(?), ca. 1470–1480

7 *Holy Trinity*   60.79

Panel (poplar), mounted on masonite, 119 × 104·5 cm
($46\frac{7}{8}$ × $41\frac{1}{8}$ inches). Painted surface: 114 × 94·5 cm ($44\frac{7}{8}$ ×
$37\frac{1}{4}$ inches).
COLLECTIONS: Camille Barrère, 1851–1940 (French
Ambassador to Italy, Rome, 1897–1924); Mme. Albert
Cousin née Barrère; Albert Cousin; (J. Seligmann & Co.,
New York).
Mr. and Mrs. William H. Marlatt Fund, 1960.

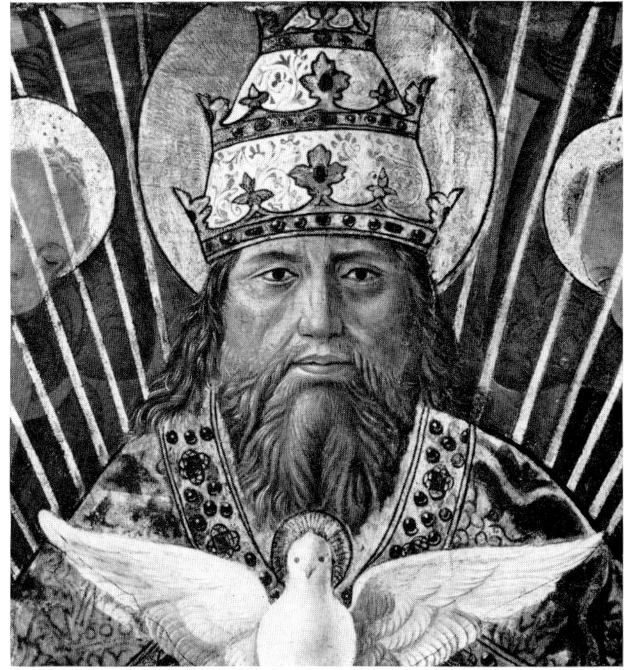

Figure 7 a. Detail.

The painting is well preserved except for slight repairs
and a few strengthened rays and lines. Some stylistic features of the panel readily point to the Loire region; the
red gloriole with cherubs is obviously derived from
Fouquet's *Virgin and Child* in Antwerp, no. 123 (Ring,
1949, pl. 74) as are other color elements, and the outer
angels foreshadow those of the Moulins altarpiece. However, other features do not point in the same direction.
The archaic type of God the Father (Fig. 7 a) who holds
the cross from above (see also Fig. 7 b) is ultimately derived from the Ghent altarpiece; it has no parallels in
Central France but can be found in Spain (*Trinity* – with
very similar Dove – in the Amiens Museum, from the
workshop of Jacomart, see *Trésors de la peinture espagnole: Eglises et musées de France*, exh. cat.; Paris, Musée
des Arts décoratifs, 1963, no. 17). The iconography of
the picture (the subject, Throne of Grace, is very rare in
France) and its composition find closer parallels in Spanish and Southern French works such as the *Trinity* of
1489 in St. Jacques, Perpignan, by the (French?) Cana-
post Master (Chandler R. Post, *A History of Spanish
Painting*, XII, 1958, 673; Sterling, letter of August 28,
1960), as well as Italian ones such as a panel once attributed to Amadeo da Pistoja, Denver Art Museum, Col-
orado (Francis, 1961, fig. 4), now given to Alunno di
Benozzo (see Fern Rusk Shapley, *Paintings from the
Samuel H. Kress Collection, Italian Schools, XIII–XV Centuries*, London, 1966, p. 118, no. K 1025), and a miniature
of 1456 with a similar extension of rays (Paris, Bibliothèque Nationale, f. it. 545; Eugène Müntz, *Pétrarque*,
Paris, 1902, pp. 101, 160, n. 2). The picture is painted on
poplar wood (verified by Mme. Marette of the Louvre
laboratory), a material extremely rare in Central France
but often used in Provence, as well as Italy and Spain
(see Jacqueline Marette, *Connaissance des primitifs par
l'étude du bois . . .*, Paris, 1961, p. 229). One is tempted

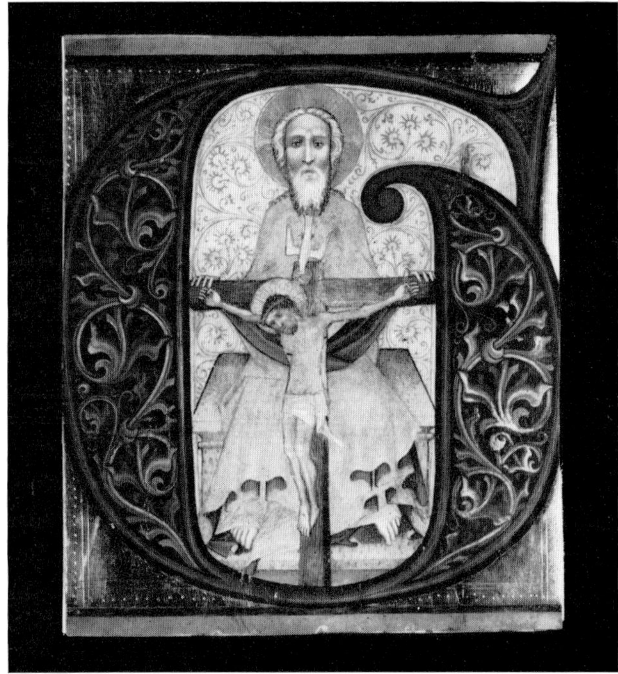

Figure 7 b. *Holy Trinity*. Tempera and gold leaf on parchment.
13 × 10·9 cm ($5\frac{1}{8}$ × $4\frac{5}{16}$ inches).
Austria, ca. 1400. Cleveland Museum of Art.
Purchase from the J. H. Wade Fund. 49.537

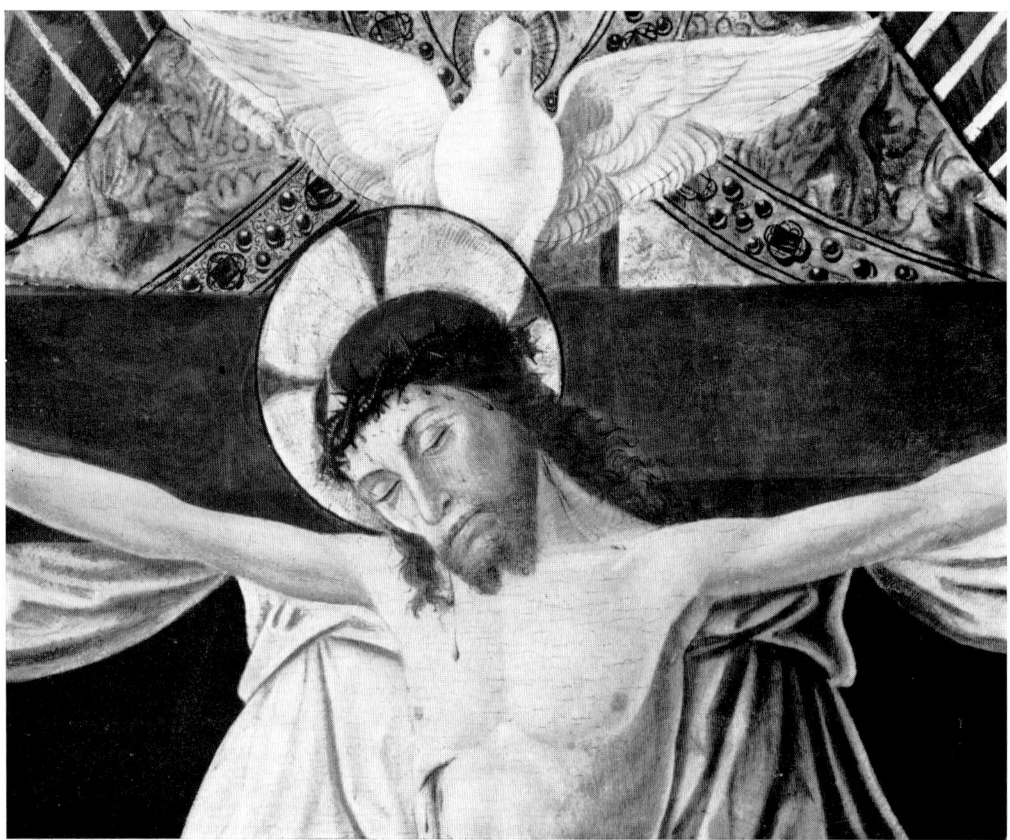

Figure 7c. Detail.

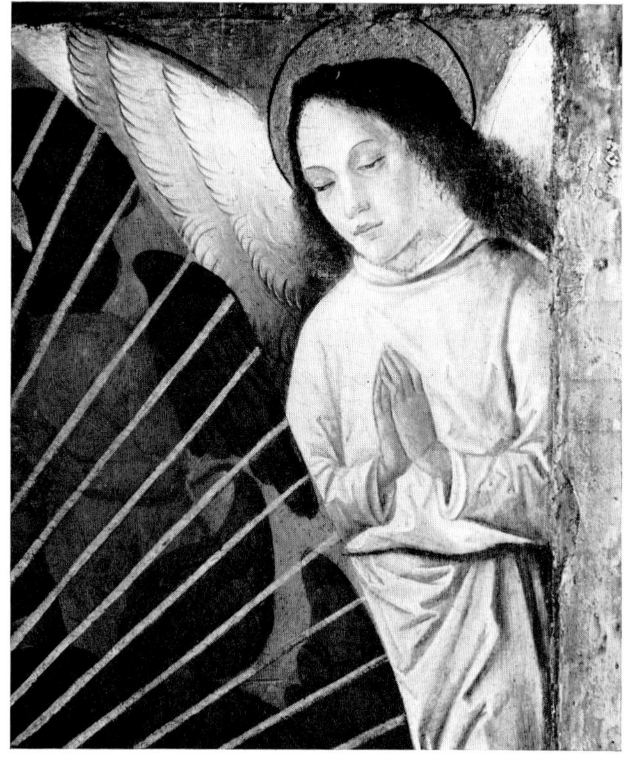

Figure 7d. Detail.

to think of a painter from the center of France working in southern Provence under some Italian and Spanish influence.

W.S.

EXHIBITIONS: CMA, December 1960: Year in Review, cat. no. 59, illus.

LITERATURE: Henry S. Francis, "The Holy Trinity," CMA *Bulletin*, XLVIII(1961), 58–62; Albert Châtelet and Jacques Thuillier, *French Painting from Fouquet to Poussin* (Geneva, 1963), p. 55; *Handbook* (1966), p. 73; Sara Jane Pearman, "The Iconographic Development of the Cruciform Throne of Grace from the Twelfth to the Sixteenth Century" (unpublished Ph.D. dissertation, Dept. of Art History, Case Western Reserve University, 1974), pp. 45–55, no. 261, fig. 5.

20

ANONYMOUS FRENCH MASTER,
Paris(?), Hainaut(?), late fourteenth century

8 *The Annunciation*   54.393

Panel (probably walnut), including original molding, 35·2 × 26·7 cm (13$\frac{7}{8}$ × 10$\frac{1}{2}$ inches). Inside frame: 30·8 × 22·5 cm (12$\frac{1}{8}$ × 8$\frac{7}{8}$ inches).

COLLECTIONS: Duke of Anhalt-Dessau, 1863 until 1925 (as Duccio); (C. A. de Burlet, Berlin); Arthur Sachs, New York and Santa Barbara, California, 1926.

Mr. and Mrs. William H. Marlatt Fund, 1954.

Inscriptions on *The Annunciation*: (on the band held by the angel) ave gracia plena dominus tecum; (on the halo of the angel) sanctus gabriel archangelus dei; (on the halo of Mary) [ecc]e ācilla domini fiat michi secūdū verbū tuum.

On the reverse is a coat of arms divided into quarters with (upper left, lower right) *d'or, au lion de sable*; (upper right, lower left) *d'or, au lion de*[*?*] within a richly tooled lozenge, surrounded by an equally rich tooled border, silver on gesso (Fig. 8a).

The painting is in a good state of preservation, including the frame. The gold has been partly renewed; there is minor retouching in the figure of Mary. The panel may have been one wing of a diptych; the tooled gesso ground found on the left edge is lacking on the right. In that case, the other must have shown, not the donor(s), but another biblical scene (cf., the "Small Bargello Diptych," Winkler, 1927, fig. 3).

The origin of the painting has been much debated; it has been ascribed to a painter active in Paris (Bazin, 1937; Sterling, 1938; Ring, 1949; Francis, 1955; Châtelet–Thuillier, 1963; Frinta, 1965), Avignon (Winkler, 1927; Dupont, 1937), Bohemia (Panofsky, 1953), the Guelders–Maastricht region (Pächt, orally 1957), and a Southern Netherlandish Master working in Paris (Wixom, 1970). The scarcity of authenticated panels from these regions makes a clear decision hazardous; however, both the Bohemian and Avignon provenances have become more and more improbable in recent years. The coat of arms (Fig. 8a) provides an important clue of a different kind, although the reduction of color makes the identification less than completely certain. The entire field still shows its golden ground, partly abraded so that the silver and gesso underneath have become visible. The black of the lions at the upper left and lower right differentiates them clearly from the other two lions which are now (or always were?) delineated mainly in

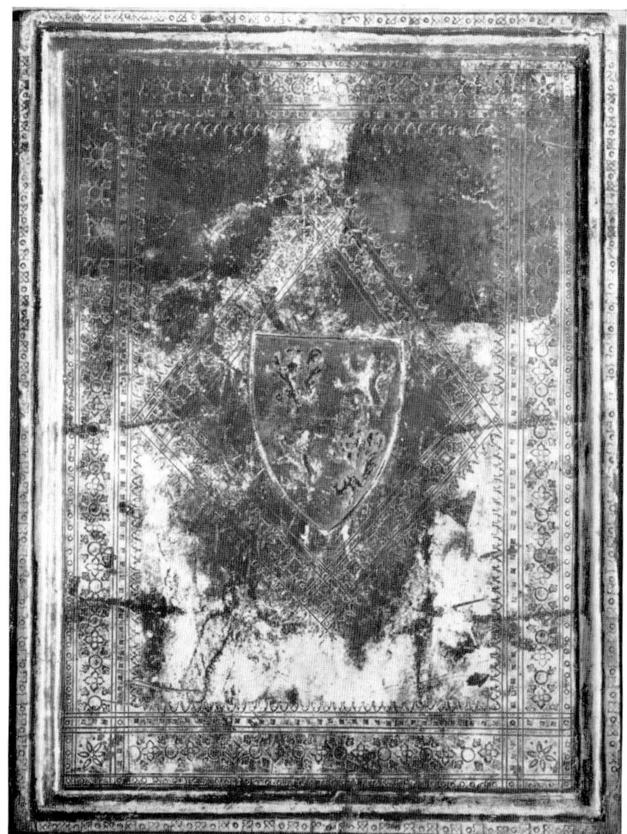

Figure 8a. Reverse side with coat of arms.

the underlying gesso. Assuming that this absence of black stands for red, the arms are identical with those of the House of Hainaut (*d'or, au lion sable*) when reigning in the country of Holland (*d'or, au lion gueules*), as was first pointed out by the late R. van Luttervelt (letter of April 18, 1961). It is true that after 1345, when the Hainaut was brought to the House of Wittelsbach, the blue-and-white crest of Bavaria was added to those arms but the old form may well have been retained under special conditions. On the catafalque of the *Messe des Morts* in the *Milan Hours* (early fifteenth century, probably by Jan van Eyck) the quartered shield corresponds essentially to the present one and was convincingly referred to as the Hainaut-Holland arms by Georges Hulin de Loo (*Heures de Milan*, Brussels, Paris, 1911, p. 65). It may be worth mentioning that the four lions are also found on the Jülich–Berg alliance arms but with gold-and-silver field under the black-and-red lions (Conrad Grünenberg, *Des C. Grünenberg, Ritter und Bürger zu Costenz, Wappenbuch* [Halle], 1840–[45], pl. XLVII b). The punched fleur-de-lis motif, which is sprinkled liberally over

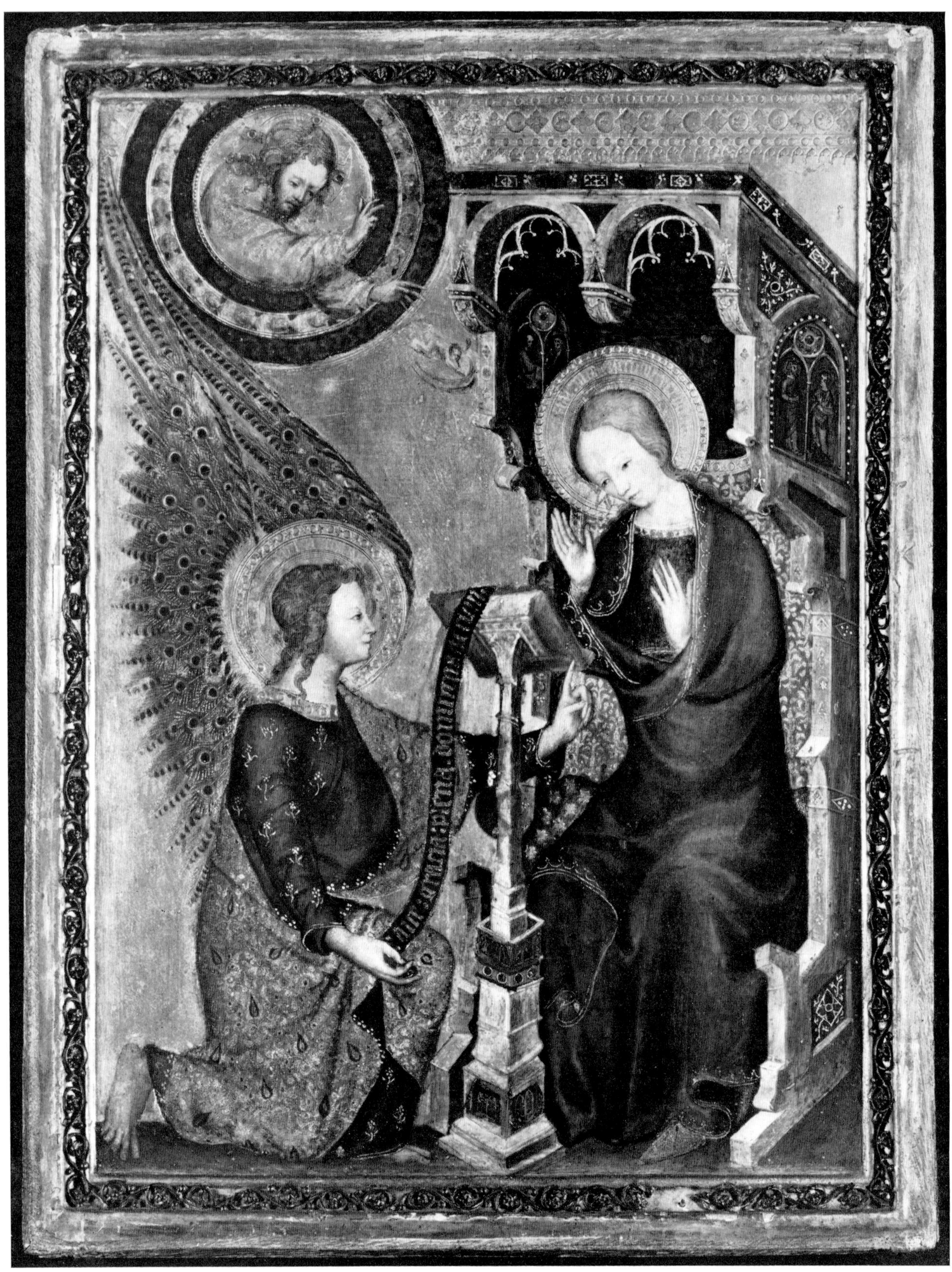

Figure 8. See also Colorplate VI.

the border of the reverse, occurs repeatedly in Sienese painting of the Trecento (Frinta, 1965) and provides no information on the place of origin.

The closest stylistic parallels are found in the "Small Bargello Diptych," as pointed out by Winkler as early as 1927, although the Cleveland panel cannot have formed part of the same ensemble. The third king of the Bargello *Adoration of the Magi* is the kin of the Cleveland Gabriel, the second king, of God the Father. The two Marys have much in common; the punching (as mentioned previously) and other decorative devices are similar, and so are the colors to a modest extent. But that they were painted by the same hand (Winkler, 1927; 1955; Pächt, 1956) is very doubtful because of a strong difference in temperament and composition; it is the present panel which looks more French. Wixom (1967) feels that the figures show a resemblance to those in the frontispiece miniatures of the *Très Belles Heures* in Brussels (MS. 11060–11061) which Meiss recently attributed to a French painter, ca. 1390, closely related to André Beauneveu (Meiss, *French Painting in the Time of Jean de Berry*, London, New York, 1967, I, pp. 207, 208; II, figs. 179, 180).

The motif of the Christ Child sliding down in bodily form to Mary, rare in French art, occurs in a tapestry in the Metropolitan Museum (Panofsky, 1953, fig. 51; James Rorimer, "The Annunciation Tapestry," MMA *Bulletin*, n.s. XX, 1961, 145–148) which is related to Broederlam and was probably woven in Arras.

As Pächt (1956) first pointed out (overlooked by Frinta, 1965), two panels in Berlin and Frankfurt, both illustrated by Stange (I, 1934, figs. 113 and 115), are related in style to the present one but they were certainly not painted in the same region and are most probably of German origin (lower Rhine?).

W.S.

EXHIBITIONS: Cambridge, Mass., Fogg Art Museum, 1927: Loan exhibition (no cat.); New York, J. Seligmann & Co., 1927: Religious Art, cat. no. 1; New York, F. Kleinberger Galleries, 1927: French Primitives, cat. no. 4; Detroit Institute of Arts, 1928: French Gothic Art, cat. no. 1; London, Royal Academy, 1932: French Art 1200–1900, no. 1 (commemorative cat., no. 6); Santa Barbara Museum of Art, Cal., 1946: Collection of Arthur Sachs; Paris, Petit Palais, 1950: La vierge dans l'art français, cat. no. 6; Pittsburgh, Carnegie Institute, 1951: French Painting 1100–1900, cat. no. 26; CMA (1963), cat. no. 19; CMA (1966–1967), see Wixom, *Treasures*.

LITERATURE: Gustav Parthey, *Deutscher Bildersaal*, I (Berlin, 1863), 216 (as Duccio di Buoninsegna); Friedrich Winkler, "Ein unbekanntes französisches Tafelbild," *Belvedere*, XI (1927), 6–8, fig. 1;

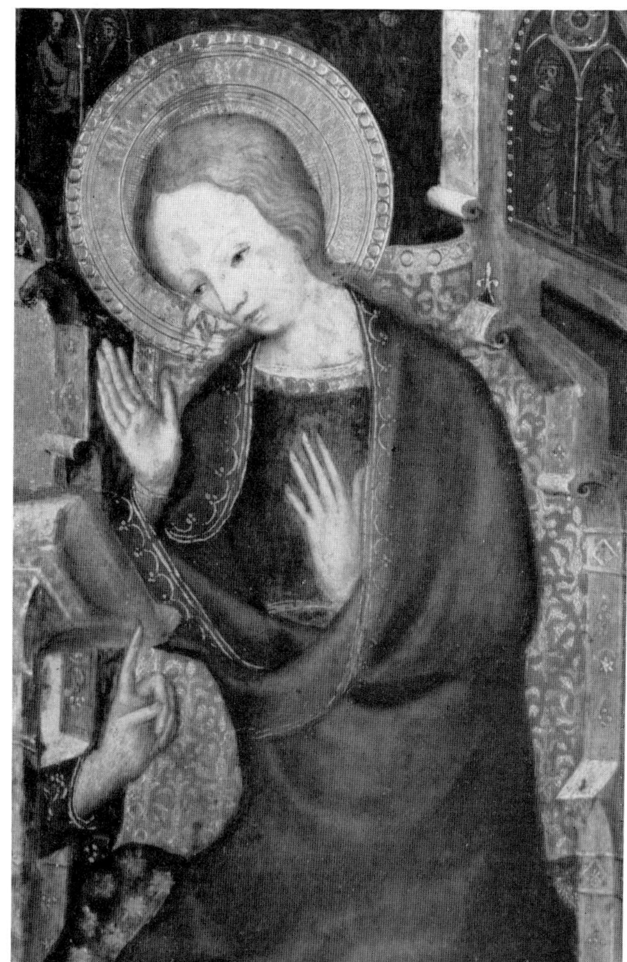

Figure 8*b*. Detail.

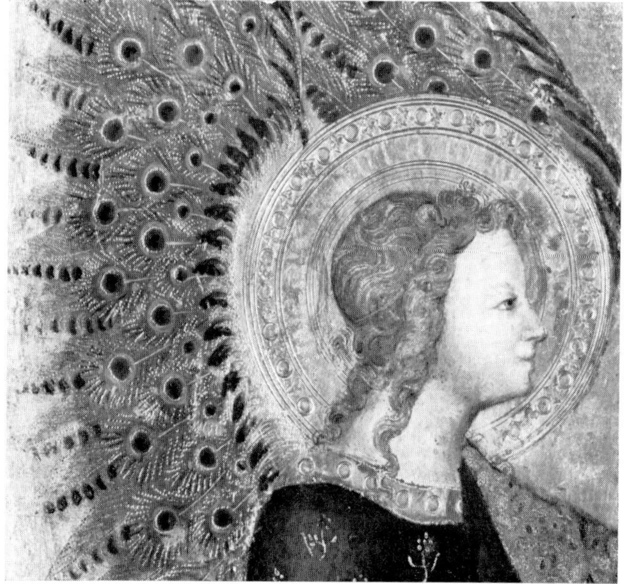

Figure 8*c*. Detail.

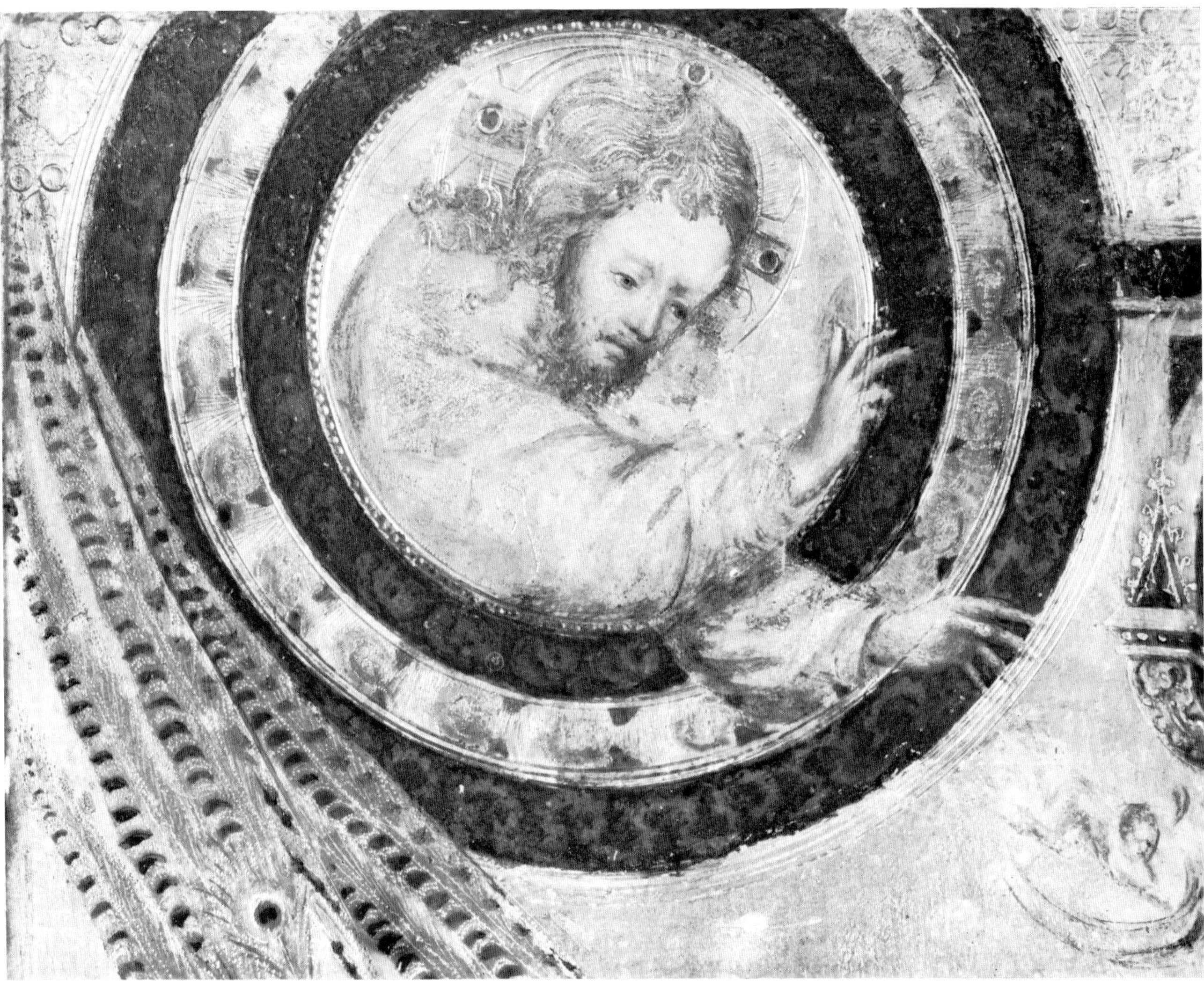

Figure 8 *d*. Detail.

W. R. Valentiner, *Unknown Masterpieces*, I (New York, 1930), 70; Paul André Lemoisne, *Gothic Painting in France* (Florence, 1931), pl. 26; Léon-Honoré Labande, *Les primitifs français: peintres et peintres-verriers de la Provence Occidentale*, I (Marseilles, 1932), 220; David M. Robb, "The Iconography of the Annunciation in the Fourteenth and Fifteenth Centuries," *Art Bulletin*, XVIII (1936), 490, fig. 13; Germain Bazin, *La peinture française des origines au XVIe siècle* (Paris, 1937), 7; Jacques Dupont, *Les primitifs français, 1350–1500* (Paris, 1937), 23; Sterling (1938), 36, n. 20; Sterling (1941), Rép. A, 3, no. 6; Ring (1949), 24, 193, no. 16; Panofsky, I (1953), 82; Dupont, *The Great Centuries of Painting: Gothic Painting* (Geneva, 1954), 126; Henry S. Francis, "A Fourteenth Century Annunciation," CMA *Bulletin*, XLII (1955), 215–219, illus. pp. 213 (color), 214, 216, 217; reprinted in *Art Quarterly*, XIX (1956), 85–87, illus. p. 84; Winkler, Review of *Early Netherlandish Painting*, by Erwin Panofsky, *Kunstchronik*, VIII (1955), 12; Otto Pächt, "Panofsky's 'Early Netherlandish Painting'—I," *Burl. Mag.*, XCVIII (1956), 113; *Handbook* (1958), no. 395; Heinrich Theodor Musper, *Gotische Malerei nördlich der Alpen* (Cologne, 1961), p. 264, fig. 226; *The International Style: The Arts in Europe around 1400* (exh. cat., Baltimore, Walters Art Gallery, 1962), p. 24; Harry Bober, "Medieval Art in Cleveland," *Apollo*, LXXVIII (1963), 456; Albert Châtelet and Jacques Thuillier, *French Painting from Fouquet to Poussin* (Geneva, 1963), p. 15; Colin Eisler, "Le Gothique International," *Art de France*, IV (1964), 290; René Guilly in *Kindlers Malerei-Lexikon*, I (Zürich, 1964), 201; Mojmír Frinta, "An Investigation of the Punched Decoration of Medieval Italian and Non-Italian Panel Paintings," *Art Bulletin*, XLVII (1965), 264, fig. 51; Michel Laclotte, *Primitifs Français* (Milan, 1966), p. 14; *Handbook* (1966), p. 63; *Selected Works* (1966), p. 95; William D. Wixom, *Treasures from Medieval France* (Cleveland, 1967), no. VI 14, 242, illus. p. 243 (color); *L'Europe Gothique XIIe–XIVe siècles* (exh. cat., Paris, Musée du Louvre, 1968), no. 300, p. 186; Wixom, "An Enthroned Madonna with the Writing Christ Child," CMA *Bulletin*, LVII (1970), 290, 297, fig. 11.

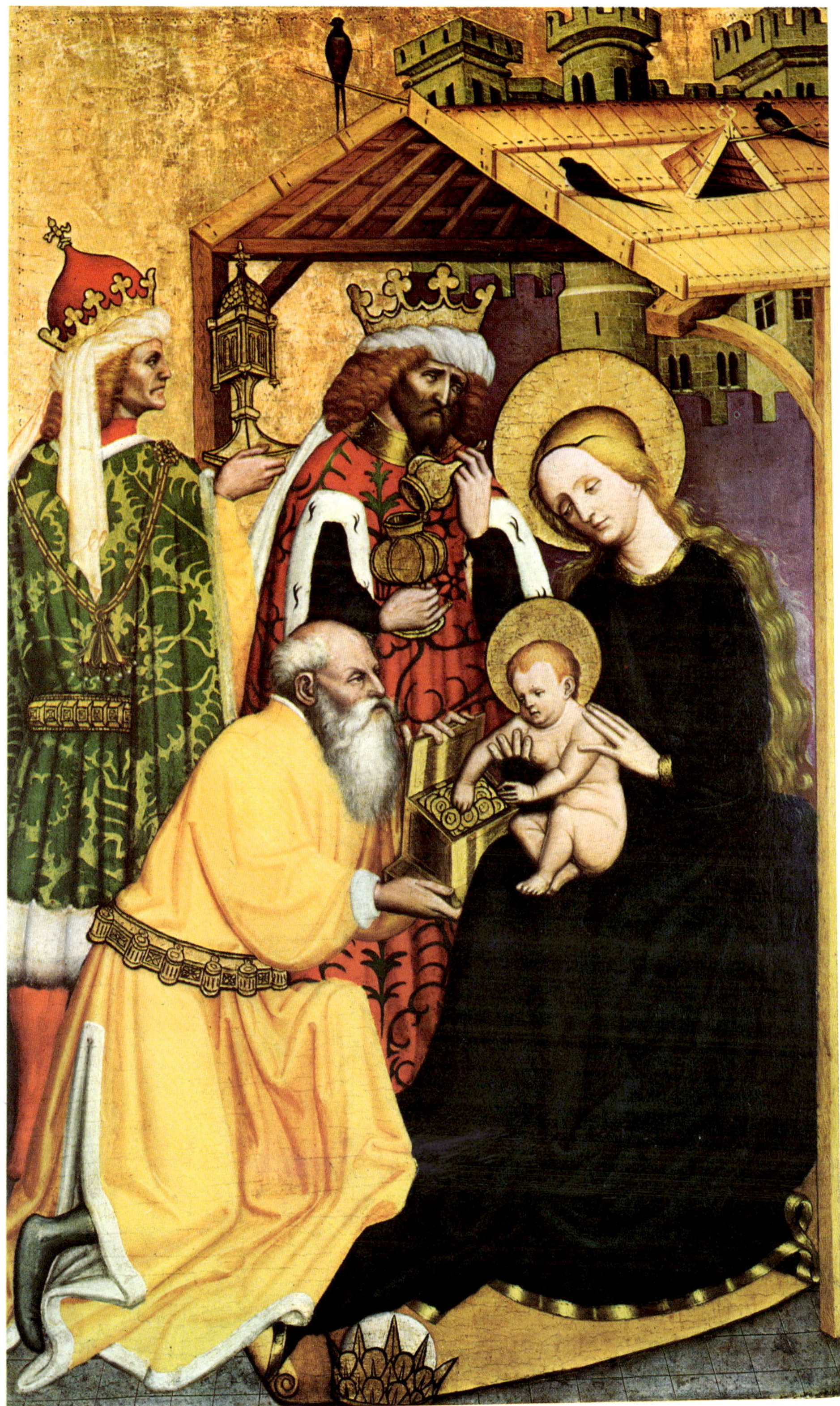

Plate 1. *The Adoration of the Magi*, Konrad Laib (Painting 1).

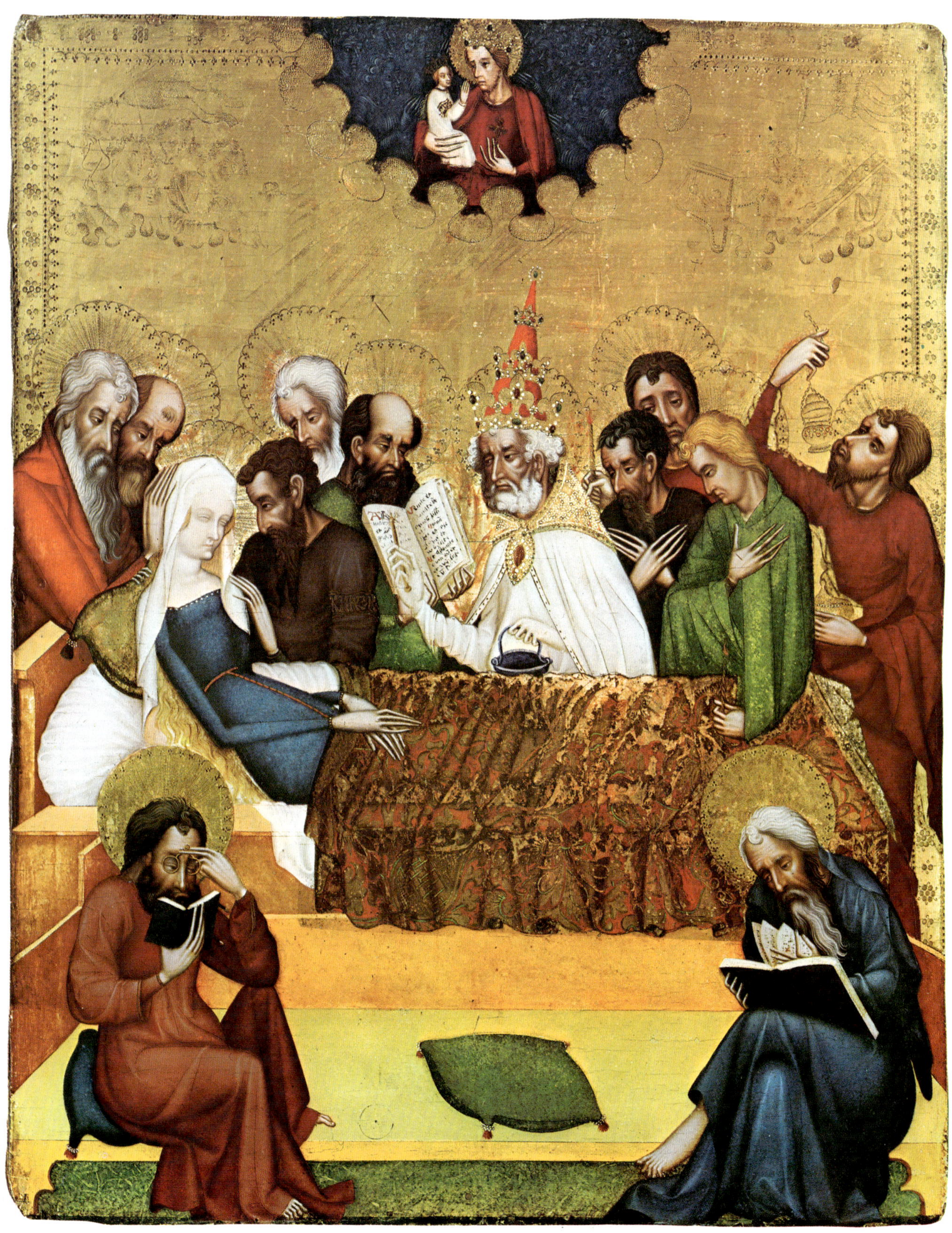

Plate II. *The Death of the Virgin*, Master of Heiligenkreuz (Painting 2).

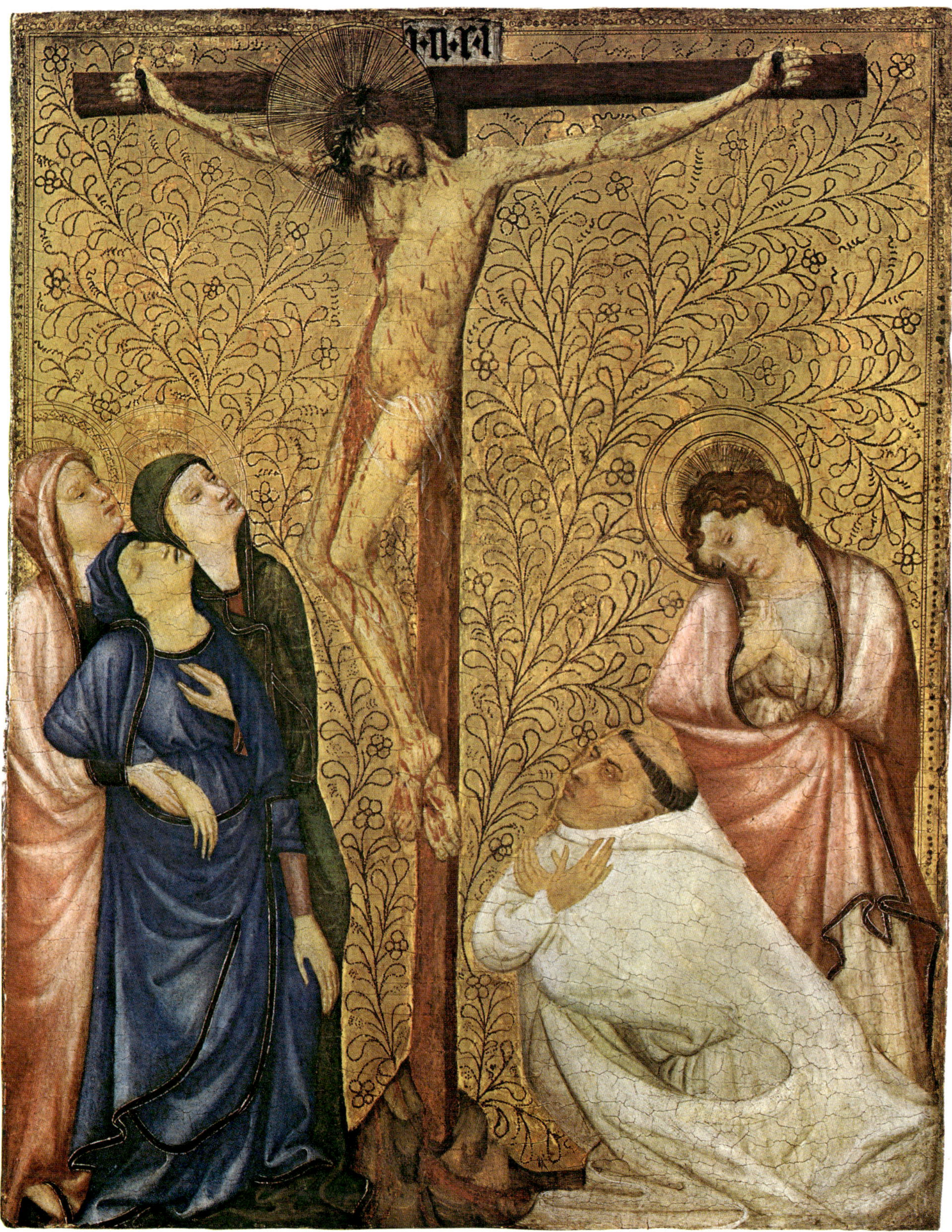

Plate III. *The Calvary with a Carthusian Monk*, Jean de Beaumetz (Painting 5).

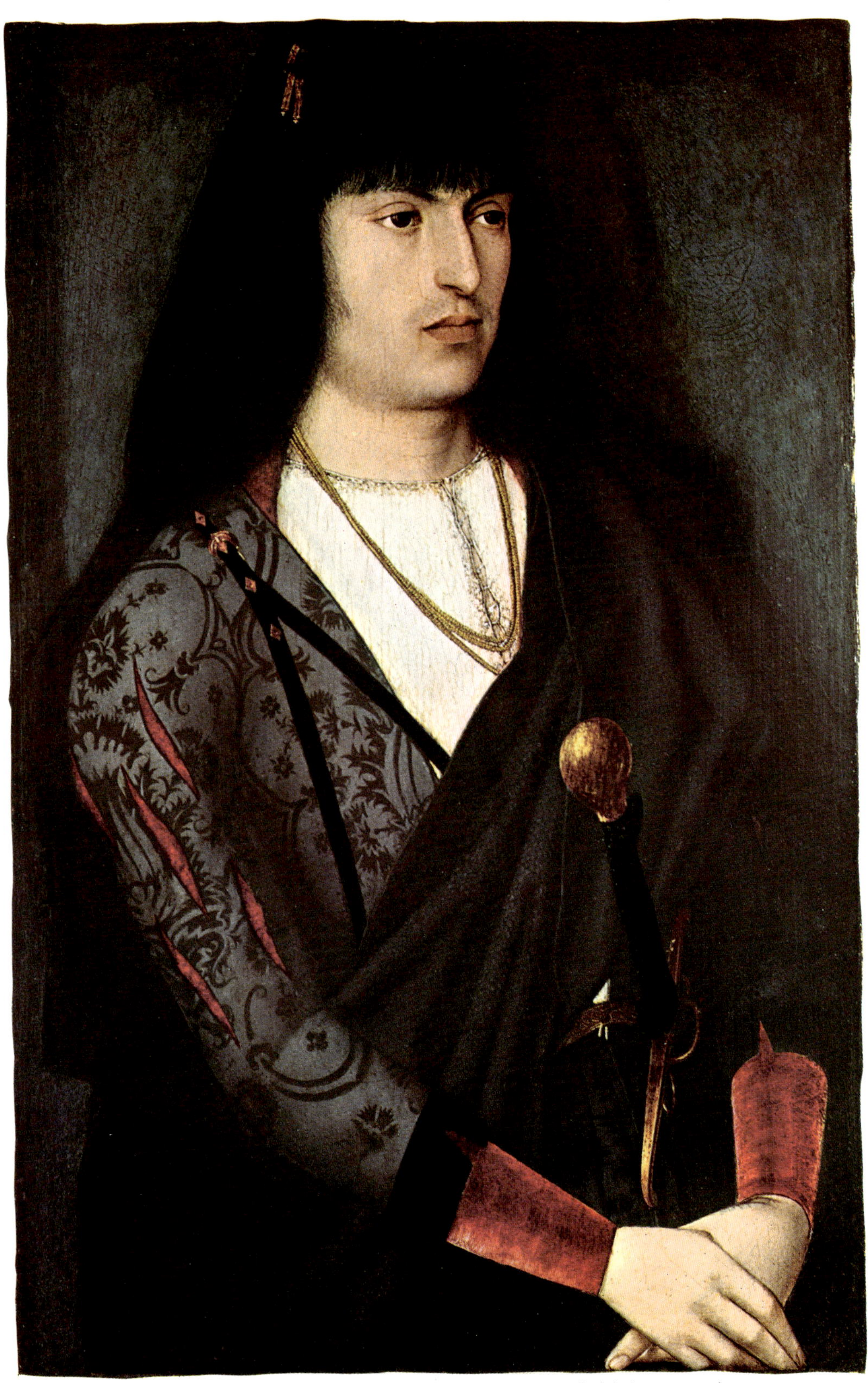

Plate IV. *Portrait of a Nobleman*, Anonymous French Master, Burgundy(?) (Painting 6).

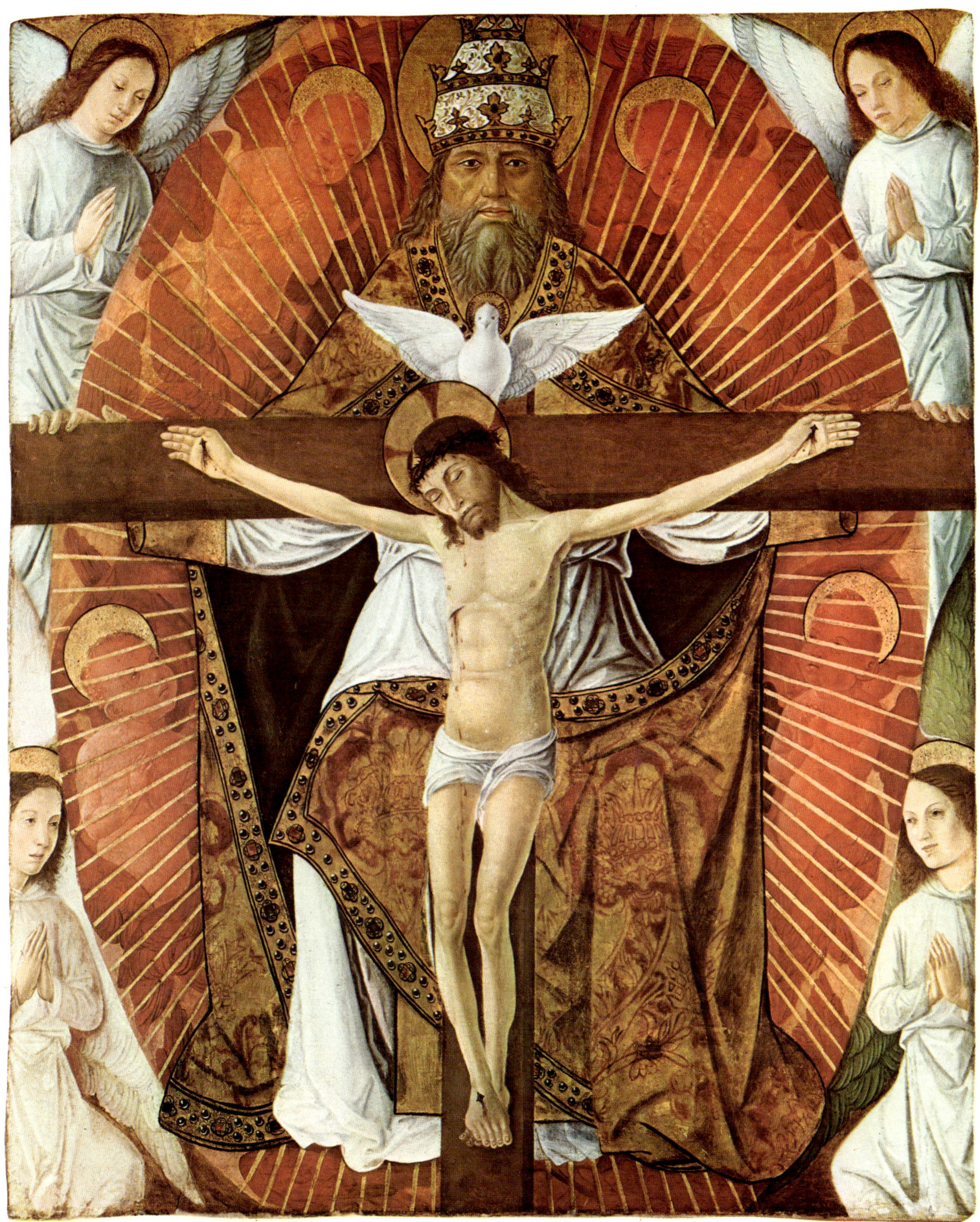

Plate v. *Holy Trinity*, Anonymous French Master, Provence(?) (Painting 7).

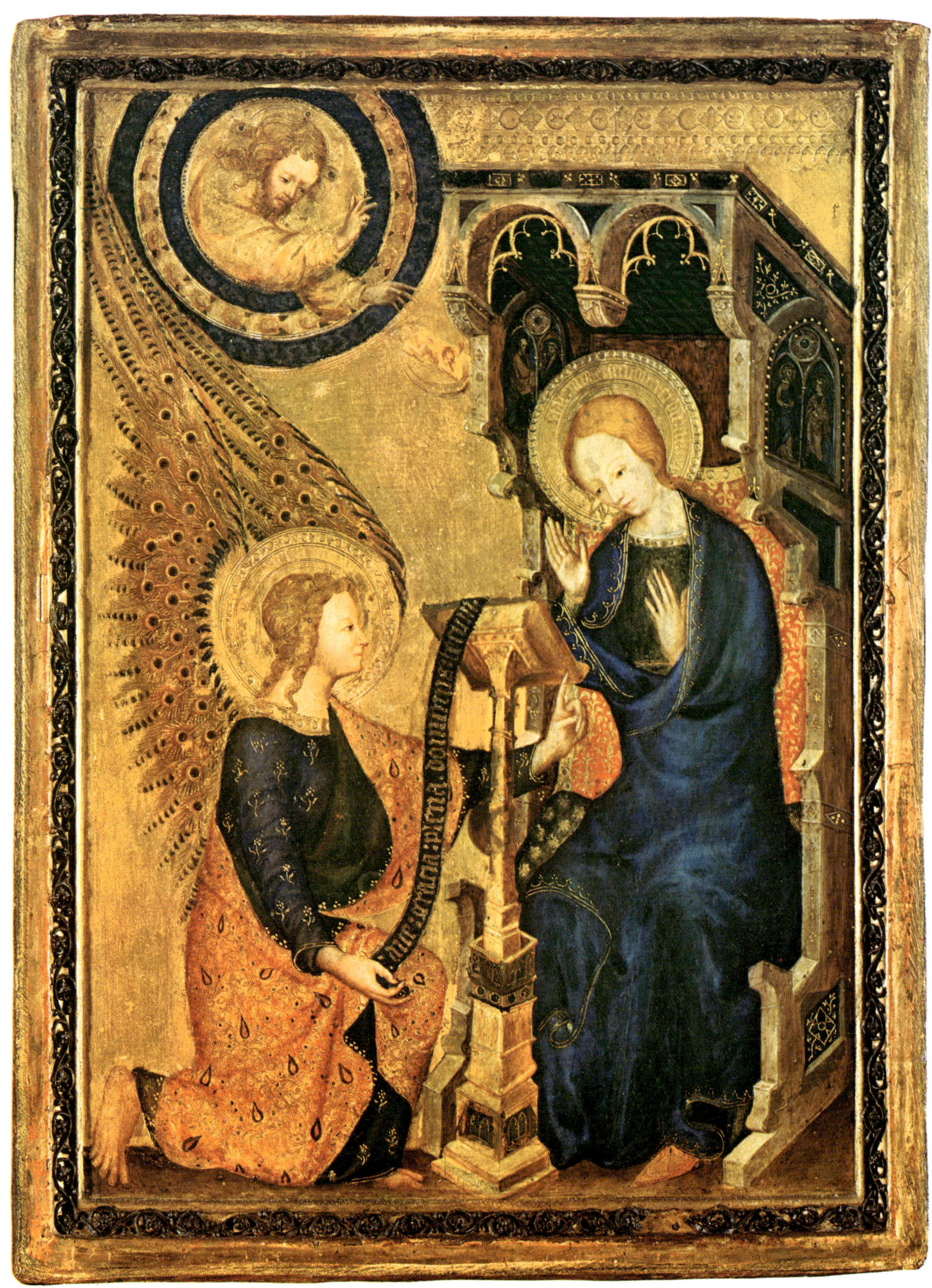

Plate VI. *The Annunciation*, Anonymous French Master, Paris(?), Hainaut(?) (Painting 8).

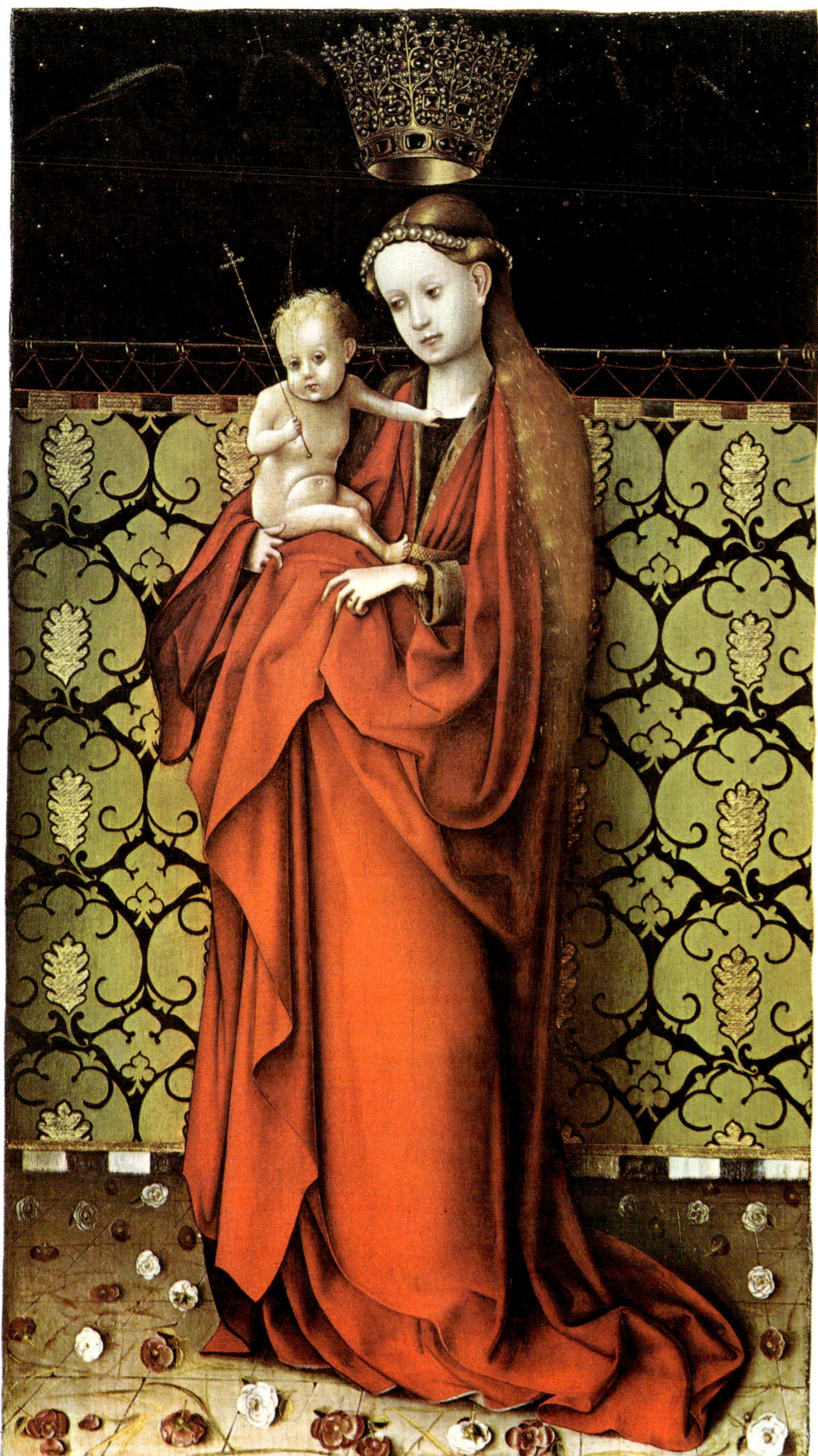

Plate VII. *Virgin Mary Crowned by Angels*, attributed to Stephen Lochner (Painting 9).

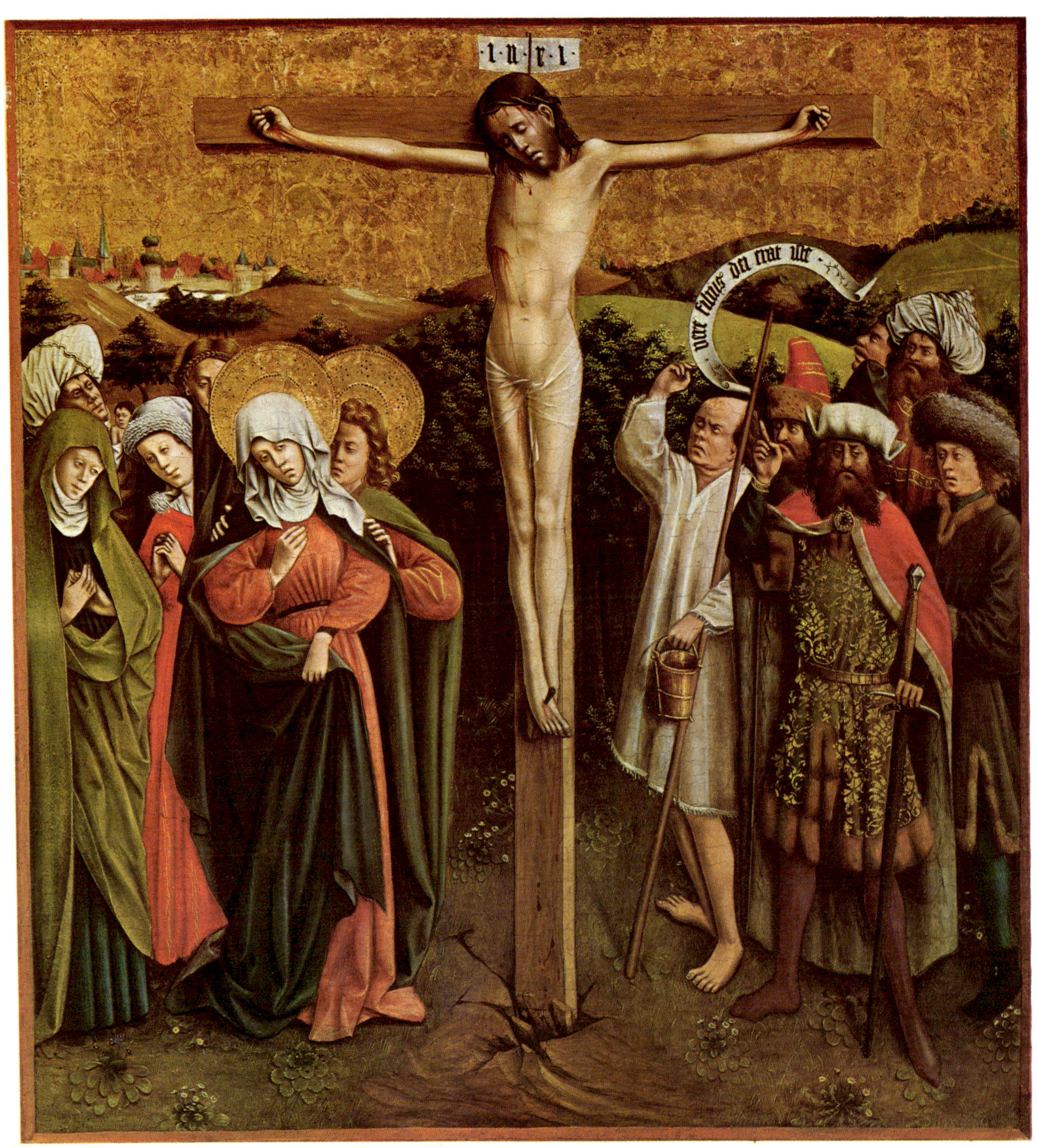

Plate VIII. *Passion of Christ*, Master of the Schlägl Altarpiece (center panel of Painting 11).

STEPHAN LOCHNER, attributed to, Cologne, died 1451

Lochner was probably born in Meersburg on Lake Constance since both his parents died there in 1451, the year of his own (most likely premature) death in Cologne. He is first mentioned in that city as a painter in 1442 under the names Meister Steffen and Stephain Loechener (Otto H. Förster, *Stefan Lochner*, Frankfurt am Main, 1938, pp. 119, 120). Albrecht Dürer passing through Cologne on his way to the Netherlands in 1520 identified the artist of the large altarpiece of the *Adoration of the Magi* as "Maister Stephan" (Förster, p. 133). This work (now in the cathedral of Cologne) marks Lochner as the major exponent of the Cologne School, revealing his affinity for the International Gothic Style developed under the influence of South German, Cologne, and above all, Netherlandish masters. There is no document attesting to an actual sojourn in the Netherlands, but his pictures offer sufficient evidence for a contact with the North.

9 *Virgin Mary Crowned by Angels* 68.20

Panel (fir), painted surface, 50·5 × 29·2 cm (19$\frac{7}{8}$ × 11$\frac{1}{2}$ inches).

COLLECTIONS: Kuno Kocherthaler, Berlin (reportedly bought on the advice of Wilhelm von Bode); (Pinakos, Inc.). John L. Severance Fund, 1968.

Except for a small filling along one joint passing through the drapery and the diminished visibility of the angels holding up the crown in the dark sky, the panel is in excellent condition.

The painting was first published by Stechow (1968) who attributed it to Stephan Lochner on the basis of style. He pointed to convincing similarities between the Virgin's head and that of the Virgin in the *Adoration of the Magi* as well as those of St. Ursula's lady companions in the sinister wing of the altarpiece in the Cathedral of Cologne (Fig. 9a) (cf., the spheric heads, rounded foreheads with high hairline, faint eyebrows, the fully-exposed ears, the small fleshy noses, the small white highlights above the lips, on noses, eyelids, etc.). Pointing to the indebtedness to Netherlandish colors in the Cleveland panel, Stechow suggests a date after Lochner's visit to the Netherlands, i.e., ca. 1440–1442. To support his argument Stechow draws convincing parallels between the Cleveland and Jan van Eyck's late Madonnas such as the *Madonna of the Fountain of*

1439 (Antwerp, Royal Museum) and the *Madonna of Nicholas van Maelbeke* begun ca. 1440 (collection of Earl of Warwick). The elaborately jewelled crown of the Cleveland *Virgin* echoes that of Van Eyck's *Madonna of the Church* (Berlin, Kaiser Friedrich Museum); with the latter she also shares the red robe coming to rest on the floor in sumptuous folds while her melancholic, meditative downward glance is more reminiscent of Robert Campin. While Urbach (1971) does not entirely dismiss the attribution to Lochner she suggests that distinct parallels with Campin's style point to a Pre-Eyckian model and may in fact reflect a lost early composition by that master.

A.T.L.

EXHIBITIONS: CMA, January 1969: Year in Review, cat. no. 67, illus.

LITERATURE: Wolfgang Stechow, "A Youthful Work by Stephan Lochner," CMA *Bulletin*, LV (1968), 305–314, illus. pp. 305 (color), 306, 307; Zsusza Urbach, Review of *Northern Painting from Pucelle to Brueghel: Fourteenth, Fifteenth and Sixteenth Centuries* by Charles D. Cuttler, *Acta Historiae Artium*, XVII (1971), 136, fig. 3.

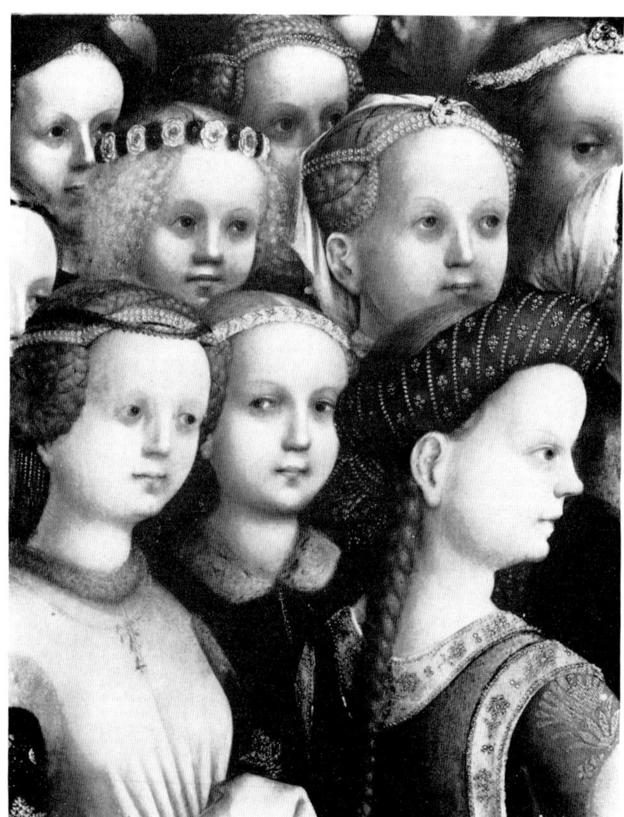

Figure 9a. *St. Ursula and Attendants* (detail of altarpiece). Lochner. Cathedral of Cologne.

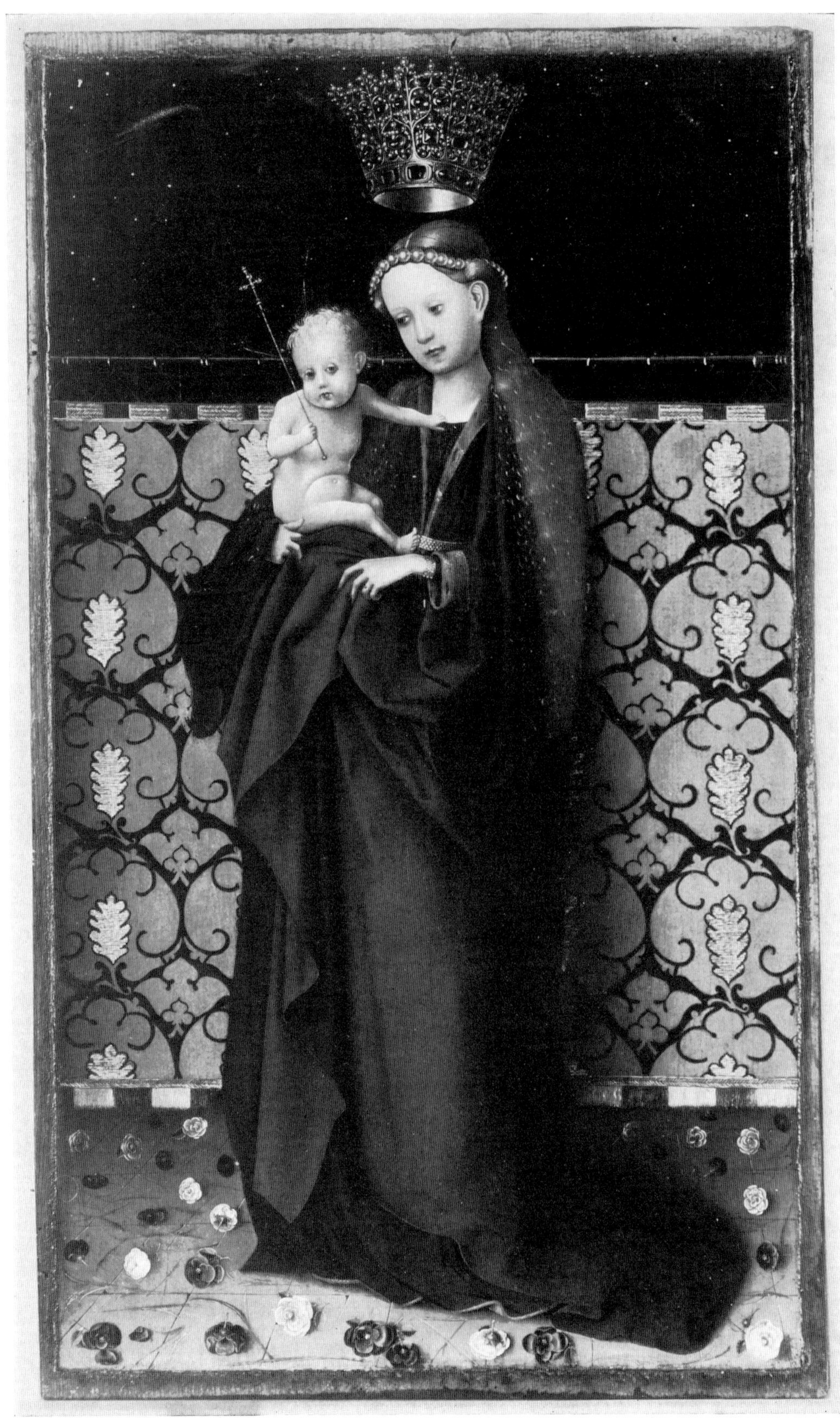

Figure 9. See also Colorplate VII.

MASTER OF THE FRÖNDENBERG ALTARPIECE, Westphalia, active early fifteenth century

The artist is named for the former high altar of the Cistercian convent at Fröndenberg on the Ruhr, of which the present panel formed a part. He was active in Westphalia in the early fifteenth century.

10 *The Coronation of the Virgin* 29.920

On the back: *St. Cecilia* (lower half only).

Panel (oak), 67·6 × 51·7 cm (26$\frac{5}{8}$ × 20$\frac{7}{16}$ inches).
Painted surface: 64·8 × 47·5 cm (25$\frac{1}{2}$ × 18$\frac{11}{16}$ inches).
PROVENANCE: Cistercian Convent, Fröndenberg.
COLLECTIONS: Haindorf, Münster, 1853; Loeb, Haus Caldenhof near Hamm, 1879 (sale: Rudolph Lepke, Berlin, June 8, 1929, no. 2); (A. S. Drey, Munich and New York).
Gift of the Friends of The Cleveland Museum of Art, 1929.

A strip about 4 inches high showing a depressed arch which had been added later, visible on the reproduction in the catalogue of the Loeb sale, has been removed. The name Stapelmann followed by the date 1816 is scribbled above CIA – all this is scratched into the surface of the paint at the center bottom edge of the panel (see Nissen, 1931).

The Fröndenberg altarpiece to which this panel originally belonged was dedicated to the Virgin Mary and ordered by Segele von Hamme whose kneeling figure appears on the *Nativity*. She was abbess of the convent between 1410 and 1422, but it is possible that she had the altar made at an earlier date, because it also contains the coat of arms of another abbess, Katharina von der Mark, who first took office in 1383 (Rensing, 1950). The main part of the altar with the central niche and eight panels from the life of Mary is still at Fröndenberg (Figs. 10*a*, *b*, *c*) with the exception of the Virgin and Child originally placed in the lower niche (now in the Museum at Dortmund, *Europäische Kunst um 1400*, exh. cat.; Vienna, Kunsthistorisches Museum, 1962, no. 48). Of the wing

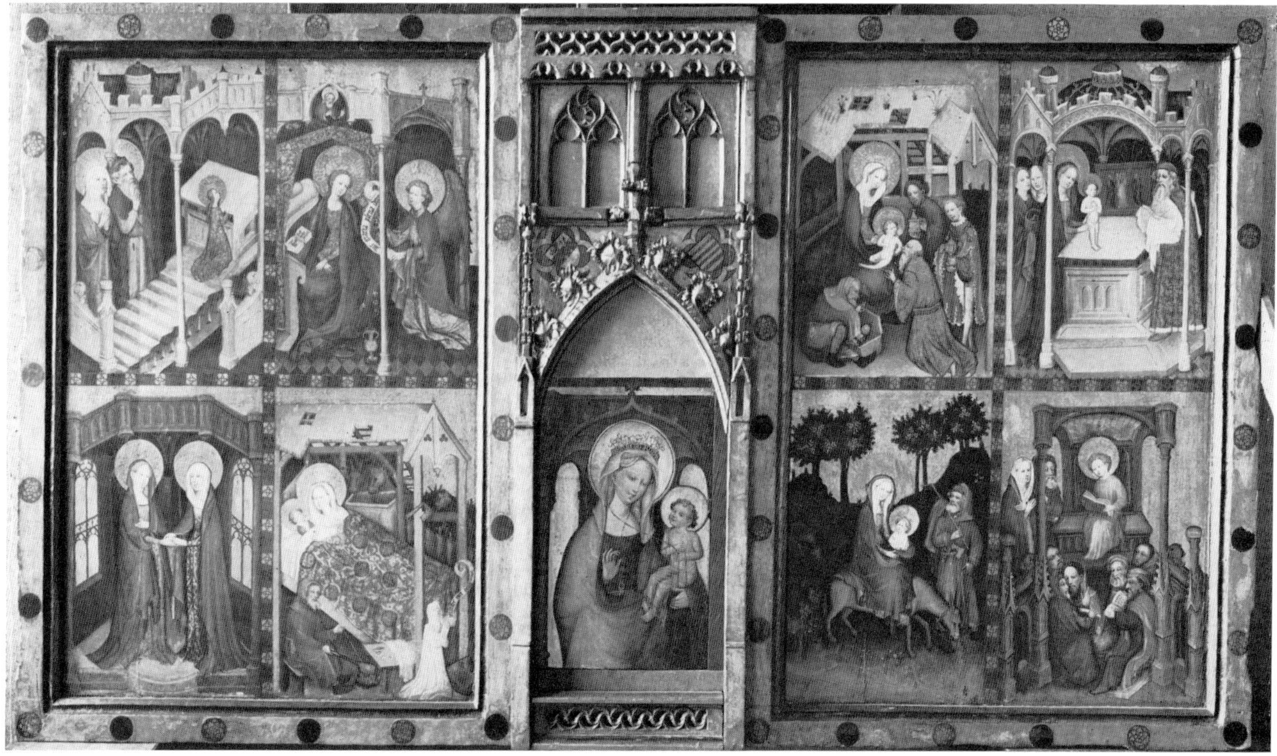

Figure 10*a*. *The Life of Mary*, main part of the altar formerly in the Cistercian convent in Fröndenberg. 168 × 300 cm (66$\frac{1}{8}$ × 118$\frac{1}{8}$ inches), including original molding. Master of the Fröndenberg Altarpiece. Museum für Kunst und Kulturgeschichte der Stadt Dortmund (central panel only); Landesmuseum für Kunst und Kulturgeschichte, Münster.

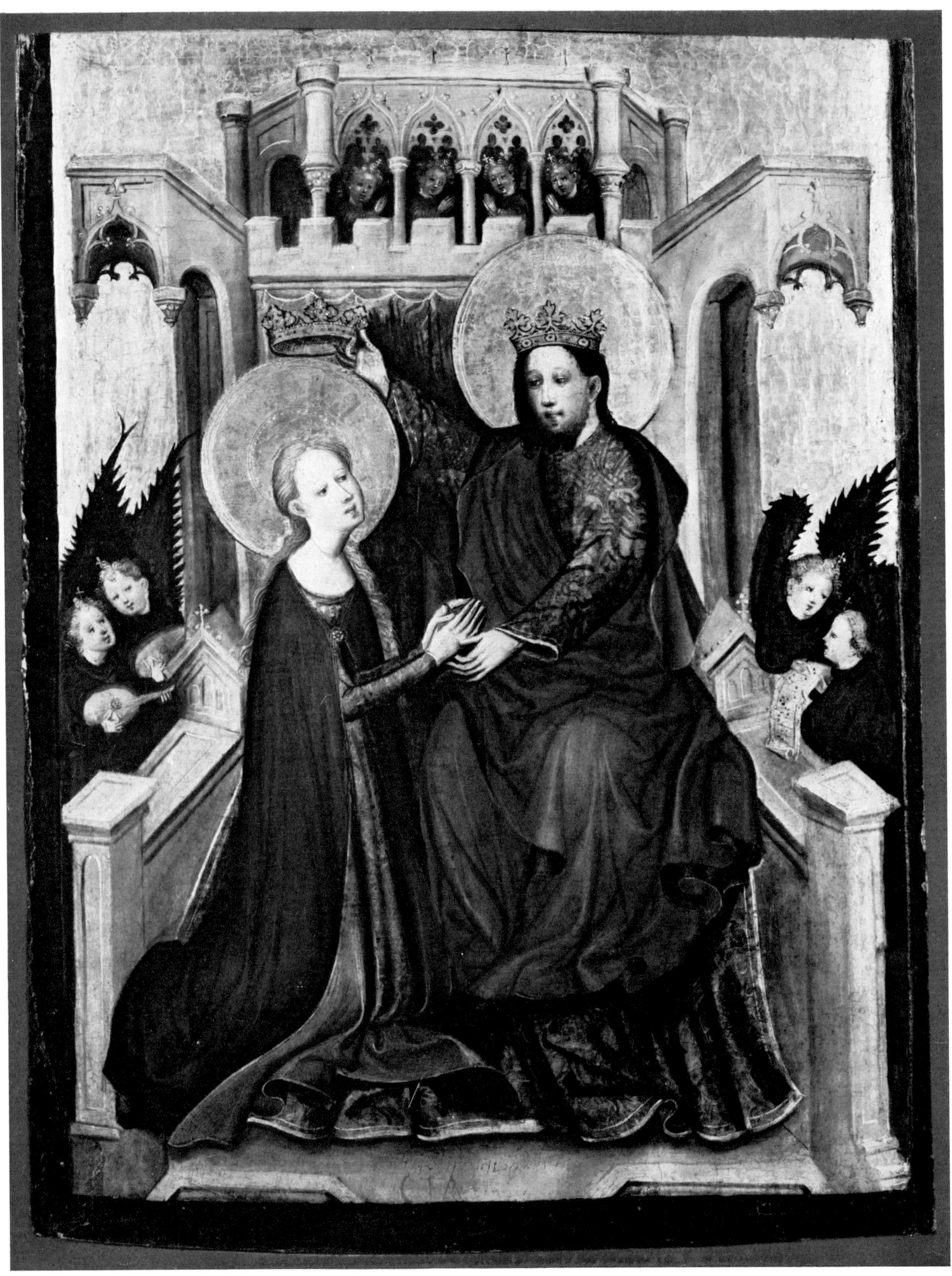

Figure 10.

panels only the *Pentecost* (Fig. 10*d*) and the Cleveland *Coronation* have survived; the former was sawed apart vertically so that its reverse, showing the upper part of the figure of St. Cecilia, now forms a separate picture whereas the Cleveland Museum painting still has the lower part of that figure intact on its reverse (see reconstruction Fig. 10*e*). This combination proves that the *Coronation* occupied the lower right corner of the sinister wing of the altar when opened. The older attribution of the altarpiece to Conrad von Soest was recently revived with an early date (shortly before 1400, Rensing, 1950) but it has little chance of being widely accepted in spite of the very close connection with the style of that master.

W.S.

EXHIBITIONS: Münster, Collegium Ludgerianum, 1879: Ausstellung westfälischer Alterthümer und Kunsterzeugnisse, cat. no. 1446; CMA (1936), cat. no. 210, pl. XLI; Boston, Museum of Fine Arts, 1940: Art of the Middle Ages, 1000–1400, cat. no. 77; Dortmund, Museum für Kunst und Kulturgeschichte, 1950: Conrad von Soest und sein Kreis, cat. no. 79; CMA (1963), cat. no. 51.

LITERATURE: Wilhelm Lübke, *Die mittelalterliche Kunst in Westfalen* (Leipzig, 1853), 344; J. B. Nordhoff, "Die Soester Malerei unter Meister Conrad," *Bonner Jahrbücher*, LXVII (1879), 126; A. Ludorff, *Die Bau- und Kunstdenkmäler von Westfalen, Kreis Soest* (Münster, 1905), 148; Hermann Schmitz in Burger–Schmitz–Beth, *Deutsche Malerei der Renaissance* (Handbuch der Kunstwissenschaft), II (Berlin, 1917), 400; Carl Hoelker, *Meister Conrad von Soest und seine Bedeutung für die norddeutsche Malerei in der ersten Hälfte des 15. Jahrhunderts*, no. 7: Beiträge zur Westfälischen Kunstgeschichte (Münster, 1921), p. 44; William M. Milliken, "Coronation of the Virgin, by Conrad von Soest," *CMA Bulletin*, XVII (1930), 19–22, illus. p. 18; Robert Nissen, "Der Meister des Fröndenberger Altares," *Westfalen*, XVI (1931), 62–65; Hans Tietze, *Meisterwerke europäischer Malerei in Amerika* (Vienna, 1935), pl. 195; Charles Louis Kuhn, *A Catalogue of German Paintings of the Middle Ages and Renaissance in American Collections* (Cambridge, Mass., 1936), no. 62; Stange, III (1938), 35–37, fig. 36; Theodor Rensing, "Rätsel um Konrad von Soest," *Westfalen*, XXVIII (1950), 164; Henry S. Francis, *American-German Review*, p. 8, illus.; *Bau- und Kunstdenkmäler von Westfalen*, XLVII: *Kreis Unna* (1959), 138; *Handbook* (1966), p. 66; Georg Troescher, *Burgundische Malerei* (Berlin, 1966), I, 64; II, pl. 59, fig. 176; Stange, *Kritisches Verzeichnis der deutschen Tafelbilder vor Dürer*, I (Munich, 1967), 143, no. 461; William D. Wixom, "An Enthroned Madonna with the Writing Christ Child," *CMA Bulletin*, LVII (1970), 297, fig. 23.

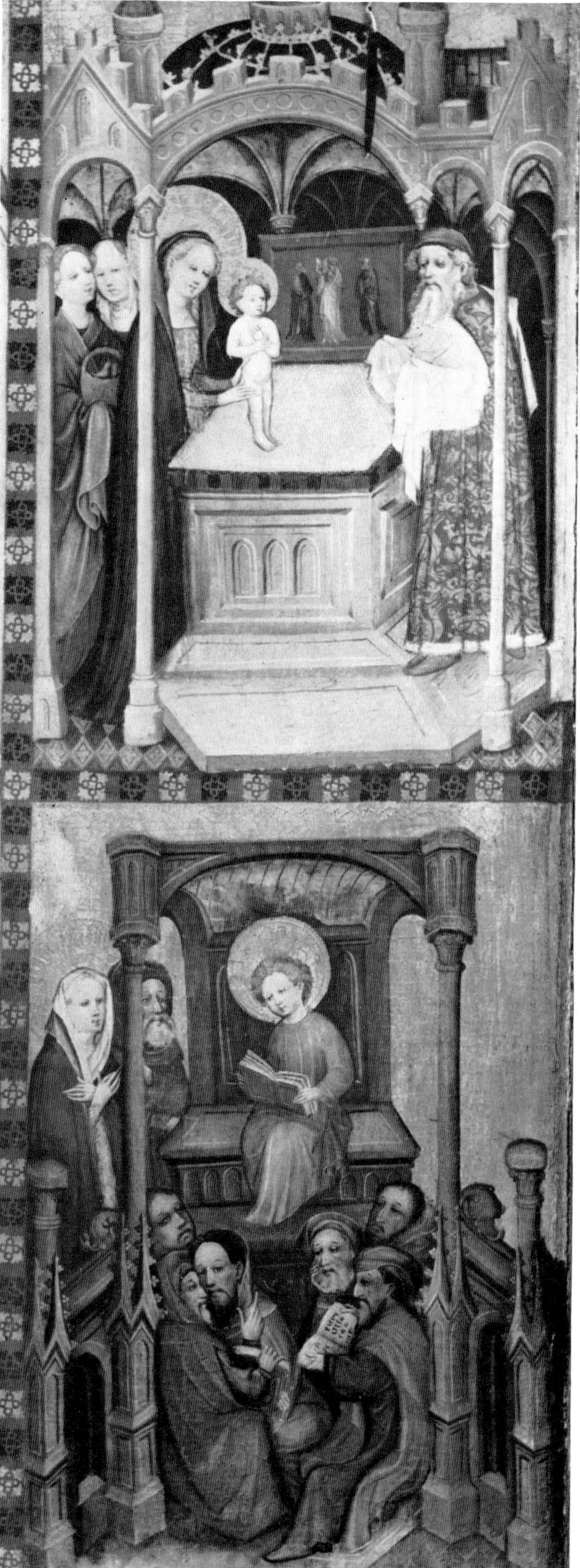

Figures 10*b, c.* Details of Figure 10*a.*

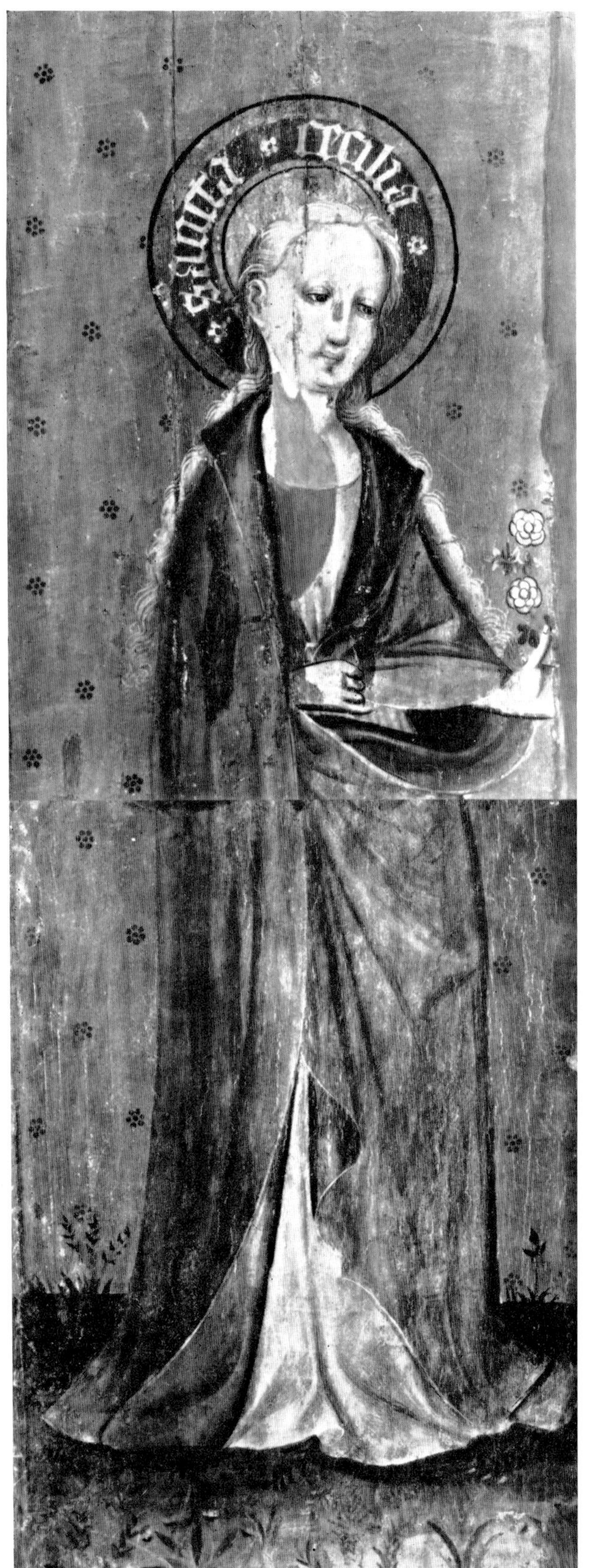

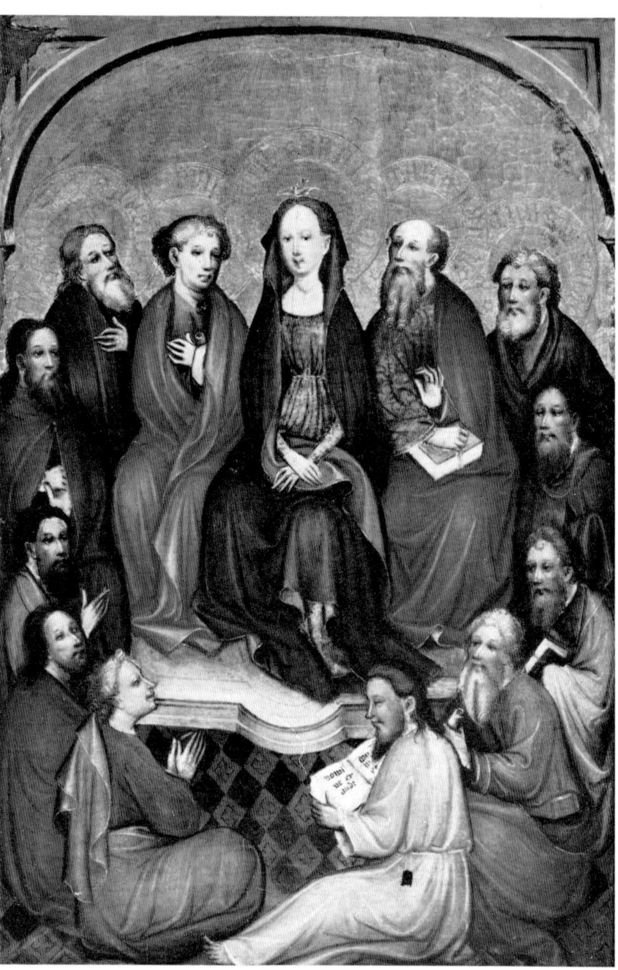

Figure 10*d*. *Pentecost*, wing panel from the Fröndenberg altar. 77 × 52 cm ($30\frac{5}{16} \times 20\frac{1}{2}$ inches).
Landesmuseum für Kunst und Kulturgeschichte.

Figure 10*e*. Reconstruction of *St. Cecilia*.
Top: Reverse (now separated) of Figure 10*d*.
Landesmuseum für Kunst und Kulturgeschichte.
Bottom: Reverse of Figure 10.

MASTER OF THE SCHLÄGL
ALTARPIECE, Westphalia, active ca. 1440–1450

11 *Passion of Christ*   51.453

Polyptych

Center panel: *Crucifixion*
Dexter above: *Agony in the Garden*; *Derision*
Dexter below: *Christ before Pilate(?)*; *Flagellation*
Sinister above: *Crowning with Thorns*; *Christ
   Bearing the Cross*
Sinister below: *Lamentation*; *Christ Falling under
   the Cross*

Panels (oak): *Crucifixion*: 74·3 × 69·8 cm (29$\frac{1}{8}$ × 27$\frac{1}{2}$ inches).
*Agony in the Garden, Christ Falling under the Cross, Christ
before Pilate, Christ Bearing the Cross,* and *Lamentation*:
36·2 × 34·9 cm (14$\frac{1}{4}$ × 13$\frac{3}{4}$ inches). *Derision, Crowning with
Thorns,* and *Flagellation*: 36·2 × 35·6 cm (14$\frac{1}{4}$ × 14 inches).
COLLECTIONS: Schlägl Abbey, Upper Austria, 1870s, still
there in the 1930s; (Rosenberg & Stiebel, New York).
Mr. and Mrs. William H. Marlatt Fund, 1951.

Comparison with the organization of related altarpieces
(Niederwildungen, Warendorf, Hildesheim, Osterwieck; see the diagrams given by P. J. Meier, "Konrad
von Soest," *Westfalen*, XVI, 1931, 43 ff.) shows that the
present distribution of the panels is not the original one.
There are no scenes pertaining to the Resurrection and
after; it is almost certain that only the dexter wing (four

panels), the *Crucifixion* of the center part, the three out of
four panels flanking it, and one panel (*Lamentation*) of the
sinister wing have survived, while the three other panels
of the sinister wing (probably *Resurrection*, *Ascension*, and
Pentecost or *Last Judgment*) and one panel of the center
part (probably *Ecce Homo*) are missing. Cracks running
through superimposed (or originally superimposed)
panels indicate that the dexter wing showed the present
sequence and that the two scenes of *Christ Bearing the
Cross* were placed on top of each other on the sinister side
of the *Crucifixion*; the *Crowning of Thorns* must have
appeared on the upper dexter side of the *Crucifixion*,
probably with the lost *Ecce Homo* underneath (Pieper,
orally 1965). The *Lamentation* probably appeared on the
upper left of the sinister wing (the *Entombment* is placed
thus on the Osterwieck altarpiece). The altarpiece is reported to have been given to the Premonstratensian Abbey of Schlägl, Upper Austria, in the 1870s by a Munich
painter named Müller. In spite of recent assumptions
about connections with the Hamburg School and with
Master Francke in particular (Busch, 1940; Stange, 1967),
its Westphalian character is obvious (already stressed
by Tietze, 1913) even though the identification of its
painter with Johann Koerbecke himself (Rensing, 1948;
1959; already tentatively proposed by Erwin Hainisch,
"Schlägl," in Georg Dehio, *Handbuch der deutschen Kunstdenkmäler*, II: *Österreich*, Vienna, Berlin, 1935, 584) is
hardly acceptable. The soft modeling of faces is most
closely related to the Haldern altarpiece of the Master of

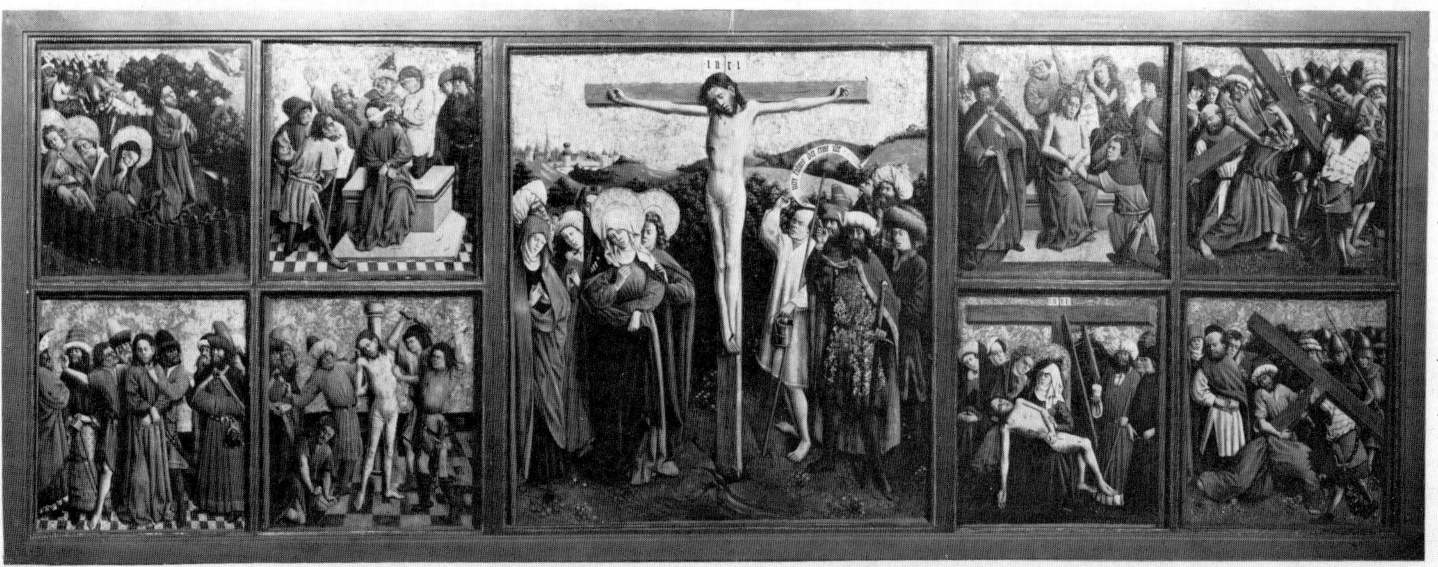

Figure 11. See also Colorplate VIII.

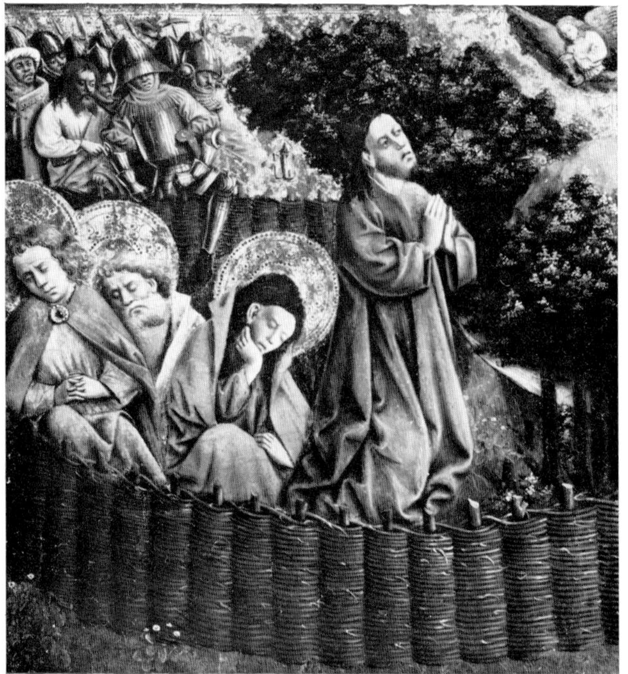

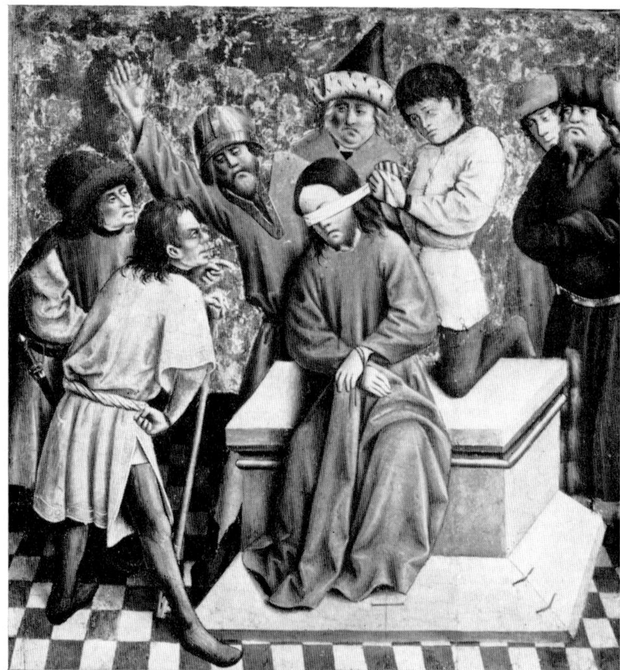

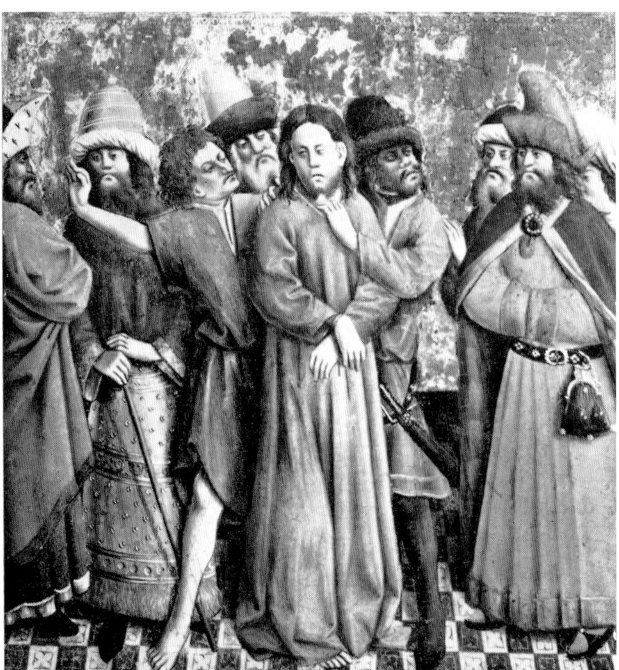

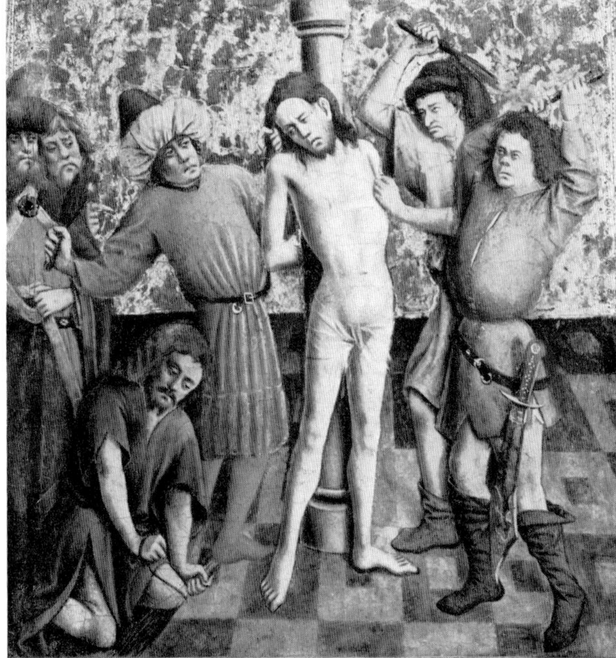

Figures 11 *a*, *b*, *c*, *d*. Panels of the dexter wing.

Schöppingen – and in choice of colors to Koerbecke's Langenhorst altarpiece, an early work of the master. The Schlägl altarpiece stands between these two, and its date probably falls in the same decade (1440s). Also closely related is the altarpiece at Steinhagen (Exh: 1952, p. 25).

W.S.

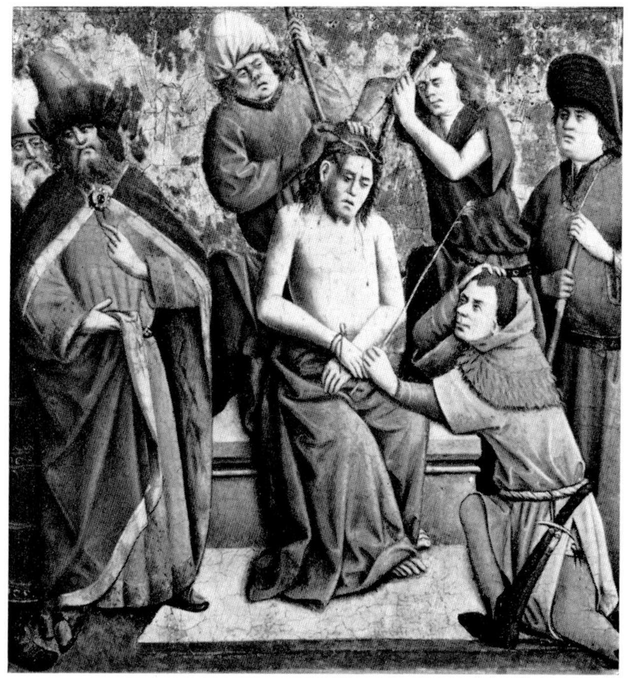

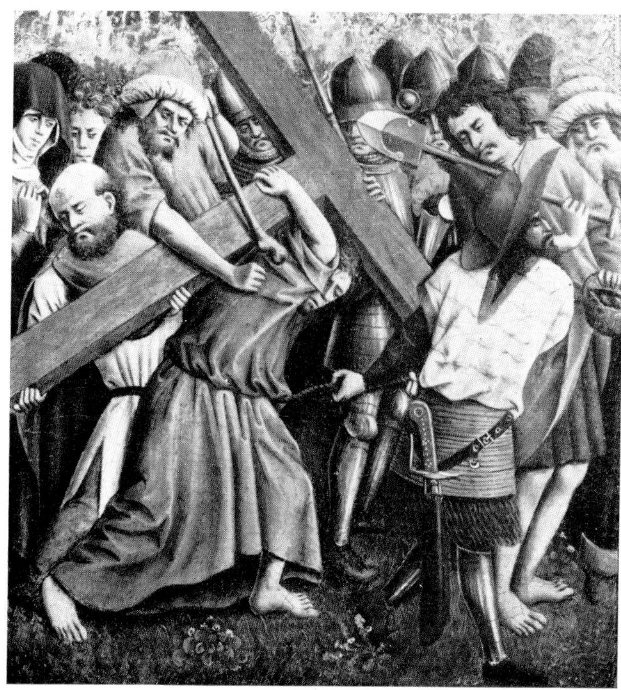

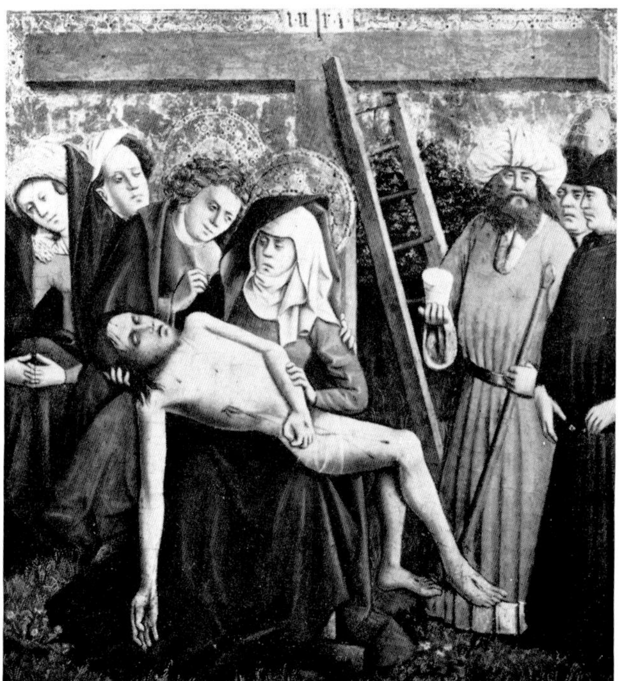

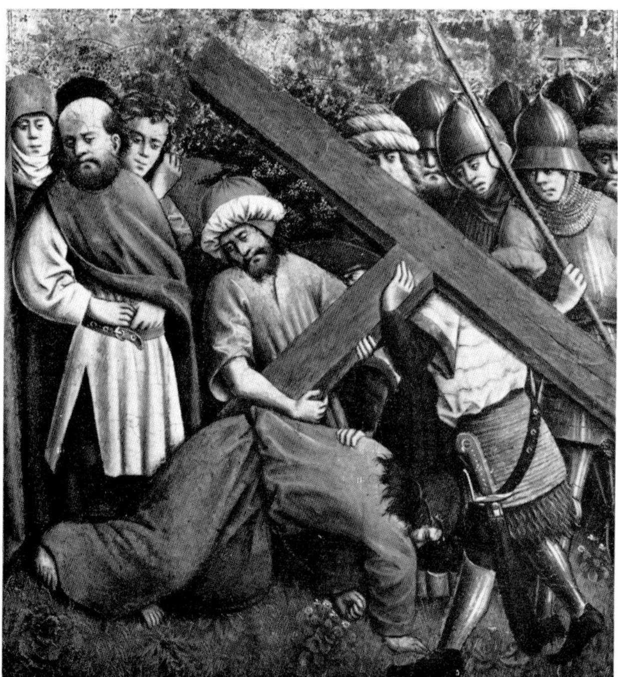

Figures 11 *e, f, g, h*. Panels of the sinister wing.

184; Johannes Sommer, "Johann Koerbecke, der Meister des Marienfelder Altares von 1457," *Westfalen*, XVI (1937), 42; Stange, III (1938), 213, figs. 273–274; Harald Busch, *Meister des Nordens* (Hamburg, 1940), p. 66, no. 11; Theodor Rensing, "Der Meister von Schöppingen," *Westfalen*, XXVII (1948), 224, 240–241; Thieme–Becker, XXXVII (1950), 301–302; Henry S. Francis, "The Schlägl Altarpiece," CMA *Bulletin*, XXXIX (1952), 213–215, illus. pp. 210–211; Stange, VI (1954), 75, 76; Francis, *American-German Review*, p. 7; Rensing, *Der Meister von Schöppingen* (Munich, Berlin, 1959), pp. 36–37; *Handbook* (1966), p. 67; Stange, *Kritisches Verzeichnis der deutschen Tafelbilder vor Dürer*, I (Munich, 1967), 178, no. 579; Paul Pieper, "Meister Francke und die niederdeutsche Kunst," *Meister Francke und die Kunst um 1400* (exh. cat.; Hamburg Kunsthalle, 1969), p. 38, illus. p. 37; Heinrich Theodor Musper, *Altdeutsche Malerei* (Cologne, 1970), pp. 49–50, illus. no. 39 (detail).

33

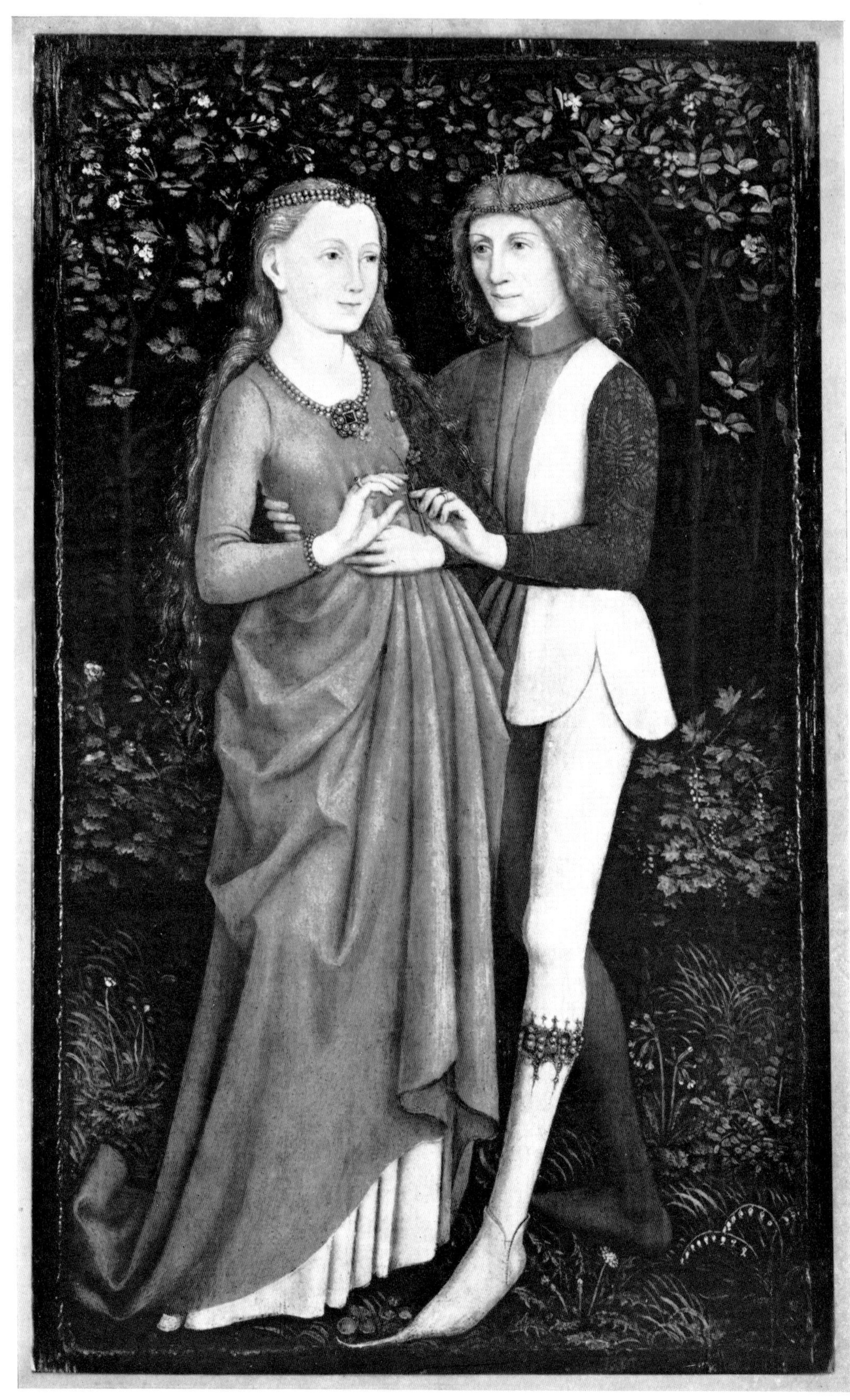

Figure 12. See also Colorplate IX.

ANONYMOUS SOUTH GERMAN MASTER, Upper Rhine Region, ca. 1470

12 *A Bridal Pair* 32.179

Panel (fir), 64·7 × 39·5 cm (25½ × 15½ inches). Painted surface: 62·3 × 36·5 cm (24½ × 14⅜ inches).

COLLECTIONS: L. Schutzenberger, 1825–1903, Strasbourg; André Weil, Paris; (Wildenstein & Co., New York).

Delia E. and L. E. Holden Funds, 1932.

The original panel has been shaved down to a thickness of about ⅛ inch (apparently after separation from its reverse), mounted on a new panel and cradled. There is some abrasion and subsequent strengthening in the faces.

The reverse of this picture showing two decaying bodies (Fig. 12 a) was published as by Grünewald (*Catalogue des peintures anciennes*, Musée des Beaux-Arts de la Ville de Strasbourg, 1938, no. 10); it, too, was in the Schutzenberger collection, then that of Hauser in Paris, and Weil. If, as is reliably reported, the Cleveland panel was in a private collection ca. 1920 in Mühlhausen on the Neckar (which would explain why the Schutzenberger collection was sometimes erroneously reported to have been located at Mülhausen in Alsace), it must have been separated from its reverse panel and reunited with it later, since Weil owned both of them. That the Cleveland and Strasbourg panels, of exactly the same size, belonged together as a Wedding–Death allegory has become more certain with the recent rediscovery of a corresponding double panel by the Master of the Aachen Cabinet Doors in Aloysius College at Godesberg (Syndicus, 1952).

The two figures are probably portraits, although the panel contains no coat of arms, inscription, or date; these may have been originally found on the frame as may also be assumed in the case of the Godesberg panel. The reversal of the customary heraldic position of groom and bride points to dependence on a tapestry or more probably a print; in fact, the composition is very closely related (Buchner, 1953) to that of an engraving by Israel van Meckenem (L. 486), which in turn reproduces a lost early work by Master E. S. The matching of the two left sleeves (brown foliated damask) continues a medieval tradition of courtly love (Francis, 1932). The circlets in the hair of the bride and groom go back to an antique custom taken up again in the fifteenth century (Hutchison, 1958); the unbound hair of the girl is part of the more formal bridal coiffure of the time and signifies

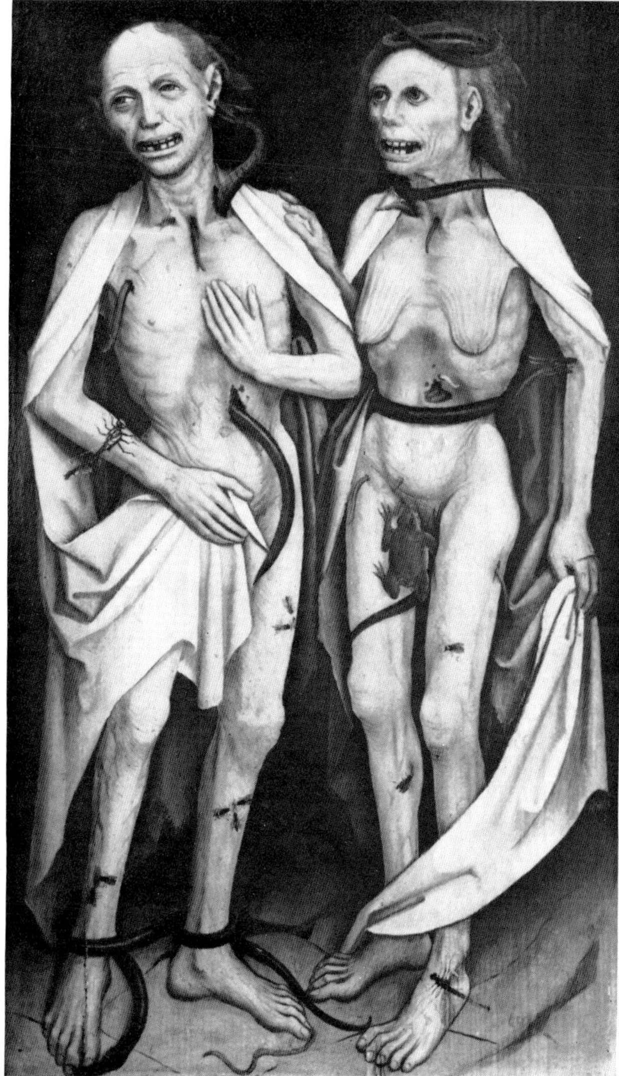

Figure 12 a. *Les Amants trépassés*.
64·8 × 40 cm (25½ × 15¾ inches).
Attributed to Grünewald, ca. 1470–1480 to 1528.
Musée des Beaux-Arts de la Ville de Strasbourg.
Formerly reverse side of Figure 12.

purity (Hutchison, 1958, after Panofsky). The flower symbolism is complex (Behling, 1957) and contains allusions to both love and death – in evidence are roses, cherry blossoms, white currant bushes, buttercups, clover, dandelions, lilies-of-the-valley, cowslip, moneywort, and valerian. The blossoms worn by the youth and tendered to his bride are probably wild chicory, a favorite love-magic symbol.

The artist may well have been related to the School of Ulm but is certainly not (as claimed by Musper, 1949; 1961, less certain in the latter), identical with the Master of the Sterzing Altarpiece; his colors and method of modeling are softer, his interpretation is more lyrical and restrained than the latter's. A distinct Upper Rhenish element is noticeable (Stange, 1957, but with attribution still to Sterzing Master), although the attribution to Schongauer (Naumann, 1935) is as unconvincing as that of its reverse to Grünewald. The provenance of the panel points in the same direction. The seeming stylistic difference between obverse and reverse is most probably due to a conscious effort to contrast the two subjects, and partly to different states of preservation. Buchner (1953) considered the *St. George*, formerly Holford collection, a work of the same master.

W.S.

EXHIBITIONS: Brooklyn Museum, 1936: European Art 1450–1500, cat. no. 38; CMA (1936), cat. no. 190, pl. XLII; New York, World's Fair, 1939: Masterpieces of Art, cat. no. 140.

LITERATURE: Henry S. Francis, "A German Primitive of the Swabian School," CMA *Bulletin*, XIX (1932), 127–131; Hans Tietze, *Meisterwerke europäischer Malerei in Amerika* (Vienna, 1935), p. 198; Hans Heinrich Naumann, "Le premier élève de Martin Schongauer: Mathias Nithart," *Archives alsaciennes*, XIV (1935), 7, 61–64, 145; Charles Louis Kuhn, *A Catalogue of German Paintings of the Middle Ages and Renaissance in American Collections* (Cambridge, Mass., 1936), no. 244; Francis, "The Lovers: A Swabian Gothic Picture of Secular Life in the Fifteenth Century," *Gaz. des B.-A.*, XXIV (1943), 343–354, illus. 353; Heinrich Theodor Musper, "Ein Ulmer Verlöbnisbild," *Die Kunst und das schöne Heim*, XLVII (1949), 204–205; Hans Kauffmann, "Rubens und Isabella Brant in der Geissblattlaube," *Form und Inhalt, Kunstgeschichtliche Studien Otto Schmitt zum 60. Geburtstag* . . . (Stuttgart, 1950), p. 260; Stange (1952), 36; Eduard Syndicus, "Hochzeit und Tod – ein wiederentdecktes Bild," *Zeitschrift für Kunstwissenschaft*, VI (1952), 48, 49; Ernst Buchner, *Das deutsche Bildnis der Spätgotik und der frühen Dürerzeit* (Berlin, 1953), pp. 170–172; Hans Haug, "Les Origines de l'élément demoniaque: Grünewald," *Atti del II Congresso Internazionale di Studi Umanistici. Part II: L'Umanesimo e il Demoniaco nell'arte* (Rome, 1953), p. 254, pl. 28; Francis, *American-German Review*, 8; Wolfgang Schöne, *Peter Paul Rubens: Die Geissblattlaube* (Stuttgart, 1956), p. 12; Lottlisa Behling, *Die Pflanze in der mittelalterlichen Tafelmalerei* (Weimar, 1957), p. 77, pl. 86; Stange (1957), 8; Jane C. Hutchison, "The Development of the Double Portrait in Northern European Painting of the Fifteenth Century" (unpublished Master's dissertation, Oberlin College, 1958), pp. 58–64, pl. XXX; *Handbook* (1958), no. 457; Victor Beyer, "La peinture alsacienne à l'aube du XVIe siècle," *L'Information d'histoire de l'art*, V (1960), 20, illus. p. 18; Musper, *Gotische Malerei nördlich der Alpen* (Cologne, 1961), p. 90, illus. p. 91 (color); Blanche Payne, *History of Costume* (New York, 1965), p. 228, illus. p. 229; Stange, *Deutsche Spätgotische Malerei, 1430–1500* (Königstein im Taunus, 1965), p. 7, illus. p. 40; *Handbook* (1966), p. 67; *Selected Works* (1966), p. 109; Alfred Schädler, "Beiträge zum Werk Hans Multschers," *Anzeiger des Germanischen Nationalmuseums* (1969), 61, n. 72; Musper, *Altdeutsche Malerei* (Cologne, 1970), p. 20, pl. 13.

School of ANDREA DI BONAIUTO DA
FIRENZE, Florence, active ca. 1343–1377

In his discussion of the painter Andrea da Firenze, painter
of the fresco cycle in the Camposanto in Pisa and the
frescoes in the Spanish Chapel in S. Maria Novella of ca.
1365–1368, J. B. Supino (Thieme–Becker, I, 1907, 452–
453) suggests that two artistic personalities are involved,
both active in Florence between 1330 and 1374. One is
Andrea di Ristoro, mentioned in the Florentine painters'
guild in 1333 and who died ca. 1392. The other, Andrea
di Bonaiuto, was a member of the guild in 1343 and the
Company of St. Luke in 1374; while it is known that he
made his testament in 1377, no death date is known.
Andrea di Bonaiuto was commissioned in 1366 to make
the model for the S. Maria del Fiore. Since it is closely
related to the Chiesa Universale which is depicted in the
frescoes of the Spanish Chapel of S. Maria Novella,
Supino is led to assume that Andrea di Bonaiuto and
Andrea da Firenze may be the same person.

13   *The Crucifixion*   16.776

Right shutter from a tabernacle

Panel (walnut), 31 × 13·4 cm ($12\frac{3}{16} \times 5\frac{1}{4}$ inches).
COLLECTIONS: Minor K. Kellogg, Paris and Cleveland,
by 1858–1889; Mrs. Liberty E. Holden, Cleveland
(acquired from Kellogg rather than Jarves as previously
thought).
Holden Collection, 1916.

The panel seems to have been cut slightly at the bottom
and was probably originally surmounted by a *Virgin
Annunciate* as in the Rothermere tabernacle (Paul George
Konody, *Works of Art in the Collection of the Viscount
Rothermere*, London, 1932, pl. 4). The paint surface is
somewhat worn. There are indications that Christ's loin-
cloth once fluttered out at the right as in the so-called
Black Crucifixion (Fig. 13 *a*) (which according to Sirén,
"Alcune note aggiuntive a quadri nella galleria vaticana," *L'Arte*, XXIV, 1921, 98, 99, has suffered from re-
painting).

    When in the Kellogg collection (1858) this *Crucifixion*
was attributed to Giottino. Rubinstein (1917) called it
Sienese School, late fourteenth century; Frank J. Mather
(written comments in the Museum's files, 1921) listed it
as "School of Simone Martini, after 1350." The Cleveland Museum (Exh.: 1936) catalogued it as Florentine,
perhaps by a follower of Giovanni da Milano, and later
(about 1940) attributed it to Allegretto Nuzi. Andrea da

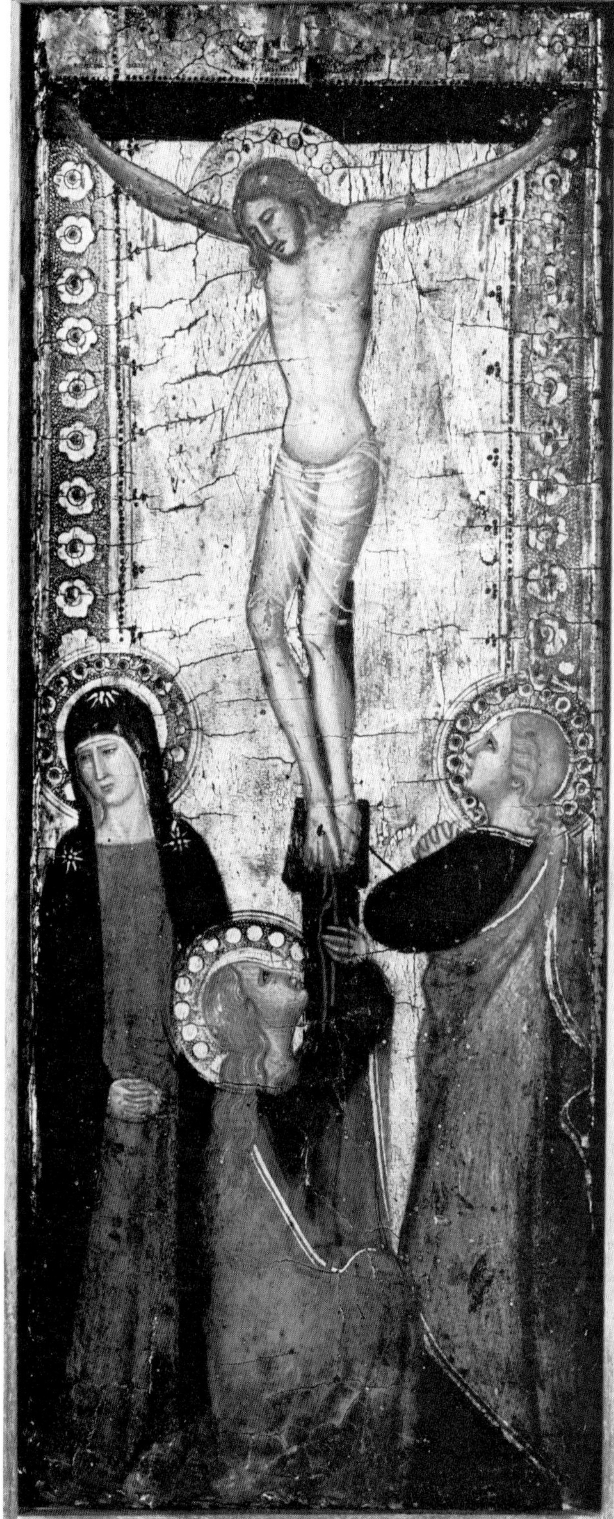

Figure 13.

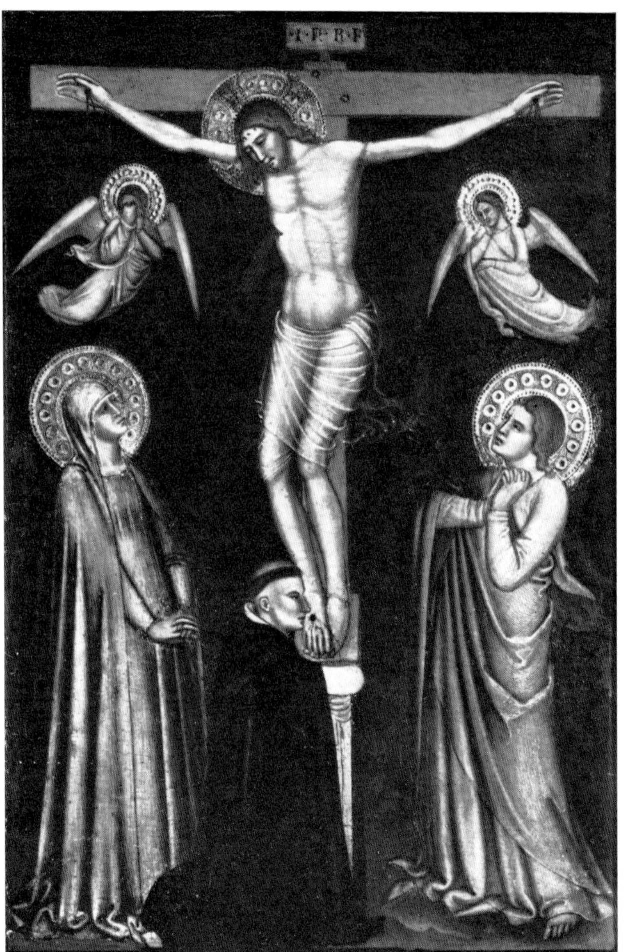

Figure 13 *a. Christ on the Cross with Saints.*
3·25 × 2·45 cm (127$\frac{7}{8}$ × 96$\frac{7}{16}$ inches). Master of
the Black Crucifixion. Florence, fourteenth century.
Pinacoteca Vaticana, 118.

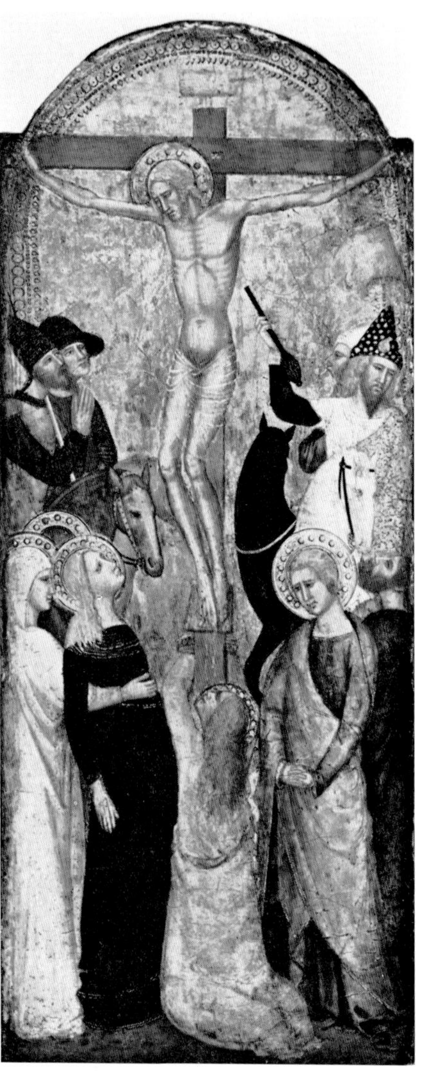

Figure 13 *b. The Crucifixion.* 39 × 16 cm (15$\frac{3}{8}$ ×
6$\frac{5}{16}$ inches). Jacopo di Cione, active ca. 1365–1398.
Museum Boymans-van Beuningen, Rotterdam, 2541.

Firenze was first suggested as the author of this *Crucifixion* by Roberto Longhi (orally, 1949). Offner, while ascribing it to Andrea's workshop, attributed it to the hand of the individual follower who painted the *Black Crucifixion*, attributed by Sirén (*op. cit.*) to Andrea himself, which apparently derives from Andrea da Firenze's fresco of the *Crucifixion* in the Spanish Chapel in S. Maria Novella, as well as the *Crucifixion* in the Museum Boymans-van Beuningen (Fig. 13 *b*) (letters of Klara Steinweg, February 2, 1964 and December 14, 1969; Offner, *Corpus*, sec. III, vol. VI, 171, n. 2). Offner also claims the same author for the tabernacle of the *Coronation of the Virgin* in the Rothermere collection which has been attributed to Bernardo Daddi (Konody, *op. cit.,*

pl. 4); to the School of Orcagna, ca. 1350 (Tancred Borenius, "Treasures from the Rothermere Collection," *Apollo*, XXII, 1935, 187); and to Niccolo di Tommaso (Berenson, *Pictures Renaiss. Florentine School,* I, 1963, 162). The attribution of the Cleveland, Vatican, and Rothermere pictures to the same hand is entirely convincing.

E.F.G.

EXHIBITIONS: CMA (1916), cat. no. 34 (Sienese, late fourteenth century); CMA (1936), cat. no. 87 (erroneously states that this was in the Jarves collection and exhibited at the Boston Exhibition of 1883).

LITERATURE: *Works of Art Composing the Collection of Mr. Minor K. Kellogg, American Painter* (Paris, 1858), no. 2 (unpublished MS. in the Museum files); Rubinstein (1917), no. 35, illus.

38

Workshop of FRA ANGELICO, Florence,
active 1417–1455

14 *The Coronation of the Virgin*   44.79

  Panel from a predella(?)

Panel (poplar), 28·3 × 38·4 cm (11⅛ × 15⅛ inches). Painted
surface: 27 × 37·2 cm (10⅝ × 14⅝ inches).
COLLECTIONS: Count Alessandro Contini-Bonacossi,
Rome; Mrs. Francis F. Prentiss, Cleveland, 1924.
Elisabeth Severance Prentiss Collection, 1944.

The original panel has been shaved down to a thickness
of ¼ inch. The gesso is thick, with raised edges indicating that it was applied while the panel was in a frame.
The edges are outlined in black. The tooled gold background is in good condition and the paint film on gar-
ments, hair, and wing is well preserved. However, the
flesh tones have suffered and much of the original drawing has been obscured. There are apparent pentimenti in
the design of the crown. The picture was cleaned in 1944
by William Suhr, and in 1960 by Joseph Alvarez.

Despite these damages, the appeal of this panel is
such that Roberto Longhi, Georg Swarzenski, August

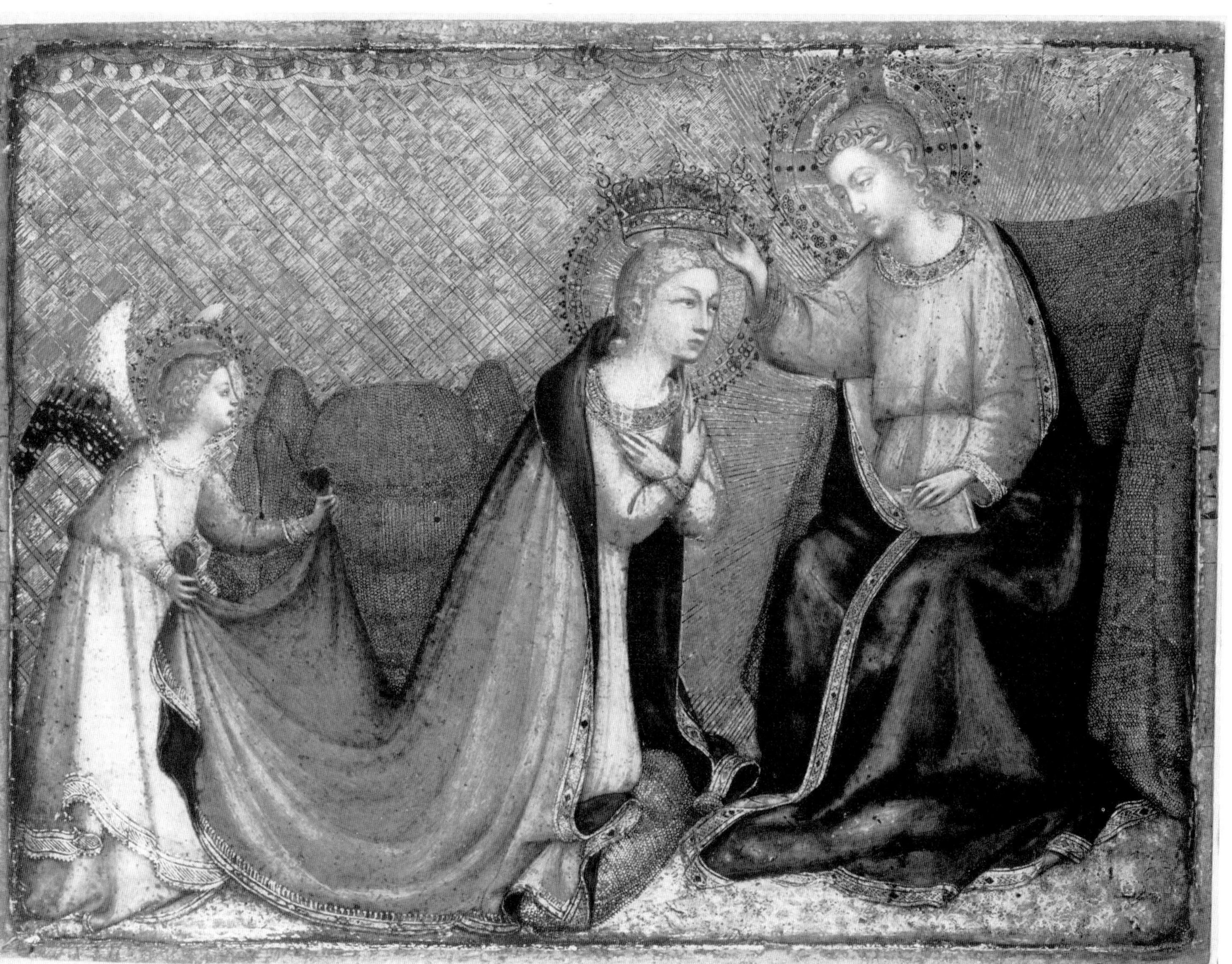

Figure 14.

Mayer (letters of 1924) and Frank J. Mather (letter of July 23, 1944) ascribed it unhesitatingly to Fra Angelico, placing it among his earliest works, noting in it the influence of Lorenzo Monaco and Gentile da Fabriano, especially in the head of Christ. Dating this panel ca. 1425–1430, Longhi compared it with the *Christ Glorified* (London, National Gallery, no. 663), and the predella to Fra Angelico's high altarpiece of S. Domenico which, like the reliquaries painted for Giovanni Masi, has been dated ca. 1420–1430.

However, others have found little connection between the Cleveland *Coronation* and Fra Angelico's authentic works. It reminded Albert Scharf (letter of July 21, 1965) of an early Benozzo Gozzoli. Pope-Hennessy (1952) and Everett Fahy (orally, 1966) found it close in style to Arcangelo di Cola da Camerino (from the Marches, active 1416–1425). (In this connection, the four predelle attributed to Arcangelo, Philadelphia, Johnson Collection, nos. 124–127, may be compared with the Cleveland panel.) Other works attributed to Arcangelo are ascribed by some to the young Fra Angelico; both were influenced by Gentile da Fabriano. Fahy (letter of October 19, 1966) noted the similarity of our panel with the *Christ Blessing* in the Royal Collection at Buckingham Palace (*Critica d'arte*, VIII, 1950, 460, fig. 384, there attributed to Zanobi Strozzi), traditionally ascribed to Fra Angelico but which Fahy has said might be by Arcangelo di Cola. Luciano Berti ("Miniature dell'Angelico e altro," *Acropoli*, III, 1963, 37, no. 9) recently attributed the London *Christ Blessing* to Fra Angelico again.

The individual parts of the Cleveland *Coronation* have their close counterparts in the paintings of Fra Angelico, but the spritely rhythm of the whole design is not characteristic of his style and suggests rather the hand of a painter-miniaturist from Fra Angelico's immediate circle, even closer to the master than Gozzoli or Arcangelo di Cola. Federico Zeri (orally, 1965) called it a studio work, close to Zanobi Strozzi. Though the flowing calligraphy of the Cleveland panel is reminiscent of his work, it does not seem quite close enough to his documented miniatures (see M. Levy d'Ancona, "Zanobi Strozzi Reconsidered," *La Bibliofilia*, LXI, 1959, 1 ff.) to warrant an attribution to Strozzi about whose panel paintings much has been said but little is known. (For the miniatures and panel paintings of Fra Angelico and his workshop, including some joint attributions to Fra Angelico and Strozzi, see Berti, *Acropoli*, II, 1961–1962, 277 ff. and III, 1963, 12 ff.)   E.F.G.

EXHIBITIONS: CMA (1936), cat. no. 112 (as Fra Angelico, ca. 1430, but associated with the school works in the National Gallery, London, *Adoration of the Magi*, no. 582, and the *Origin of the Dominican Habit*, no. 3417); CMA (1963), cat. no. 79 (School of Fra Angelico).

LITERATURE: Henry S. Francis, "Paintings in the Prentiss Bequest," CMA *Bulletin*, XXXI (1944), 87 (a school work, contemporary with Fra Angelico's early activity); *Prentiss Coll. Cat.* (1944), cat. no. 1, pl. 1, p. 21 (contemporary and directly from the workshop of the master); John Pope-Hennessy, *Fra Angelico* (London, 1952), p. 197.

BERLINGHIERO (Berlinghiero di Milanese the Elder), Lucca, active ca. 1200–1240

Berlinghiero was first recorded in a Lucchese document of 1228 and mentioned as already dead by 1243. Crowe and Cavalcaselle's mistranslation of the document of 1228 (known only from a seventeenth-century transcription) gave rise to the apparently mistaken assumption that Berlinghiero came from Milan and that his last name was Berlinghieri. These misconceptions persist despite the thorough review and corrected interpretation of the available sources published by Garrison (1951, 11 ff.). Berlinghiero introduced Byzantine elements into the style of painting in Lucca which dominated that school during the first three-quarters of the thirteenth century and strongly influenced painting in Pisa and Florence. Attributions to Berlinghiero are based on his one signed work, a *Crucifix*, probably painted ca. 1210–1220 (Fig. 15 b). Three sons were trained by Berlinghiero and works by two of them, Bonaventura and Marco, are known.

15 *The Madonna and Child with Saints* 66.237

Triptych (tabernacle)

Dexter wing: *The Crucifixion of St. Andrew;
    St. Francis and St. Paul(?)*
Sinister wing: *The Last Judgment; St. Stephen
    and St. Lawrence*
Exterior wings: *Byzantine Cross*

Panel (poplar), over-all: 42·6 × 51·5 cm (16$\frac{13}{16}$ × 20$\frac{1}{4}$ inches).
Center: 42·6 × 27 cm (16$\frac{13}{16}$ × 10$\frac{5}{8}$ inches).
Dexter wing: 42·6 × 12·5 cm (16$\frac{3}{4}$ × 4$\frac{7}{8}$ inches).
Sinister wing: 42·2 × 12 cm (16$\frac{5}{8}$ × 4$\frac{11}{16}$ inches).
COLLECTIONS: (Theodore Bonjean, Paris); (Peter Matthiessen, Matthiessen Gallery, London, until 1938); Adolphe Stoclet, Brussels, after 1938; Mme. Michele Stoclet, Barcelona; (sale: Sotheby, London, June 30, 1965, no. 21, repr. p. 20 as by Berlinghiero); (Rudolf J. Heinemann).
Gift of The John Huntington Art and Polytechnic Trust, 1966.

Inscribed on central panel flanking Virgin: MP OV. On back of panel: XC IC ES NI.

The wings are slightly cut at the edges. Some retouching was evident in faces on dexter wing and in the face of Christ on the right (cf., Garrison, 1946; 1949). It was cleaned by Mario Modestini in 1965 and found to be in excellent condition (Stechow, 1966).

This tabernacle was discovered (while in the Stoclet

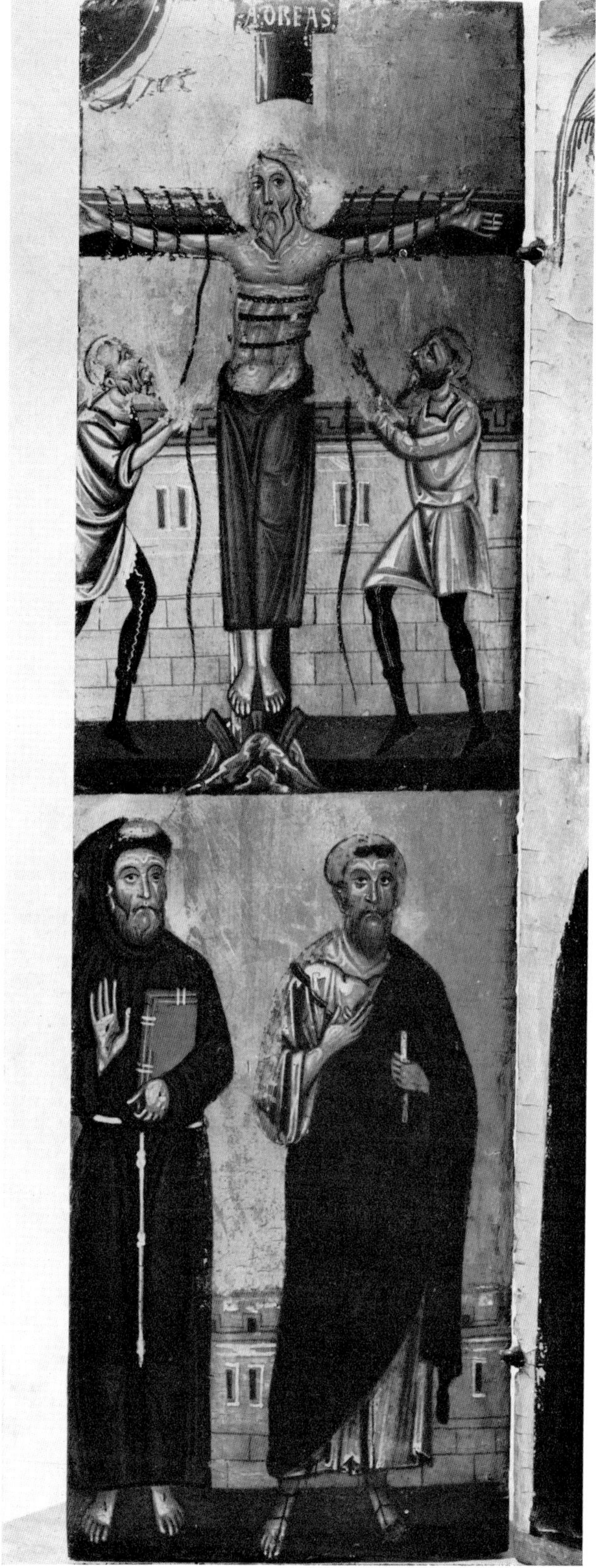

Figure 15 a. Dexter wing.

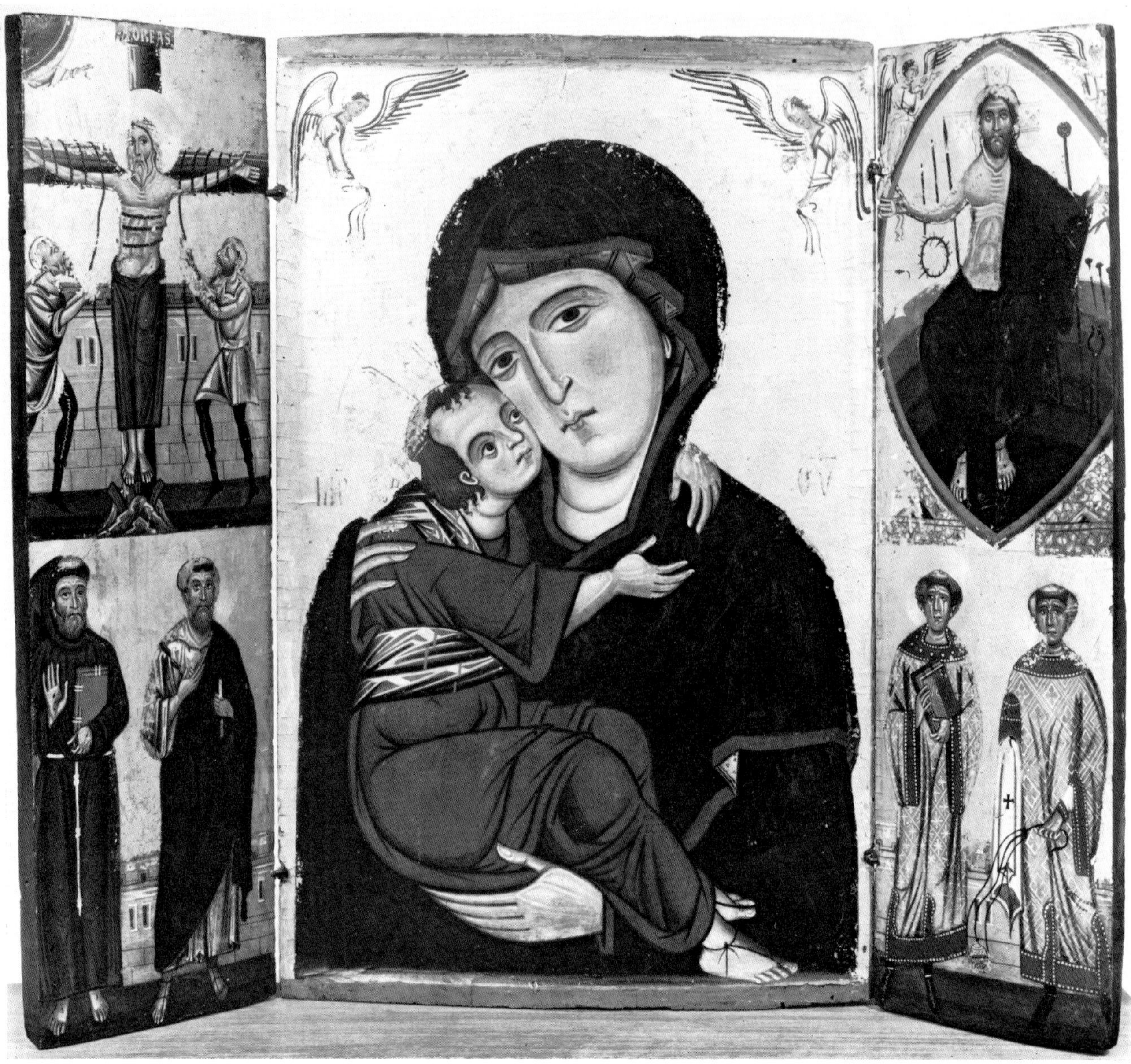

Figure 15. See also Colorplate X.

collection) and recognized as Berlinghieresque by Offner. It was first published by Garrison (1946, p. 215) as
by an advanced follower of Berlinghiero, painted ca.
1240–1250 and showing the influence of Bonaventura's
S. Francesco Pescia altar panel of 1235, but also related
to the later (ca. 1255–1260) diptych by the Master of the
Oblate Crucifixion, Florence, Accademia (nos. 8575,
8576).

The doubts expressed in the literature about Berlinghiero's authorship of this tabernacle are not corrobo-
rated by actual comparison with Berlinghiero's *Crucifix*;
this comparison is sufficiently convincing evidence that
both paintings are by the same hand although the Cleveland panel may be of a later date, ca. 1230–1240 (Stechow, 1966). It may also be compared with the two
attributed by Garrison to Berlinghiero himself, the *Madonna di Sotto gli Organi* of ca. 1200–1220, Pisa, Duomo
(Garrison, 1947, p. 177); and the *Madonna and Child*
of ca. 1230–1240 in the collection of Mrs. J. I. Straus,
New York (Garrison, 1949, p. 59, no. 96). According to
Garrison (1958, pp. 261 ff.) the Cleveland painting is
chronologically closest to the once heavily overpainted
Lucchese *Madonna* now in the North Carolina Museum
of Art at Raleigh (Valentiner, 1957) attributed by Offner
and Valentiner to Berlinghiero himself – but by Garrison to a close follower, painted about 1235–1245. This
was also once part of a tabernacle like the Cleveland triptych although the arch suggested in the latter by the
censing angels is actually inscribed in the Raleigh panel.
A variant of the CMA *Madonna* now in the Abegg-
Stiftung, Berne, was called by Garrison (1949, p. 52)
School of Berlinghiero, 1250–1260. The Madonna of the
Cleveland tabernacle is of the *Glykophilousa* or affection-
ate type, deriving from a Byzantine prototype such as
the early twelfth-century *Virgin of Vladimir* in Moscow.

E.F.G.

EXHIBITIONS: CMA (1966), cat. no. 56, illus.; CMA (1971), cat.
no. 1.

LITERATURE: Edward B. Garrison, Jr., "A Berlinghieresque
Fresco in St. Stefano, Bologna," *The Art Bulletin*, XXVIII (1946),
215–219, fig. 7; Garrison, "Post-War Discoveries – III: The
Madonna di Sotto gli Organi," *Burl. Mag.*, LXXXIX (1947), 279;
Offner, *Corpus*, sec. III, vol. V (1947), 48, n. 1 (a fine example by
Berlinghiero of ca. 1235), 56–57, n. 3, 207–208, n. 1, 252, n. 6, 259
(the earliest Tuscan representation of the Last Judgment); Garrison,
Italian Romanesque Panel Painting (Florence, 1949), pp. 12, 112, no.
284; Garrison, "Addenda ad indicem II," *Bollettino d'arte*, XXXVI
(1951), 294, 296, no. 6 (cf., no. 1); George Kaftal, *Iconography of
Saints in Tuscan Painting* (1952), p. xxiii, n. 7, cols. 40, 613, 949
(identifies the two deacon saints in sinister wing of triptych, calls it

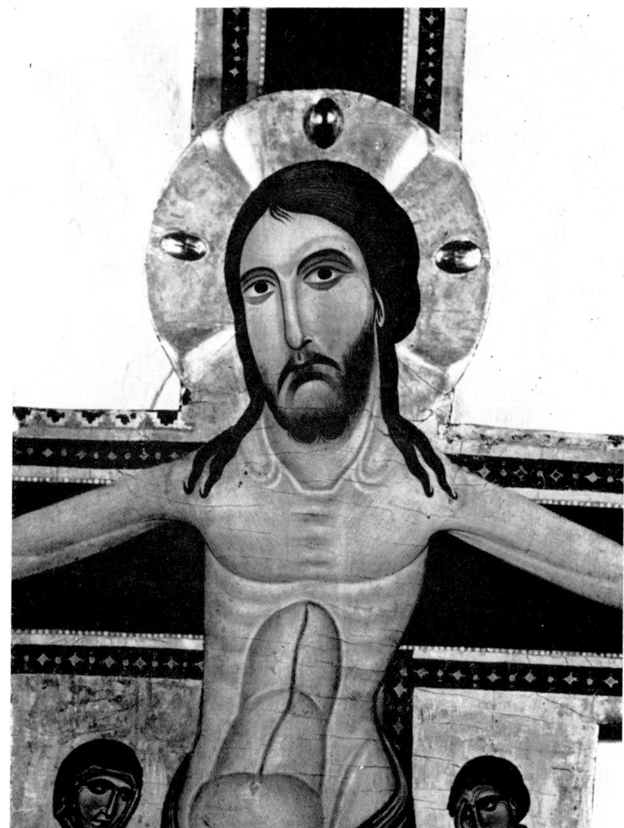

Figure 15 b. *Crucifix* (detail). 175 × 140 cm
($68\frac{7}{8}$ × $55\frac{1}{8}$ inches). Berlinghiero.
Museo Nazionale di Villa Guinigi, Lucca, 39.

variously, Berlinghiero, ca. 1235, and School of Berlinghiero,
1240–1250); W. R. Valentiner, "A Madonna by Berlinghiero Ber-
linghieri," *The North Carolina Museum of Art Bulletin*, I (1957), 1–3
(Lucchese school); Garrison, *Studies in the History of Medieval
Italian Painting* (Florence, 1958), III, 261–264 (compares Raleigh,
N.C., Madonna with CMA and other Berlinghieresque Madonnas); James H. Stubblebine, *Guido da Siena* (Princeton, 1964), p. 78
(School of Berlinghiero), p. 88 (discussion of iconography of Last
Judgment in Dugento painting, of which the scene in the CMA
tabernacle is an example of the French formula for this scene, here
called "stylistically close to Berlinghiero; second-quarter of thirteenth century," fig. 109); Wolfgang Stechow, "Cleveland's
Golden Anniversary Acquisitions," *Art News*, LXV (September
1966), 32, illus. (remarks on "nearly impeccable" preservation, and
on similarity to Berlinghiero's signed *Crucifix*); *Handbook* (1966),
p. 51; Henry S. Francis, "Berlinghiero – The Stoclet Tabernacle,"
CMA *Bulletin*, LIV (1967), 92–96, illus. p. 89 (color), figs. 4–6;
Berenson, *Pictures Renaiss.*, *Central and North Italian Schools*, I
(1968), 46.

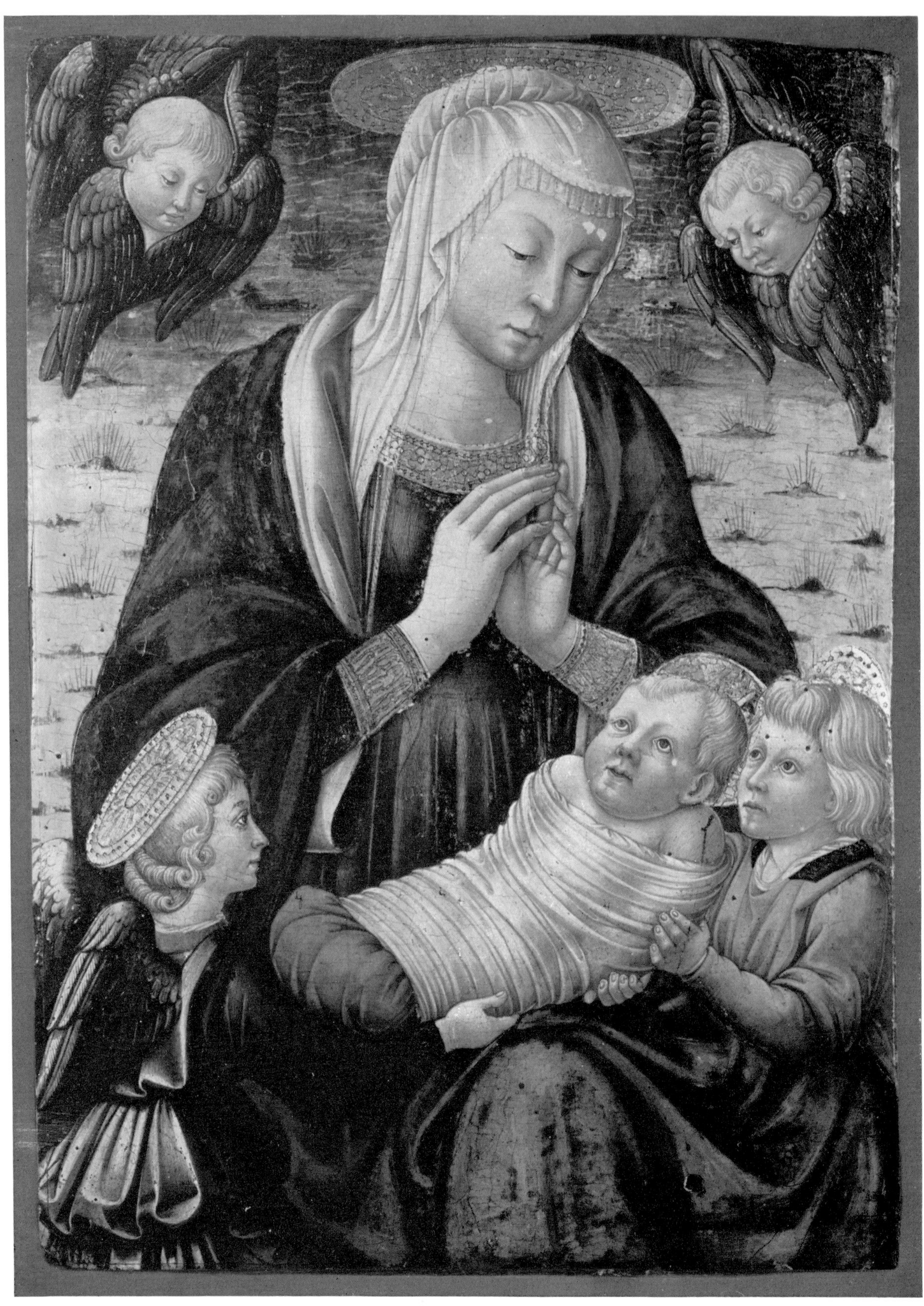

Figure 16.

NERI DI BICCI, Florence, 1419–ca. 1491

Neri was the pupil of his father Bicci di Lorenzo (see Painting 18) and was influenced by the works of Fra Angelico and Fra Filippo Lippi. His earliest documented work is datable ca. 1444 but he must have been active as a painter before then. A record of Neri's works from 1453 to 1475 is preserved in his Libro di Ricordanze in the Uffizi Library. This prolific painter maintained a large workshop whose main assisting members have yet to be clearly distinguished from Neri's own hand.

16 *Madonna and Child with Angels* 16.798

Panel (poplar), 64 × 45·5 cm ($25\frac{3}{16}$ × $7\frac{7}{16}$ inches).
COLLECTIONS: James Jackson Jarves; Mrs. Liberty E. Holden, Cleveland, 1884.
Holden Collection, 1916.

Annotation on the back: Fra Filippo Lippi.

Although slightly warped and worm-eaten, this panel is well preserved. A thick coat of soiled and discolored varnish was removed by William Suhr in 1943 together with discolored retouchings in the sky, in the darker areas of the rose madder of the Virgin's dress, and in her blue mantle. The infra-red photograph (Fig. 16a) compared with the photograph taken before cleaning (Fig. 16b) shows the extent of the distortion of the paint surface caused by old restorations, especially in the faces; removing these revealed the true character of the original.

While in the Jarves collection this panel was ascribed to Fra Filippo Lippi from whose art the motif of the angels supporting the Christ Child derives (cf., Uffizi no. 1598, ca. 1455–1457, and Painting 31). M. L. Berenson (1907) was the first to attribute the picture to Neri di Bicci, calling it one of his best works and mentioning a then current attribution to Benozzo Gozzoli. B. Berenson (1932; 1963) accepted the picture as by Neri himself although it was called a school work by Van Marle (1928) and C. Collins Baker (letter of October 25, 1930), and a Cosimo Rosselli by Mather (written comments in the Museum files, 1921). The Cleveland *Madonna* may be compared with a Neri di Bicci painting in the Lee of Fareham collection (Van Marle, 1928, 535, fig. 319), where the tooling is identical and the amplitude of the forms similar. The profile of the angel in the Holden picture is also identical with that of the St. John in the *Adoration of the Child*, Brussels, Van Gelder collection (Van Marle, fig. 322). Both the Lee of Fareham and the Van Gelder pictures are dated after 1460 by Van Marle, and the Cleveland picture would appear to be no earlier.

E.F.G.

EXHIBITIONS: Boston (1883), cat. no. 443; MMA (1912), cat. no. 3, illus. p. 175; CMA (1916), cat. no. 4 (compared with Neri's *Madonna*, Budapest, no. 1228, and *Annunciation*, Accademia, Florence, no. 8622 of 1464); CMA (1936), cat. no. 76.
LITERATURE: Jarves (1884) cat. no. 9; M. L. Berenson (1907), p. 2; Georg Gronau in Thieme–Becker, III (1909), 606; Rubinstein (1917), no. 4, illus.; Van Marle, X (1928), 542, 545; Berenson, *Pictures Renaiss.* (1932), p. 386; Berenson, *Pictures Renaiss., Florentine School*, I (1963), p. 153.

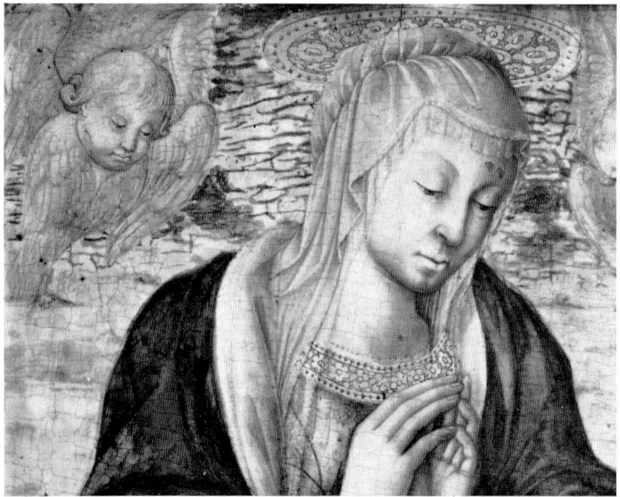

Figure 16a. Infra-red photograph.

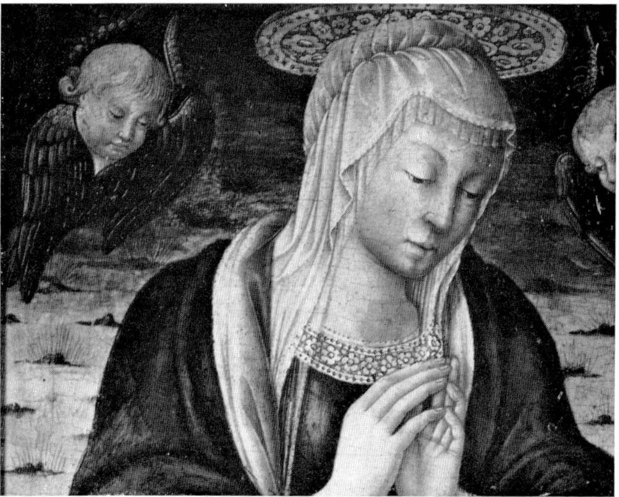

Figure 16b. Before cleaning.

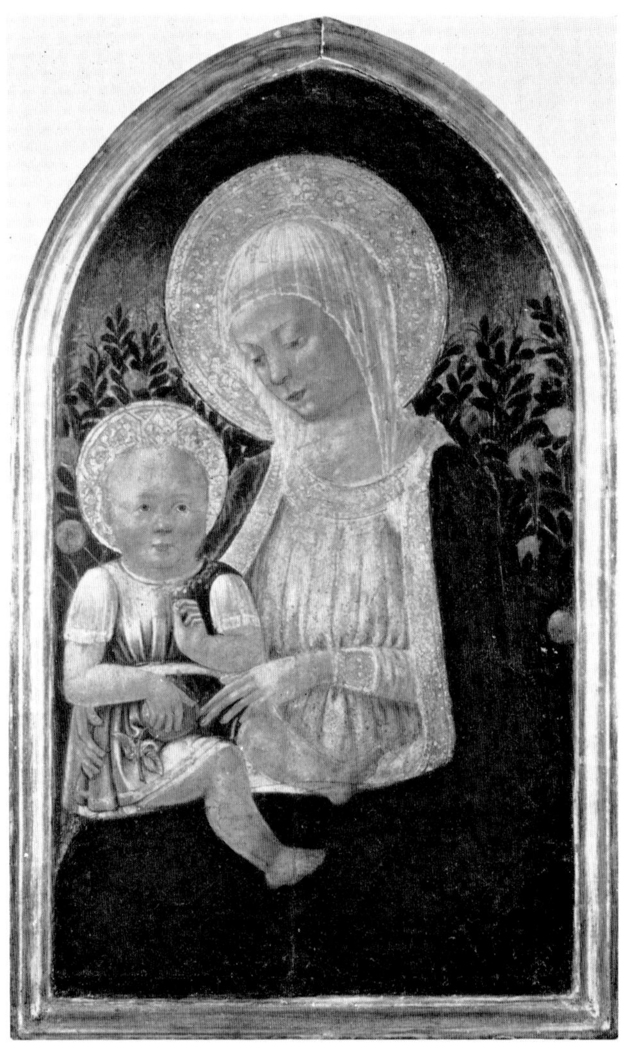

Figure 17*a*. With overpaint, before cleaning.

NERI DI BICCI, Florence

17 *Madonna and Child*   46.242

Panel (poplar), including original molding, 59×35 cm ($23\frac{1}{4} \times 13\frac{3}{4}$ inches). Inside frame: $54 \times 30 \cdot 8$ cm ($21\frac{1}{4} \times 12\frac{1}{8}$ inches).

COLLECTIONS: Francesco Sparagni, Florence; acquired from a street shrine in Florence by H. W. Cannon, through Berenson, and presented to the future Mrs. Cannon, Miss Myrta L. Jones, by 1928.

Gift of Mrs. Henry White Cannon, 1946.

Inscribed on back of the panel: Questa Venabile Immagine di proprieta di Fra[nces]co Sparagni e stata collocata in detto Logo nell S[ette]mbre 1797.

Cleaning in 1947 revealed extensive overpaint in the background of this panel. A modern hedge with orange trees behind the Virgin (Fig. 17*a*) disappeared entirely, revealing a lighter blue background with clumps of grass and sunrays at the top. The Virgin's costume had suffered considerably and lines in faces and hands had been strengthened. When the overpaint was removed and the damage attenuated, the painting assumed a more monumental aspect, although traces of repairs may still be seen in the Virgin's face, the upper contour of the Child's head, in the top of His tunic, and the outline of the Virgin's halo.

The picture was attributed to Neri di Bicci by Berenson at the time of its purchase by Cannon and seems to be a characteristic work of ca. 1454–1460 (cf., Van Marle, X, 1928, figs. 317–318).

E.F.G.

EXHIBITIONS: CMA, 1928: Representative Art through the Ages.

LITERATURE: Henry S. Francis, "Recent Gifts to the Museum," CMA *Bulletin*, XXIV (1947), 14; Berenson, *Pictures Renaiss., Florentine School*, I (1963), 153.

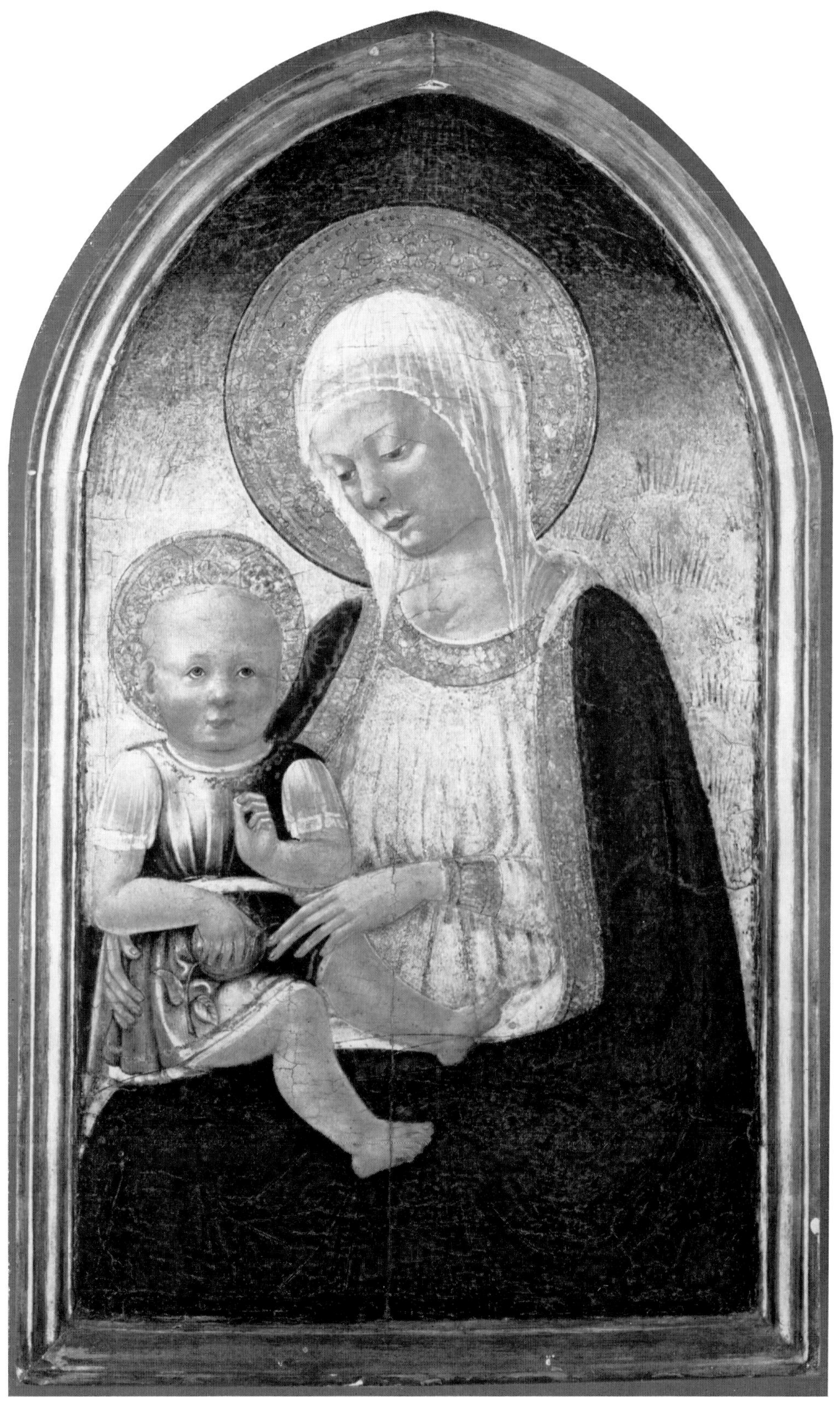

Figure 17.

BICCI DI LORENZO, Florence, 1373–1452

He was born in Florence and died in Arezzo. The activity of this prolific painter is well documented from 1416, the date of his earliest work when he participated in the decoration of the Palazzo dei Capitani del Bigallo, until 1450, the date of his altarpiece in the cathedral of Fiesole. He was trained in the workshop of his father, the painter Lorenzo di Bicci, and was himself the father of Neri di Bicci (see Painting 16). Although somewhat influenced by Lorenzo Monaco, Fra Angelico, Gentile da Fabriano, and Domenico Veneziano, he remained fundamentally a trecentesque artist continuing the tradition of Agnolo Gaddi.

18 *St. Francis Receiving the Stigmata* 16.787

Panel (poplar), including original molding, 21·7 × 32 cm (8½ × 12⅝ inches). Inside frame: 17·9 × 27 cm (7 1/16 × 10⅝ inches).

COLLECTIONS: James Jackson Jarves; Mrs. Liberty E. Holden, Cleveland, 1884.

Holden Collection, 1916.

Cleaned in 1960 by J. Alvarez, the panel was found to be in excellent condition with no visible retouches.

This panel comes from the predella of an unidentified altarpiece. M. L. Berenson (1907) challenged Jarves' attribution to Fra Angelico, calling it a work of the early Florentine school, and it was thus labeled by the Museum. Frank J. Mather (written comments in the Museum files, 1921) noted that it must be by a close follower of Lorenzo Monaco, and F. Mason Perkins (unpublished opinion, 1923) pointed out its trecentesque character, doubting that it could be later than 1425. This panel is very similar in size and shape to two predella panels by Bicci di Lorenzo in the Vatican (Figs. 18 *a, b*) depicting *St. Anthony Feeding the Poor*, and *St. Francis at the Deathbed of the Miser of Celano* (each 22·5 × 32 cm) which, according to Zeri (letter of July 12, 1962) belong to the same predella. The composition of the Cleveland panel is close to the *Stigmatization* in the spandrel of Bicci's triptych in Perugia (Pinacoteca, no. 5666), usually considered a late work. Another predella attributed to Bicci with the same subject composed in reverse is in the Capitoline Museum, Rome. The Cleveland predella panel seems later than those dated 1423 formerly in the Berlin Museum (no. 1064 A), but earlier than the Perugia triptych and comparable in style to the predella of the altarpiece at Pieve di S. Ippolito, Bibbiena, dated 1435.

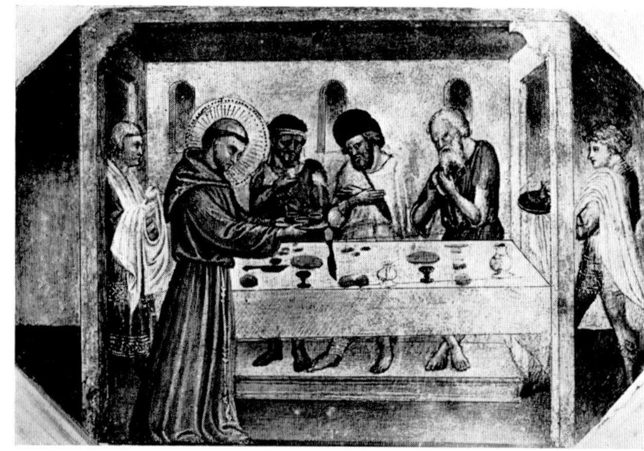

Figure 18 *a. St. Anthony Feeding the Poor*. 22·5 × 32 cm (8⅞ × 12⅝ inches). Bicci di Lorenzo. Pinacoteca Vaticana, 89.

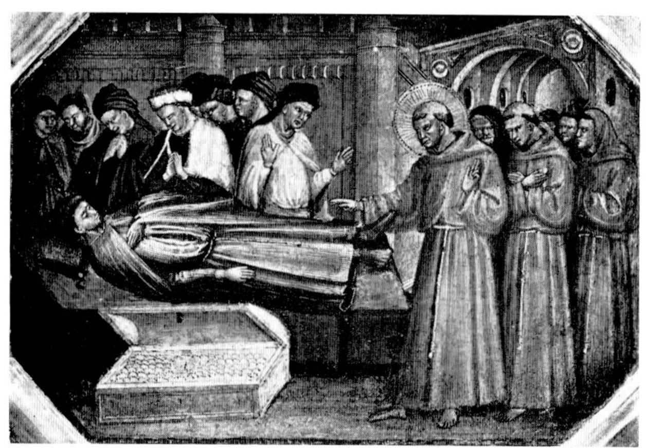

Figure 18 *b. St. Francis at the Deathbed of the Miser of Celano*. 22·5 × 32 cm (8⅞ × 12⅝ inches). Bicci di Lorenzo. Pinacoteca Vaticana, 100.

The latter are all reproduced in Berenson (*Pictures Renaiss., Florentine School*, 1, 1963, pls. 499, 500, 511).

E.F.G.

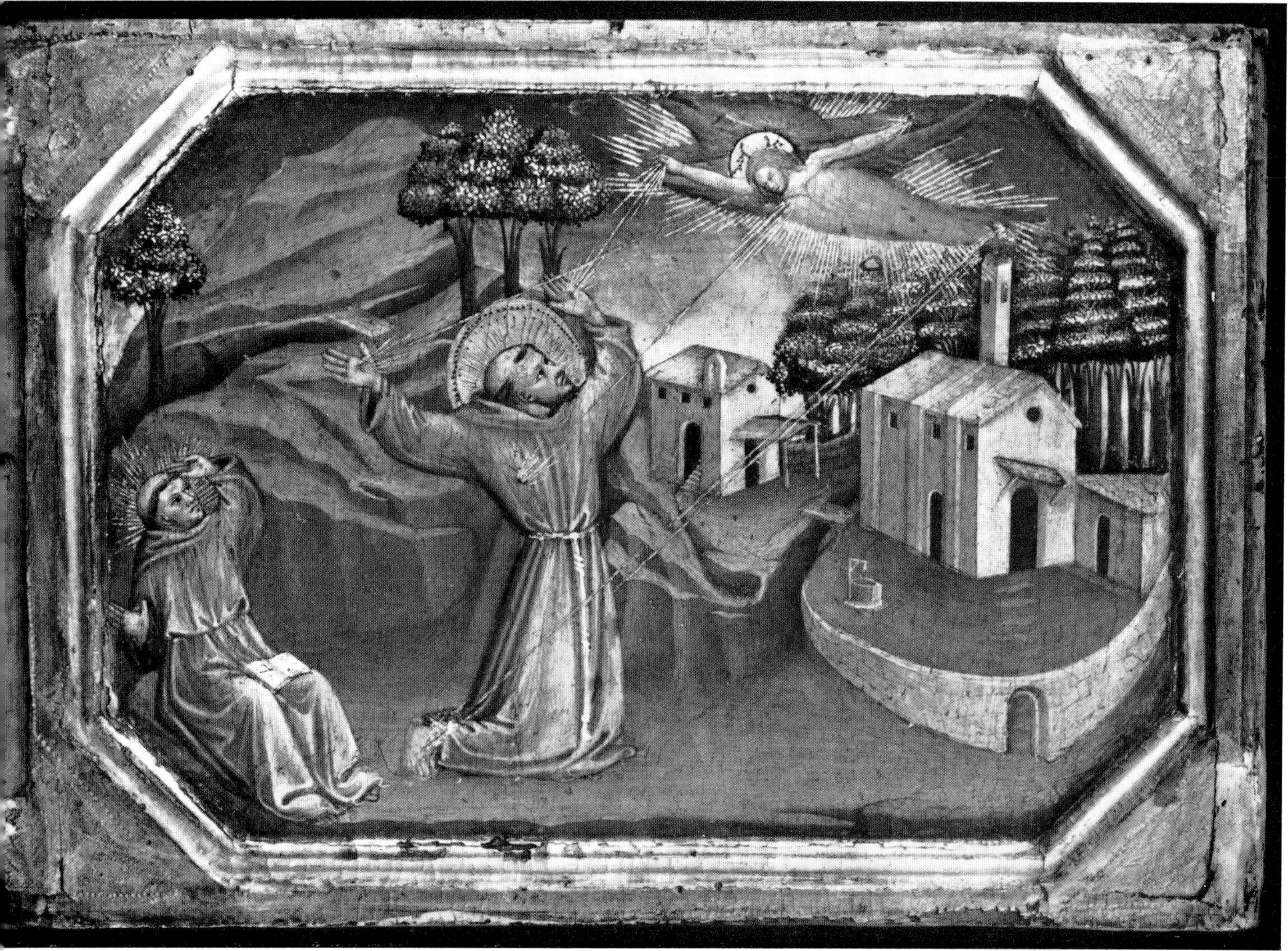

Figure 18.

EXHIBITIONS: Boston (1883), cat. no. 408; MMA (1912), cat.
no. 7 (as Florentine, mid-fifteenth century); CMA (1916), cat. no.
18; CMA (1936), cat. no. 89 (Florentine, early fifteenth century);
CMA (1963), cat. no. 77.
LITERATURE: Jarves (1884) cat. no. 5 (as by Fra Angelico); M. L.
Berenson (1907), 2; Rubinstein (1917), no. 18; Henry S. Francis,
"Sassetta – Crucifixion with St. Francis," CMA *Bulletin*, L (1963),
46, fig. 2.

SANDRO BOTTICELLI (Alessandro Filipepi),
Florence, 1444–1510

The youngest son of Mariano di Giovanni of Florence,
like the rest of his family, eventually adopted his oldest
brother's nickname Botticelli as his surname. In the
late 1450s, after a brief apprenticeship as a goldsmith,
Sandro became the pupil of the most famous of the
Florentine painters at the time, Fra Filippo Lippi, whose
naturalism and wistful lyricism influenced his early style
and set the mood for his figures until the late 1480s. Botticelli's full and rounded drapery folds, expressive of
movement, revealed influences from Verrocchio, while
the intense naturalism of certain of his works such as
his *St. Sebastian* of the mid-1470s (Berlin, Staatliche
Museen) approximate the style of the Pollaiuoli. After
Fra Filippo Lippi's death Botticelli developed a style
increasingly dependent on line and its abstract qualities
to create rhythm and compositional unity without sacri-
ficing his figures' tactility. His pupil and collaborator
Filippino Lippi combined his father's (Fra Filippo Lippi)
sense of bulk and plasticity with Botticelli's rhythmical
line and movement. After 1490, affected by the
religious teaching of Savonarola, Botticelli's figures
grew increasingly anti-naturalistic, eager and feverish
in their movement, their former wistful sadness turning
into brooding melancholy.

19   *Madonna and Child with*   70.160
     the Young St. John

> Tondo, diameter, 68 cm (26¾ inches).
> COLLECTIONS: Possibly M. de la Rozière, Paris (see Plunkett,
> 1900; Gebhart, 1907, in following); Robert Hoe, New
> York (sale: Mendelsohn Hall, New York, February 17,
> 1911, no. 101); A. Haviland; Arthur I. Hoe, Bedford Hills,
> New York; (Ehrich collection, New York); Baron
> Lazzaroni; (Iolanda d'Antoni, Lugano, Switzerland).
> Purchase, Leonard C. Hanna Jr. Bequest, 1970.

The tondo underwent a series of restorations, affecting
mainly the Madonna's left sleeve. A photograph from
the Berenson archives (Fig. 19 *b*), taken when the picture
was on loan from Arthur Hoe to the Fogg Art Museum
between 1914 and 1916, is the earliest known proof
of the picture's original state supported by the existence
of a nearly exact copy in Montpellier (Fig. 19 *c*). Both the
Berenson photograph and the Montpellier copy, as well
as one in the Galleria Estense in Modena, show traces of a
carved armrest close to the lower right edge of the tondo
inside the triangular loop formed by the Madonna's left

sleeve; it disappeared when Baron Lazzaroni's restorer
changed the Madonna's left sleeve into a flat dark-blue
shape with a gold border (Fig. 19 *d*) fashioned after the
Madonna of the Magnificat in the Uffizi. During this restoration the Madonna's original halo was removed and
replaced by golden rays. The landscape was flattened
out on the right and trees removed from the rocky ter-
rain on the left. The Child's hair was dressed up, slight
changes were made on His shawl, and the small triangular gap between the Madonna's and Infant's cheeks was
tampered with. A second restoration at a later date re-
turned the Madonna's left sleeve to its original yellow
color and close to its original shape. Before the Museum
acquired the tondo it was restored by Modestini; the
painting was stripped of its most obvious overpaint, revealing faint outlines of rising hills on the right and the
substructure of the original left sleeve (Fig. 19 *e*). Following traces of the landscape, the restorer freely reconstructed the background and painted in the yellow sleeve
with its sensitive curving folds with watercolor simulat-
ing the brilliance of tempera, leaving the underdraw-
ing easily accessible for any further investigation.

De la Rozière's name as the owner of the tondo
appeared in the Robert Hoe sales catalogue of 1911. To
date no documentary evidence has been found attesting to his ownership or his lending it to the Palais Bourbon in Paris in the 1880s as that catalogue entry states.
His name as the owner of a tondo, *Madonna and Child
and St. John* (as school of Botticelli), is first listed in 1900
with no reproduction of the work (Count Plunkett,
Sandro Botticelli, London, 1900, p. 105) and again by
Emile Gebhart (*Sandro Botticelli*, Paris, 1907, p. 249), who
writes that the tondo in the De la Rozière collection is
close to the *Madonna with Angels and St. John*, formerly
in the hospital of S. Maria Nuova, now in the Uffizi
(painted about twenty years earlier than the CMA tondo!). After Hoe's death in 1911 the next owner of this
tondo, his son Arthur I. Hoe, probably bought it back
(letter of April 9, 1914, from Mr. Forbes, Director of the
Fogg Art Museum, to Arthur Pope), possibly through a
Mr. A. Haviland whose name appears next to the annotated sales catalogue entry of 1911. Hoe lent his picture to
the Fogg Art Museum from 1914 to 1916; it was included
in their loan exhibition of Italian paintings when it was
published by Edgell (1915) who observed that while the
tondo strongly suggested Botticelli he found it even
more reminiscent of the youthful work of his pupil
Filippino Lippi. No early records of the Ehrich collection have been found, so the exact date of this sale is not

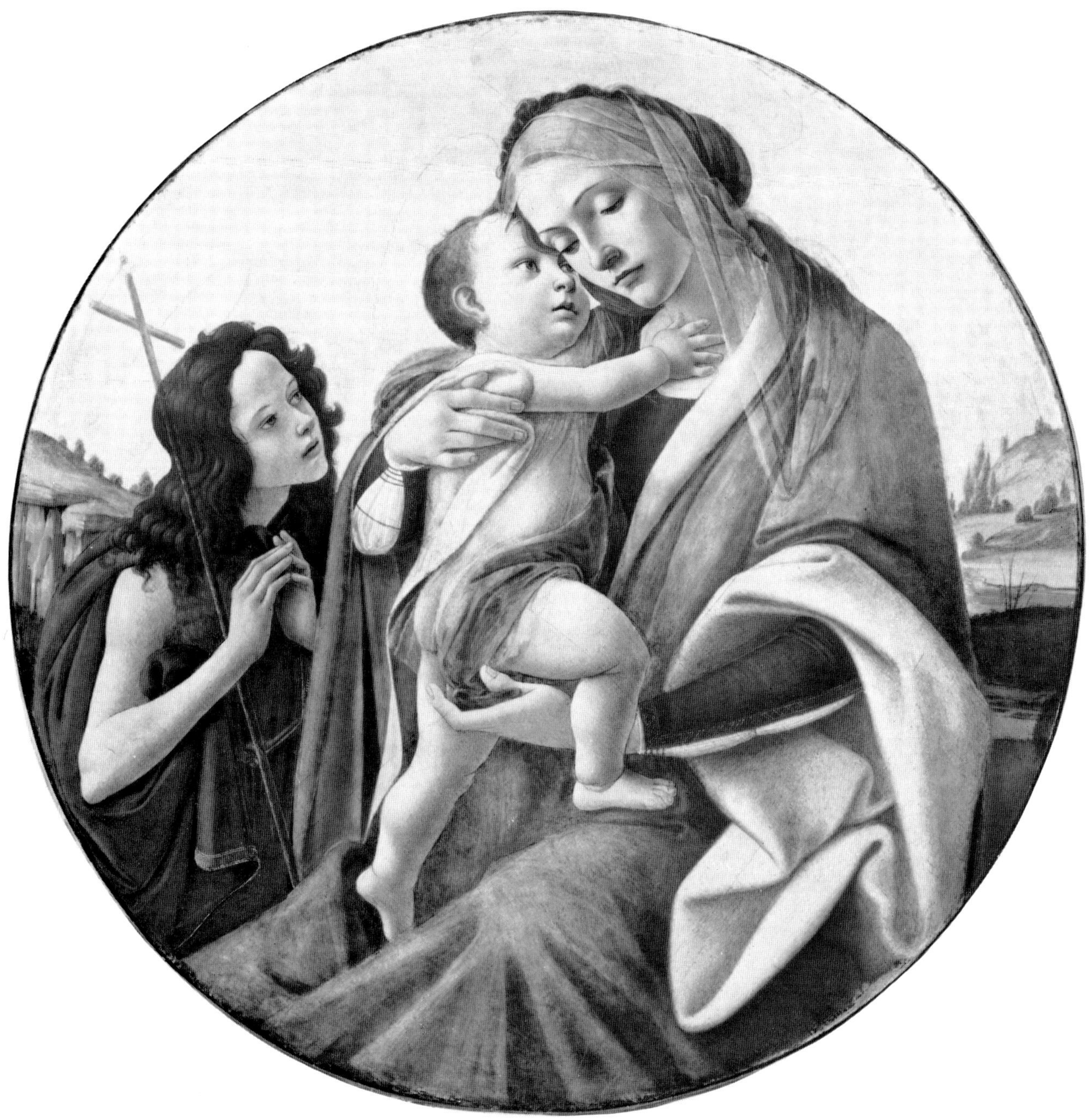

Figure 19. See also Colorplate XI.

known. However, Baron Lazzaroni owned the tondo when Yashiro (1925) published it under the heading "Contemporary Copies and Versions," listing it among a group of related tondi: one in the Galleria Estense, Modena; one in the Musée Fabre, Montpellier (Fig. 19*c*); and one in the R. von Kaufmann collection sale, Berlin, December 4–5, 1917, no. 20 (Yashiro believes the latter freely combined the Montpellier and Liechtenstein versions, see Stix and Strohmer, *Die Fürstlich Liechtensteinsche Gemäldegalerie*, Vienna, 1938, p. 92). He also convincingly related the types of Madonna and Child in these tondi to ones in a drawing in the British

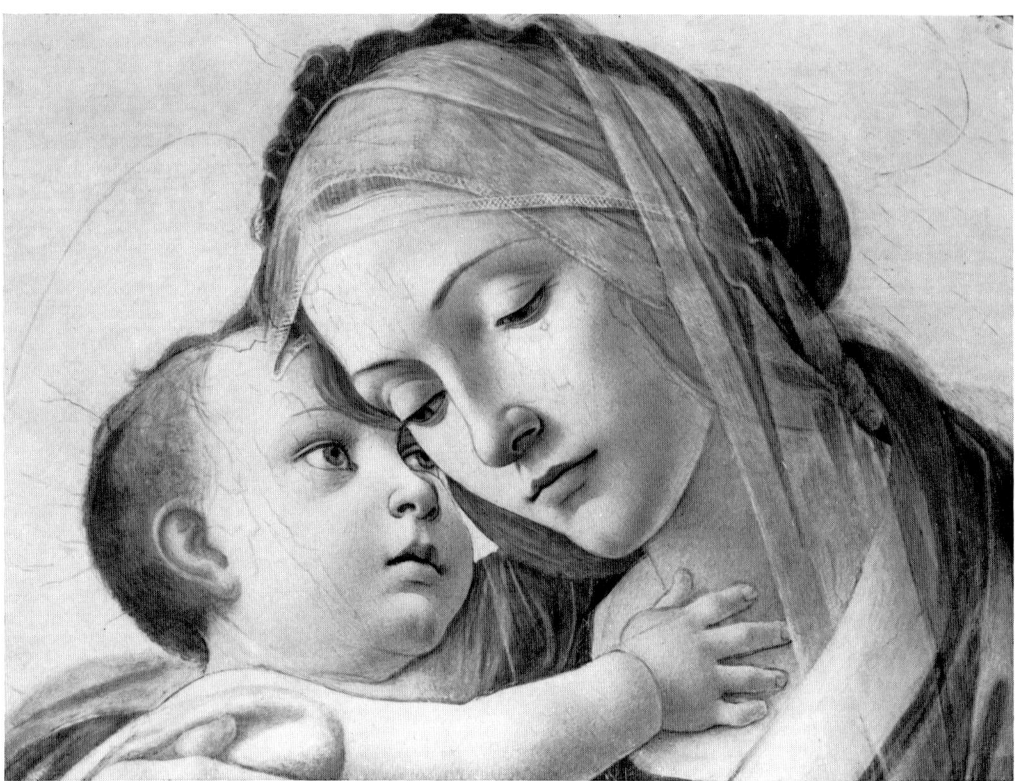

Figure 19a. Detail.

Museum (A. E. Popham and Philip Pouncey, *Italian Drawings in the Department of Prints and Drawings in the British Museum*, I, London, 1950, pl. XXVII).

Tigram (1926), A. Venturi (1927), Van Marle (1931), Gamba (1936), and Bettini (1942) accept the tondo as a work by Botticelli. Salvini (1958), believing the tondo to be largely Botticelli's work, rejected Mesnil's (1938) argument that the tondo was only invented by Botticelli and painted by his workshop. While Van Marle (1931) and Mesnil (1938) date the tondo ca. 1490 – the period when Botticelli's works reflected a strong influence from Savonarola's teachings – Salvini (1958), Gamba (1936), and Bettini (1942; 1947) group it with the *Madonna of the Magnificat*. It is safe to say that the tondo dates from the latter part of the 1480s and that it represents one step in his stylistic development from the *Madonna of the Magnificat* and the Berlin *Madonna Enthroned with the Two St. Johns* (commissioned for the Bardi Chapel of S. Spirito, ca. 1485), to the *Coronation of the Virgin* in the Uffizi (commissioned for the church of S. Marco) and finally to the *Annunciation* painted for the S. Maria Maddalena dei Pazzi, now in the Uffizi, both ca. 1489–1490. While the quiet calm of the Cleveland Madonna and her half-dreaming expression seem

to warrant a date closer to the mid-1480s, the intricate curving of her sleeve opening, the eager movement of the Child towards His Mother, and the intensely yielding pose and expression of the adoring St. John anticipate the hasty movements and exaggerated gestures of the S. Maria Maddalena dei Pazzi *Annunciation* of ca. 1489–1490.

A.T.L.

EXHIBITIONS: Possibly Paris, Expositions du Palais Bourbon, 1880s; Cambridge, Mass., Fogg Art Museum, 1915: Loan Exhibition of Italian Paintings; CMA, February 1971: Year in Review, cat. no. 35, illus. p. 21 (color); CMA (1971), cat. no. 8.

LITERATURE: George H. Edgell, "The Loan Exhibition of Italian Paintings in the Fogg Museum, Cambridge," *Art and Archeology*, II (1915), 17, fig. 6; Yukio Yashiro, *Sandro Botticelli*, I (London, Boston, 1925), 247; Tigram, "C'è una crisi dell'arte in Italia? La Confederazione nazionale degli amici dell'arte," *Vita artistica*, I (1926), pp. 2–3, illus. p. 3; Adolfo Venturi, *Botticelli* (London, 1927), p. 116, pls. CLXXXVII, CLXXXVIII, CLXXXIX; Van Marle, XII (1931), 171, 229; Carlo Gamba, *Botticelli* (Milan, 1936), p. 148, pl. 101; Jacques Mesnil, *Botticelli* (Paris, 1938), p. 163, pl. LXXXIX; Sergio Bettini, *Botticelli* (Bergamo, 1942), pp. 33, 49, pl. 84; (2nd ed. rev., 1947), pp. 34, 51, pl. 84; Roberto Salvini, *Tutta la pittura del Botticelli*, II (Milan, 1958), 40, pl. 6; Gabriele Mandel, *The Complete Paintings of Botticelli* (New York, 1967), p. 100, no. 99.

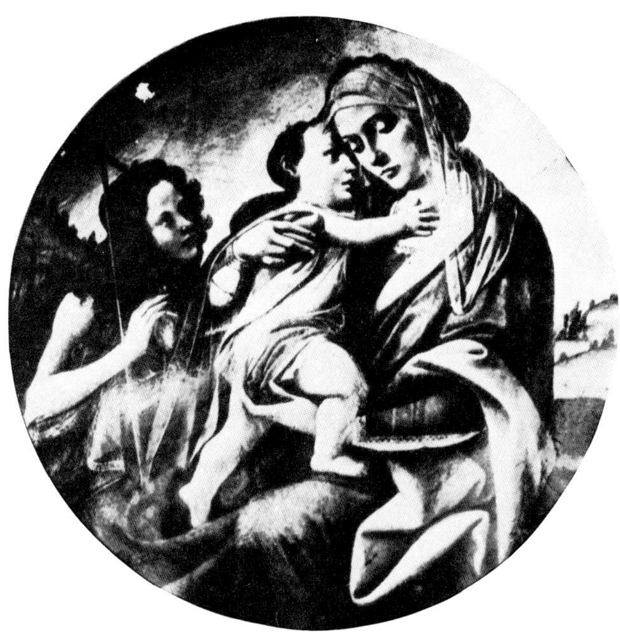

Figure 19 b. *Madonna and Child with the Young St. John*
as it appeared in a photograph of 1914.

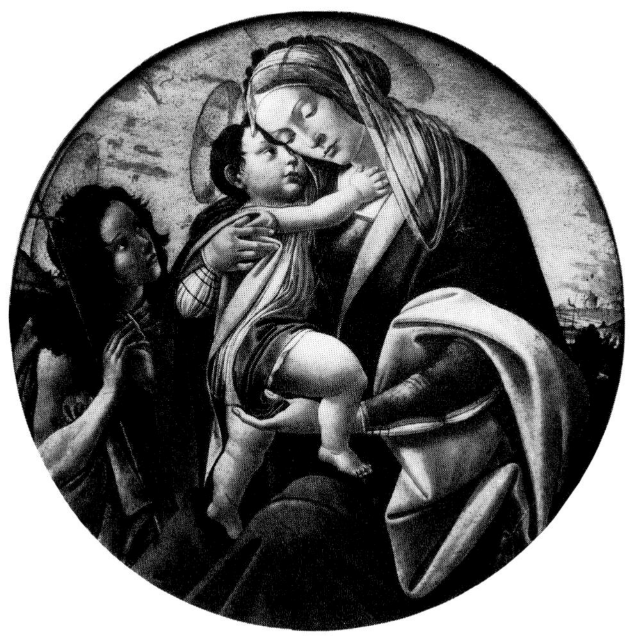

Figure 19 c. *Madonna and Child with the Young St. John.*
Attributed to Botticelli. Musée Fabre, Montpellier.

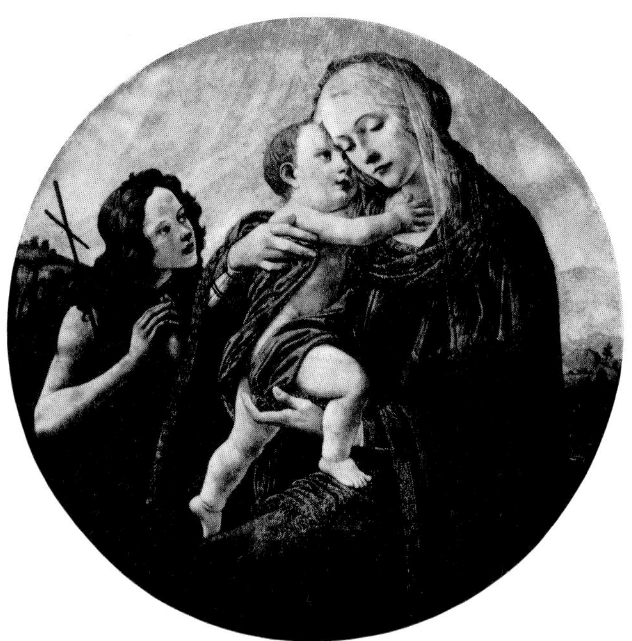

Figure 19 d. *Madonna and Child with the Young St. John*
after restoration while in the Lazzaroni collection.

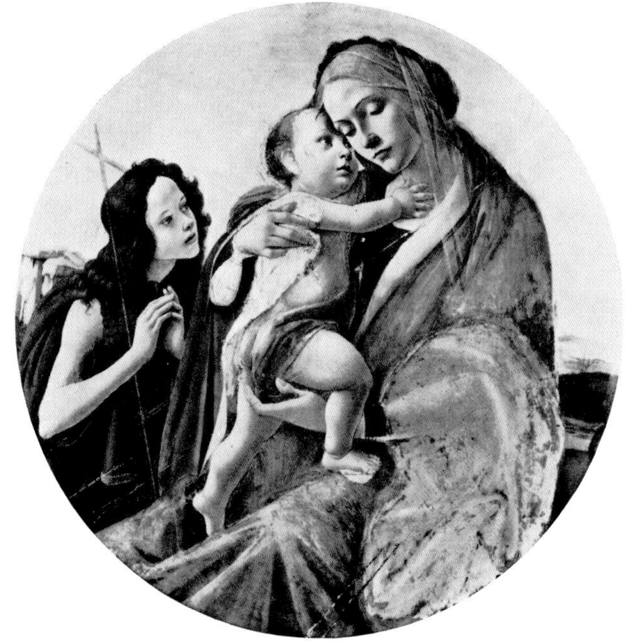

Figure 19 e. *Madonna and Child with the Young St. John*
stripped of overpaint.

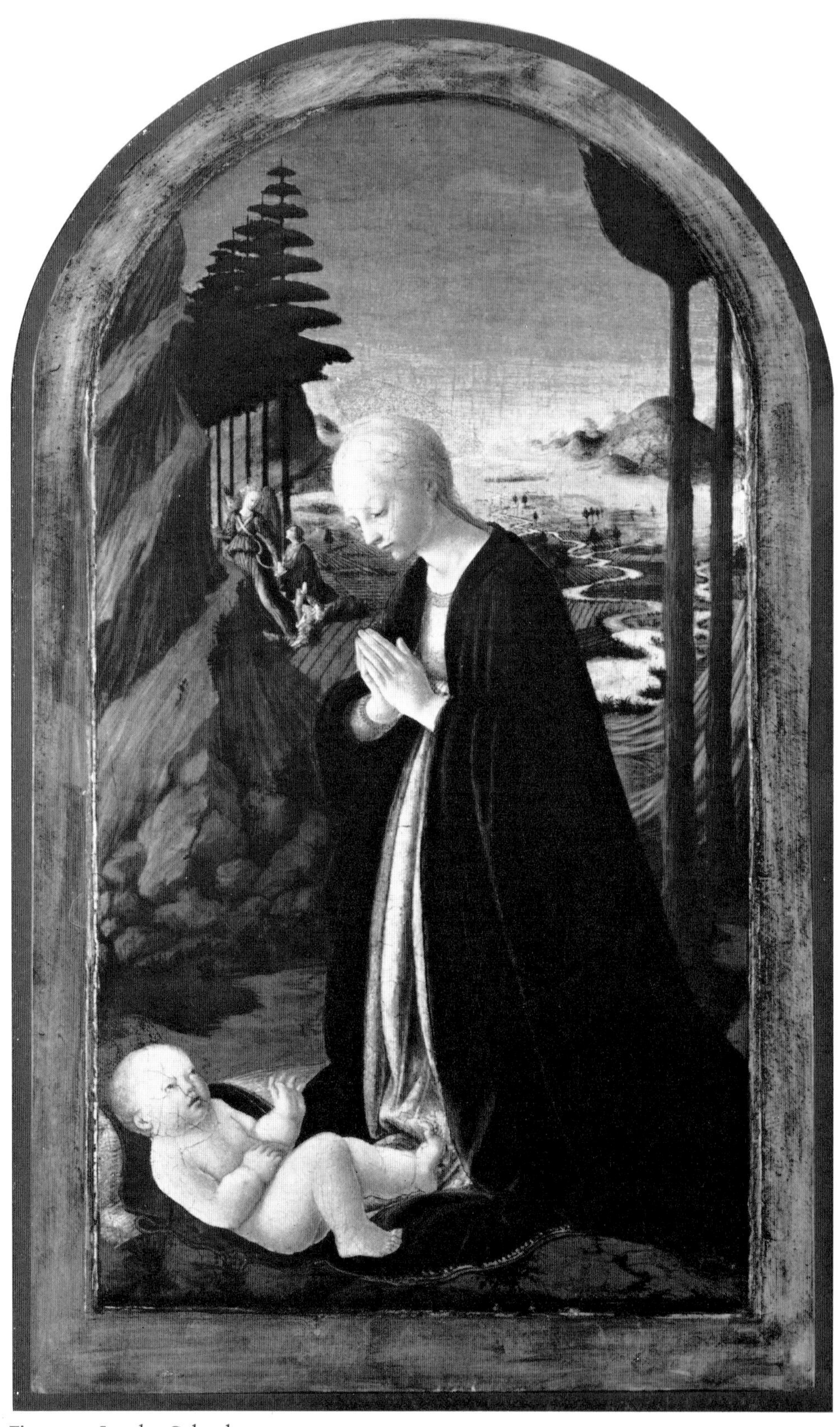

Figure 20. See also Colorplate XII.

FRANCESCO BOTTICINI, Florence, ca. 1446–1497

He was the son of Giovanni di Domenico, a painter of playing cards, and the father of Raffaello Botticini (1477–1520, last recorded date). The documents call him Francesco di Giovanni. He probably is the painter who entered the studio of Neri di Bicci in October 1459. His eclectic painting follows in the tradition of his master, Neri di Bicci, and after the style of several of his contemporaries such as Cosimo Rosselli, Fra Filippo Lippi, Botticelli, and Verrocchio. The group of paintings ascribed to him is diversified enough and in some cases so vernacular as to cause some question as to its homogeneity. His one documented work is a tabernacle at Empoli, commissioned in 1484 and more or less finished by 1491.

20 *Madonna and Child* 16.789

Panel (transferred from poplar to plywood), 96·7 × 59 cm (38$\frac{1}{8}$ × 23$\frac{1}{2}$ inches). Painted surface: 84·6 × 47 cm (33$\frac{5}{16}$ × 18$\frac{1}{2}$ inches).
COLLECTIONS: James Jackson Jarves; Mrs. Liberty E. Holden, Cleveland, 1884.
Holden Collection, 1916.

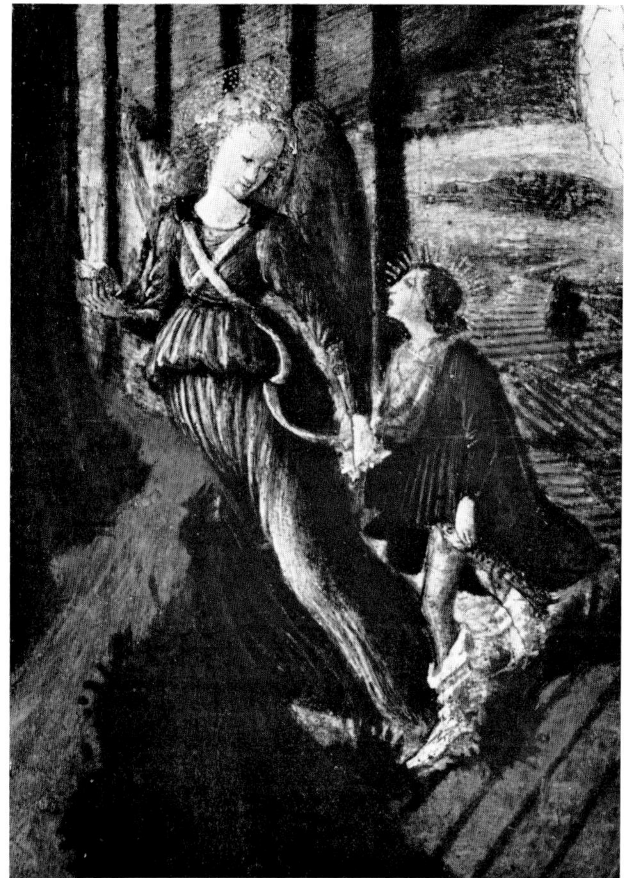

Figure 20*a*. Detail.

This painting was transferred by William Suhr in 1947 from its original panel which had several vertical cracks, one down the entire length of the panel at the left of the Virgin's head. Unfortunately, it has lost much of the original surface and has been rubbed, particularly in the areas of the Virgin's head and the figure of the Christ Child.

The archangel Raphael and Tobias, taken from the deuterocanonical Book of Tobit, are introduced into the background of this Adoration scene (Fig. 20*a*) to emphasize the concept of divine guardianship. This was a very popular theme in quattrocento Florentine painting particularly between 1465 and 1485. Raphael Societies, their individual members, and merchants were responsible for the numerous commissions of this subject (made to protect individuals while traveling). This story was usually treated as an independent subject but occasionally was included in the background of other scenes. The early attribution of this panel to Jacopo del Sellaio and Francesco Botticini (who was himself a member of one of the more important of these lay societies, the Campagnia dell'Arcangelo Raffaelo in San Spirito) was due in part to the appearance of Tobias and

Raphael, a favorite subject of these two painters and their workshops. (For a discussion of the iconography of this theme and examples, see Gertrude M. Achenbach, "The Iconography of Tobias and the Angel in Florentine Painting in the Renaissance," *Marsyas*, III, 1943–1945, 71–84.)

Bought by Jarves as a Piero della Francesca, M. L. Berenson (1907) gave the picture to Botticini although she felt it looked like a Jacopo del Sellaio and had a landscape derivative from Baldovinetti. Rubinstein (1917) was the first to publish the panel as School of Baldovinetti, followed by Van Marle (1929), and this Museum has agreed with their attribution until very recently. Kennedy (1938) attributed the painting to "Anonimo," a personality not clearly defined but influenced by Botticini because of the Tobias theme and sympathetic with Baldovinetti's touch as well. She also gives to this same Anonimo a *Madonna and Child with St. John* formerly in the Gamberini collection (Kennedy, fig. 90) which now seems to be quite different from the Cleveland panel and closer to a follower of Filippo Lippi (in the circle of Pier Francesco Fiorentino).

Like Berenson (1932), Everett Fahy (orally, 1971) attributed this painting to the early Botticini, dating it about 1470. There is a close similarity in the river valley landscape backgrounds of the Cleveland picture, Botticini's early *Madonna* in the Galleria Estense in Modena (Rodolfo Pallucchini, *I dipinti della Galleria Estense di Modena*, Rome, 1945, no. 497, fig. 192), and his *Madonna and St. John Adoring the Christ Child* in the Universitätsgalerie in Göttingen (Van Marle, XIII, 1931, fig. 275). Among other early paintings by Botticini that are closely related to the Museum's are the *Madonna in a Rocky Landscape* from the Prince Golimicheff-Koutousoff collection (*Art News*, XIV, April 15, 1916, illus. p. 1) and the *Madonna Adoring the Child* in the Fitzwilliam Museum in Cambridge. Goodison and Robertson (1967) relate the Cleveland painting to the Fitzwilliam Botticini as well as examples in the Ca'd'Oro in Venice (Gino Fogolari, *Regia Galleria Giorgio Franchetti alla Ca' d'Oro di Venezia*, No. 56: *Itinerari dei musei e monumenti d'Italia*, Rome, 1936, p. 39); the Hoden collection; the ex-Dreyfus collection, Paris; the ex-Bloudoff collection, Moscow (*Trésors d'art en Russie*, v, 1905, pl. 26); and the ex-Hurd collection, New York (sale: Kende, New York, October 29, 1945, no. 21).

N.C.W.

EXHIBITIONS: Boston (1883), cat. no. 402; MMA (1912), cat. no. 10 (close to Sellaio or Botticini); CMA (1916), cat. no. 2; CMA (1936), cat. no. 74, pl. X; CMA (1971), cat. no. 9.

LITERATURE: Jarves (1884), cat. no. 3 (as Piero della Francesca); M. L. Berenson (1907), p. 2 (as Botticini); Berenson, *The Florentine Painters...* (1909), pp. 119, 192 (as Botticini?); Crowe and Cavalcaselle, *History of Painting in Italy*, IV (1911), 183 (as Sellaio); Underhill (1917), 20, illus. p. 33 (as School of Baldovinetti); Rubinstein (1917), no. 2, illus. pp. 11–12 (as School of Baldovinetti); Van Marle, XI (1929), 282, fig. 181; XIII (1931), 418; Berenson, *Pictures Renaiss.* (1932), p. 107 (as Botticini?); Ruth Wedgwood Kennedy, *Alesso Baldovinetti: A Critical and Historical Study* (New Haven, London, 1938), p. 96, fig. 91; *Handbook* (1958), no. 400; *Handbook* (1966), p. 80; J. W. Goodison and G. H. Robertson, *Catalogue of Paintings*, Vol. II: *Italian Schools* (Fitzwilliam Museum, Cambridge, 1967), p. 23.

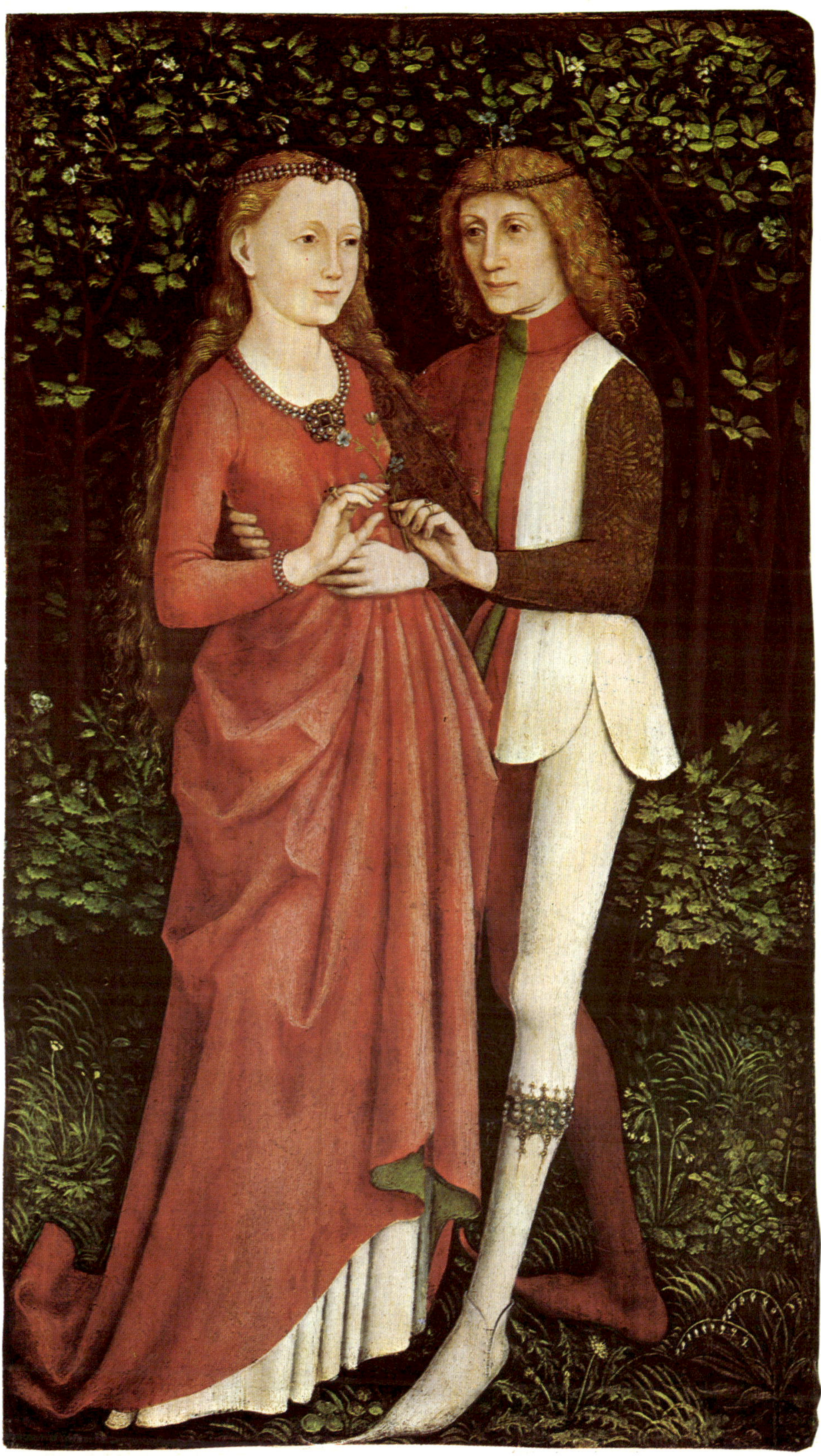

Plate IX. *A Bridal Pair*, Anonymous South German Master, Upper Rhine Region (Painting 12).

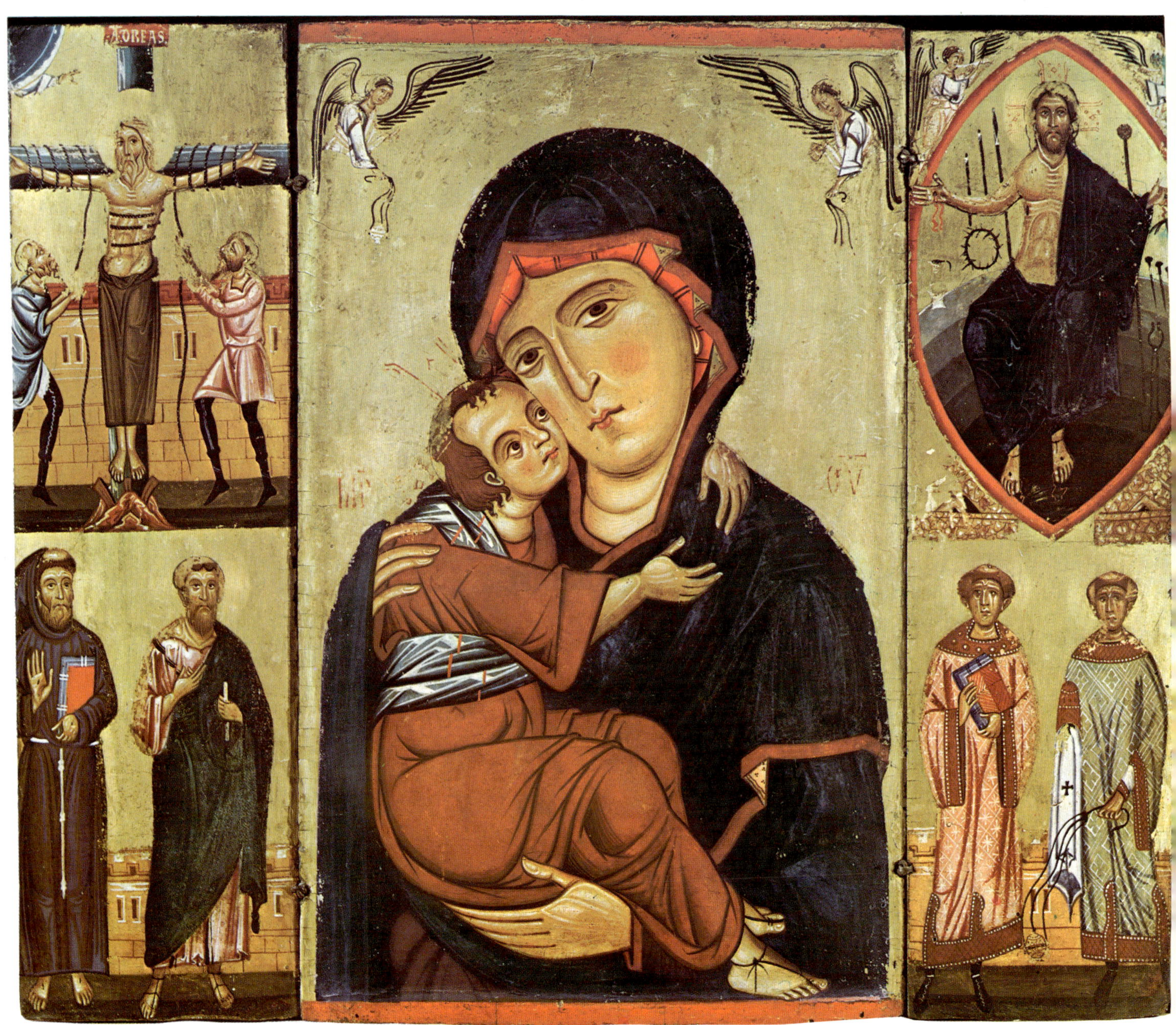

Plate x. *The Madonna and Child and Saints*, Berlinghiero (Painting 15).

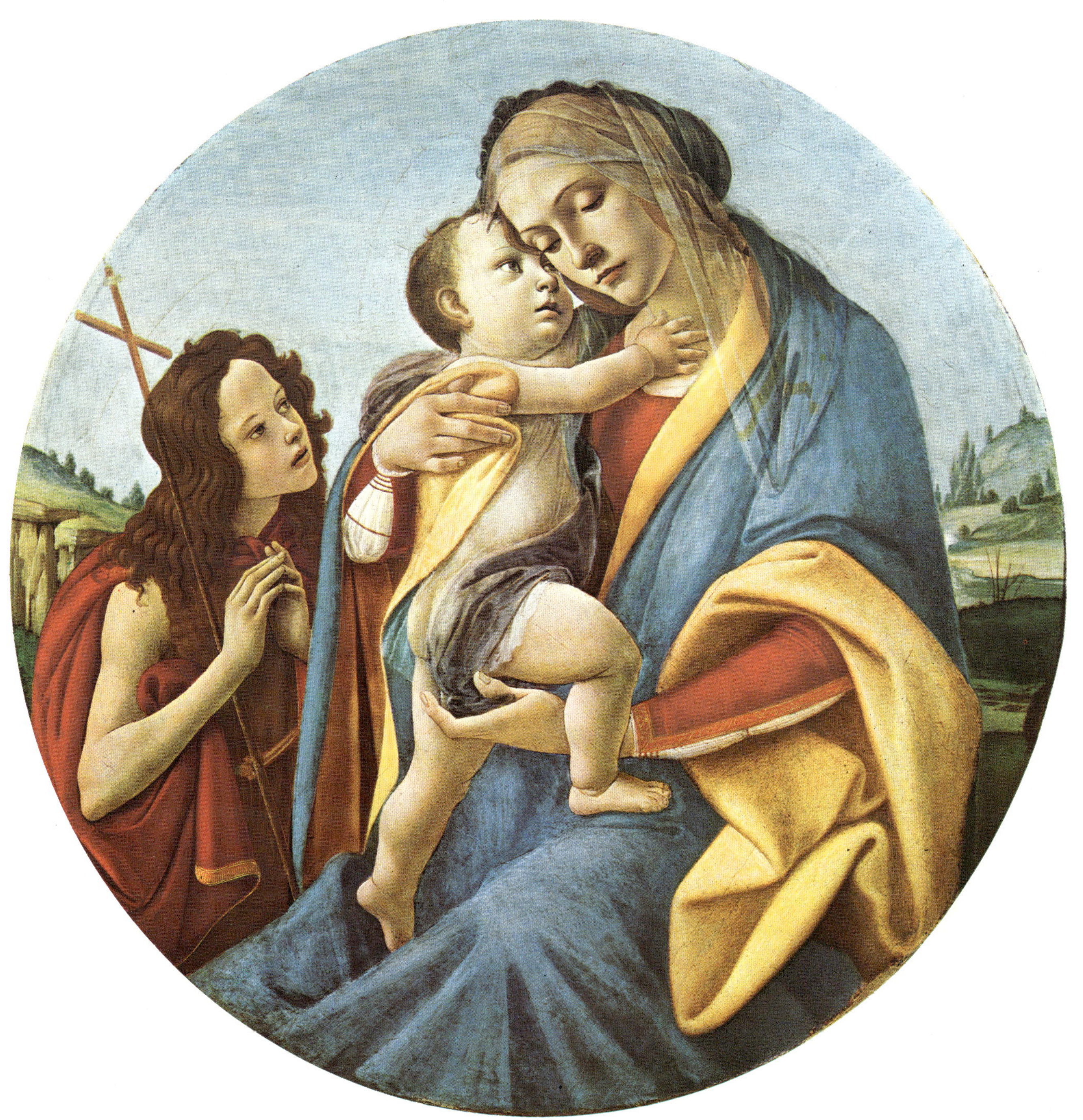

Plate XI. *Madonna and Child with the Young St. John*, Sandro Botticelli (Painting 19).

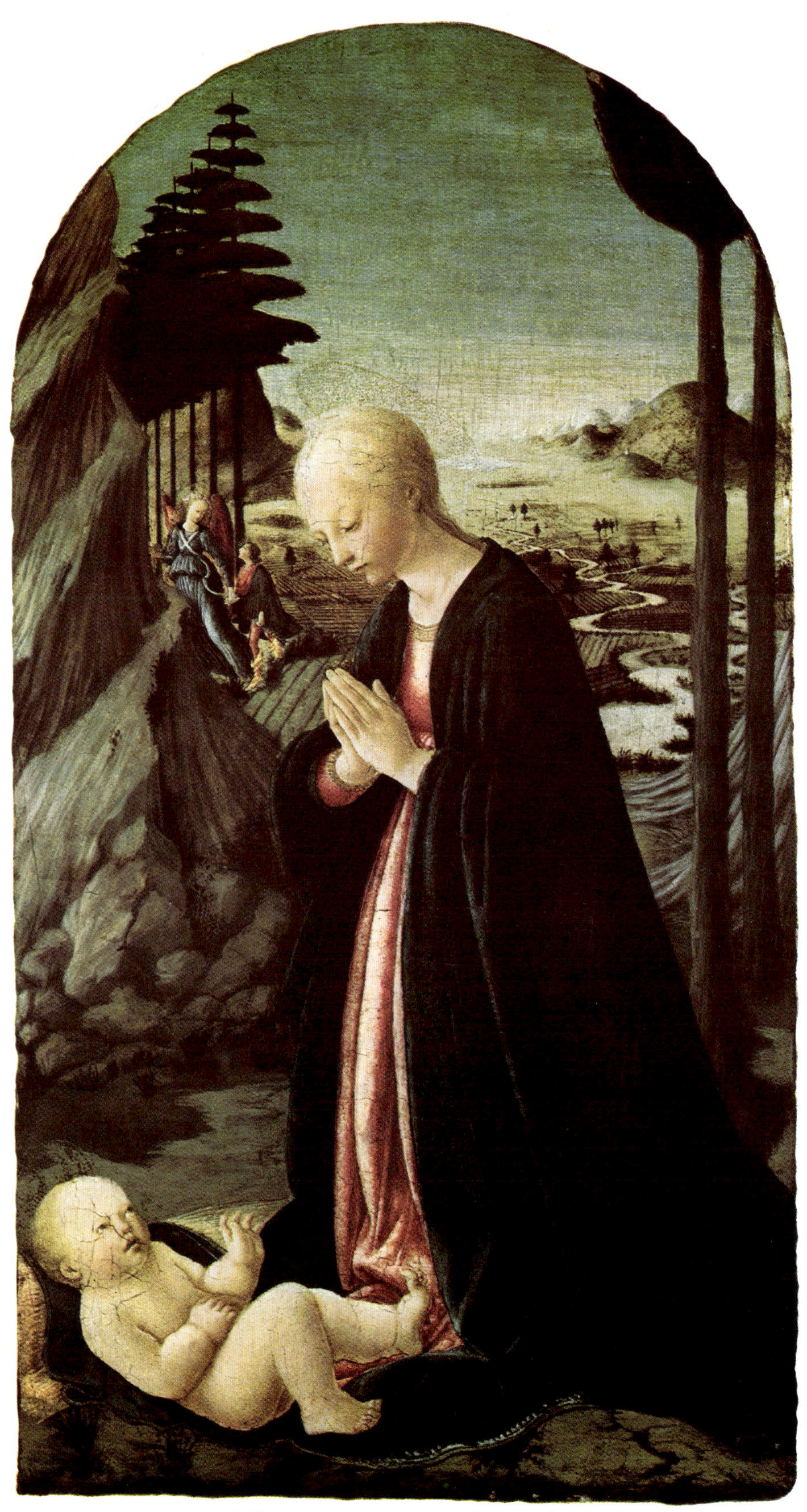

Plate XII. *Madonna and Child*, Francesco Botticini (Painting 20).

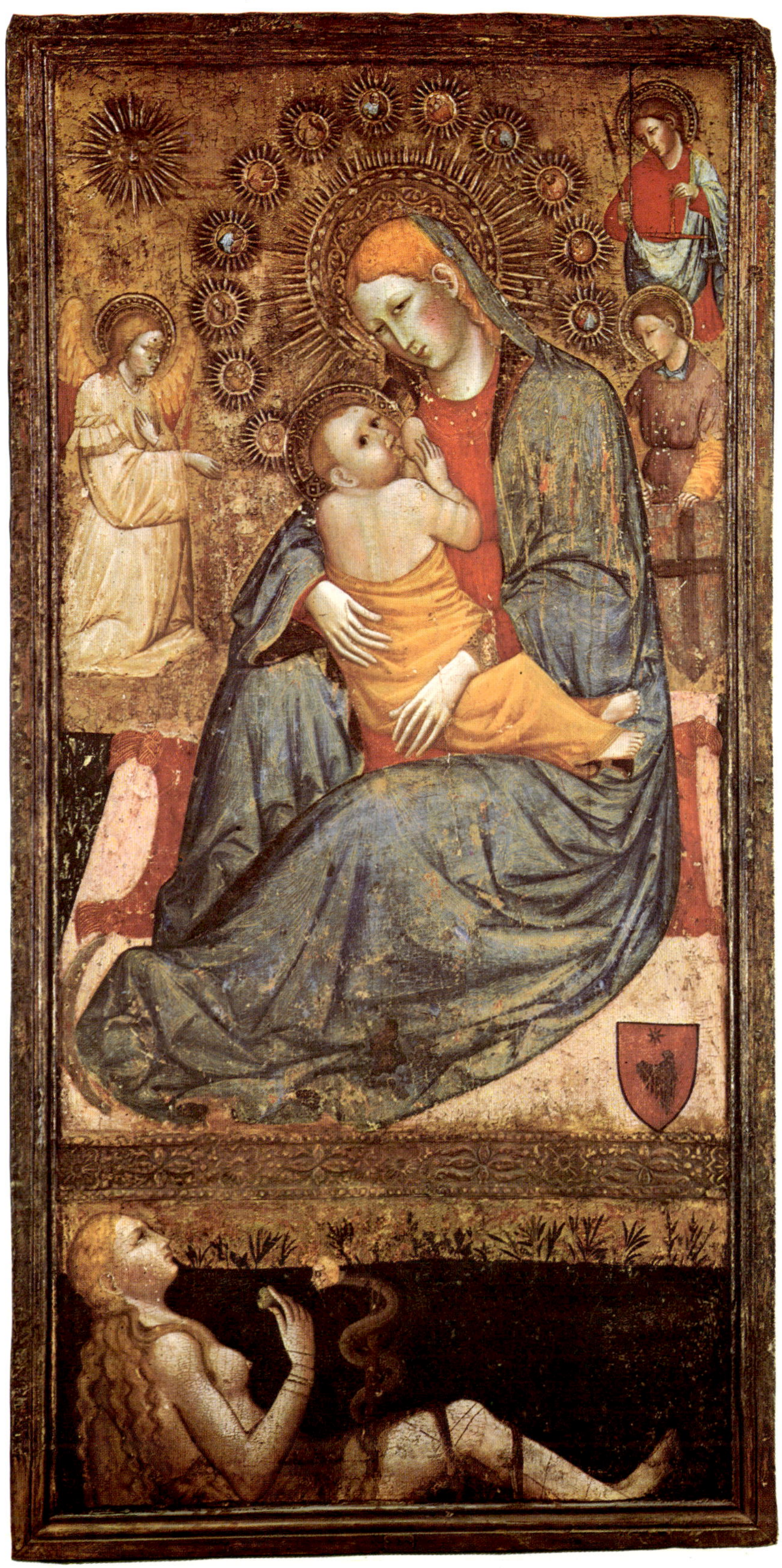

Plate XIII. *The Madonna of Humility with the Temptation of Eve*, Carlo da Camerino (Painting 22).

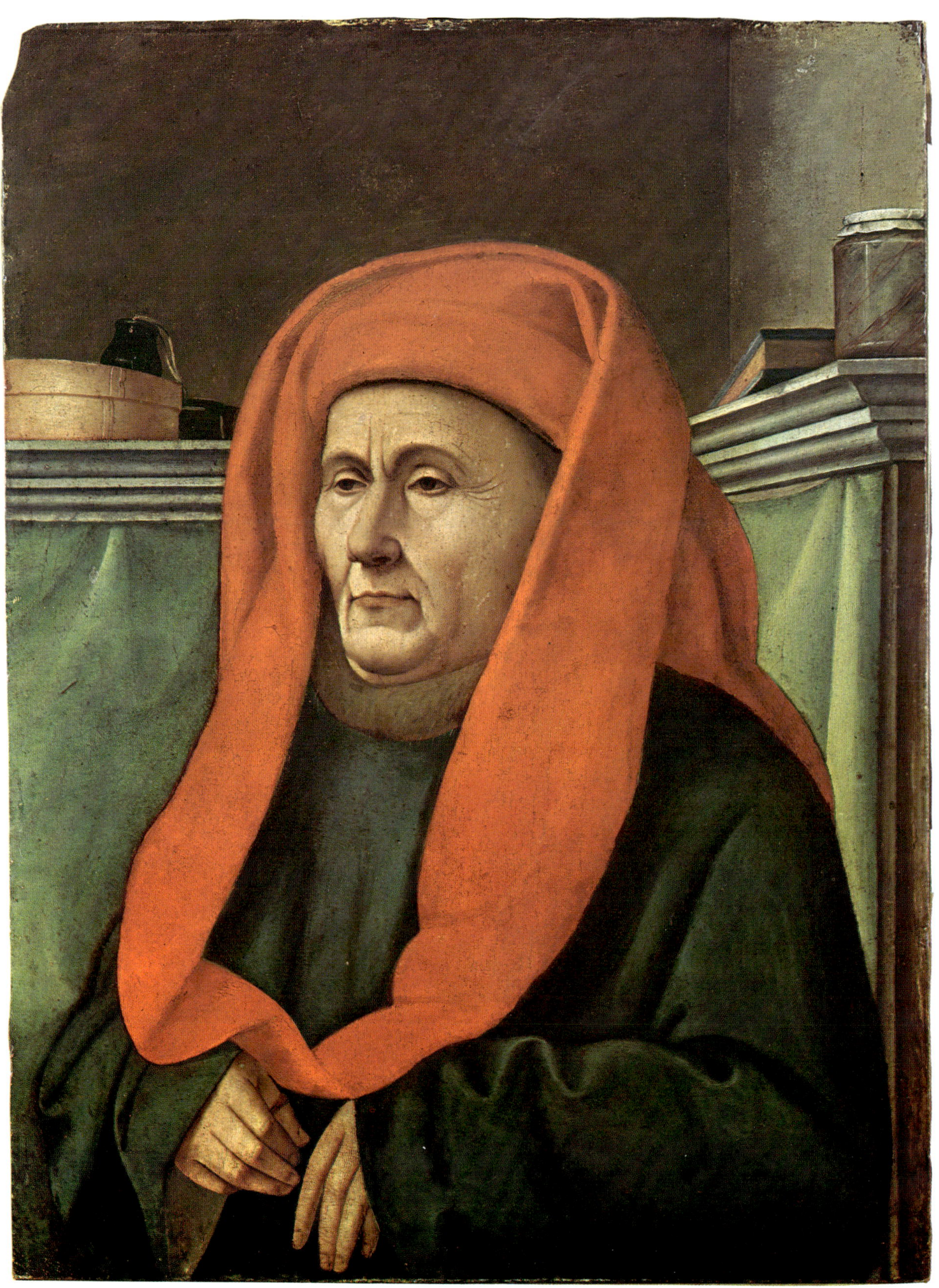

Plate xiv. *Portrait of a Man*, Colantonio(?) (Painting 24).

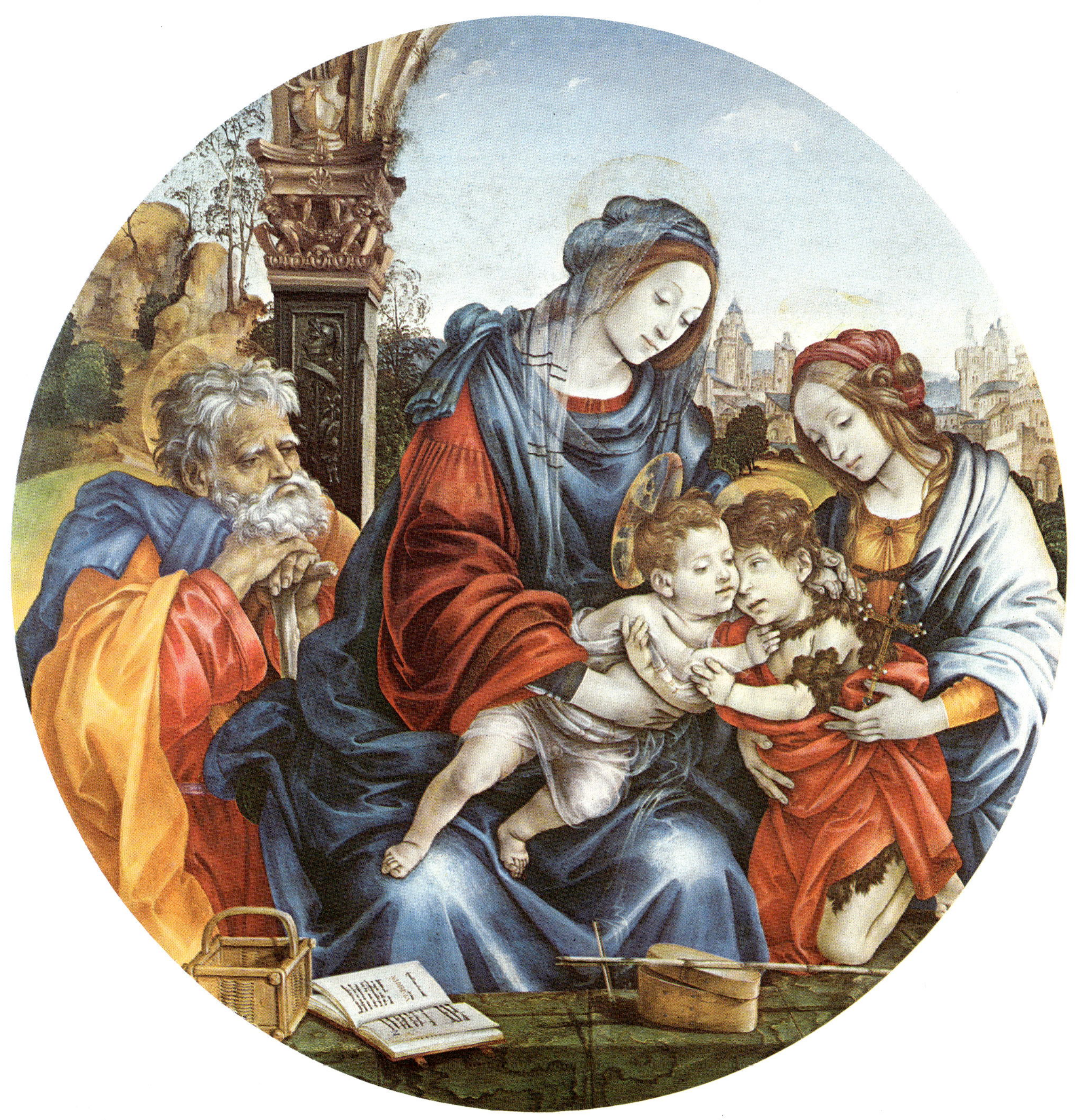

Plate xv. *The Holy Family with the Infant St. John and St. Margaret*, Filippino Lippi (Painting 29).

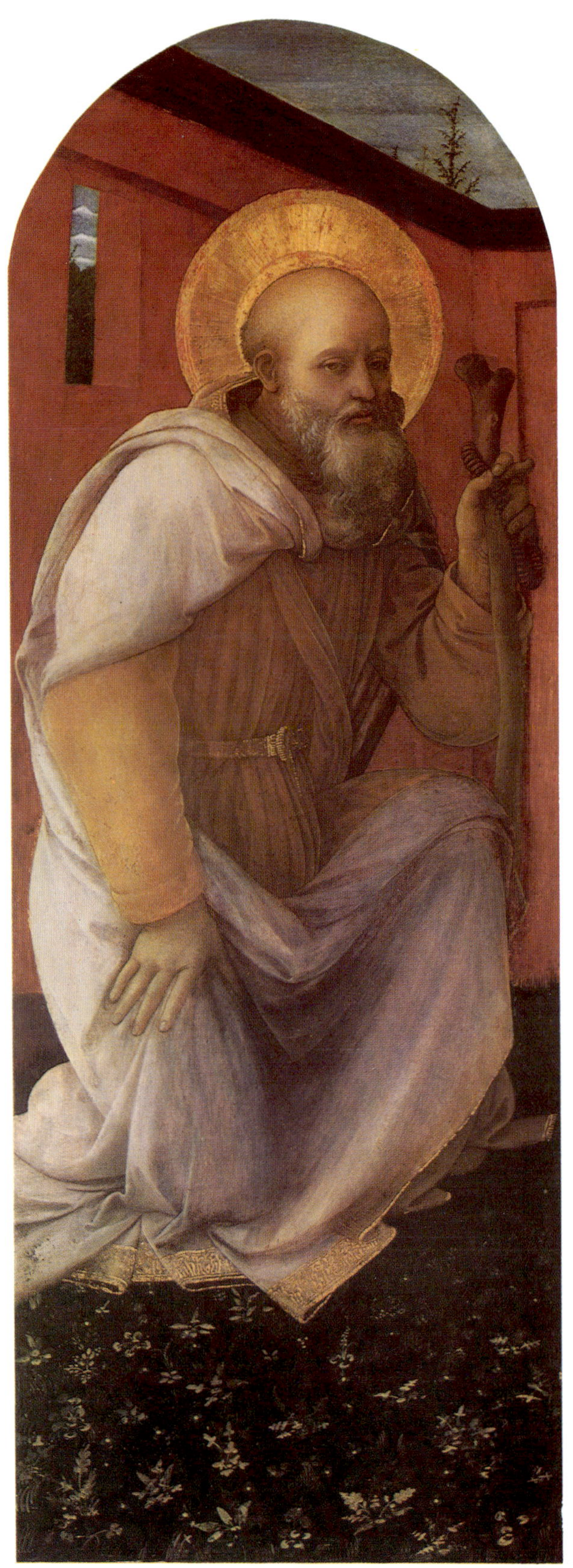 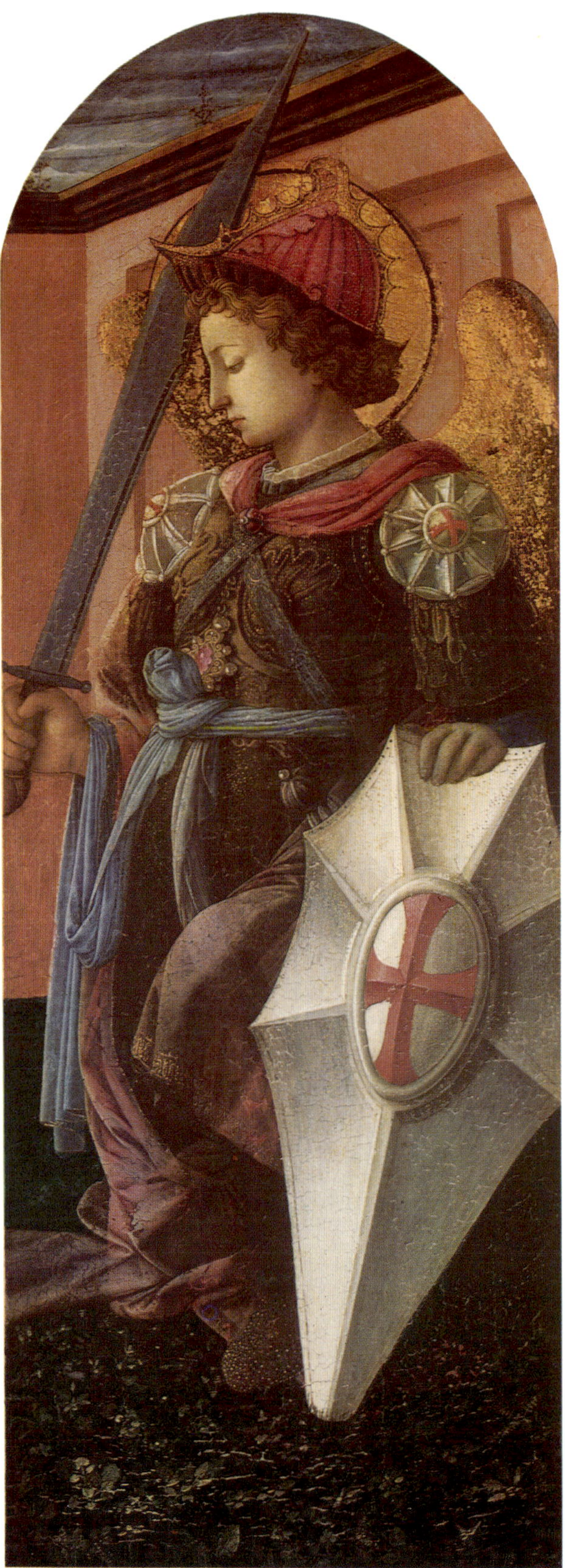

Plate XVI. *St. Anthony Abbot* (left) and *St. Michael*, Fra Filippo Lippi (Paintings 30 A, B).

FRANCESCO BOTTICINI

21 *Madonna and Child*   16.788

Panel (poplar), 67·2 × 46 cm ($26\frac{1}{2} \times 18\frac{1}{8}$ inches).
Painted surface: 64·6 × 45 cm ($25\frac{3}{8} \times 17\frac{1}{2}$ inches).
COLLECTIONS: James Jackson Jarves; Mrs. Liberty E.
Holden, Cleveland, Ohio, 1884.
Holden Collection, 1916.

The condition of this panel is fair. There are minor losses
of paint throughout with some abrasion to the paint
surface, particularly in the Christ Child's head and hand.
The gold decoration is missing in the Madonna's veil
and the haloes, and the entire blue of her robe has been
repainted. The original edges of the paint surface are
visible.

This panel was first attributed to Domenico Ghirlandaio by Jarves (1884) in the Boston Exhibition of 1883.
This catalogue also states that Baron Liphart thought
the painting was by Verrocchio. M. L. Berenson first
considered this painting to be by Francesco Botticini in
1907. B. Berenson (1909) gave the painting to Francesco
Botticini(?), Frank J. Mather (written comment in the
Museum Files, 1921) agreed with this attribution and
dated the painting about 1470. Van Marle (1931) gave
the painting to Botticini(?), saying that it is almost
too Verrocchiesque for this attribution. Because of the
strong influence of Verrocchio in this painting, it would
seem to date ca. 1475–1480. One of the paintings which
is most closely related to the Museum panel is the *Madonna and Child with St. John* in Boston (Fig. 21 a). The
hilly landscape with a lake and boats behind the Cleveland Madonna varies from the craggy mountains and
winding river of the Boston painting but the rendering
of the Madonna's face and head-covering, the expression
of the faces, the proportions, and general composition
are very close as in another variant of the subject in the
collection of Viscount Rothermere, London, in which
the position of the Madonna's hands is also the same.
Berenson uses the Virgin from the *Nativity* at the Pitti
Gallery in Florence (no. 347), the University Gallery in
Göttingen (no. 16), the Louvre (no. 1683), and the Cleveland picture, as well as others, for the basis of his attribution to Botticini of the drawing in the Louvre (Berenson, 1961, pl. xxv).

N.C.W.

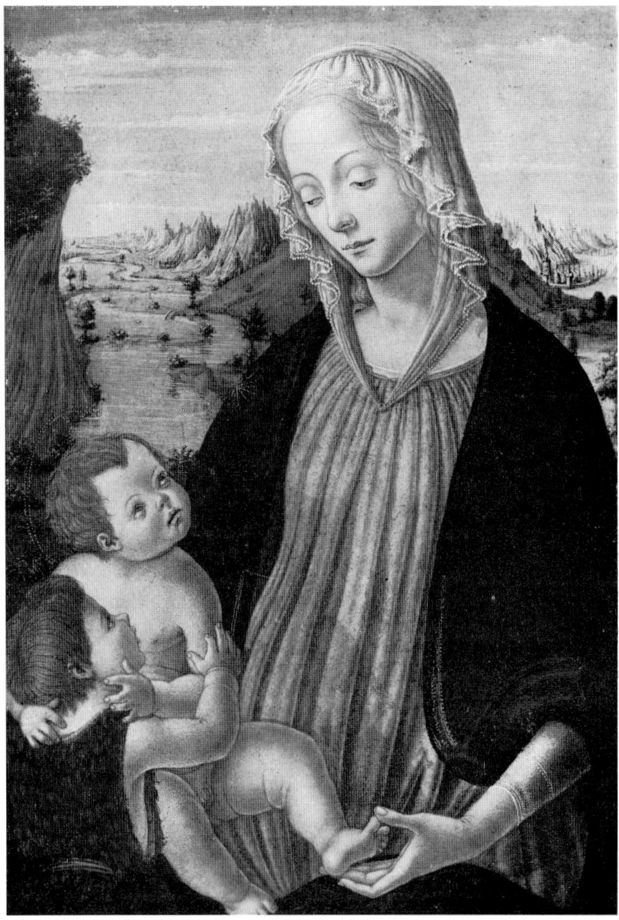

Figure 21 a. *The Madonna and Child with St. John.*
67 × 47 cm ($26\frac{1}{4} \times 18\frac{1}{2}$ inches). Botticini.
Isabella Stewart Gardner Museum, Boston.

EXHIBITIONS: Boston (1883), cat. no. 444; MMA (1912), cat. no.
4; CMA (1916), cat. no. 6; CMA (1936), cat. no. 77, pl. x.
LITERATURE: Wilhelm Bode, "Die Italienischen Sculpturen der
Renaissance in den Königlichen Museen," *Jahrbuch der Königlich-
Preussischen Kunstsammlungen*, III (Berlin, 1882), 238, 240, 244, 252;
Jarves (1884), cat. no. 13; M. L. Berenson (1907), p. 2; Berenson,
The Florentine Painters... (1909), pp. 119, 192; Underhill (1917),
p. 20, illus. p. 18; Rubinstein (1917), no. 6, illus. pp. 14–15; Van
Marle, XIII (1931), 409, fig. 278; Paul George Konody, *Works of
Art in the Collection of Viscount Rothermere* (London, 1932), pl. 11;
Berenson, *Pictures Renaiss.* (1932), p. 107; Berenson, "Un dessin de
Botticini au Musée du Louvre," *Gaz. des B.-A.*, VIII (1932), 278;
Berenson, *I Disegni...*, I (1961), 112; Berenson, *Pictures Renaiss.,
Florentine School*, I (1963), 39.

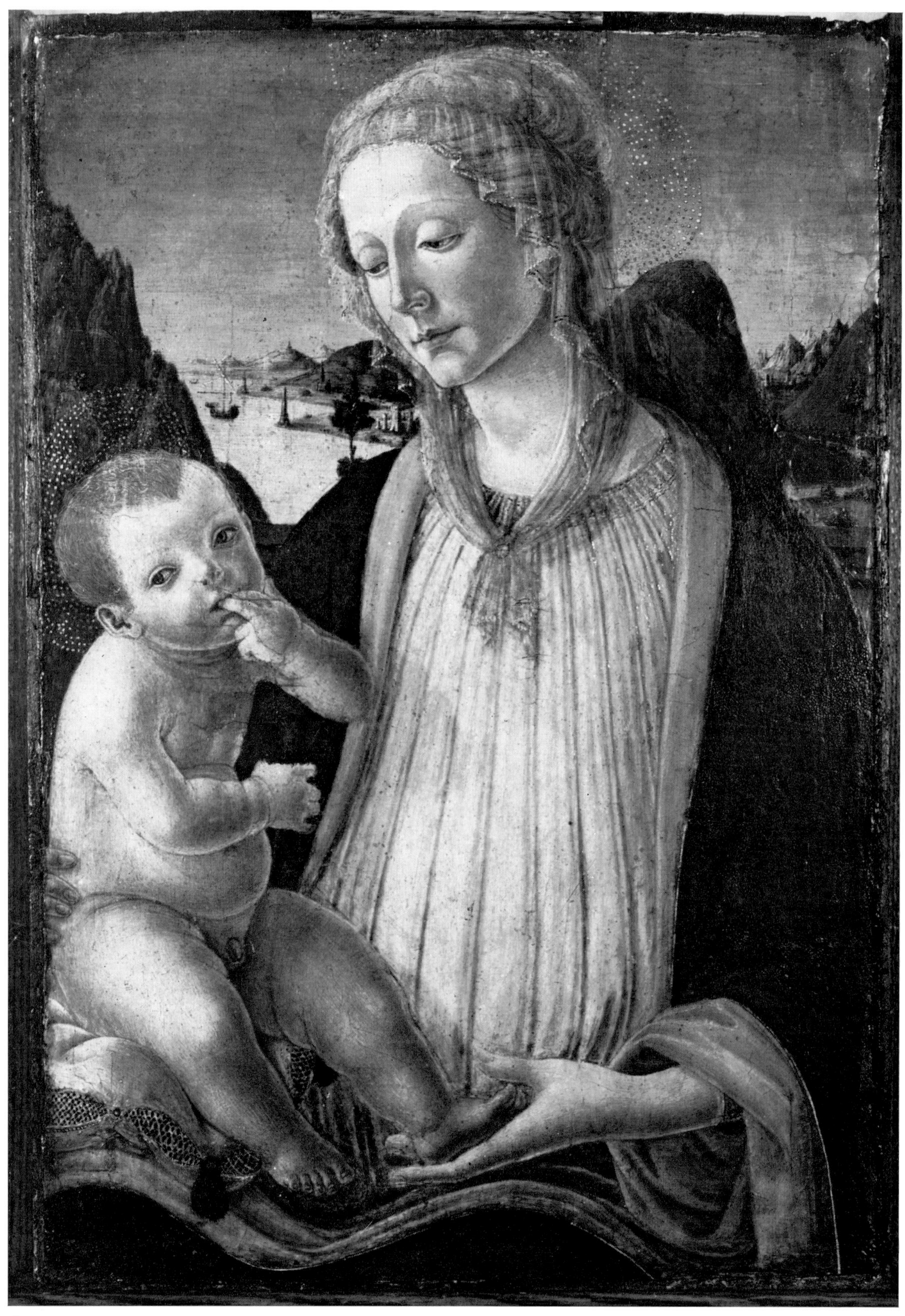

Figure 21.

CARLO DA CAMERINO, The Marches,
active ca. 1380–1420

This artist was working in the Marches ca. 1380–1420. His signature appears on a cross dated 1396 in the church of S. Michele in Marcerata Feltria. He was influenced by local painting in the Marches, by Sienese painting, and by Andrea da Bologna. Zeri (1950) also attributed to this artist the *Annunciation* in the Galleria Nazionale delle Marche in Urbino; the *Madonna* in the Municipality of Mondavia; a *Triptych* (37.699) in the Walters Art Gallery, Baltimore; the *Death of the Virgin* and the fragment of the *Virgin Crowned by Two Angels*, both from the Museum in Ancona. With the exception of the *Death of the Virgin* which Longhi attributes to Andrea da Bologna, both he and Offner agree with the attribution of this group to Carlo da Camerino. Zeri also attributes the *Circumcision* in the Ancona Museum to the same artist.

22   *The Madonna of Humility with*   16.795
     the Temptation of Eve

Panel (poplar), including molding, 191·2 × 98·7 cm (75½ × 38¹³⁄₁₆ inches). Inside frame: 181·5 × 88·6 cm (71⁷⁄₁₆ × 34¾ inches).

COLLECTIONS: James Jackson Jarves; Mrs. Liberty E. Holden, Cleveland, Ohio, 1884.

Holden Collection, 1916.

In its present stripped-down condition, the painting is reasonably well preserved, with general over-all but minor abrasions of time. There is a major area of refill in the figure of Eve. The lower part of the figure of Eve has been cut off, shortening the original height of the panel. The lower part of the frame (5½ inches on the left, 6½ inches on the right, and the bottom) is modern.

On the Virgin's right is the archangel Gabriel with a representation of the sun above, which appears less frequently in fourteenth-century painting the Marches. On the Madonna's left is St. George below with St. Michael above. Around the Madonna's halo there is another celestial halo of twelve raised stars with portrait busts of the apostles (Figs. 22 *a*, *b*). By the Madonna's feet, the moon is at one side and an unidentified coat of arms at the other. Below the horizontal decorative border, Eve is shown reclining in a simple landscape with the snake coiled around her leg and extending upward, its human head peering at the apple in her hand (Fig. 22 *c*).

The *Madonna of Humility* (a representation of the Madonna sitting on the ground nursing the Christ Child) first appeared as a subject independent of the Nativity in Italian trecento painting. Meiss (1936) points out that its origins may also be found in the figure of Eve nursing her Child after the expulsion from the Garden of Eden (see *Adam and Eve*, MS. 183, f. 13, Liège, eighth century, New York, Morgan Library), which is particularly interesting in relation to the iconography of the Museum panel. He notes the paradoxical combination in the subject of the Madonna of Humility - " the tender, humble image of the mother nursing her child with the awesome celestial Woman described in the twelfth chapter of the Apocalypse: 'And there appeared a great wonder in heaven; a woman clothed with the sun, and the moon under her feet, and upon her head a crown of twelve stars…'" (for further discussion of the iconography of the Madonna of Humility, see Meiss, 1936, 435–464).

Although the subject of the Madonna of Humility became an established tradition in the Marches in the last half of the fourteenth and the fifteenth century (the earliest known example is the dated panel of 1359 by Francescuccio Ghissi in S. Domenico, Fabriano, probably copied from an earlier example by Allegretto Nuzi), the Cleveland panel is unusual in the combination of the Madonna of Humility with the Temptation of Eve.

A lost painting by Simone Martini may have been the earliest depiction of the combination of the two subjects, the earliest extant example being the Ambrogio Lorenzetti fresco at S. Galgano at Monte Siepi (see Giulia Sinibaldi, *I Lorenzetti*, 1929, pl. XXXIV). There is an interesting little-known group of at least ten examples from the last half of the Trecento related iconographically by the inclusion of the figure of Eve in either a Coronation of the Virgin or a Madonna of Humility scene by followers of Ambrogio Lorenzetti or followers of Paolo di Giovanni Fei in Umbria. The Museum example is the only one known from the Marches.

The painting has had various attributions. Jarves felt that it was painted for the family of Dante (because of the coat of arms which is at present still unidentified) and attributed it to Giotto. Based on the iconography M. L. Berenson suggested the Sienese School showing the influence of Bartolo di Fredi. Aru (1921) was of the opinion that it was a Ligurian work imitating more-or-less the manner of Bartolommeo da Camoglie, derived from his *Madonna of Humility* in the National Museum

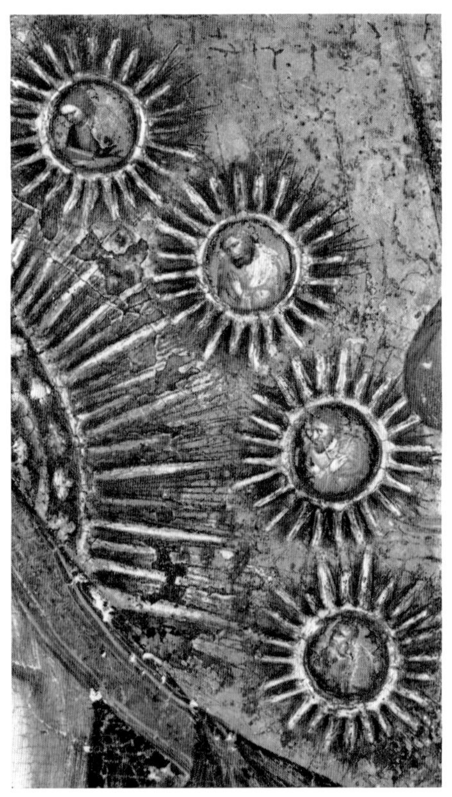

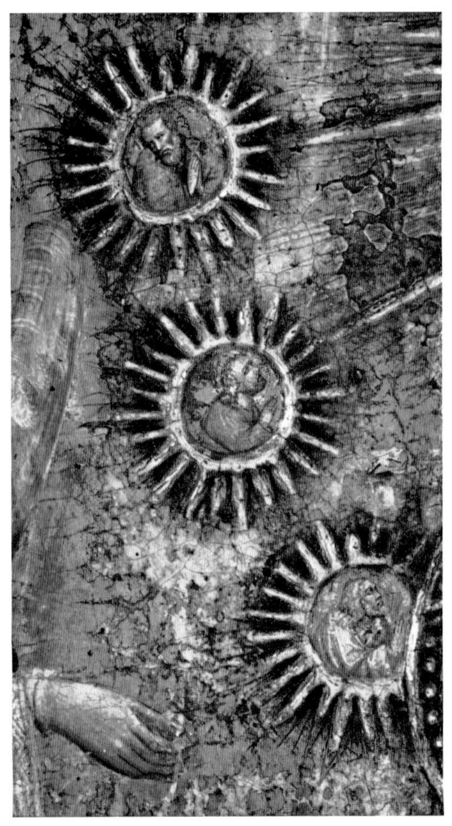

Figures 22 *a* and *b*. Details of the Apostles.

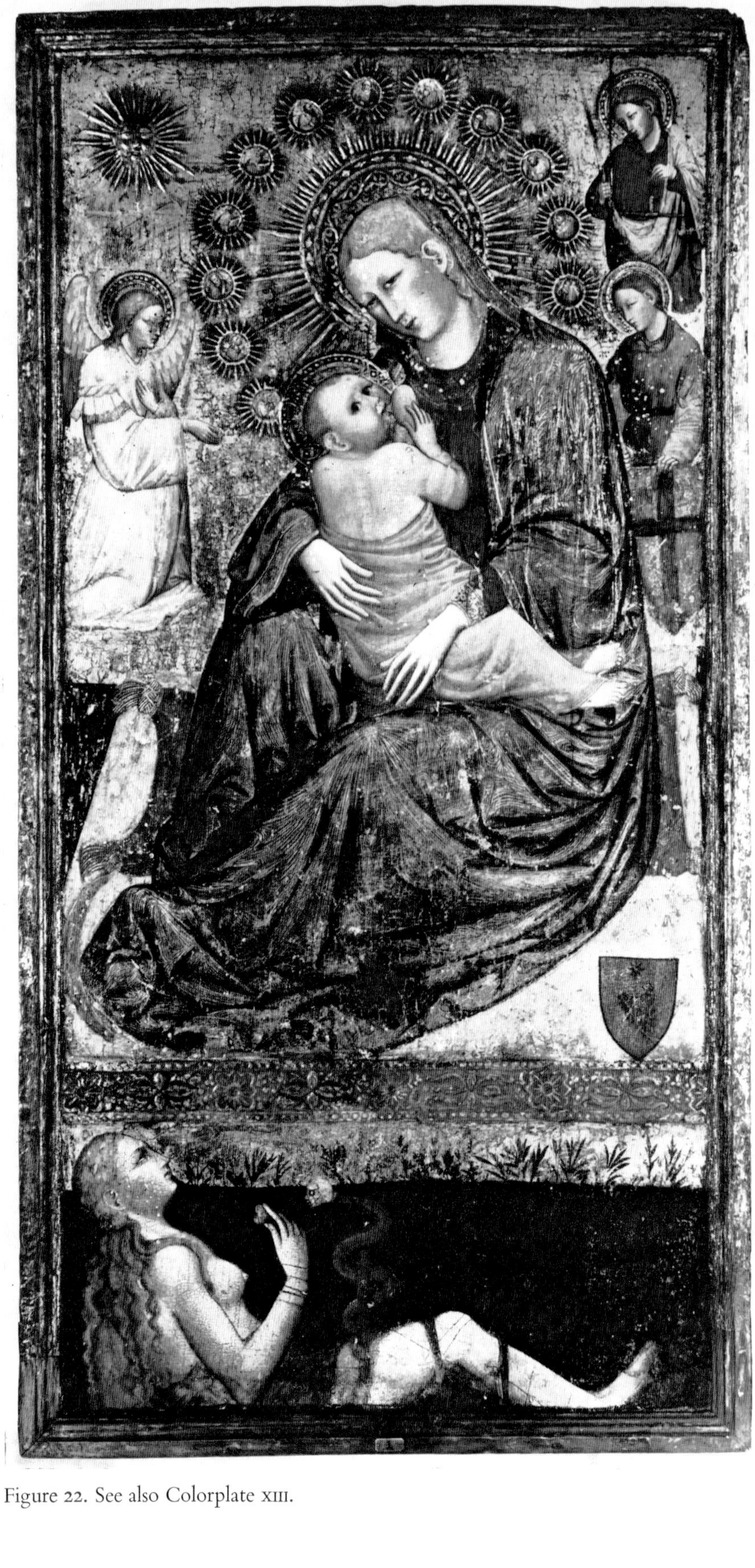

Figure 22. See also Colorplate XIII.

in Palermo. Mather (1923) called it Andrea da Bologna before 1380 because of its similarity to the signed and dated *Madonna of Humility* in S. Agostino, Pàusola. Van Marle felt it was closer to the style of Allegretto Nuzi than to Francescuccio Ghissi. Evelyn Sandberg-Vavalà in an unpublished manuscript in the files of the Museum dated April 3, 1945, stated that the painter of the Museum panel stylistically falls between the *Madonna* by Andrea da Bologna at Pàusola, signed and dated 1372, and the *Madonna* by Lippo Dalmasii in the church of the Misericordia at Bologna, signed and dated 1397. She felt that the Cleveland picture might possibly be a direct imitation of the Pàusola painting. However, Zeri (1950), Meiss (1951), and Offner (letter of February 2, 1965) have given the painting convincingly to Carlo da Camerino, the most important and appealing painter in the Marches in the late Trecento before Gentile da Fabriano. Another painting of the Madonna of Humility by the same artist is in the collection of Paolo Lampugni in Milan (see *Italienische Kunst*, exh. cat.; Milan, Biblioteca Ambrosiana, Lucerne, Kunstmuseum, 1946, pl. XVIII, no. 77). Although it is related to the Museum painting and has the same apostle medallions terminating the halo, the forms are flatter and Zeri has stated that it is a more feeble and later work by Carlo da Camerino.

N.C.W.

EXHIBITIONS: Boston (1883), cat. no. 399; MMA (1912), cat. no. 12, illus.; CMA (1916), cat. no. 16; CMA (1936), cat. no. 90, pl. XI; CMA (1963), cat. no. 76, illus. p. 185.

LITERATURE: Jarves (1884), cat. no. 1; M. L. Berenson (1907), p. 2, illus. p. 1; Frank J. Mather, *The Nation*, XCV (1912), 392; Underhill 1917), p. 23, illus.; Rubinstein (1917), cat. no. 16, illus.; Carlo Aru, "Bartolomeo Pellarano da Camogli," *Bollettino d'arte*, XV (1921), 271; Mather (1923), p. 271, fig. 170; Van Marle, V (1925), 164, 168, fig. 105; Chandler R. Post, *A History of Spanish Painting*, II (Cambridge, Mass., 1930), 232, n. 1; Milliken (1932), illus. p. 149; George Harold Edgell, *A History of Sienese Painting* (New York, 1932), p. 169, n. 48; Millard Meiss, "The Madonna of Humility," *Art Bulletin*, XVIII (1936), 441, n. 23, 459, n. 76, 460, n. 88, 462, n. 105; Federico Zeri, "Arcangelo di Cola da Camerino," *Paragone*, I (1950), 38; Meiss (1951), p. 137, n. 20, p. 151, n. 84, p. 154, nn. 99, 101, p. 149, n. 72; E. Siegfried, "Maria auf der Mondsichel. Ein Beitrag zur Ikonographie der apokalyptischen Muttergottes" (unpublished Ph.D. dissertation, Göttingen, 1955), p. 40; *Handbook* (1958), no. 405; Ewald M. Vetter, "Mulier Amicta sole und Mater Salvatoris," *Münchner Jahrbuch der Bildenden Kunst*, IX/X (1958–1959), 39, fig. 9; Giuseppe Marchini, *La Pinacoteca Comunale "Francesco Podesti" di Ancona* (Ancona, 1960), p. 25; Otto Goetz, *Der Feigenbaum in der religiösen Kunst des Abendlandes* (Berlin, 1965), p. 108, fig. 81; *Handbook* (1966), p. 56; Ernst Guldan, *Eva und Maria: Eine Antithese als Bildmotiv* (Cologne, 1966), pp. 132, 218, pl. 148; G. Vitalini Sacconi, *Pittura marchigiana la scuola Camerinose* (Trieste, 1968), p. 63, pl. XV.

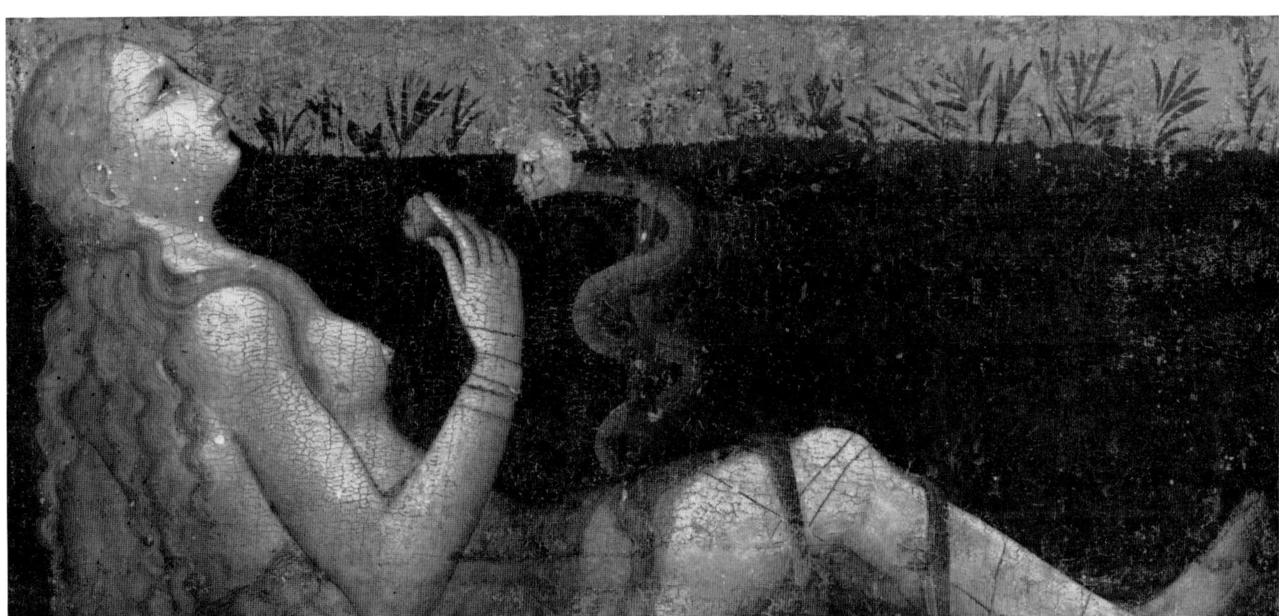

Figure 22 *c*. Detail.

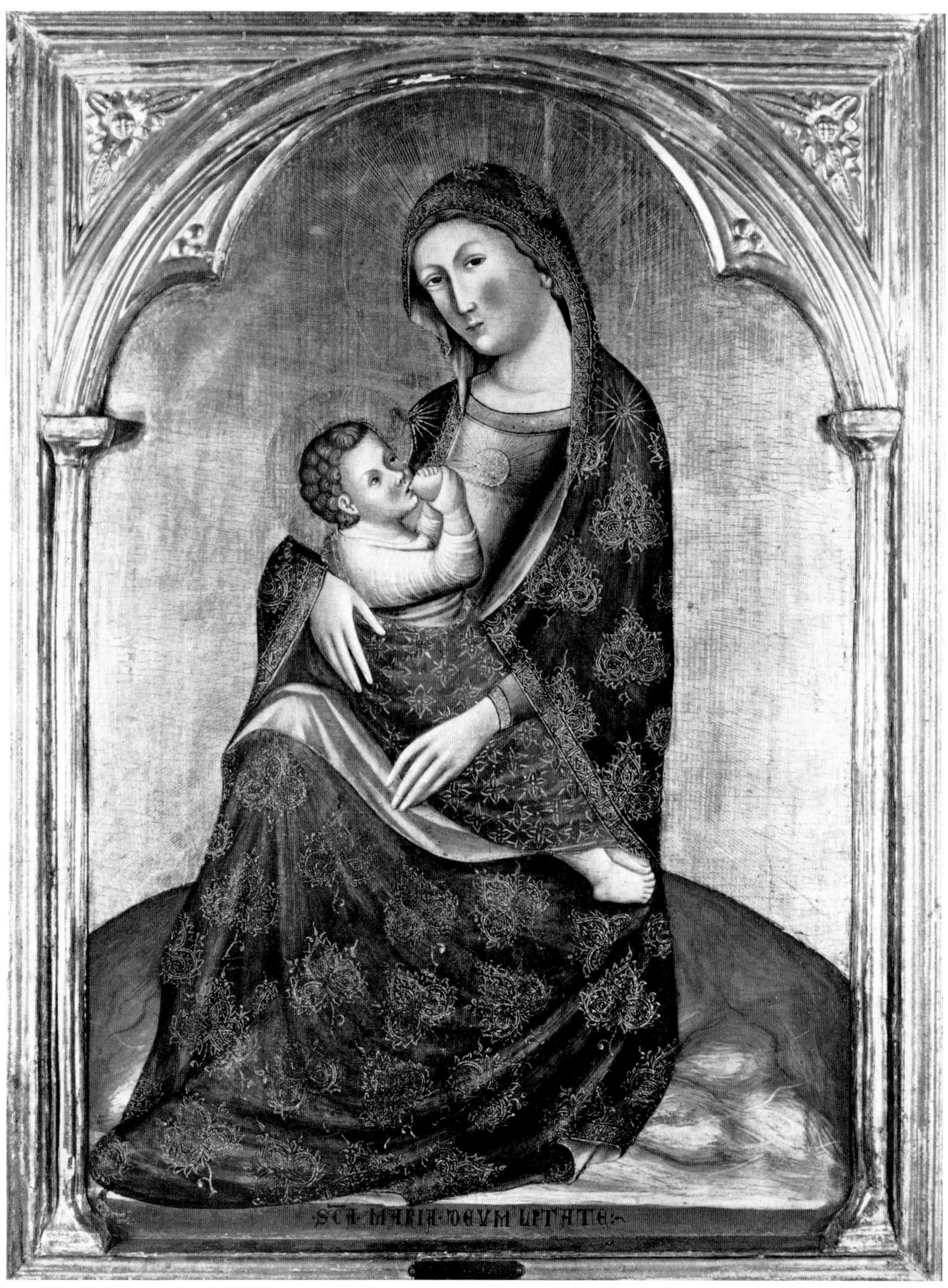

Figure 23.

CATERINO VENEZIANO, Venice,
recorded 1362–1382

Caterino was a Venetian painter, a contemporary of Lorenzo Veneziano, and not to be confused with Caterino di Andrea Moranzoni, a Venetian sculptor mentioned in 1394 who died ca. 1412. Two documented paintings by Caterino are lost; however, five documented paintings by his hand are still extant. In 1372 he executed, with Donato di San Vitale, the *Coronation of the Virgin* now in the Querini-Stampalia Gallery in Venice. He alone painted the signed and dated *Coronation of the Virgin* in the Accademia in Venice (n. 16) of 1375, and another signed *Coronation of the Virgin with St. Lucy and St. Nicolo da Tolentino* in the same Museum (n. 702). Two signed paintings of the *Madonna of Humility* are in the Worcester Art Museum and the Walters Art Gallery, Baltimore (37.468), the latter being the central panel of a polyptych. He is last mentioned in the records in 1382 when he lived in the quarter of San Luca in Venice. Among other paintings closely related to him are a polyptych of a *Madonna of Humility with Saints* in S. Maria a Mare, Torre di Palme, Fermo (see Laudedo Testi, *Storia della pittura veneziana*, I, Bergamo, 1909, 246; Van Marle, IV, 1924, fig. 44, p. 89; Meiss, 1951, p. 136, n. 18) and a painting of an *Enthroned Madonna and Child with Two Saints* in the Akademie der bildenden Künste in Vienna, no. 51 (see Testi, *op. cit.* p. 246, and Georg Ludwig, "Documente über Bildersendungen von Venedig nach Wien in den Jahren 1816 und 1838...," *Jahrbuch der Kunsthistorischen Sammlungen des Allerhöchsten Kaiserhauses*, XXII, 1901, p. xii, no. 68).

23 *Madonna of Humility*   63.500

Panel (transferred from poplar to plywood), including molding, 92·1 × 70·2 cm (36¼ × 27⅝ inches). Inside frame: 79·7 × 54·6 cm (31⅜ × 21½ inches).
COLLECTIONS: Private collection, Italy; Baron Thyssen, Schloss Rohoncz, Lugano, by 1930; Rudolf J. Heinemann. Gift of Dr. Rudolf J. Heinemann, 1963.

Inscribed at bottom of panel: $\overline{\text{SCA}}$. MARIA. DEUM LITATE.

This painting was undoubtedly the central panel of a larger altarpiece. The panel was split vertically in two places about four inches apart possibly caused by the strain of a vertical support on the back some time in the past. The painting has been restored recently and sealed into its present nineteenth-century frame. There are minor retouchings and reinforcements in the linear design and inscription. However, the area upon which the Madonna is seated appears to have been entirely repainted in a disturbing flesh-color with peculiar and prominent brushwork which detracts from the quality of the rest of the painting; the flowered arched hillock, characteristic of all the other *Madonnas of Humility* by Caterino, is unfortunately not present.

The painting style and iconography is typical of the known work of Caterino. The serrated network of Byzantine gilt lines in the blue mantle of the Madonna found in his earlier work done in collaboration with Donato di San Vitale has developed into an over-all gold pattern of pomegranate, typical of Venetian silks of the period, indicating that he became more influenced by Western painting styles as well as Tuscan iconography. The Museum panel must have been executed between ca. 1375 and ca. 1382. The iconography of the *Madonna of Humility* (see Painting 22) derives from Sienese painting, specifically that of Simone Martini. The subject was introduced into Venice as early as ca. 1355–1365 as can be seen in such examples as those in the Thyssen collection, Lugano; S. Anastasia, Verona; and the National Gallery, London (no. 3897), ascribed to Lorenzo Veneziano (Meiss, 1951, p. 136). The Museum's panel along with the other examples signed by or related to Caterino mentioned in the preceding continue the tradition of this subject in the latter part of the Venetian Trecento.

N.C.W.

EXHIBITIONS: Munich, Neue Pinakothek, 1930: Sammlung Schloss Rohoncz, cat. no. 67; CMA (1963), cat. no. 75; CMA, December 1963: Year in Review, cat. no. 85, illus.
LITERATURE: August L. Mayer, "The Exhibition of the Castle Rohoncz Collection in the Munich New Pinakothek," *Apollo*, XII (1930), 95–96, illus.; Raimond van Marle, "I Quadri italiani della raccolta del Castello Rohoncz," *Dedalo*, XI (1931), 1371–1372, illus.; Meiss (1951), p. 136, n. 18.

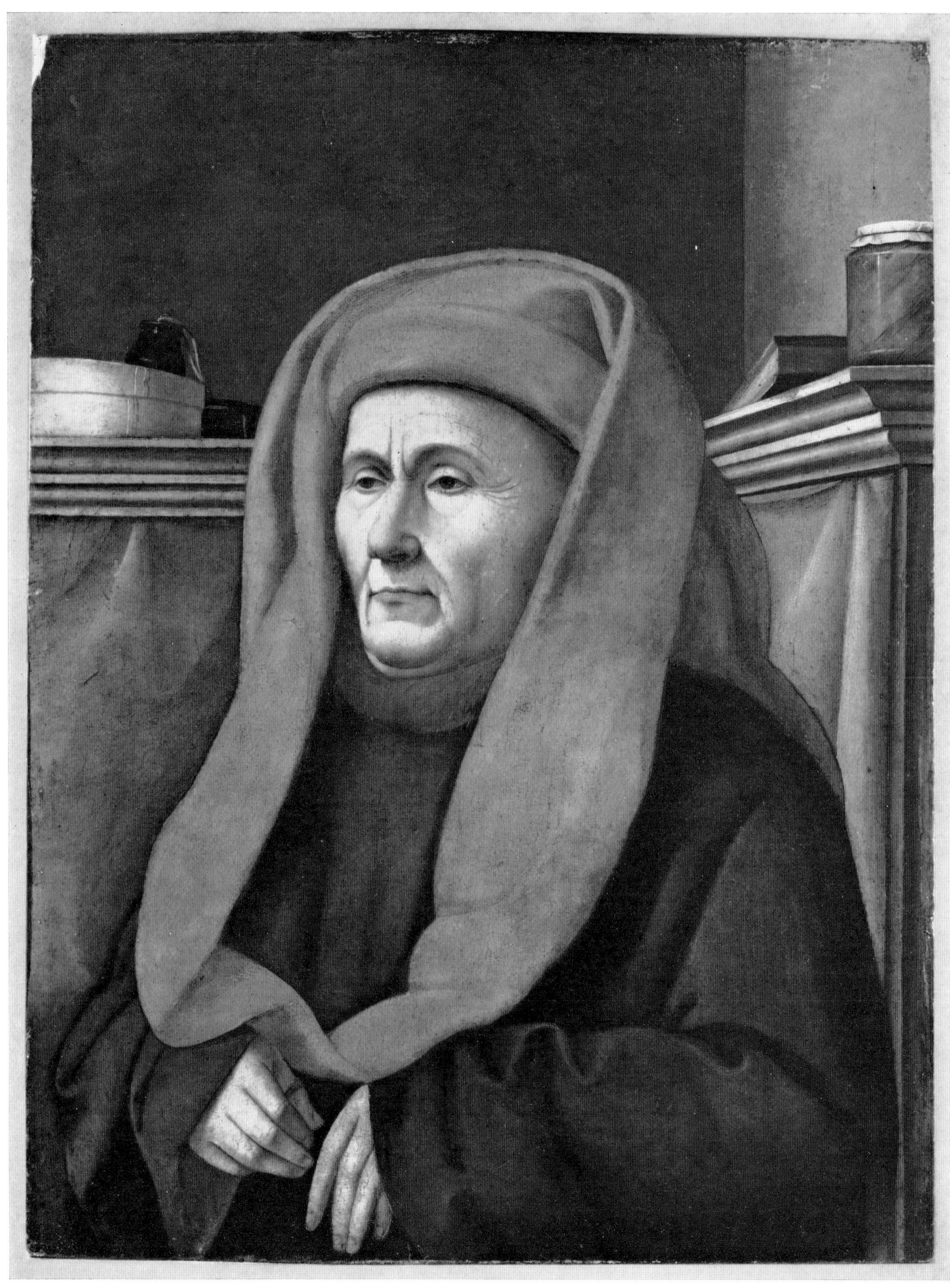

Figure 24. See also Colorplate XIV.

COLANTONIO(?), Naples, active from
ca. 1430–1440 to ca. 1460–1470

According to Pietro Summonte writing in 1524 to Marcantonio Michiel (Emmanuele A. Cicogna, *Memorie dell'I. R. Istituto Veneto die Science, Lettere ed Arti*, IX, Venice, 1860, 415–417), Colantonio was the painter of an altarpiece for S. Lorenzo, the main parts of which are now in the Naples Museum, and of the altarpiece with the life of St. Vincent Ferrer, still in S. Pietro Martire in Naples. The teacher of Antonello da Messina, he has been wrongly identified by some with the French Master of the Aix Annunciation.

24   *Portrait of a Man*   16.811

Panel (walnut), 60 × 45·4 cm (23⅝ × 17⅞ inches).
COLLECTIONS: James Jackson Jarves, Florence, after 1872; Mrs. Liberty E. Holden, Cleveland, 1884.
Holden Collection, 1916.

On the back inscribed by seventeenth- or eighteenth-century hands: Gabriele Giuseppa Olivierj.

There are some abrasions in the curtain at the left; the wrinkles on the left eye and a few other lines have been strengthened, otherwise the painting is well preserved.

The picture has been listed as Follower of the Master of the Aix Annunciation, ca. 1450–1470, since 1961 but its former attribution to Colantonio, first made by L. Venturi (1930), must still be very seriously considered. In contrast to the Aix *Annunciation*, wrongly attributed to Colantonio (Demonts, 1931; Aru, 1931), this looks more like an Italian work under northern influence; while the choice of support (walnut) is unusual in Italy, the inscriptions in back establish early Italian connections. The similarity to the near-authenticated paintings of Colantonio (Summonte, *op. cit.*) is impressive – particularly the S. Lorenzo altarpiece – although perhaps not so much to the famous *St. Jerome* which formed its lower part, as to the portrait-like heads and the drapery of the Franciscans in its upper part (see Ferdinando Bologna, "Il Maestro di San Giovanni da Capestrano," *Proporzioni*, III, 1950, pl. XCVI). This work can be dated ca. 1445 (see Roberto Longhi, "Una 'Crocefissione' di Colantonio," *Paragone*, VI, 1955, no. 23, 6) and the Cleveland panel is certainly more closely related to it than is the *Dominican Monk* of the Kisters collection in Meersburg (*Antonello da Messina*, exh. cat.; Palazzo Comunale di Messina, 1953, no. XXXVIII). Colantonio's St. Vincent

Ferrer altarpiece of ca. 1460, while less convincingly related to the present picture, nevertheless contains some comparable portraits. The color gamut of the panel (dark green and red against light green) is perhaps the chief difficulty in attributing it to Colantonio; it is somewhat reminiscent of the Aix *Annunciation* and some other southern French panels. Could it be that the Neapolitan painter studied in or visited Southern France? The suggestion of Ring (1949) that this is "perhaps not a pure portrait but rather...the representation of a prophet" can hardly be accepted. We also know that Colantonio copied Flemish portraits. Sterling (1941) sees a close relationship with the drawing of a standing clergyman, now in the Rotterdam Museum and usually attributed to the Aix Master (Ring, 1949, no. 95, pl. 53).

W.S.

EXHIBITIONS: Boston (1883), cat. no. 436; MMA (1912), cat. no. 15 (as Justus van Ghent?); CMA (1936), cat. no. 82, pl. XII.
LITERATURE: Jarves (1884), cat. no. 15 (as Ghirlandaio); M. L. Berenson (1907), 5 (as Justus van Ghent); Rubinstein (1917), no. 15, illus. (as Flemish); Lionello Venturi, "Contributi a Colantonio," *L'Arte*, XXXIII (1930), 291, 292; L. Venturi (1931), pl. CCLXXIX; Carlo Aru, "Colantonio, ovvero il 'Maestro della Annunciazione di Aix,'" *Dedalo*, XI (1931), 1140; Louis Demonts, "Le Maître de l'Annonciation d'Aix et Colantonio," *Mélanges Hulin de Loo* (Brussels, Paris, 1931), 124, 127, pl. XVI; Henry S. Francis, "A Picture Newly Attributed to Colantonio," CMA *Bulletin*, XIX (1932), 35–37, illus. p. 33; Van Marle, XV (1934), 348, n. 1 (as French); Hans Tietze, *Meisterwerke europäischer Malerei in Amerika* (Vienna, 1935), pl. 50; M. Marignane, *Le Maître de la Pietà de Villeneuve, de l'Annonciation d'Aix...révélé Engverrand Charonton* (Paris, 1938), pp. 67–69; Sterling (1941), Rep. B, p. 26, no. 44 (pupil of the Master of the Aix Annunciation); Ring (1949), p. 206, no. 98 (probably Colantonio); Giuseppe Fiocco, "Colantonio e Antonello," *Emporium*, CXI (1950), 52; *Handbook* (1958), no. 410; Michel Laclotte, *L'Ecole d'Avignon* (Paris, 1960), p. 122, n. 47 (neither Maître d'Aix nor Colantonio; listed on p. 125 as "Italian XV Century?"); *Handbook* (1966), p. 78; Liana Castelfranchi Vegas, "I rapporti Italia-Fiandra," *Paragone*, n.s. XXI (1966), 46.

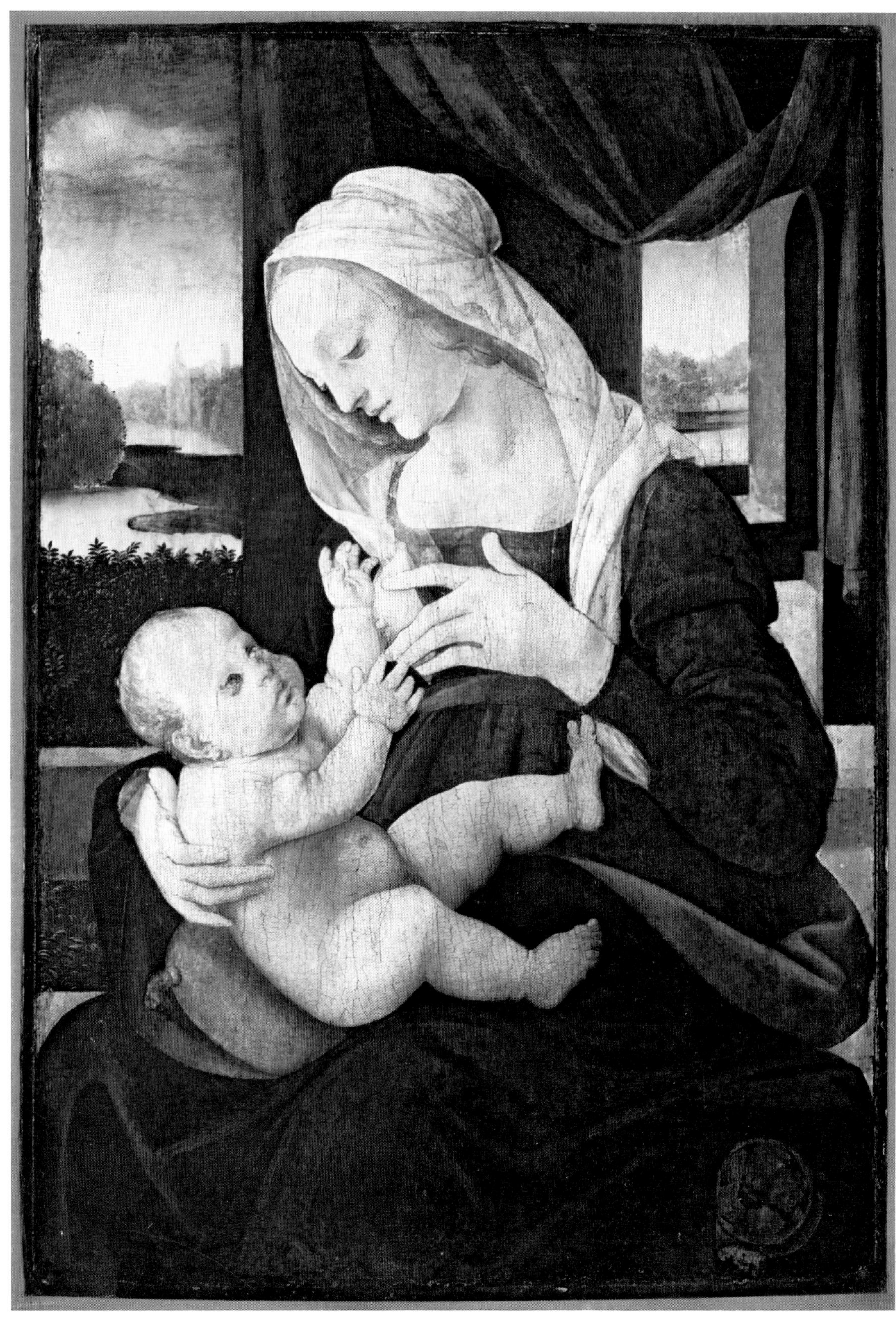

Figure 25.

LORENZO DI CREDI, Florence,
ca. 1458–1537

A Florentine painter probably born in 1458 who was
the son of Andrea, a goldsmith. He is recorded in Verrocchio's studio in 1480–1486 and was probably there
until Verrocchio's death in 1488. Like Leonardo da Vinci (who was in Verrocchio's workshop in 1476) he collaborated on paintings from his workshop. Because of
lack of documentation on the early work of Leonardo
and Lorenzo di Credi there has been a great deal of discussion and difference of opinion about the part Lorenzo
di Credi took in the paintings around the workshop of
Verrocchio from 1475–1485 although it is universally
agreed that he was very much influenced by Leonardo.
There are more records concerning his later work which
shows little development or innovation. He had several
students and close followers in the sixteenth century. He
worked in Florence and Pistoia and died on January 12,
1537.

25 *Madonna and Child*   16.826

   Panel (poplar), 78·4 × 54·5 cm (30$\frac{7}{8}$ × 21$\frac{11}{16}$ inches).
   Painted surface: 77 × 53·2 cm (30$\frac{5}{16}$ × 20$\frac{15}{16}$ inches).
   COLLECTIONS: James Jackson Jarves; Mrs. Liberty E.
   Holden, Cleveland, 1884.
   Holden Collection, 1916.

There has been considerable damage to the thin, exposed underpainting particularly in the body of the
Christ Child and the neck and face of the Madonna.
The appearance of the panel suggests that it might have
been left unfinished, however, it has been argued that
the picture was finished but badly abraded (Everett
Fahy, orally 1971).

In its published history after leaving the Jarves collection in 1884, it has been attributed to Lorenzo di Credi.
It would seem to date from about 1480 when Credi was
in Verrocchio's workshop and greatly under the influence of Leonardo. The Christ Child and general composition follow the Verrocchiesque type such as the *Madonna and Child* in Berlin or in the National Gallery,
London; the face of the Madonna shows the influence
of Leonardo and is reminiscent of the profile of Leonardo's study for the *Madonna del Latte* in the Louvre (no.
2376) of about 1480 or another drawing attributed to
Leonardo in the Uffizi (no. 428 E). It comes from the
same early period as the *Adoration of the Magi*, National
Gallery, London.   N.C.W.

EXHIBITIONS: Boston (1883), cat. no. 451; MMA (1912), cat.
no. 5; CMA (1916), cat. no. 12; CMA (1936), cat. no. 81; CMA
(1971), cat. no. 11.

LITERATURE: Jarves (1884), cat. no. 14; M. L. Berenson (1907),
repr. p. 3; Berenson, *The Florentine Painters…* (1909), pp. 131,
192; A. Venturi, VII (1911), 817, n. 1; Georg Gronau in Thieme–
Becker, VIII (1913), 75; Crowe and Cavalcaselle, *History of
Painting in Italy*, VI (1914), 42, n. 1; Underhill (1917), p. 20, illus.
p. 34; Rubinstein (1917), no. 12, illus.; Van Marle, XIII (1931), 277;
Bernhard Degenhart, "Die Schüler des Lorenzo di Credi," *Münch-
ner Jahrbuch der Bildenden Kunst*, Ser. 2, IX (1932), 157; Berenson,
Pictures Renaiss. (1932), p. 296; Berenson, *I Pittori italiani del
Rinascimente*, trans. Emilio Cecchi (Milan, 1935), p. 117, illus.;
Berenson, *Pictures Renaiss., Florentine School*, I (1963), 115; Gigetta
dalli Regoli, *Lorenzo di Credi* (Pisa, 1966), no. 8, p. 103, fig. 11;
Robert Brewer, *A Study of Lorenzo di Credi* (Florence, 1970),
pp. 46–47, pl. v.

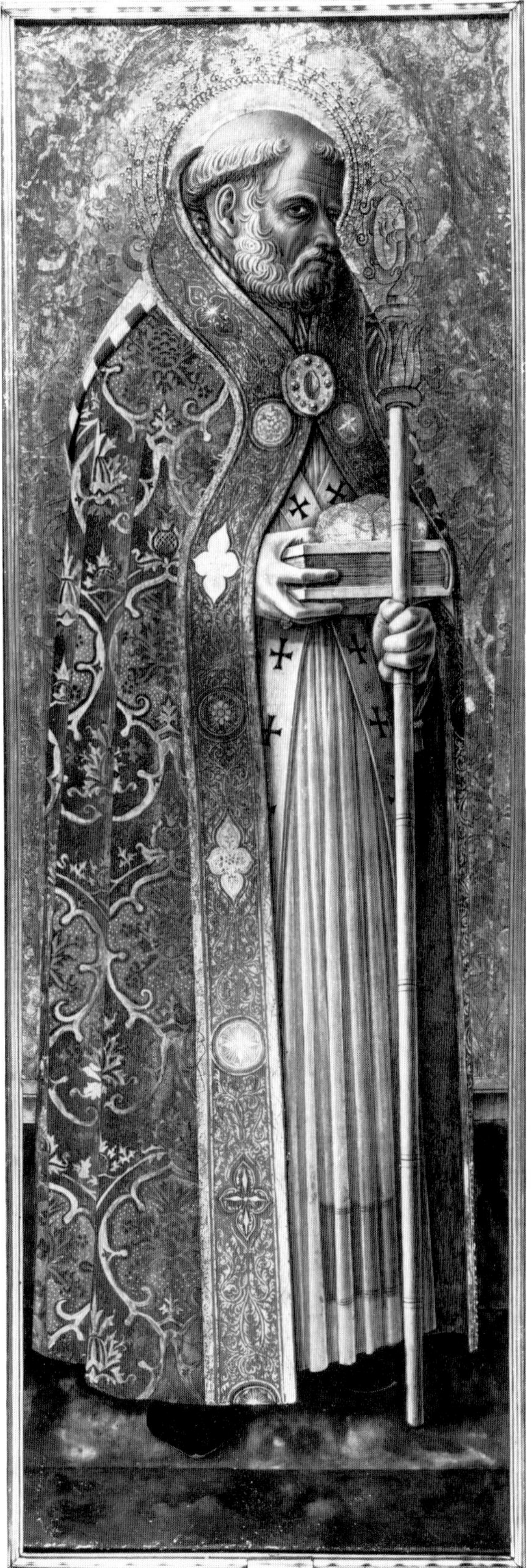

Figure 26.

CARLO GIOVANNI CRIVELLI, Venice, born ca. 1430–1435, died ca. 1495

His father was Jacopo Crivelli, a Venetian. A brother, Vittorio, was his collaborator and imitator. Although he lived elsewhere most of his life, Crivelli was trained in the Venetian tradition of Giambono, the elder Bellini, and Vivarini, and usually signed himself VENETUS. After imprisonment for a misdemeanor in 1457 he left Venice – perhaps for Padua, as his style reflects close contact with the Paduan School. He was in Zara in 1465 and subsequently worked in the Marches, having settled at Ascoli in 1478. He was knighted by Prince Ferdinand of Capua in 1490 and thereafter added MILES to his signature. He was still alive in 1494, but in 1500 his wife is mentioned as widowed.

26   *St. Nicholas of Bari*   52.111

Panel, 97·3 × 33 cm (38⅝ × 13 inches).
COLLECTIONS: Cardinal Fesch, Palazzo Falconieri, Rome; (sale: Rome, March 17, 18, 24 ff., 1845, cat. p. 76, no. 1780, with four companion saints and the Madonna, no. 1777, bought by Bromley for forty lire); Mr. Davenport Bromley, Wooton Hall, near Ashbourne; the Rev. Walter Davenport Bromley; (sale: Christie's, London, June 12–23, 1863, no. 69); Baroness Kerbreck, Paris; (M. Knoedler & Co., New York).
Gift of Hanna Fund, 1952.

Except for some wear on the gold ground, the panel is in good condition. The only major repairs are those of two vertical splits extending about three-quarters of the length of the panel. A half-inch strip along the bottom edge and the area around the saint's left foot have been repainted.

This panel is part of the dismembered and fragmentary Erickson polyptych (Fig. 26a), so-called after the former owners of the central panel, a *Madonna and Child*, signed and dated 1472. The Erickson panel then was acquired by Jack Linsky at the Erickson sale (Parke-Bernet Galleries, New York, November 15, 1961, p. 36, no. 9). The other panels which belonged to the ancona were first associated with the Erickson *Madonna* by L. Venturi (II, 1933, pls. 364–366). Francis (1952) and Berenson (1957) recognized the Cleveland *St. Nicholas* as belonging to the same complex. Berenson thought it occupied the position at the extreme left of the main tier of the ancona next to the *St. James* which he placed at the Virgin's right hand. However, Venturi (II, 1933, pl. 366) says "according to Crivelli's custom the two

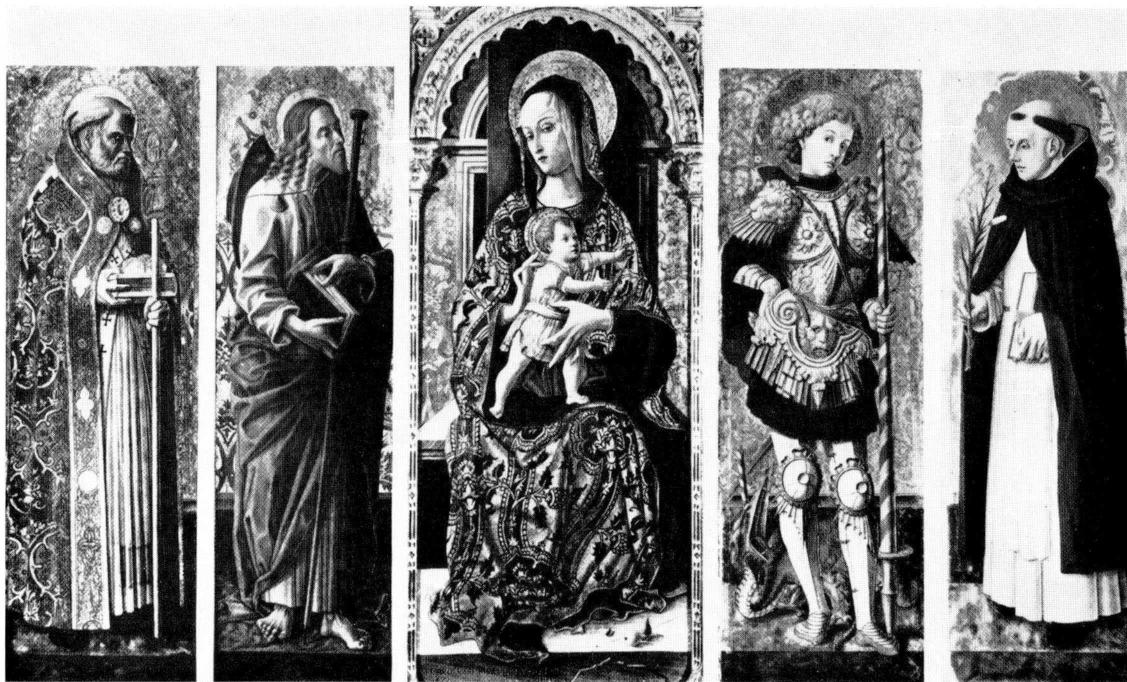

Figure 26 a. Reconstruction of the polyptych of 1472 by Crivelli. Left to right: *St. Nicholas of Bari*,
Cleveland Museum of Art. *St. James*, Brooklyn Museum, New York. *Madonna and Child*, signed and dated 1472,
Mrs. A. W. Erickson, New York. *St. George* and *St. Dominic*, Metropolitan Museum of Art.

saints nearest the Madonna were not placed so decid-
edly in profile as the saints at the extremities" and
Zampetti's reconstruction reverses the positions of SS.
Nicholas and James. The four saints and the Madonna
were separated after the Fesch sale. The former are probably those seen together by Waagen (1854) in the Davenport Bromley collection although he ascribed them
to Jacobello del Fiore. Van Marle (1926) was unable to
trace the four "Jacobello del Fiore" saints from the
Davenport Bromley collection and since all four Crivelli saints were in that collection it seems reasonable to
assume that Waagen's Jacobellos and the ex-Fesch Cri-
vellis are identical. Other panels which have been associated recently with the Erickson polyptych are: the
Pietà, Philadelphia Museum of Art (by Zeri, 1961, p.
162; which Zampetti includes as the top center panel of
his reconstruction); and five predella panels, (1) *The Sav-
iour Blessing* (El Paso, Texas Museum of Art, Kress Collection); (2) *St. Peter* (New Haven, Yale Art Gallery);
(3) *St. Bartholomew*; (4) *St. John the Evangelist* (both in
Milan, Castello Sforzesco); (5) *St. Andrew* (Amsterdam,
E. Proehl). The last four had been associated with the
Montefiore dell'Aso polyptych (Franz Drey, *Carlo Crivelli und seine Schule*, 1927, pp. 125 ff.; William Suida,

"Italian Primitives in the Marinucci Collection in Rome,"
Apollo, XX (1934), 120). Bovera (1961, pp. 67–69) related all five to the "Second San Domenico Polyptych"
and the Esterhazy *Madonna*. Martin Davies (*The Earlier
Italian Schools*, London, National Gallery, 1961, p. 156,
n. 7) denied their association with the Montefiore polyptych, and Zeri (1961) tentatively identified them as
parts of the predella from the Erickson polyptych which
he believes post-dates the Montefiore complex. Bovera
sees in the *St. Nicholas* a prototype for the same figure in
the Monte San Martino altar and for the *St. Peter* in the
Brera triptych.

E.F.G.

EXHIBITIONS: None.
LITERATURE: Waagen, III (1854), 377; Van Marle, VII (1926), p.
352; Harry B. Wehle, *A Catalogue of Italian, Spanish and Byzantine
Paintings* (New York, MMA, 1940), p. 178; Henry S. Francis, "St.
Nicholas by Carlo Crivelli," CMA *Bulletin*, XXXIX (1952), 187–
189; Berenson, *Pictures Renaiss., Venetian School* (1957), I, 69, II,
137; *Handbook* (1958), no. 398; Federico Zeri, "Cinque schede
per Carlo Crivelli," *Arte antica e moderne*, nos. 13–16 (1961), p. 162;
Anna Bovera, *Tutta la pittura del Crivelli* (Milan, 1961), p. 60, pl.
29A; Pietro Zampetti, *Carlo Crivelli* (Milan, 1961), pp. 16, 24, 76,
figs. 24, 27; *Handbook* (1966), p. 88.

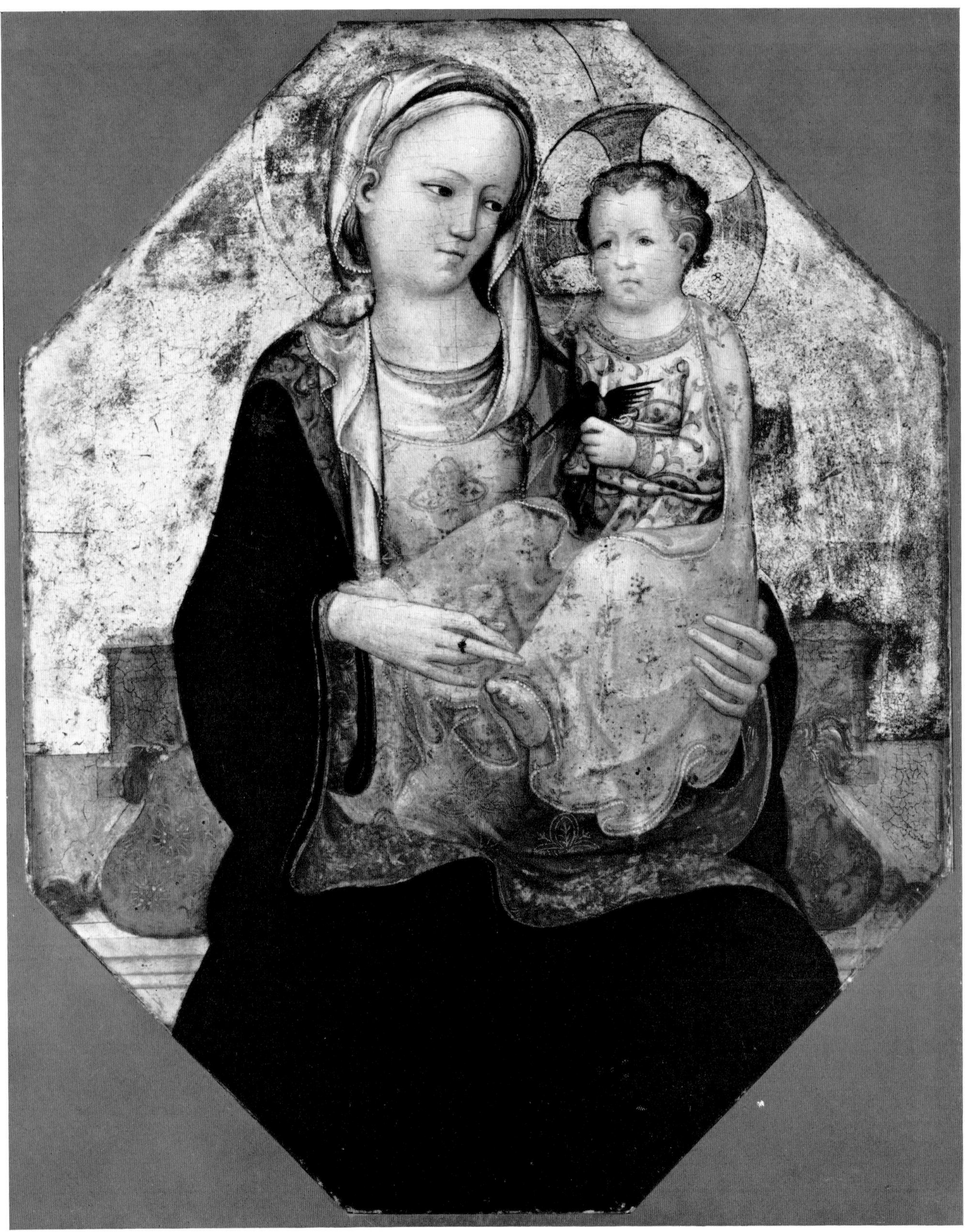

Figure 27.

ROSSELLO DI JACOPO FRANCHI, Florence, ca. 1376–1457

He was probably born in 1376 as the inscription on his tombstone in S. Lorenzo in Florence states that he died at eighty years of age in 1457. There are several records documenting the life and work of this painter. He worked with his brother Giunta di Jacopo Rosselli (born 1379) for the Bigallo in Florence in 1426, and in 1445–1446 again with his brother, and later with Ventura di Moro. He was probably a pupil of Mariotto di Nardo (active 1394–1431) who painted the central panel of the altar in the Museo Civico in Pistoia; Rossello di Jacopo Franchi executed the lateral wings. He left three signed works: a triptych with the *Coronation of the Virgin*, dated 1420, in the Accademia in Florence; the *Coronation of the Virgin with Two Angels*, dated 1439 in Siena; and the *Virgin and Child Enthroned with Two Angels*, stolen in 1920 from S. Maria Assunta in Staggia, Poggibonsi. He represents the conservative tradition in early fifteenth-century Florentine painting, influenced by Lorenzo Monaco and later by Gentile da Fabriano. His work is close to the style of Bicci di Lorenzo with whom he worked in 1433.

27 *Madonna and Child* 16.814

Panel (poplar), now octagonal, 69·5 × 55·5 cm ($27\frac{3}{8}$ × $21\frac{7}{8}$ inches).

COLLECTIONS: James Jackson Jarves; Mrs. Liberty E. Holden, Cleveland, 1884.

Holden Collection, 1916.

The original panel unfortunately has been cut down to its present octagonal shape. There are major losses in the blue mantle and brown lining of the Madonna's robe. The gilding on the background is modern. Aside from minor scratches in the face of the Christ Child and the Virgin, the rest of the paint film is in good condition.

Jarves assigned this painting to Starnina. M. L. Berenson (1907) gave it to Rossello di Jacopo Franchi shortly after the artist emerged as a documented personality in Florentine painting (see Osvald Sirén, "Campagno di Bicci," *L'Arte*, VII, 1904, 352–355; Berenson, "Due quadri inediti a Staggia," *Rassegna d'arte*, V, 1905, 9–11). The painting is assigned to the later work of Rossello by Van Marle and is characteristic of the less schematic style of his work in the late 1430s or later. The facial type of the Madonna and Child and the lyrical color illustrates the formula that Rossello repeated over and over again in his painting.

N.C.W.

EXHIBITIONS: Boston (1883), cat. no. 405; MMA (1912), cat. no. 24; CMA (1916), cat. no. 29; CMA (1936), cat. no. 84; CMA (1963), cat. no. 80; CMA (1971), cat no. 5.
LITERATURE: Jarves (1884), cat. no. 4; M. L. Berenson (1907), p. 2; Thieme–Becker, XII (1916), 315–316; Rubinstein (1917), no. 30, illus.; Van Marle, IX (1927), 64, fig. 38; Berenson, *Pictures Renaiss.* (1932), p. 493; Berenson, *Pictures Renaiss., Florentine School*, I (1963), 192.

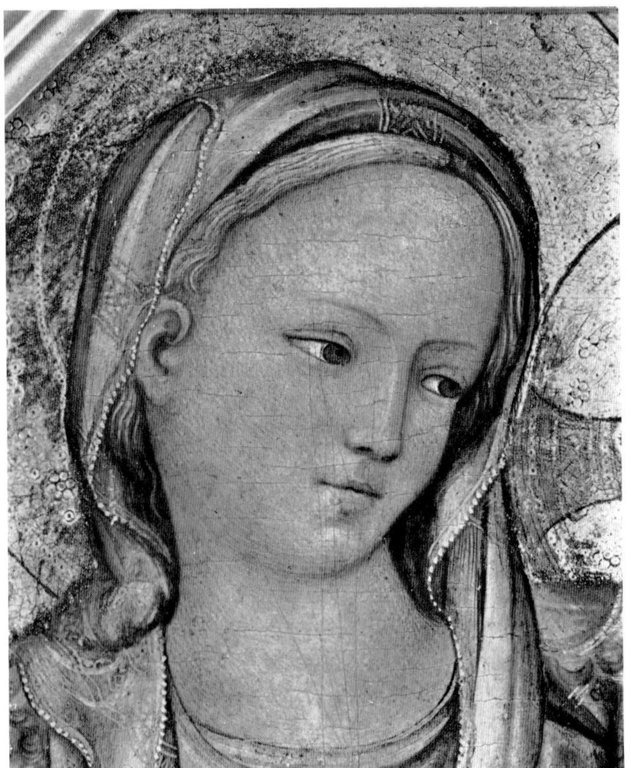

Figure 27a. Detail.

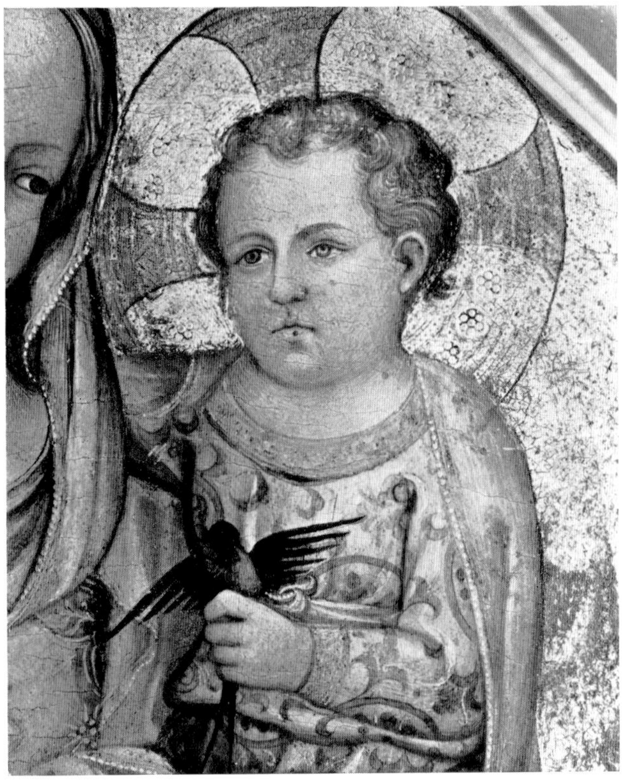

Figure 27b. Detail.

GIOVANNI DI PIETRO (Master of the
Ovile Annunciation), Siena, ca. 1432–before 1479

Giovanni di Pietro was a Sienese painter and probably
the brother of Lorenzo di Pietro, called Vecchietta. Although a number of documents exist concerning his life
and work, none of the recorded paintings is preserved.
His name was first recorded in 1432 and in 1453 it appears on the property tax return of the Sienese painter,
Matteo di Giovanni. He was a partner in Matteo's workshop from 1452 until after 1461. He was sharing a house
with his daughter in 1478 at the end of his life, and he
had two sons, Galgano Michelangelo (born 1441) and
Pietro Paolo.

John Pope-Hennessy ("The Development of Realis-
tic Painting in Siena – II," *Burl. Mag.*, LXXXIV, 1944,
143) was the first to ascribe the *Annunciation* in S. Pietro
Ovile in Siena and the predella panels of the *Marriage of
the Virgin* and the *Visitation* in Philadelphia (Johnson
Collection, 107, 108) to the painter Giovanni di Pietro.
In an unpublished monograph on Matteo di Giovanni
(1951, pp. 9–21) he associated the Ovile *Annunciation*
with documents of 1460 in which both Matteo di Giovanni and Giovanni di Pietro were commissioned to
paint an altarpiece for the church of S. Pietro Ovile.
Everett Fahy (unpublished research) also includes in the
work of Giovanni di Pietro the six small saints in the
pilaster of the right frame, the two scenes on the right
in the predella (*The Baptist Preaching to Herod* and
Salome's Dance) of the polyptych largely executed by
Matteo di Giovanni in the Duomo of Borgo San
Sepolcro (which formerly included Piero della
Francesca's *Baptism of Christ*, now in the National
Gallery, London), and the following painting in the
Cleveland Museum collection.

28 *Madonna and Child with Angels* 56.719
    between St. Jerome and
    St. Catherine of Alexandria

Panel (poplar), including original molding, 68 × 48 cm
(26¾ × 18⅞ inches). Inside frame: 59·5 × 39 cm (23⅜ ×
15⅜ inches).

COLLECTIONS: Achillito Chiesa, Milan; (sale: American
Art Galleries, New York, November 27, 1925, no. 50); Mr.
and Mrs. Ralph King, Cleveland, 1925.
The Fanny Tewksbury King Collection, 1956.

The panel is somewhat warped and worm-eaten. Ex-
amination under ultra-violet rays shows several layers
of past restoration. The contours of the Virgin's face and
the stems of the flowers have been strengthened; the
green of the angels' wreaths has been repainted as well
as the border of the Child's robe and the Virgin's right
sleeve. Pentimenti are visible in the fingers of her left
hand. There are scattered small repairs in the faces of the
Virgin, the Child, and the angel at the right. The picture
was cleaned by William Suhr in June, 1933.

At the time of the Chiesa collection sale (Eglington,
1925), this panel was published as an early Sano di Pietro
influenced by Sassetta, and Van Marle (1925) accepted it
as an early Sano, dating it before 1450. When it was lent
to the Museum (Exh: 1936) it was described as superior
to Sano and reminiscent of Neroccio de' Landi and Matteo di Giovanni and related to Andrea di Niccolo. Pope-
Hennessy (letter of February 13, 1940) thought it by a
"quite distinct Sano di Pietro pupil," and Zeri (orally,
October 1965) also thought it a school work of ca. 1470.
Everett Fahy (letter of November 8, 1966) first attributed the Cleveland panel to the author of the *Annunciation* in the church of S. Pietro a Ovile, Siena (Fig. 28 *b*)
and more recently (letter of February 4, 1971) sent further
convincing information on the comparative works of
Giovanni di Pietro, called the Master of the Ovile
Annunciation. Enzo Carli (letter of December 12, 1966)
agrees that the Cleveland *Madonna* is a work stylistically closest to the Ovile *Annunciation* but is not con-
vinced that both are by the same hand.

N.C.W.

EXHIBITIONS: CMA, 1928: Representative Art through the
Ages; CMA (1936), cat. no. 141.

LITERATURE: Guy Eglington, "Chiesa Collection," *Art News*,
XXIV (November 21, 1925), 14; Van Marle, IX (1925), 484, n. 1.

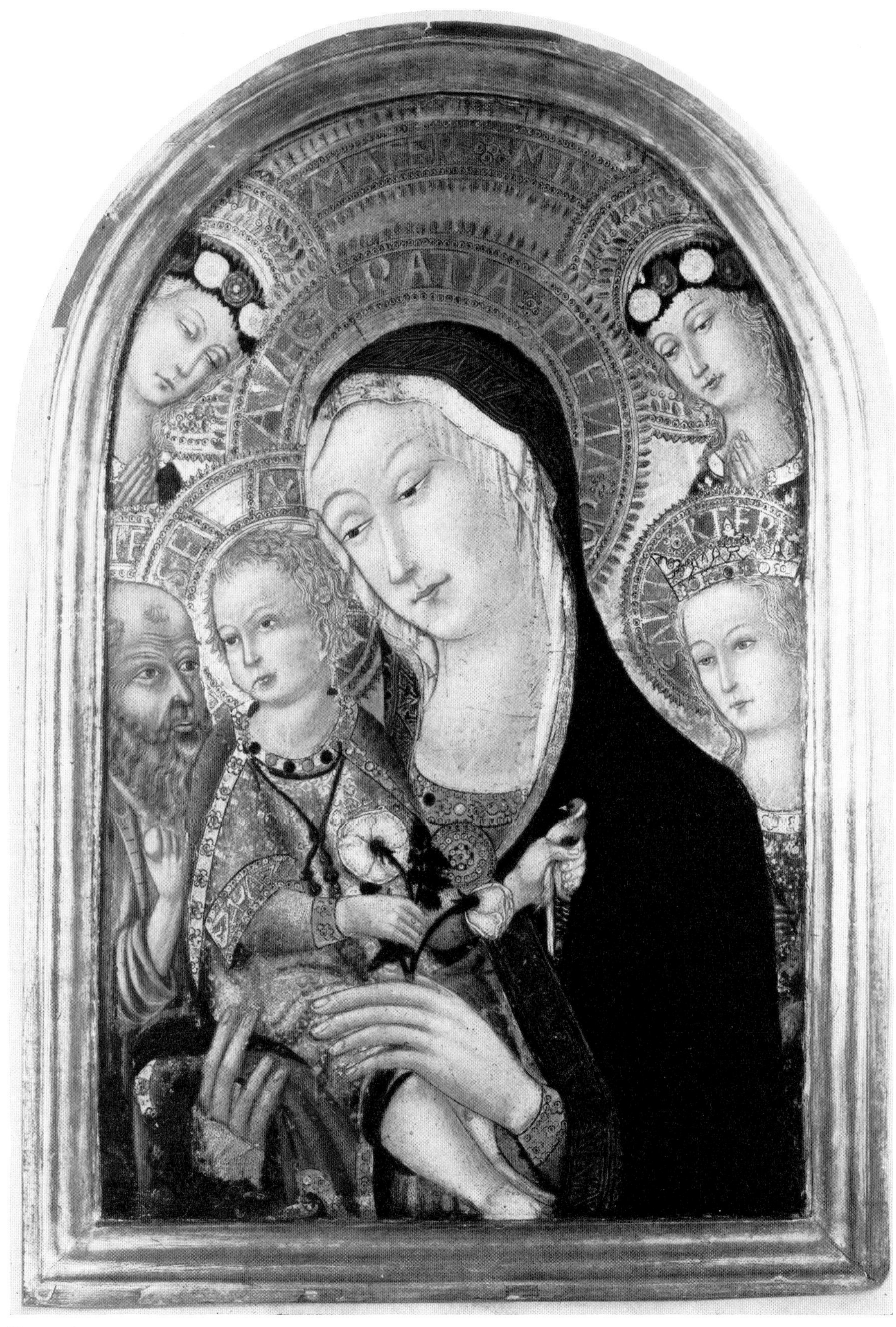

Figure 28.

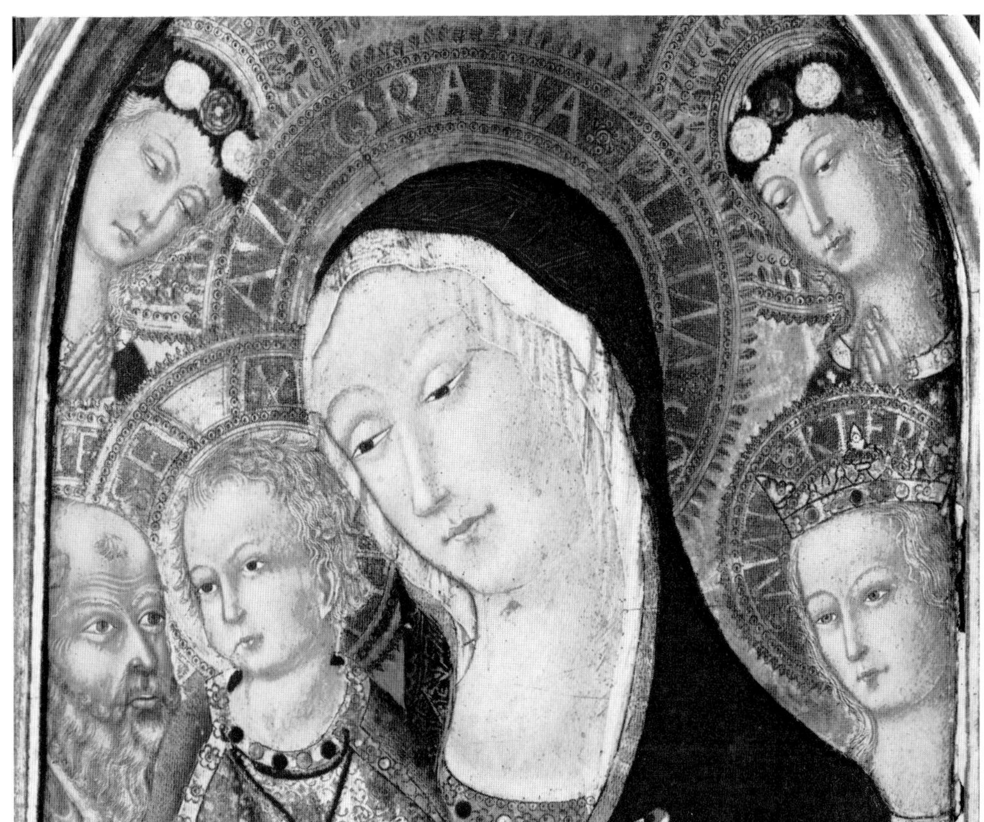

Figure 28 *a*.
Detail.

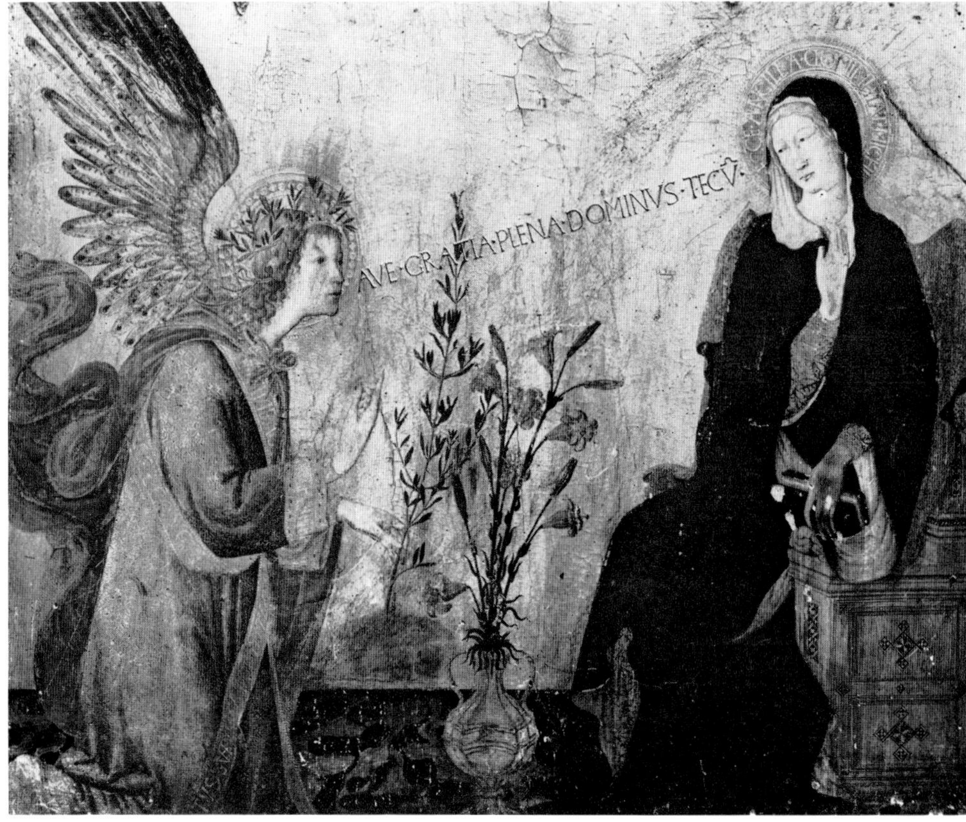

Figure 28 *b*.
The Annunciation (detail).
Giovanni di Pietro.
Church of S. Pietro a Ovile,
Siena.

FILIPPINO LIPPI, Florence, ca. 1457–1504

It is generally believed that Filippino Lippi was born in Prato in 1457 (although Gronau, 1929, considers the date to be ca. 1452), the natural son of Filippo Lippi and Lucrezia Buti. He was in Spoleto with his father from 1467 until his father's death and left in 1469 or in early 1470. He may have been in Botticelli's workshop in Florence and was living with him ca. 1472. He worked mostly in Florence, but also in Pavia and Rome. There are several recorded or dated paintings and frescoes in existence. He completed the frescoes of Masaccio in the Brancacci Chapel, and he was commissioned by Lorenzo de' Medici to decorate his villas. He devoted several years to painting the frescoes in the Strozzi Chapel in S. Maria Novella. He died in Florence in 1504.

29   *The Holy Family with the Infant*   32.227
     St. John and St. Margaret

   Tondo (oak?), diameter, 153 cm (61¼ inches).
   COLLECTIONS: Caraffa family, Castel Sant'Angelo, Naples; Mrs. Samuel D. Warren, Boston, 1898–1901; Cornelia Warren, d. 1921, co-owner from 1901 with Edward P. Warren, Lewes, Sussex, d. 1929; H. Asa Thomas, 1929; (Harold Parsons).
   Purchase from the Delia E. Holden Fund and a fund donated as a memorial to Mrs. Holden by her children: Guerdon S. Holden, Delia Holden White, Roberta Holden Bole, Emery Holden Greenough, Gertrude Holden McGinley, 1932.

Inscribed on crossbands across the bodice of St. Margaret: S. MARGHARITA VIR.

The painting was cleaned in 1912 although unfortunately there are no records of the condition (see annotated pamphlet in the Museum files, *A Masterpiece of Filippino Lippi: Representing the Madonna and Child, The Infant St. John the Baptist, St. Joseph and St. Margaret*, ca. 1912, 8 pp.). Apparently at one time the sky was painted over with a gray-blue which was later removed, possibly in 1912. Some traces of the gray-blue remain in the lower sky. A number of small areas in the haloes of the Virgin and St. Margaret were slightly abraded. In 1970 a layer of yellowed varnish was removed and the abrasions retouched. Except for these very minor restorations the painting was found to be in remarkably good condition.

Crowe and Cavalcaselle identified this painting as by Filippino Lippi in 1864 and corrected the earlier Ghirlandaio attribution. It was published several times as

Filippino by Berenson who brought the painting, then in the collection of the Castel Sant'Angelo in Naples, to the attention of Edward P. Warren of Boston in 1898 (letter of June 6, 1898, in the files of the Museum of Fine Arts, Boston).

Berenson suggested (1900) that the presence of St. Margaret, rare iconographically in Florentine painting, might indicate that the painting was commissioned by the Convent of St. Margaret in Prato where his mother, Lucrezia Buti, had lived, or by a family in that city which was particularly devoted to this saint. Another possible provenance presents itself. According to Vasari, in 1488, upon the recommendation of Lorenzo de' Medici, Filippino received an invitation from Oliviero Caraffa, Cardinal of Naples, to paint frescoes in his family chapel in S. Maria sopra Minerva in Rome. This commission kept him in Rome from 1488 until probably 1491 or 1493. As the earliest provenance for the painting is the Castel Sant'Angelo in Naples (the palace of the Caraffa family) it seems possible that Filippino Lippi could have executed the picture during the years that he was in close contact with the Caraffa family, and that it entered their collection at that time.

In the past there has been some difference of opinion as to the date of the painting. Crowe and Cavalcaselle (1911) have dated it as early as the Nerli altarpiece but Scharf (1935) dated it as late as 1497; it is generally agreed that it dates from the first half of the decade of the 1490s. Berenson consistently put it soon after 1490, and in the edition of 1961 it is dated ca. 1495. L. Venturi (1933) and Neilson (1938) place it ca. 1496 because of its stylistic proximity to the dated *Adoration of the Magi* of 1496 in the Uffizi. It seems logical that it dates toward the end of Filippino's work on the Caraffa Chapel in Rome or soon after his return to Florence. The possibility that it was painted in Florence is strengthened by the fact that there are four Florentine copies of the Museum tondo (the author is indebted to Everett Fahy for information concerning the existence of two); two of these are direct copies after the Cleveland painting with simplification of the architecture at the right and the town in the background. One of these replicas is in the Strossmayer Bildergalerie in Agram (see Frizzoni, 1904, 428, fig. 2) and the other in the collection of Lord Crawford of Balcarres. A third version with the same general composition of figures without St. Joseph is in the Accademia in Florence (see Ugo Procacci, *La Galleria dell' Accademia di Firenze*, Rome, 1951, repr. p. 98, as school of Lorenzo di Credi). The fourth tondo is *The Madonna*

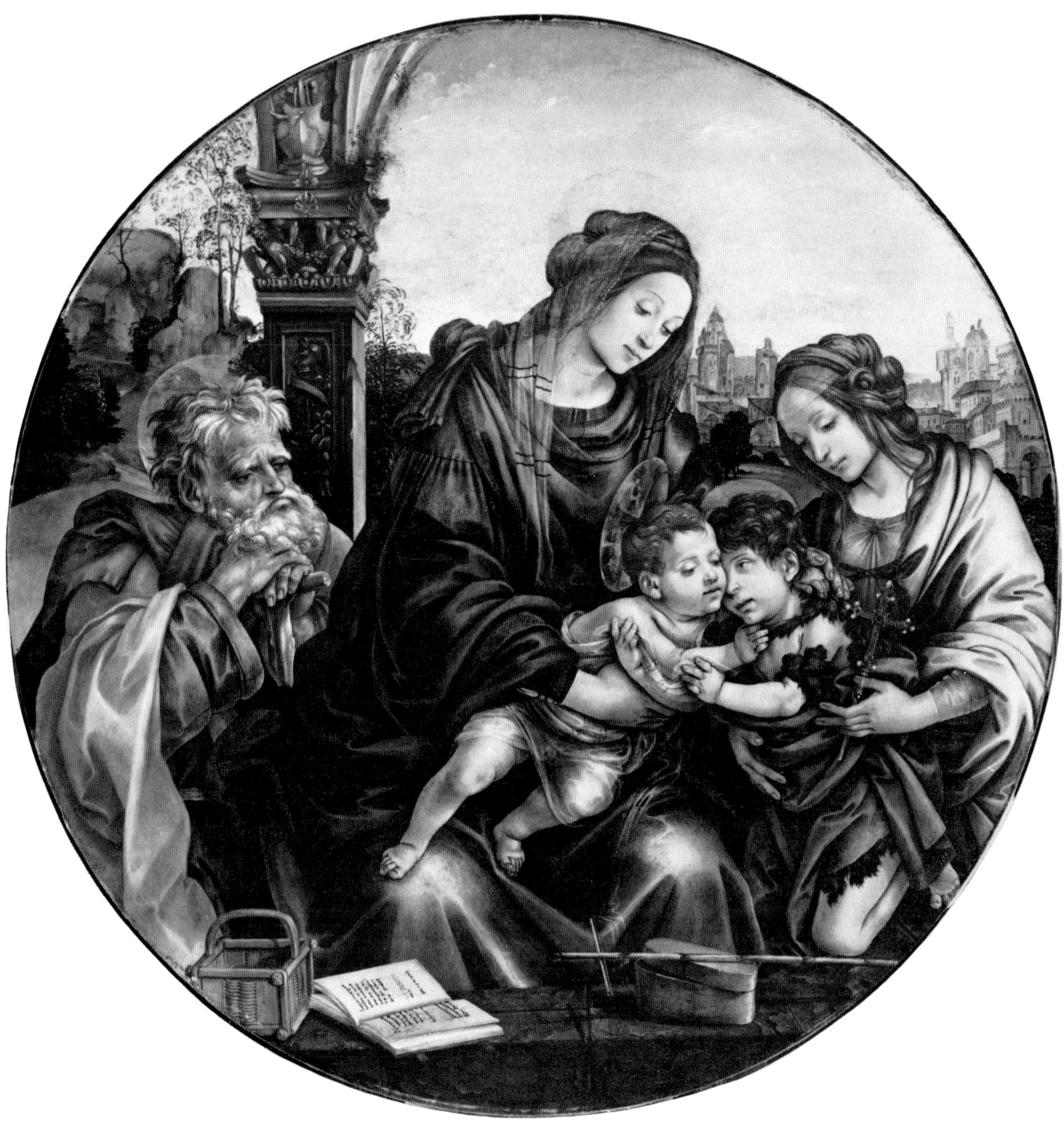

Figure 29. See also Colorplate xv.

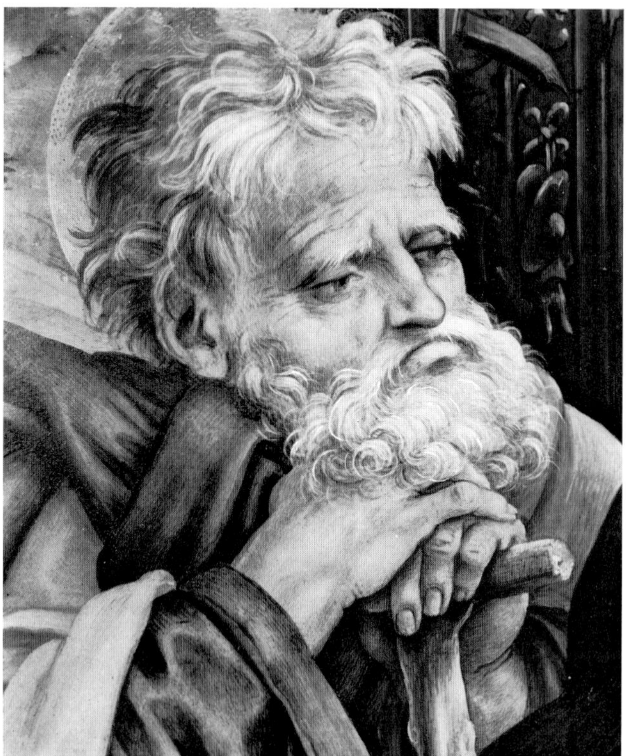

Figure 29 a. Detail of Joseph.

and Child with St. John between Two Angels in the Glasgow Art Gallery and Museum. This painting has been variously attributed to Botticelli, Filippino Lippi, and Raffaellino del Garbo and is certainly closely related to the Cleveland panel in style and composition (see Scharf, 1933, 158–159, fig. 6; Denys Sutton, *The Art of Painting in Florence and Siena from 1250–1500*, exh. cat.; London, Wildenstein & Co., 1965, no. 64).

There is no drawing extant which is precisely a study for the Museum tondo. One of the closest, however, is the verso side of a drawing of an inclined head in the Galleria Corsini, very similar to the St. Margaret in the Museum painting (see Scharf, 1935, no. 190, pl. 108, fig. 167).

N.C.W.

EXHIBITIONS: Boston, Museum of Fine Arts, April 1902: Special Exhibition of Paintings from the Collection of the late Mrs. S. D. Warren, cat. no. 87; London, Royal Academy, Burlington House, 1904: Exhibition of Old Masters, cat. no. 13; CMA (1971), cat. no. 10.

LITERATURE: Carlo Celano and Giovanni Battista Chiarini, *Notizie del bello dell'Antico e del Curioso della citta di Napoli*, III (Naples, 1858), 691, as Domenico Ghirlandaio; Crowe and Cavalcaselle, *A New History*..., II (London, 1864), 450; John Murray, *A Handbook for Travellers in Southern Italy* (London, 1868), p. 183;

Berenson, *The Florentine Painters*... (1899), pp. 121, 144; Berenson, "Un Chef-d'œuvre Inédit de Filippino Lippi," *Revue Archéologique*, XXXVII (Paris, 1900), 238–243, pl. XI; Arduino Colasanti, "Miscellanea: Nuovi Dipinti di Filippo e di Filippino Lippi," *L'Arte*, VI (1903), 299–304; Colasanti, "Two Unpublished Pictures by Fra Filippo and Filippino Lippi," *The Connoisseur*, VII (1903), 233 (reprint of article in *L'Arte*, VI (1903), 304, listed above); Gustavo Frizzoni, "La Pinacoteca Strossmayer nel'Accademia di Scienze ed Arti in Agram," *L'Arte*, VII (1904), 427–429, fig. 3; Louise M. Richter, "Correspondence d'Angleterre: Les Maîtres Anciens à Burlington House," *Gaz. des B.-A.*, XXXI (1904), 424, 426, illus.; Paul George Konody, *Filippino Lippi* (London, 1905), pp. xii, xv–xvi, xxiii; Berenson, *The Florentine Painters*... (1909), pp. 149, 200; Berenson, "An Unpublished Masterpiece by Filippino Lippi," *The Study and Criticism of Italian Art*, Ser. 2 (London, 1910), pp. 92–96, illus.; A. Venturi, VII (1911), 658; Crowe and Cavalcaselle, *History of Painting in Italy*, IV (London, 1911), 290–291; Algernon Graves, *A Century of Loan Exhibitions, 1813–1912*, II (London, 1913), 709; Berenson, "Un Possibile Antonello da Messina ed uno impossibile," *Dedalo*, IV (1923–1924), 32; Berenson, "Un Botticelli Dimenticato," *Dedalo*, V (1924), 22, illus. p. 24; Berenson, "A Neglected Altarpiece by Botticelli," *Three Essays in Method* (Oxford, 1927), p. 78, fig. 76; Berenson, "A possible and an impossible 'Antonello da Messina,'" *Three Essays in Method* (Oxford, 1927), 107; Georg Gronau in Thieme–Becker, XXIII (1929), 270; Van Marle, XII (1931), 326, 373, fig. 208; Henry S. Francis, "A Tondo by Filippino Lippi," CMA *Bulletin*, XIX (1932), 146–154, illus. pp. 141, 142; Berenson, *Pictures Renaiss.* (1932), p. 285; Urbain Mengin, *Les deux Lippi* (Paris, 1932), p. 240; Alfred Scharf, "Tondi von Filippino Lippi," *Pantheon*, XII (1933), 329–335, illus.; L. Venturi, II (1933), pl. 264; Scharf, "Die Frühen Gemälde des Raffaellino del Garbo," *Jahrbuch der Preussischen Kunstsammlungen*, LIV (1933), 158–159; Hans Tietze, *Meisterwerke europäischer Malerei in Amerika* (Vienna, 1935), no. 61; Scharf, *Filippino Lippi* (Vienna, 1935), pp. 58, 109, no. 38; Moritz Hauptmann, *Der Tondo* (Frankfurt am Main, 1936), pp. 222–223; Katherine B. Neilson, *Filippino Lippi: A Critical Study* (Cambridge, Mass., 1938), pp. 116, 121–125, 133–134, 195, fig. 54; *Katalog Strossmayerove Galerije I* (Zagreb, 1939), no. 24, p. 54; Berenson, *The Drawings of the Florentine Painters*, I (Chicago, 1938), 105; Osbert Burdett and E. H. Goddard, *Edward Perry Warren, the Biography of a Connoisseur* (London, 1941), pp. 72, 80, 130, 209, 228, 411; Scharf, *Filippino Lippi* (Vienna, 1950), pp. 34, 55, pls. 81–85; Luciano Berti and Umberto Baldini, *Filippino Lippi* (Florence, 1957), pp. 46, 88–89, no. 63; Fiammetta Gamba, *Filippino Lippi nella storia della critica* (Florence, 1958), pp. 55, 103, n. 36; Milliken (1958), illus. p. 31; *Handbook* (1958), no. 41; John Canaday, *Metropolitan Seminars in Art: Great Periods in Painting, Portfolio E: The World in Order: The High Renaissance* (New York, MMA, 1959), p. 7, pl. E2; Berenson, *I Disegni*... (1961), I, 162, 169–171; II, 252, 268; Ira Moskovitz, *Great Drawings of all Times*, I (New York, 1962), no. 126; Berenson, *Italian Pictures Renaiss., Florentine School* (1963), I, 108; II, pl. 1150; *Handbook* (1966), p. 91; *Selected Works* (1966), p. 121; Albert Schug, "Zur Ikonographie von Leonardos Londoner Karton, II. Teil," *Pantheon*, XXVII (1969), 31, illus. no. 29; Jack Wasserman, "The Dating and Patronage of Leonardo's Burlington House Cartoon," *Art Bulletin*, LIII (1971), 314, fig. 3.

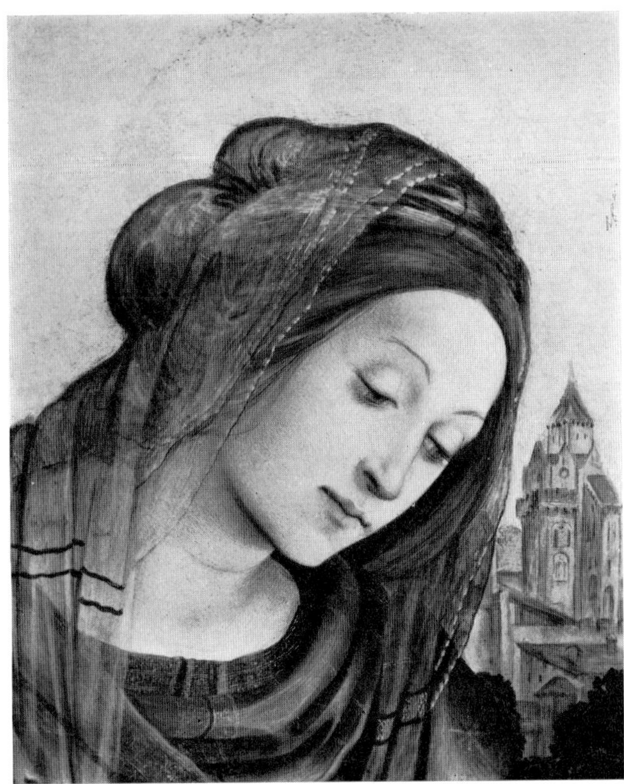

Figure 29*b*. Detail of the Madonna.

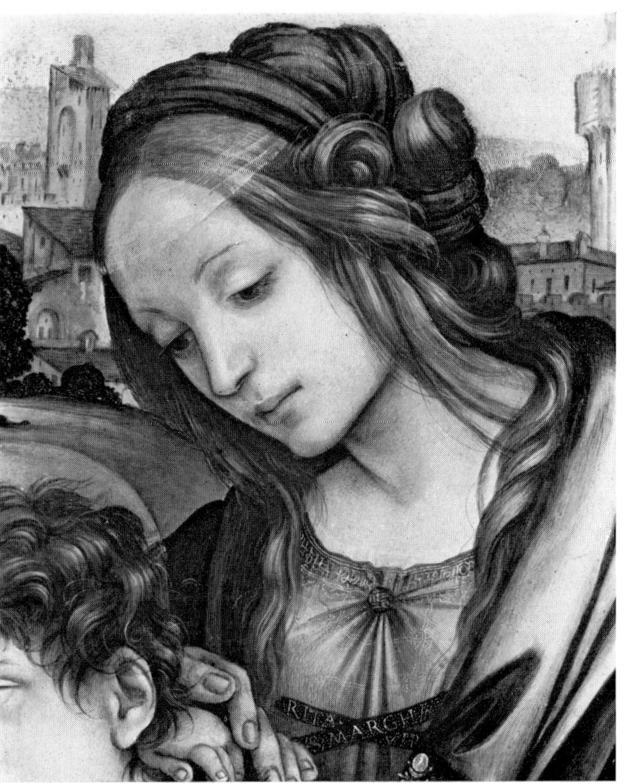

Figure 29*c*. Detail of St. Margaret.

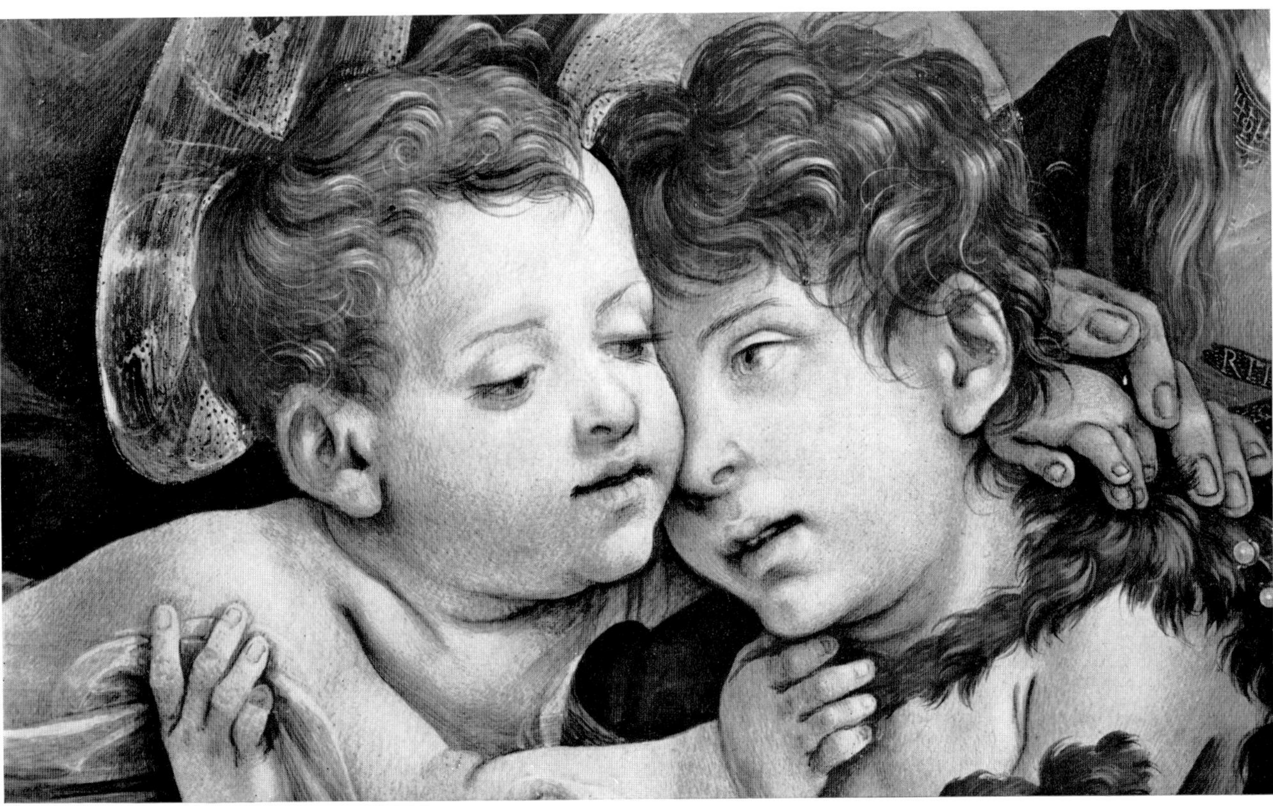

Figure 29*d*. Detail of the Infant St. John (left) and the Christ Child.

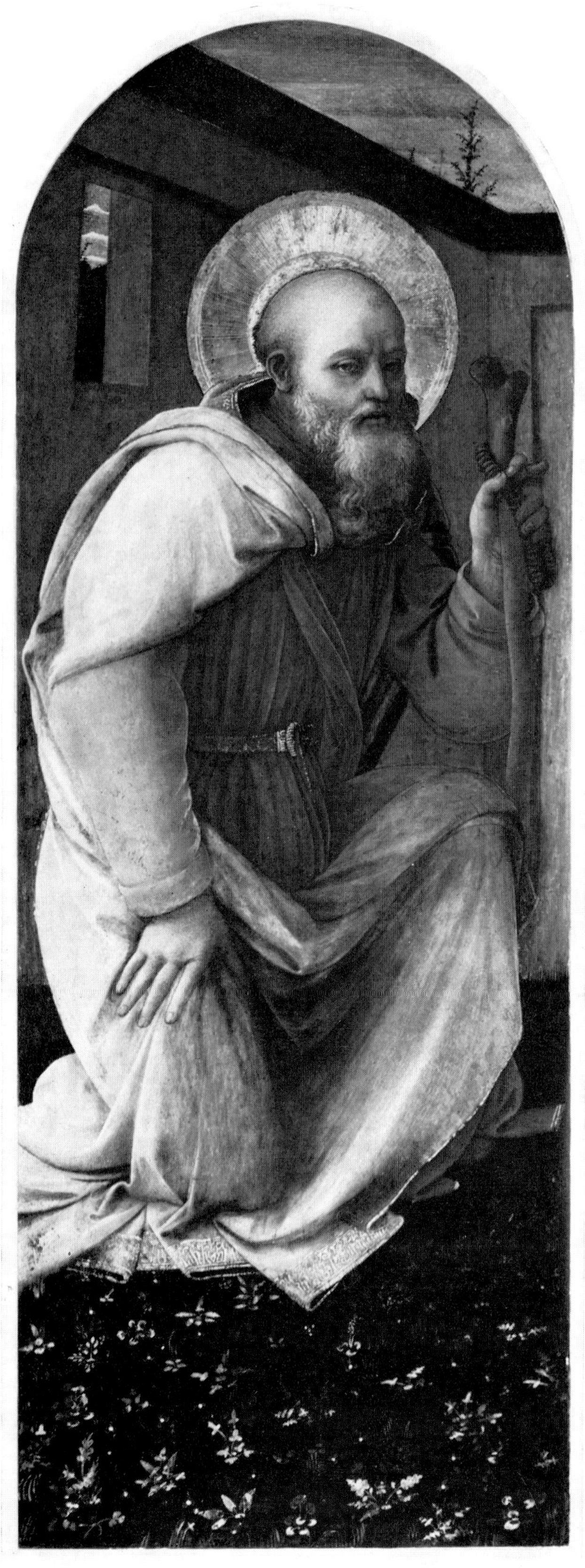

Figure 30A. See also Colorplate XVI.

80

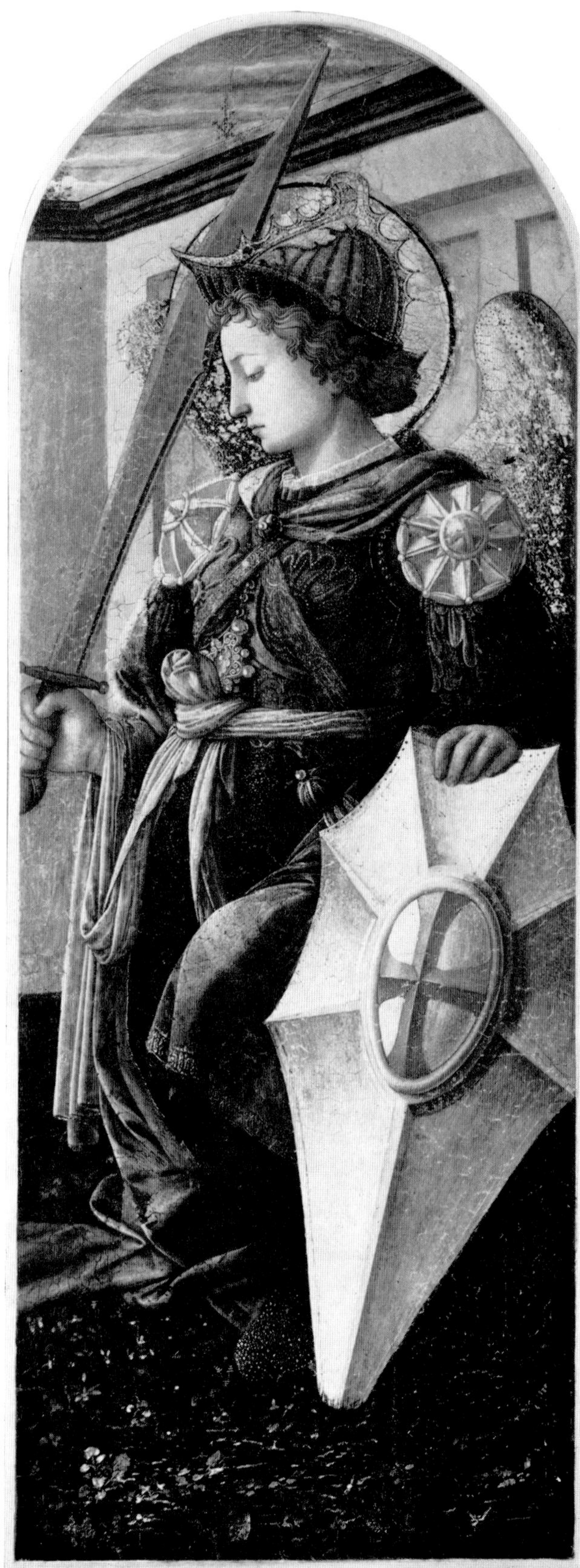

Figure 30B. See also Colorplate XVI.

FRA FILIPPO LIPPI, Florence, ca. 1406–1469

He took his vows as a Carmelite monk in Florence in 1421 and is first mentioned as a painter in the Carmine in 1431. In 1434 he is mentioned as being at Padua and in Florence again in 1437. From 1452 he worked intermittently at Prato and in 1467 and 1469 in Spoleto where he died. He was very much influenced in his early work by Masaccio and gradually developed a more delicate style. Many of his later works were executed at least in part by pupils.

30A	*St. Anthony Abbot*	64.151
30B	*St. Michael*	64.150

Panels, each, 81·3 × 29·8 cm (32 × 11 11/16 inches).

PROVENANCE: Painted for Giovanni di Cosimo de' Medici who ordered it as a gift for Alfonso V of Aragon.

COLLECTIONS: Alfonso V of Aragon (Alfonso I of Naples); Condesa Pacheco, Madrid (wife of the Spanish Ambassador to Rome); bought from her in 1871 by Sir John Charles Robinson for Sir Francis Cook; Sir Francis, Sir Frederick, and Sir Herbert Cook, Cook Collection, Doughty House, Richmond, Surrey; (Rosenberg & Stiebel Inc., New York).

Purchase, Leonard C. Hanna Jr. Bequest, 1964.

In 1965 both pictures were cleaned by Mario Modestini and restored by William Suhr. The worm-eaten poplar panel was removed and the facing mounted to a tempered masonite board with poplar veneer on its back and edges, with cradling for additional support. The condition of the surfaces of the two paintings differs considerably although neither suffered serious damage to the faces or the major portion of the figures. Both had two diagonal cracks bisecting the upper curved edges of the panels. In the *St. Anthony* there was a long crack about an inch and a half from the left edge of the panel extending from the bottom on through the window in the background, interrupted only in the sleeve which is covered by an earlier restoration. There was a large loss in the top center of the panel in the sky. Smaller losses were across the saint's left sleeve, on the three fingers which curve over the beads on the left hand, on the right wrist, in the inner circle of the halo directly surrounding the top of the head, and scattered losses across the forehead and in the beard. There is crackle over much of the surface of the *St. Michael*, with a large loss on the left edge above the hand holding the sword, scattered small losses around the edges of the panel, in the wings, and on both pauldrons. All the larger losses were restored by Suhr.

Pentimenti in the *St. Michael* indicate numerous changes by Fra Filippo. The left hand was added after the top edge of the shield was painted. However, the lighter area of blue to the right of his hand immediately above the shield seems to be a later addition. The crimson garment was arranged differently around the lower part of the figure and extended further downward; crimson shows through crackle in the grass and flowers in the area directly below the figure and shield, suggesting the possibility that the figure originally had both knees on the ground. This is borne out by the artist's sketch of his original intentions for the triptych (Fig. 30*e*) which also makes it apparent that some time later both panels were cut down at the sides and tops to their present size and shape. The entire triptych ornately framed in a flamboyant Gothic cornice was sketched by Fra Filippo Lippi in a letter dated Florence, July 20, 1457, to Giovanni di Cosimo de' Medici who had commissioned the work as a gift to Alfonso V of Aragon (Alfonso I, King of Naples). A transcription of the letter appears in Gaye (1839–1840, I, 175, no. LXVI), Crowe and Cavalcaselle (1911, II, 155), and Berenson (1961, III, fig. 176).

Work on these paintings was probably begun in Florence by June, 1457, and completed before May, 1458. In a letter of August 31, 1457, from Francesco Cantasanti [agent] to Giovanni de' Medici (see Gaye, I, 176–177, no. LXVII) the former says he has been in Fra Filippo's shop trying to make him work at finishing the picture. The triptych is subsequently mentioned in two letters from Giovanni de' Medici to his agent in Naples, Bartolommeo Serragli, confirming the arrival of the painting in Naples. The first, dated May 27, 1458 (Gaye, I, 180, no. LXX), states: "I understand you have presented the picture to the King's Majesty and that it pleases him fairly . . . ," and the second dated June 10, 1458 (Crowe and Cavalcaselle, 1911, II, 153, n. 4), says "I note that you write respecting the high esteem in which his Majesty holds the picture. . . ." Both Berenson (1961, I, 129) and Pittaluga (1949, p. 205) suppose that Vasari knew of this triptych; however, Vasari tells only a confused story that Fra Filippo himself "was brought safely to Naples where he painted for King Alfonso a panel in distemper for the Chapel of the Castel where the guard room is now" (*Le Opere di Giorgio con nuove annotazio i e commenti di Gaetano Milanesi*, II, Florence, 1906, 515).

These two panels are the only known parts of a well-documented triptych whose lost central panel represented a kneeling Madonna adoring the Christ Child Who is carried by two angels. The *Madonna and Child*

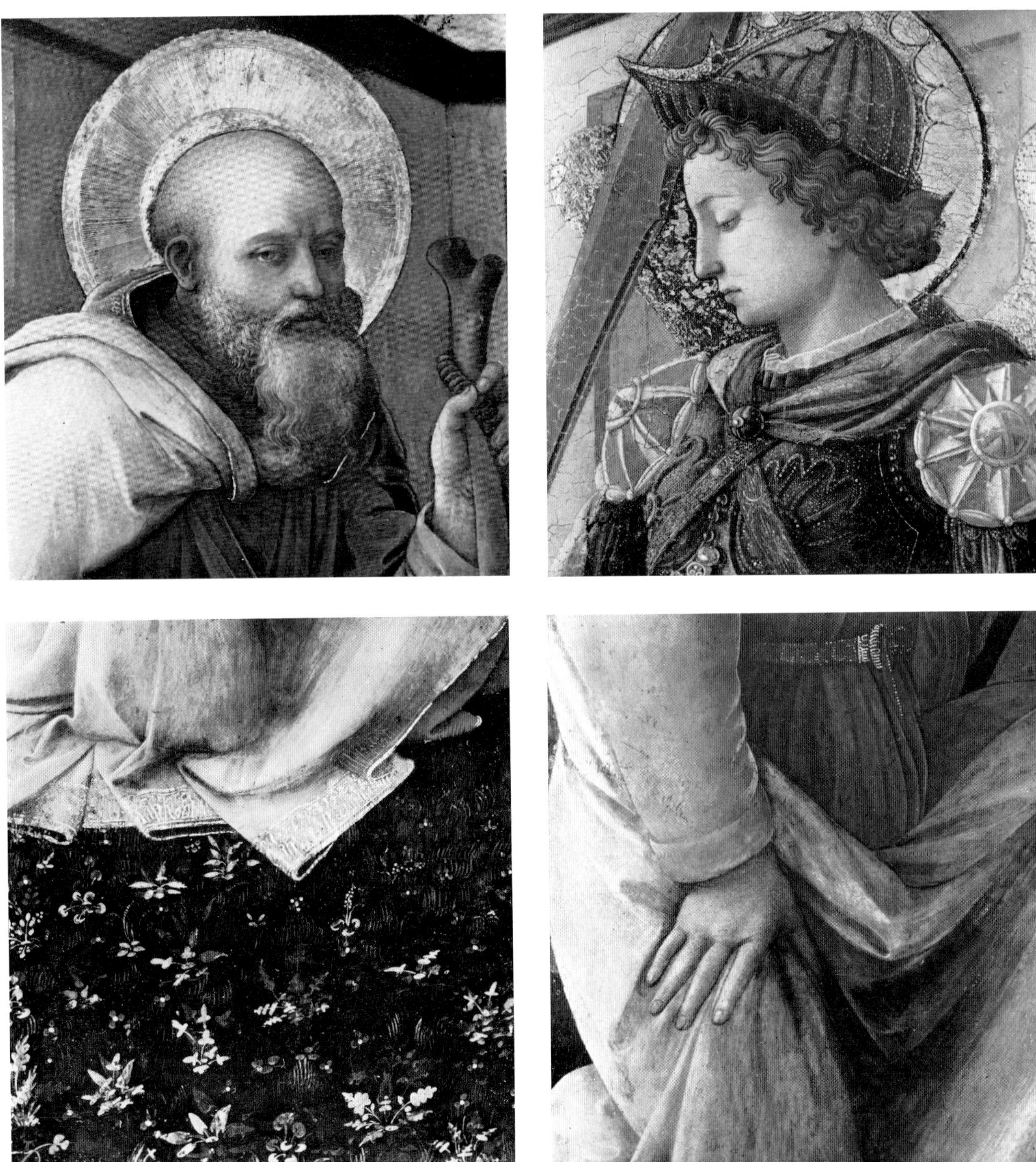

Figures 30 *a*, *b*, *c*, *d*. Details of Figures 30 A, B.

with Angels after Fra Filippo Lippi (Painting 31) has been suggested as one of the closest copies of this lost central panel. According to Berenson (1938; 1961) the panels were first identified as parts of the lost triptych by Roger Fry, and according to Oertel (1942) they were first associated with the triptych by Henriette Mendelsohn; however, the earliest publication of the two wings as part of the lost triptych was by Cook (1905). The iden-

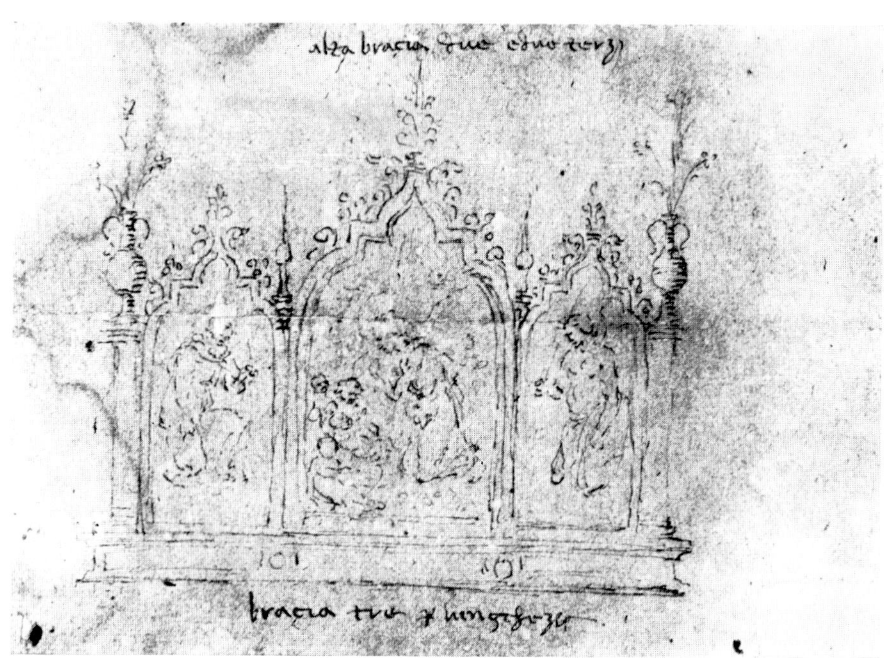

Figure 30e.
Sketch for a triptych
by Fra Filippo Lippi
in a letter to Giovanni
di Cosimo de'Medici,
dated July 20, 1457.
Archivio di Stato,
Florence.

tity of Archangel St. Michael is firmly established in the letter of July 20, 1457, where Fra Filippo said "the St. Michael is so far advanced that it only awaits the ornaments of gold and silver to its armour..." (Crowe and Cavalcaselle, 1911, II, 155). The dexter saint has been variously called St. Anthony Abbot and St. Bernard of Clairvaux. It seems probable that the saint is meant to be St. Anthony Abbot, who is frequently represented as an elderly bearded monk holding a stick and beads, wearing a cowl and cloak of different colors.

N.C.W.

EXHIBITIONS: London, Burlington Fine Arts Club, 1902: cat. no. 16 (as St. Anthony and St. George); London, Grafton Galleries, 1909–1910: National Loan Exhibition, cat. no. 69, pl. 105; London, Burlington Fine Arts Club, 1920: Exhibition of Florentine Paintings, cat. no. 15, pp. 21, 22, pl. xv; London, Royal Academy of Arts, Burlington House, 1930: Exhibition of Italian Art 1200–1900, cat. no. 98 (see Balniel, Clark and Modigliani, 1931); CMA, December 1964: Year in Review, cat. nos. 80 and 81, illus. 233, 268 (color); CMA (1971), cat. no. 6.

LITERATURE: Giovanni Gaye, *Carteggio inedito d'artisti dei secoli XIV, XV, XVI* (Florence, 1839–1840 [Turin, 1961 reprint]), p. 175, no. LXVI, pp. 176–177, no. LXVII, p. 180, no. LXX; Crowe and Cavalcaselle, *A New History...*, II (1864), 328–331; Crowe and Cavalcaselle, *History of Painting in Italy*, IV (1911), 153–156; Berenson, *The Florentine Painters...* (1899), pp. 123, 153; Edward C. Strutt, *Fra Filippo Lippi* (London, 1901), pp. 118, 178–179; Igino Benvenuto Supino, *Les Deux Lippi* (Florence, 1904), pp. 18, 81, 88; Herbert Cook, Bart., "La Collection de Sir Frederick Cook, Visconde de Monserrate a Richmond," *Les Arts*, IV (1905), i, ii, illus. p. 4; Giovanni Poggi, "Di due tavole di Fra Filippo Lippi nella raccolta Cook a Richmond," *Rivista d'arte*, IV, Ser. 1 (1906), 39; Herbert Horne, *Sandro Botticelli* (London, 1908), 6–8; Berenson, *The Florentine Painters...* (1909), pp. 151, 209; Henriette Mendelsohn, *Fra Filippo Lippi* (Berlin, 1909), pp. 154, 156, docs. XIX–XXII; Roger E. Fry, "La Mostra di antichi dipinti alle 'Grafton Galleries' di Londra," *Rassegna d'arte* X (1910), 35–36; Algernon Graves, *A Century of Loan Exhibitions 1813–1912*, II (London, 1913), 710; Tancred Borenius, *Italian Schools*, vol. I of Sir Frederick L. Cook, *A Catalogue of the Paintings at Doughty House, Richmond, and elsewhere in the Collection of Sir F. Cook...*, ed. Herbert Cook (London, 1913), 23, no. 17, pl. III; A. Venturi, VII (1914), 378; Gustavo Frizzoni, "Rivelazioni della Galleria Cook a Richmond," *Rassegna d'arte antica e moderna*, I (1914), 123; Van Marle, X (1928), 397–398, 436, fig. 263; Georg Gronau in Thieme–Becker, XXIII (1929), 271–272; Lord Balniel, Kenneth Clark, and Ettore Modigliani, eds., *A Commemorative Catalogue of the Exhibition of Italian Art Held in the Galleries of the Royal Academy, Burlington House, London, Jan.–March, 1930* (London, 1931), no. 108, p. 37; Berenson, *Pictures Renaiss.* (1932), p. 288; Maurice W. Brockwell, *Abridged Catalogue of the Pictures at Doughty House, Richmond, Surrey, in the Collection of Sir Herbert Cook, Bart.* (London, 1932), p. 27, no. 17, pl. XI; Urbain Mengin, *Les Deux Lippi* (Paris, 1932), pp. 32–37; Georg Pudelko, "Per la datazione delle opere di Fra Filippo Lippi," *Rivista d'arte*, VIII, Ser. 2 (1936), 52, n. 3; Berenson, *The Drawings of the Florentine Painters* (Chicago, 1938), p. 81; Robert Oertel, *Fra Filippo Lippi* (Vienna, 1942), pp. 28–29, 41, cat. nos. 99, 100; Mary Pittaluga, *Filippo Lippi* (Florence, 1949), 120–121, 164, 205–207, figs. 141–142; Pietro Toesca, *Enciclopedia italiana*, XXI (Rome, 1949), 238; Berenson, *I Disegni...*, (1961), I, 129; III, figs. 175–176; Pittaluga, "Lippi," *Enciclopedia universale dell'arte* (extract from vol. VIII), (1962), 626; Berenson, *Pictures Renaiss., Florentine School*, (1963), I, 113; II, fig. 840; Henry S. Francis, "Fra Filippo Lippi: St. Michael and St. Anthony Abbot," CMA *Bulletin*, LI (1964), 234–235, illus. pp. 233 (color, 268; *Handbook* (1966), p. 79; *Selected Works* (1966), p. 116 (color).

AFTER FRA FILIPPO LIPPI,
Florence, ca. 1406–1469

This copyist was a productive and technically accomplished painter, gifted in the rendering of flowers. He has often been mistaken for Pier Francesco Fiorentino who is known from two signed works; one dated 1494 in the church of S. Agostino in San Gimignano and the altarpiece of 1497 in the Gallery of Montefortino in the Marches. He was a close follower of Benozzo Gozzoli and Fra Filippo Lippi. Berenson created a new name for him, Pseudo-Pier Francesco Fiorentino, an attribution too precise to encompass the varying styles of the many religious productions made to meet the demand of the Florentine public in this period. The painter of the Museum panel would seem to have been working a generation earlier. He pieced together his compositions from the works of Fra Filippo Lippi, Pesellino, and their followers in the 1460s and 1470s and also made some copies of Fra Filippo's works in a precise but dry style such as the copy of the *Adoration* panel of ca. 1459 in the Medici Chapel of the Palazzo Riccardi in Florence, a replica made to replace the original.

31   *Madonna and Child with Angels*   16.802

> Panel (poplar), 97·2 × 54·9 cm (38¼ × 21⅝ inches).
> Painted surface: 94·9 × 53 cm (37⅜ × 20⅞ inches).
> COLLECTIONS: James Jackson Jarves; Mrs. Liberty E. Holden, Cleveland, 1884.
> Holden Collection, 1916.

The panel is in exceptionally good condition although warped and undoubtedly thinned down at some earlier date. There are minute scattered losses of paint of no serious consequence. The right leg of the Christ Child has the only considerable area of surface damage and the face of the angel at the lower left is slightly rubbed. It was cleaned in 1934 and 1946 by William Suhr.

In 1883 Jarves attributed this painting to the early manner of Fra Filippo Lippi or his school. M. L. Berenson (1907) was the first to call it Pier Francesco Fiorentino and this opinion was seconded by Van Marle (1931). In 1932 Berenson attributed it to a new master, the so-called Pseudo-Pier Francesco Fiorentino. F. Mason Perkins (letter of March 25, 1923) protested against this attribution. He felt it to be one of many paintings lacking in originality although possessed of great charm from a Florentine studio of the mid-fifteenth century showing the influence of Fra Filippo Lippi and to a lesser degree

Pesellino and Baldovinetti. Martin Davies (*The Earlier Italian Schools*, London, National Gallery, 1961, p. 420) also feels that the attributions to Pier Francesco Fiorentino and the Pseudo-Pier Francesco Fiorentino are too precise to include such a varying group.

There are countless versions of the subject of the Museum's panel with variations of background and figure grouping. Among the closest in composition are the paintings in the Horne Museum in Florence and the Städelsche Kunstinstitut in Frankfurt am Main although both these paintings have a rose-arbor backdrop rather than a landscape as in the Museum panel. Pudelko (1936) has suggested that the CMA panel is a copy of the lost central panel of Fra Filippo's triptych of 1457. A pen-and-ink sketch of this altar is preserved at the bottom of a letter from Fra Filippo to Giovanni di Cosimo de' Medici, dated July 20, 1457, now in the Archivio di Stato in Florence (Fig. 30 e). The wings of this altar are in The Cleveland Museum of Art (see Paintings 30A, B). The painting seems to have been directly inspired by the lost central panel, if not copied directly after it. Of all the variants of this composition, the Museum's would seem to be the closest in following the composition of the figures and the landscape.

N.C.W.

EXHIBITIONS: Boston (1883), cat. no. 403; MMA (1912), cat. no. 9, illus.; CMA (1936), cat. no. 83; CMA (1971), cat. no. 7.
LITERATURE: Jarves (1884), cat. no. 8; M. L. Berenson (1907), p. 2; Berenson, *The Florentine Painters...* (1909), pp. 167, 192; Berenson, *Catalogue of a Collection of Paintings and some Objects: Italian Paintings*, I (Philadelphia, 1913), 26; Rubinstein (1917), no. 14, illus.; Underhill (1917), mentioned p. 19; Fogg Art Museum, *Collection of Medieval and Renaissance Paintings* (Cambridge, Mass., 1927), p. 70; Magda Oberschall, "Un élève inconnu de Fra Filippo Lippi," *Gaz. des B.-A.*, IV (1930), 220; Van Marle, XIII (1931), 435, 459, 463, fig. 291; Berenson, *Pictures Renaiss.* (1932), 450; Georg Pudelko, "Per la datazione delle opere di Fra Filippo Lippi," *Rivista d'arte*, Ser. 2, VIII (1936), 51, n. 3; Mary Pittaluga, *Filippo Lippi* (Florence, 1949), p. 206; Berenson, *Pictures Renaiss., Florentine School* (1963), I, 172; II, pl. 840; Henry S. Francis, "Fra Filippo Lippi: St. Michael and St. Anthony Abbot," CMA *Bulletin*, LI (1964), 235, fig. 2, n. 7; *Handbook* (1966), p. 78.

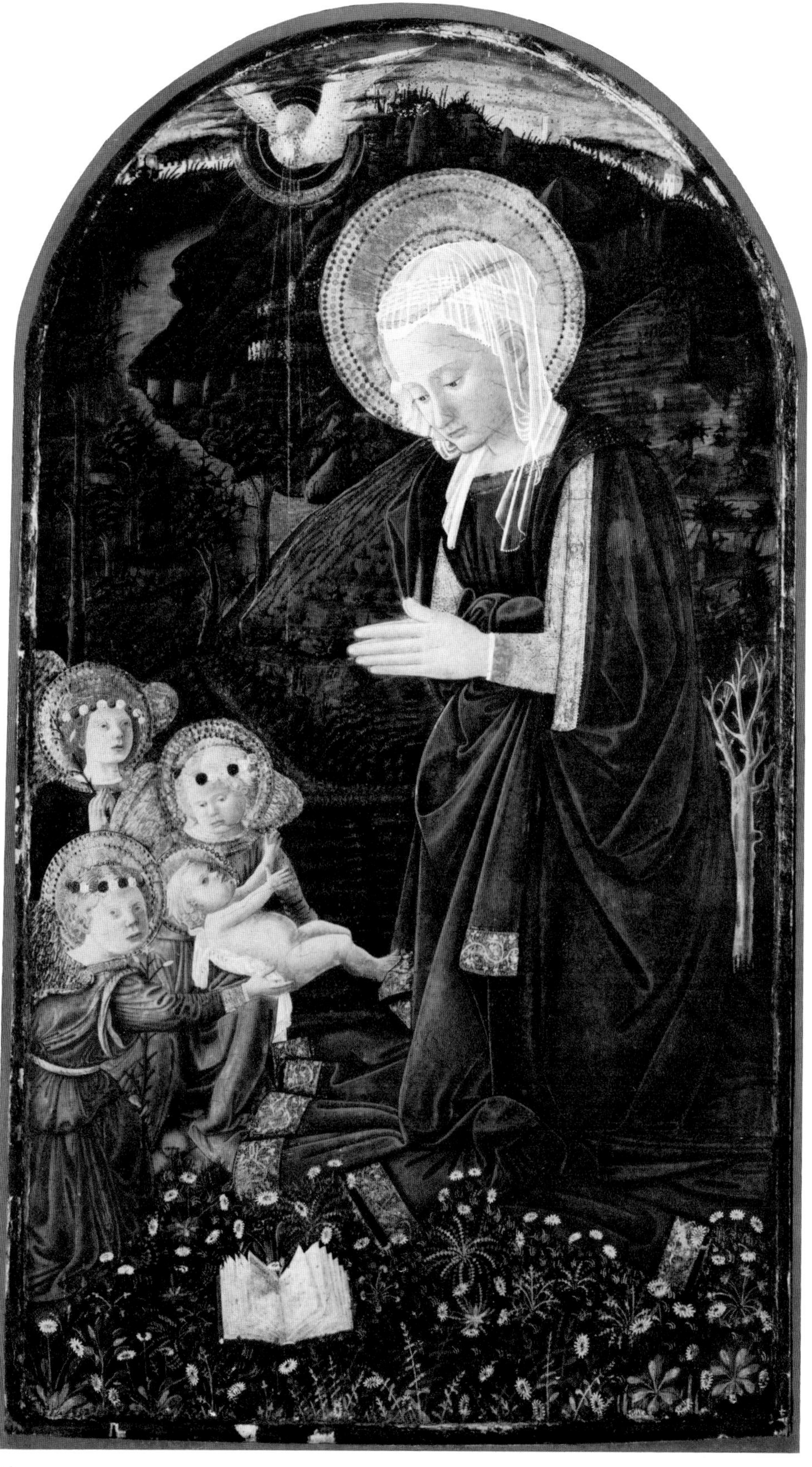

Figure 31.

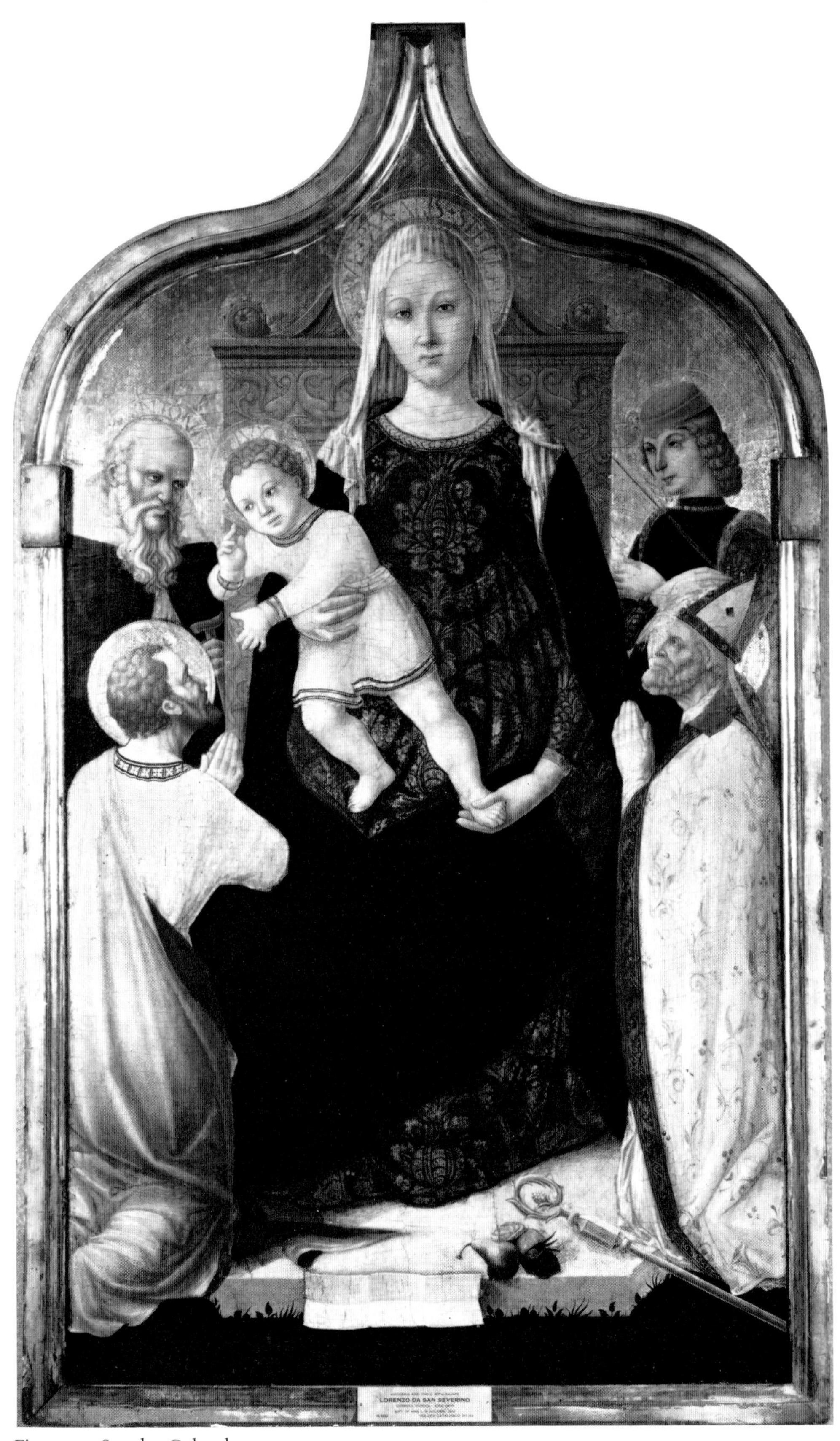

Figure 32. See also Colorplate XVII.

LORENZO D'ALESSANDRO DA SANSEVERINO, Umbria, active 1468–1503

First mentioned in 1468 in a document of Sanseverino, he apparently never travelled for any length of time from his home town southeast of Fabriano inland on the Polenza River in the Marches. Four signed and dated works from his hand are extant (see Berenson, 1968, II, figs. 958, 959, 961, 962). He was influenced by Niccolo di Liberatore, Carlo Crivelli, and others. He is not to be confused with an earlier painter from the Marches, Lorenzo Salimbeni da Sanseverino, ca.1374–ca. 1420.

32 *Madonna and Child with*   16.800
St. Anthony Abbot, St. Sebastian,
St. Mark, and St. Severino

Panel (transferred from poplar to masonite with poplar veneer back), including original molding, 143·5 × 84·2 cm ($56\frac{1}{2} \times 33\frac{1}{8}$ inches). Inside frame: 128·9 × 76 cm ($50\frac{7}{8} \times 29\frac{15}{16}$ inches).

PROVENANCE: Ancient cathedral of S. Severino.

COLLECTIONS: Venanzo Biglioli, San Severino, 1834; James Jackson Jarves; Mrs. Liberty E. Holden, Cleveland, 1884.

Holden Collection, 1916.

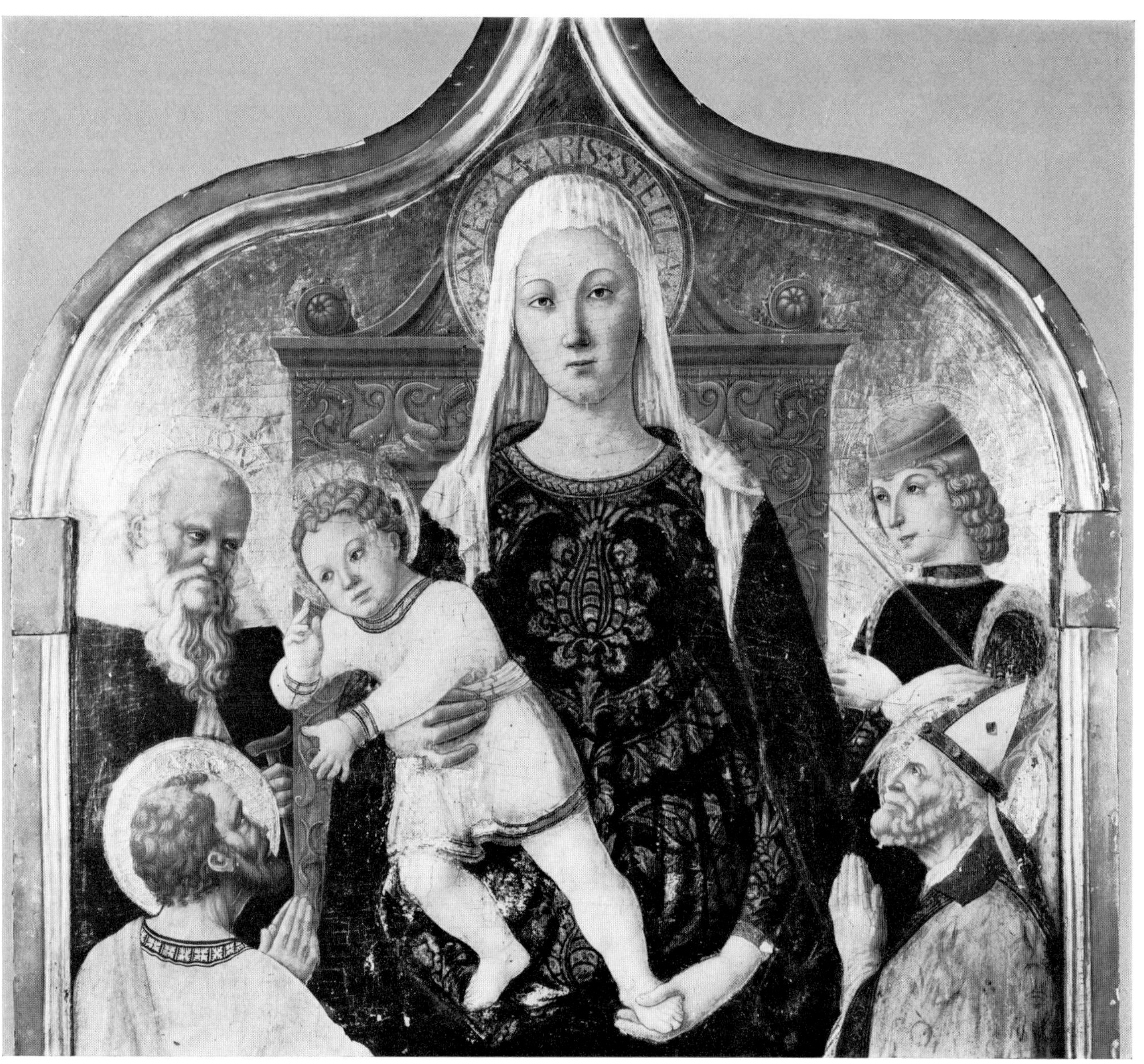

Figure 32a. Detail, before restoration.

The Virgin is seated in the center holding the Christ Child on her lap. Her halo is inscribed: AVE MARIS STELLA. At her right St. Anthony Abbot is standing, his halo inscribed: S. ANTONIVS AB... At her right St. Mark is kneeling, his halo inscribed: SANCTVS MARCUS. At her left is St. Sebastian, his halo inscribed: S. SEBASTIANVS. At her left is a kneeling bishop saint, traditionally called St. Severino because of the original site of the painting (Kaftal, 1965, says incorrectly that the name is in the halo). The inscription in his halo is: SANCTVS... On the cartolina at the base of the throne is written in gold script: AVE MARIA GRATIA PLENA. Traces of illegible inscription are behind.

This painting is first mentioned by Ricci (1834) who says that it was formerly on the altar at the left as you entered the ancient cathedral of S. Severino and that it was purchased by Venanzo Biglioli. Rossi (1875) commends Venanzo Biglioli for trying to preserve the painting but adds that the noble deed of trying to preserve it from further injury of time and man was useless because of his heir. However, the present condition of the painting on the whole is good. Considerable repaint was removed in 1933 and the painting was transferred from its original poplar panel in 1954. The faces are all intact. Most of the important deterioration can be found in the darkened cloak of the Virgin; there is considerable loss below the hand of the Virgin and under the right knee of the Christ Child. Rossi speaks of damage particularly to the robes of the kneeling saints when removing the painting from the altar; these areas are rubbed, but nevertheless are in fair condition.

The painting has been universally attributed to Lorenzo d'Alessandro da Sanseverino (with the exception of Colasanti, 1932, who assigns it to Girolamo di Giovanni of Camerino). It is generally dated in the early 1490s, based upon its stylistic reference to two signed and dated works by the artist, the *Madonna and Child with Eight Saints and the Donors* in the church of the Madonna del Monte at Caldarola, 1491, and *St. Anthony of Padua*, 1496, in the parish church of S. Francesco at Pollenza, near Monte Milone. His early style, verified by two dated works in the early 1480s, is closer to Niccolo da Foligno (ca. 1430–1520) and Carlo Crivelli. In the 1490s his style becomes more placid and fuller in form with characteristic oval, frontal faces and more voluminous drapery as in the *Virgin and St. Anne* in the Vatican Museum and *The Mystical Marriage of St. Catherine* in the National Gallery in London.

N.C.W.

88

EXHIBITIONS: Boston (1883), cat. no. 400; MMA (1912), cat. no. 18, illus.; CMA (1916), cat. no. 33; CMA (1936), cat. no. 104, pl. XI.

LITERATURE: Amico Ricci, *Memorie storiche delle arti e degli artisti della Marca di Ancona*, I (Macerata, 1834), 194–195; Adamo Rossi, "M. Lorenzi di M. Alessandra pittore severinate," *Giornale di erudizione artistica*, IV (Perugia, 1875), 362; Jarves (1884), cat. no. 7; M. L. Berenson (1907), 3, illus.; Crowe and Cavalcaselle, *History of Painting in Italy*, V (1914), 216–217, n. 5; L. Venturi, "A Traverso le Marche," *L'Arte*, XVIII (1915), 195; *Internationale Bibliographie der Kunstwissenschaft*, XIV (1915–1916), 29; Rubinstein (1917), no. 34, illus.; Underhill (1917), p. 20, illus. p. 24; Mather (1923), p. 272, fig. 172; F. Mason Perkins in Thieme–Becker, XXIII (1929), 390; L. Venturi, *Pitture italiane in America* (Milan, 1931), pl. CCXLII; Berenson, *Pictures Renaiss.* (1932), p. 305; Arduino Colasanti, *Italian Painting of the Quattrocento in the Marches* (Florence, Paris, 1932), pp. 58, 139; L. Venturi, II (1933), pl. 317; Van Marle, XV (1934), 58, fig. 37; Luigi Serra, *L'Arte nelle Marche: il periodo del Rinascimento*, II (Rome, 1934), 272, 276, fig. 351; Berenson, *Ital. Painters...* (1952), pl. 294; *Handbook* (1958), no. 394; George Kaftal, *Saints in Italian Art: Iconography of the Saints in Central and Southern Italian Schools of Painting* (Florence, 1965), p. 1019; *Handbook* (1966), p. 84; Berenson, *Pictures Renaiss., Central and North Italian Schools*, I (1968), 222.

MASTER OF 1419, Tuscany, active in the early fifteenth century (so named for the inscription on the picture)

33 *Madonna and Child Enthroned* 54.834

Panel (poplar), including original molding, 196·2 × 68·2 cm (77¼ × 26 13/16 inches). Inside frame: 129·1 × 59 cm (50 13/16 × 23¼ inches).

PROVENANCE: Painted for the church of S. Maria a Latera (above the plain of Cavallina); in 1516 transferred to the Oratory of the church of S. Jacopo alle Cavallina.

COLLECTIONS: William Wetmore Story, Rome; R. T. Crawshay, Rome, ca. 1900; Major W. R. Crawshay, Rome; (Thomas Agnew and Sons, Ltd., London).

Gift of Hanna Fund, 1954.

Inscribed at bottom: QUESTA TAVOLA AFATO FARE ANTONIO DI DOMENICHO GIUGNI P(ER) RIMEDIO DELA SUA ANIMA ANI DNO MCCCCXVIIII. The general condition of the panel is good. There is a damage of two inches in diameter on the face of the Madonna, the loss caused by drilling a hole through the panel from the back. This repainted area includes the tip and nostrils of the Madonna's nose, her mouth, half of her chin, and her left cheek. There is some abrasion and repaint in her blue mantle, particularly the single brushstrokes which highlight the folds. The frame molding of the gable, and the horizontal molding at the bottom of the panel are not original. The painting was cleaned just before it was placed on the London art market in 1954 and the false signature of Gentile da Fabriano on the base of the throne was removed.

The painting was fully documented by Cohn (1956); he found that the altar was referred to as follows in the will of Antonio di Domenico Giugni in 1414: "Item amore Dei pro remido anime sue reliquit et legavit ecclesie S. Marie de latera de mucello comitatis florentie florenos auro quinquaginta . . . quos spendi et eroghari voluit pro faciendo et quod de eis fieri voluit quadam tabula virginis ad altare et pro altare decte ecclesie cum illis picturis et ornamentis et aliis necessariis et opportunis ad dictam tabulam prout melius fieri poterit de dictis flor aui L." (Firenze, Archivio de Stato, Archivio Notarile. *Rogiti di Ser Guido di Domenico Pucci*, p. 575, inserto III, cc. 129–130.)

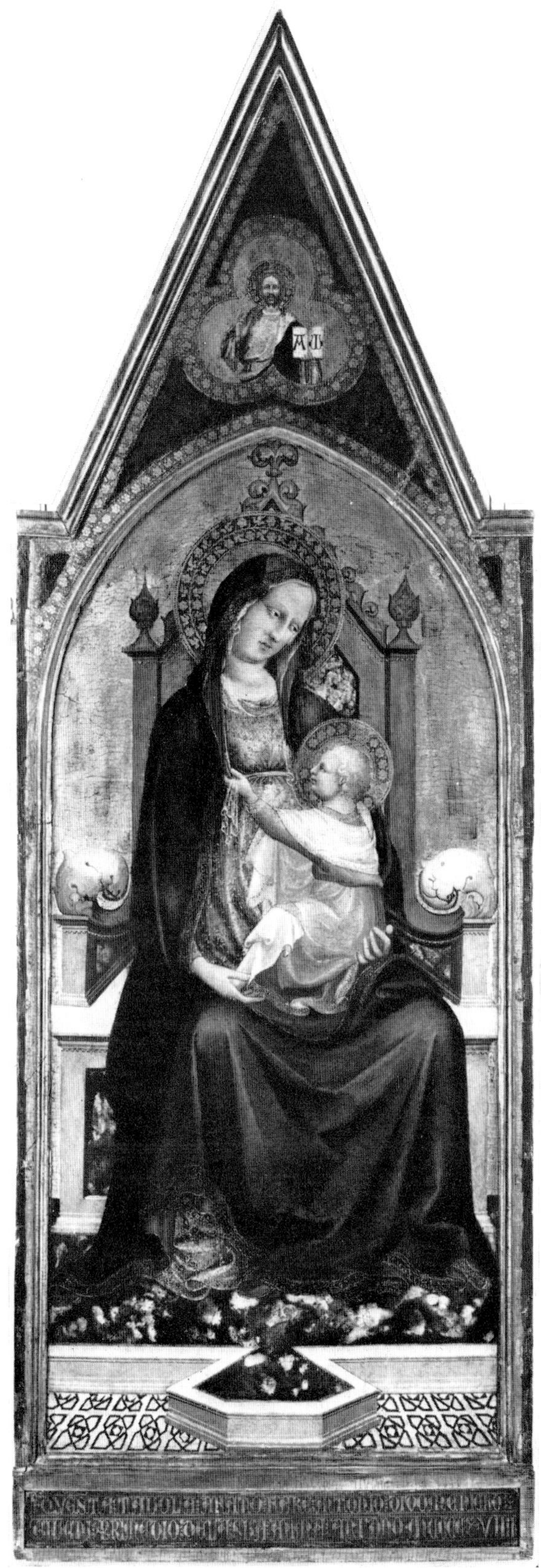

Figure 33. See also Colorplate XVIII.

It was painted for the old church of S. Maria a Latera (above Cavallina). The painting was moved to the oratory of the church of S. Jacopo alle Cavallina, two kilometres south of Barberino in the Mugello in Tuscany when the parochial seat was transferred in 1516. Cohn (1956) also quotes the description of the altarpiece from Brocchi (1748, p. 179) translated here as follows, "The ancient painting of said Oratorio (that belonging to the Marchesi Giugni) behind the high altar, in the arms of the aforesaid gentlemen, under which are written these words: S. Julianus, S. Jacobus, S. Maria, S. Joannes Baptista, S. Antonius. And in the middle is written: Questa Tavola a fatto fare Antonio di Domenico Giugni per rimedio dell'anima sua. MCCCCXVIIII." Thus the opinion of Pudelko (1938) who suggested that the panel of *St. John the Baptist and St. Anthony Abbot*, formerly in the Victor Hahn collection, Berlin (sale: Munich, A. S. Drey, 1936, no. 1, table 2, under the name of Spinello Aretino, present whereabouts unknown), might be the right wing of this altar, and of Pouncey (1954, fig. 30) who published the *St. Julian and St. James the Greater with the Angel of the Annunciation*, private collection, as by the same hand and possibly from the same altar as the CMA *Madonna* (see reconstruction, Fig. 33 *b*) has been confirmed by Cohn with his publication of the Brocchi description of the entire altar. The triptych of *St. Julian Enthroned between SS. Anthony Abbot and Martin* (Fig. 33 *c*) is by the same hand as is probably the *Madonna of Humility* formerly in the Contini Bonacossi collection in Florence (Berenson, 1963, I, pl. 552). The Cleveland panel has been called Arcangelo da Camerino by Van Marle; however, most authorities agree that although this painter carries on the decorative tradition of Lorenzo Monaco he is closest to the early work of Masolino in such paintings as the *Madonna of Humility*, dated 1423, in the Kunsthalle, Bremen. Sacconi (1968, p. 231) suggested it was painted in the circle of Masolino in the area of such close followers as Arcangelo di Cola, Bicci di Lorenzo, and Giovanni Toscani (Master of the Griggs Crucifixion).

N.C.W.

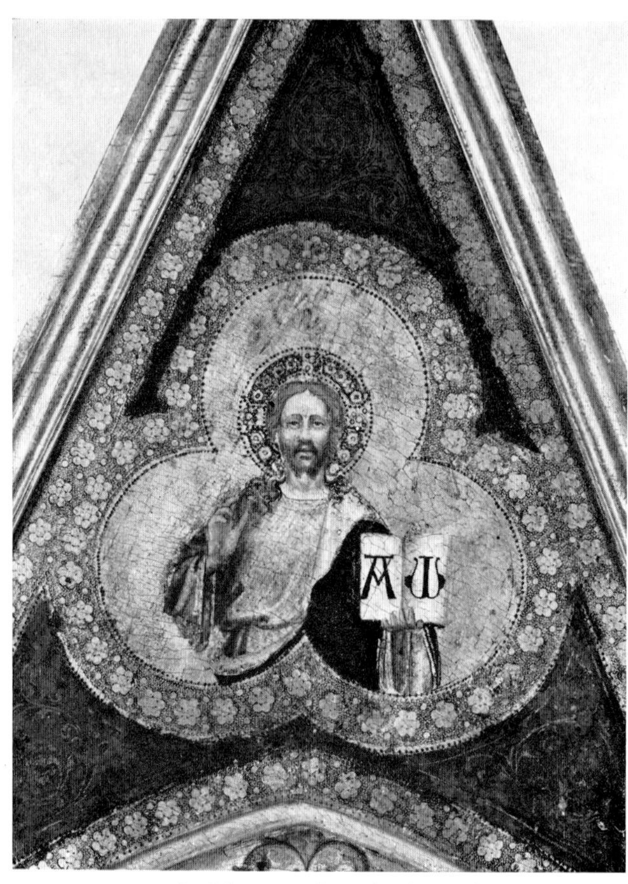

Figure 33 *a*. Detail of the pinnacle with Christ Blessing.

EXHIBITIONS: Rome, Castel Sant'Angelo, 1911: Esposizione internazionale: Mostre Retrospettive, p. 197, as Gentile da Fabriano (?); CMA (1963), cat. no. 79, illus. p. 197; CMA (1971), cat. no. 3.

LITERATURE: G. M. Brocchi, *Descrizione del Mugello* (Firenze, 1748), p. 179; Van Marle, VIII (1927), pp. 256, 258, fig. 154; Georg Pudelko, "The Maestro del Bambino Vispo," *Art in America*, XXVI (April, 1938), 63, fig. 6; Roberto Longhi, "Fatti di Masolino e di Masaccio," *La Critica d'arte*, XXV–XXVI (1940), 185, n. 21; Benedict Nicolson, "The Master of 1419," *Burl. Mag.*, XCVI (1954), 181, fig. 1; Philip Pouncey, "A New Panel of the Master of 1419," *Burl. Mag.*, XCVI (1954), 291–292, fig. 31; Henry S. Francis, "Master of 1419," CMA *Bulletin*, XLIII (1956), 211–213, illus. p. 209; Werner Cohn, "Notizie storicho intorno ad alcune tavole fiorentine del '300 e '400," *Rivista d'arte*, XXXI, Ser. 3 (1956), 49–52, fig. 2; *Handbook* (1958), no. 399; Berenson, *Pictures Renaiss., Florentine School*, I (1963), 217, pl. 550 (entire altarpiece); Alessandro Parronchi, *Studi su la dolce Prospectiva* (Milan, 1964), p. 133; *Handbook* (1966), p. 61; G. Vitalini Sacconi, *Pittura marchigiana: La Scuola camerinese* (Trieste, 1968), p. 89, 231, n. 190, fig. 49.

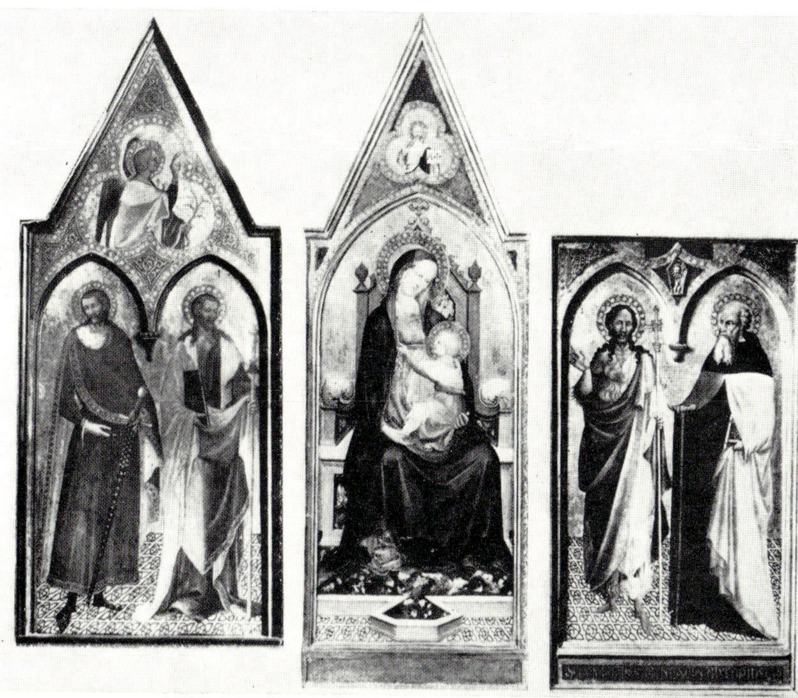

Figure 33 *b*.
Reconstruction of the altarpiece
painted for the Church
of S. Maria a Latera.
Master of 1419.
Left to right:
*St. Julian and St. James the Greater
with the Angel of the Annunciation*,
private collection.
Madonna and Child,
The Cleveland Museum of Art.
*St. John the Baptist and
St. Anthony Abbot*,
formerly Victor Hahn collection;
present whereabouts unknown.

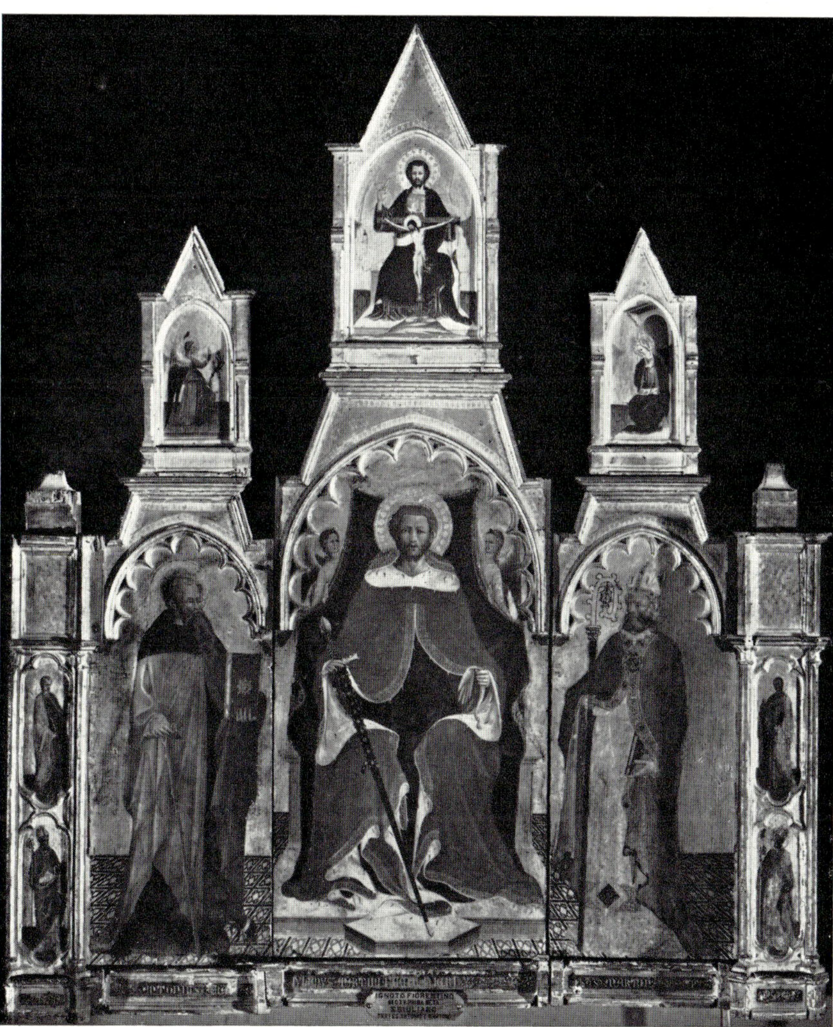

Figure 33 *c*.
*St. Julian Enthroned between SS.
Anthony Abbot and Martin*.
Attributed to Master of 1419.
Museo Civico, San Gimignano.

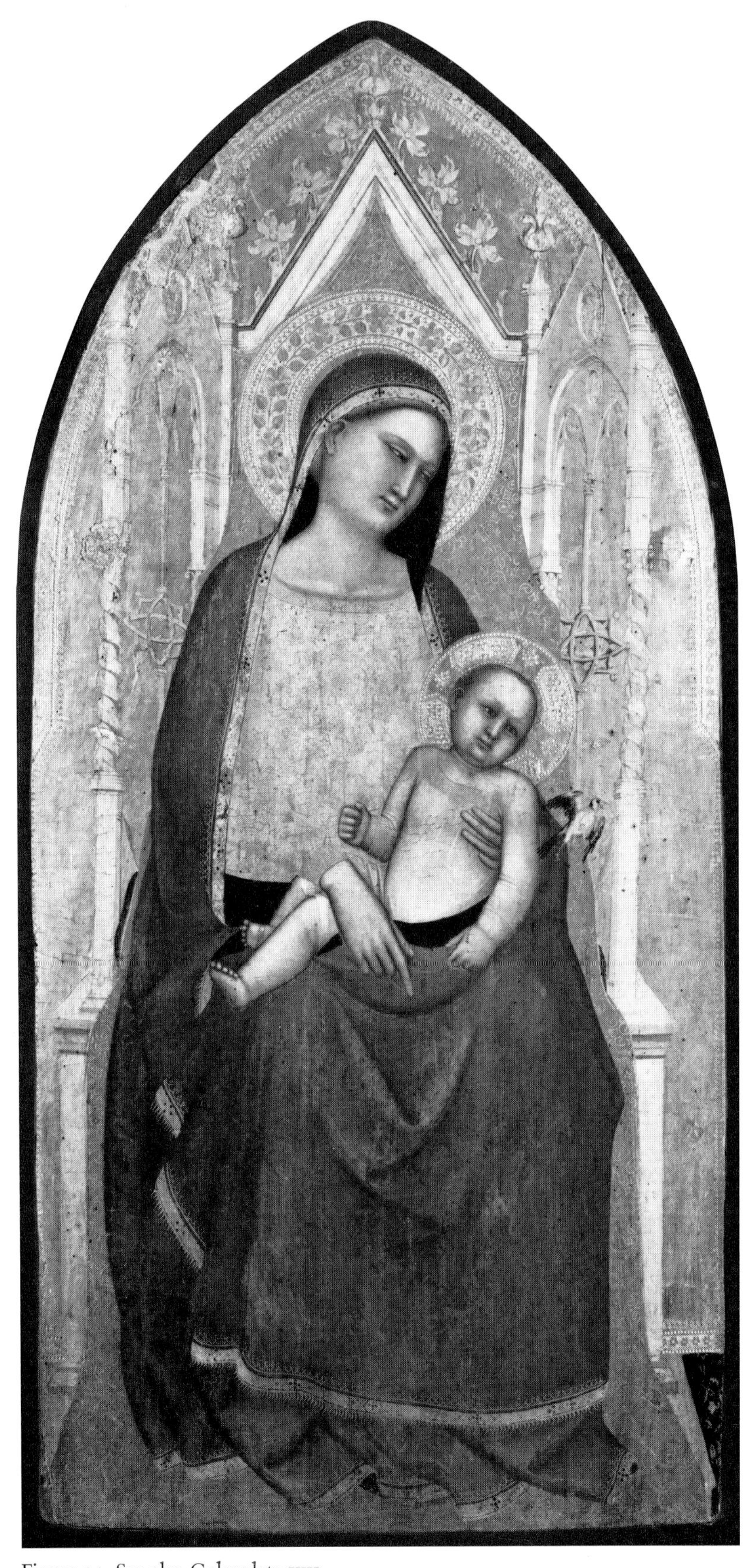

Figure 34. See also Colorplate XIX.

MASTER OF THE SAN LUCCHESE
ALTARPIECE, attributed to, Florence, mid-
fourteenth century

34 *Madonna and Child Enthroned* 68.206

Panel (poplar), 113·7 × 54 cm (44¾ × 21¼ inches).
COLLECTIONS: possibly Ignazio Enrico Hugford,
1703–1778, Florence; Alexis-François Artaud de Montor,
1772–1849, Paris; M. Challamel (to whom it was given
by Artaud de Montor ca. 1845); heirs of M. Challamel;
(sale: Palais Galliera, Paris, June 16, 1967, no. 191, by an
anonymous owner, as workshop of Bernardo Daddi);
(Wildenstein & Co., New York).

Purchase, Leonard C. Hanna Jr. Bequest, 1968.

The panel is in very good condition with the gold and
all the colors, especially the lapis lazuli blue, remarkably
well preserved. About one inch of the panel has been
trimmed off both sides from about the middle of the
panel to the bottom (the original shape of the panel can
be seen in the lithograph published by Artaud de
Montor (Fig. 34*a*). It was cleaned in 1968 by Mario
Modestini who removed the grime and exposed one
small spot of the original clean white tempera (between
the first and second spirals from the bottom, on the
dexter column) which had been protected by a drop of
wax, presumably spilled on the panel from an altar
candle. Some minor losses were filled in, while others
were purposely left unrestored. The two circular marks
on either side of the Madonna's shoulders, for example,
were left alone. They were caused by two large nails in
the back of the panel. The one on the left was extracted
some time ago, causing the paint to come off exposing
the canvas lining the panel; the nail on the right, which
was not removed, caused a round bulging blister.

The painting once belonged to Artaud de Montor,
one of the first collectors of early Italian art. He probably purchased it (between 1801 and 1807) during his
travels in Italy. It may have been among the twenty-five
pictures collected and later given up by Ignazio Enrico
Hugford (1703–1778, an English–Italian dilettante),
which became the nucleus of Artaud de Montor's collection (see De Montor, 1843, p. 14, n. 1). The panel
was included in the latter's descriptive and illustrated
catalogue, reproduced in a lithograph (Fig. 34*a*) and
attributed to Guido da Siena (De Montor, 1843, pl. 6).

This plate served most scholars in their search for an
attribution. Schmarsow (1898) was the first to mention
the panel, associating it tentatively with Bernardo

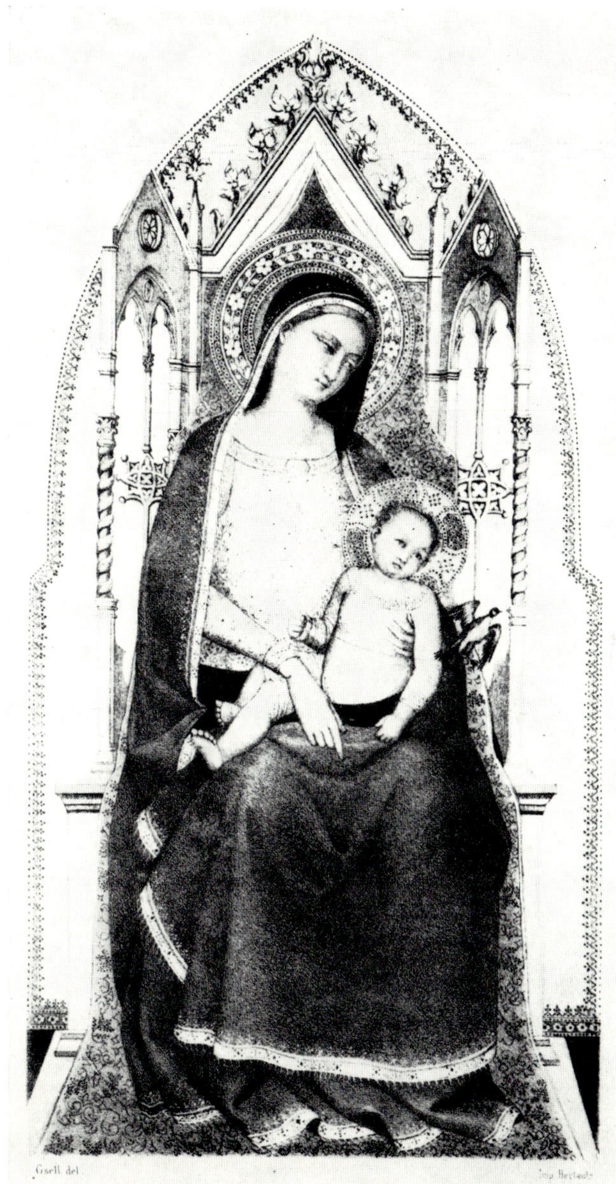

Figure 34*a*. Reproduction of *Virgin and Child Enthroned*
in the catalogue of the collection of Artaud de Montor,
Peintres primitifs, published in 1843, pl. 6.

Daddi. Suida (1905) included it among the works of
Giovanni da Milano; Venturi (1907) and Van Marle
(1924) withheld their opinions, recognizing the inade-
quacy of an attribution from a bookplate. Offner (1930)
listed it under works wrongly attributed to Bernardo

Daddi with no alternative suggestion. The first to illustrate the panel with a photograph was Berenson (1931) attributing the Madonna to the early Jacopo di Cione (documented 1365–1398), noting that the Christ Child showed influences from Allegretto Nuzi (ca. 1315–1373). The design and tooling of the halo of the Cleveland Madonna is very close to that of the *Madonna of Humility* in the National Gallery in Washington (Kress Collection, 1366) attributed to Jacopo di Cione, except that in the latter the garland is arranged counterclockwise. The halo of the Christ Child in the latter panel also has the rhombic division of the Cleveland one although the tooling itself differs.

The textile design on the Cleveland Madonna's blouse is common in works by followers of Giotto (Brigitte Klesse, *Seidenstoffe in der italienischen Malerei des 14. Jahrhunderts*, Bern, 1967, nos. 415, 417) many of which share the three- or five-part grapes indicated with small dark dots along the stems, their curving ends crossing or joining with those of a floral vine ending in palmette-like blossoms (at times with a trefoil nucleus). The goldfinch also appears frequently in depictions of the Madonna and Child by Giotto's immediate followers, including Taddeo Gaddi (e.g., *Virgin and Child Enthroned with SS. Mary Magdalen and Catherine and Four Angels* in the Uffizi).

Everett Fahy (1969) found Berenson's attribution more convincing than all preceding ones but felt that the style was too individual for Jacopo di Cione to have evolved in his early period (as Berenson implied) when he was still working with his brothers, Nardo and Andrea. Initially Fahy ascribed the picture to Giottino and it was under this name that the panel was tentatively catalogued in the Museum's collection (Exh: 1969). But in an article on the painting Fahy (1969) cautiously suggested instead that it was painted by an artist influenced by Jacopo di Cione's softer and more feminine interpretation of Nardo's and Andrea's styles, namely the Florentine Bonaccorso di Cino. This attribution was supported by the stylistic similarities between the Cleveland Madonna and the *Madonna del Parto*, a fresco in the church of S. Lorenzo in Florence, which was attributed to Bonaccorso di Cino by Procacci and Baldini (*Great Age of Fresco: Giotto to Pontormo*, exh. cat.; New York, MMA, 1968, p. 47).

More recently, however, Fahy (1971) changed his opinion. In the addendum to his first article he proposed attributing the painting to an anonymous artist,

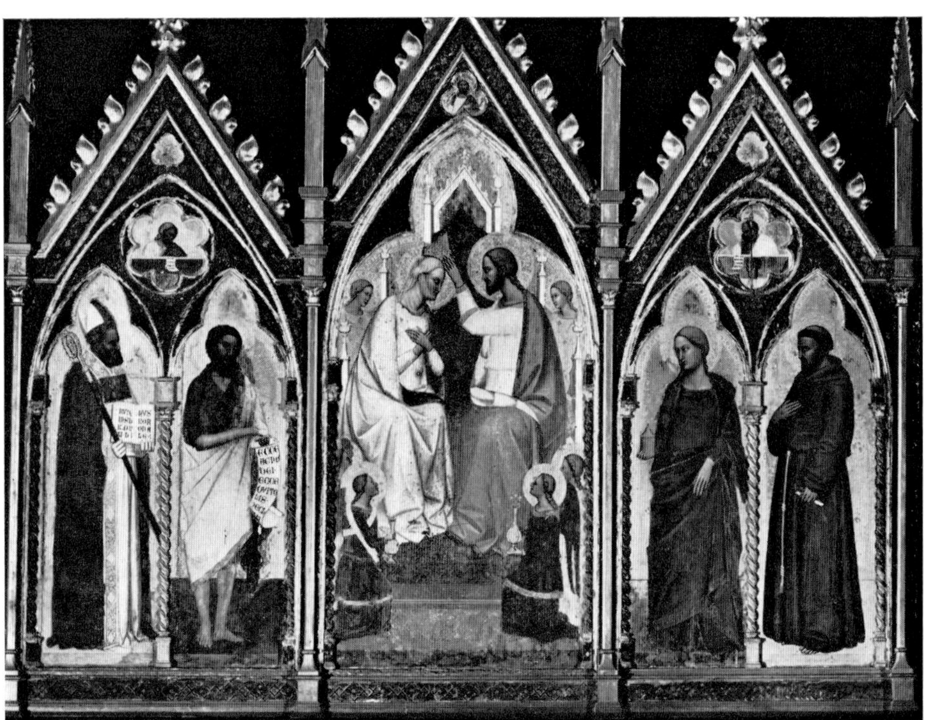

Figure 34*b. Coronation of the Virgin with Six Angels and SS. John the Baptist, Mary Magdalen, Francis, and a Bishop Saint.* Triptych. Master of the San Lucchese Altarpiece, Tuscany, ca. 1350. (Destroyed; formerly Church of San Lucchese, Poggibonsi.)

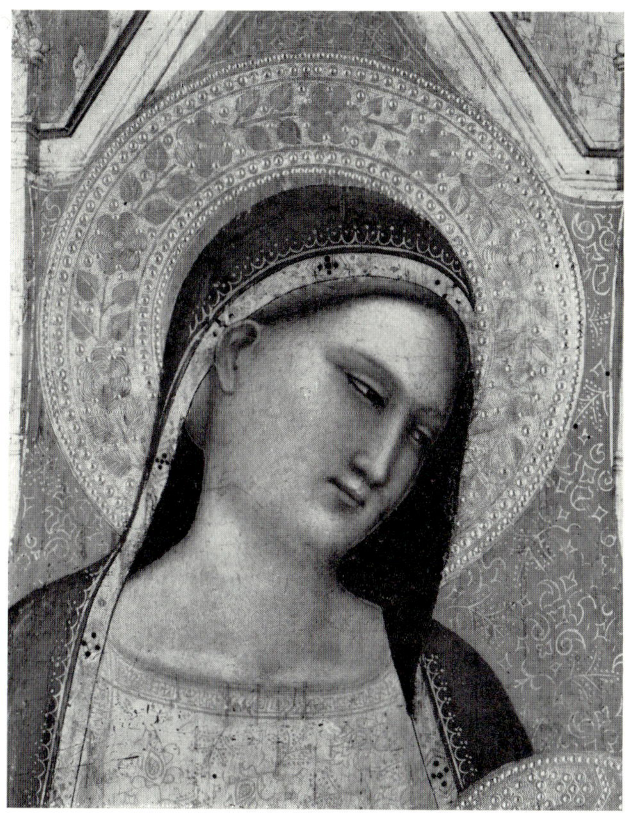

Figure 34c. Head of the Virgin (detail of Figure 34).

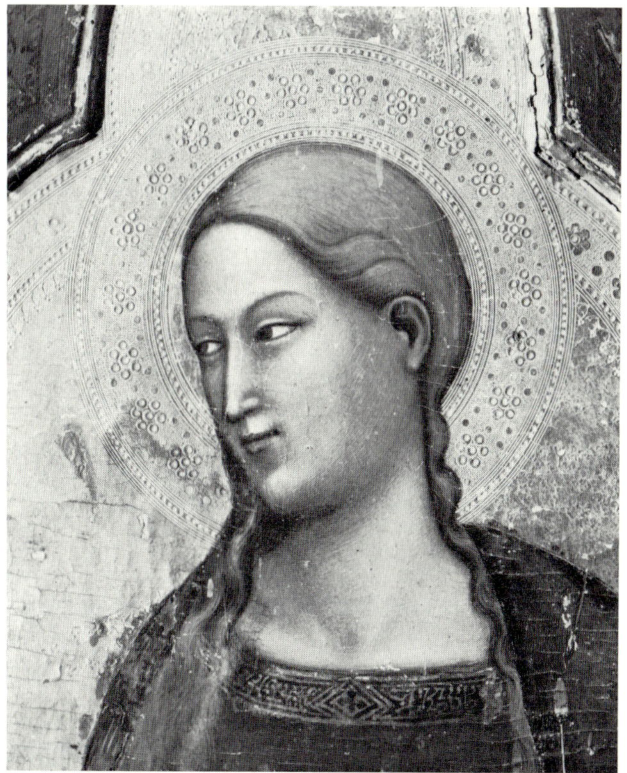

Figure 34d. Head of Mary Magdalen (detail of Figure 34b).

the Master of the San Lucchese Altarpiece. This is a little known mid-fourteenth century Tuscan painter who is named after a large triptych with the *Coronation of the Virgin with Saints and Angels* (Fig. 34b) formerly in the church of S. Lucchese at Poggibonsi, destroyed during World War II. That the Cleveland Madonna was painted by the same artist was also recognized by the late Richard Offner (who, however, never published his opinion), Miklòs Boskovits, Millard Meiss, and Federico Zeri. The slight differences in facial features and modeling between the Cleveland Madonna and the figures by the Master of the San Lucchese Altarpiece may be accounted for by a difference in dates. The former's face (Fig. 34c) shows softer lines describing rounder features, while the features of the Poggibonsi Mary Magdalen (Fig. 34d) are somewhat more sharply delineated, and perhaps more stylized, pointing to a later date for these panels.

A.T.L.

EXHIBITIONS: CMA, January 1969: Year in Review, cat. no. 65, illus. p. 52; CMA (1971), cat. no. 2.

LITERATURE: Alexis-François Artaud de Montor, *Considérations sur l'état de la peinture en Italie, dans les quatre siècles qui ont précédé celui de Raphael* (Paris, 1808), pp. 21–22, no. 18; Artaud de Montor, *Peintres primitifs: Collection de tableaux rapportée d'Italie* (Paris, 1843), pp. 27–28, pl. 6, no. 22 (as Guido da Siena); August Schmarsow, "Maîtres Italiens à la galerie d'Altenburg et dans la collection A. de Montor," *Gaz. des B.-A.*, XX (1898), 496; Georg Graf Vitzthum von Eckstädt, *Bernardo Daddi* (Leipzig, 1903), p. 10, n. 5; William Suida, "Studien zur Trecentomalerei," *Repertorium für Kunstwissenschaft*, XXVII (1904), 386 (refers to a group from Artaud de Montor collection); Suida, *Florentinische Maler um die Mitte des XIV. Jahrhunderts* (Strassburg, 1905), p. 38, pl. XXVII (after reproduction in Artaud de Montor catalogue, see 1); A. Venturi, V (1907), 915; Van Marle, IV (1924), 240, n. 2 (as close to Giovanni da Milano); Richard Offner, *Studies in Florentine Painting: The Fourteenth Century* (New York, 1927), p. 80, no. 6, p. 107, no. 11; Offner, *Corpus*, III (1930), 11 (attributed to Daddi); Berenson, "Quadri senza casa, Il Trecento fiorentino, II," *Dedalo*, XI (1931), 1045, illus. p. 1048 (original photo); *Art and Auctions, International Art Dealers' and Collectors' Guide*, XI (Rotterdam, August 1967), illus. (atelier de Bernardo Daddi); "International Saleroom," *Connoisseur*, CLXVI (1967), illus. p. 115, fig. 4; Berenson, *Homeless Pictures of the Renaissance* (London, 1969), p. 101, fig. 154; Everett Fahy, "A Masterpiece of Early Italian Painting," CMA *Bulletin*, LVI (1969), 347–353, illus. p. 347 (color), fig. 1; Fahy, "Second Thoughts about the Artaud de Montor Madonna," CMA *Bulletin*, LVIII (1971), 251–254, fig. 1; William D. Wixom, "A Masterpiece Attributed to Andrea Pisano," CMA *Bulletin*, LIX (1972), 282, fig. 44.

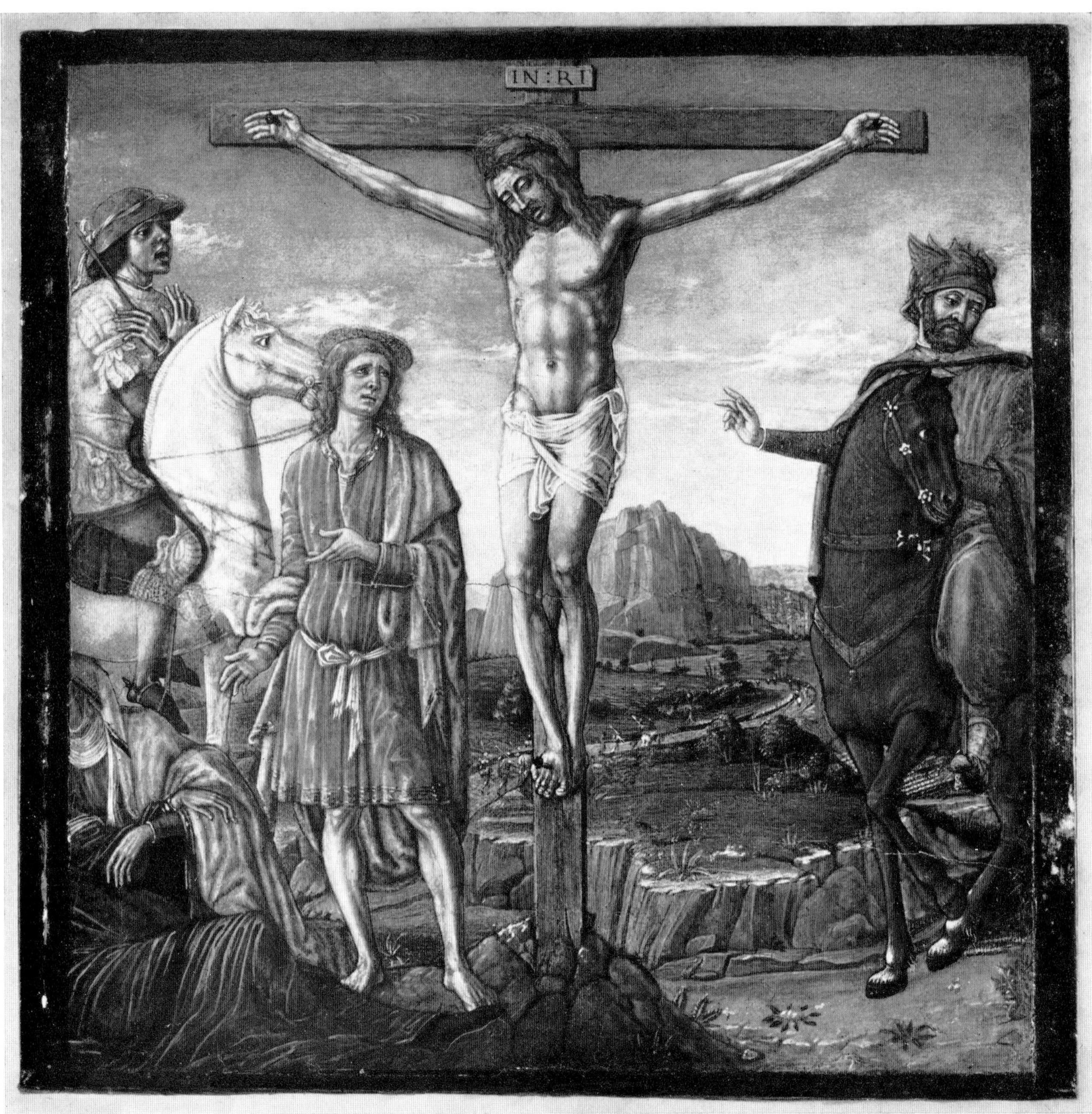

Figure 35. See also Colorplate xx.

MATTEO DI GIOVANNI DI BARTOLO,
Siena, ca. 1430–1495

Although his father was from Borgo San Sepolcro which
was probably Matteo's birthplace, the latter spent most
of his life in Siena where his activity as a painter is documented from 1452. His early works reflect an admiration
for Vecchietta which persists through his maturity. His
interest in the classical is evident in the CMA *Crucifixion*,
which reflects Mantegna's northern classicism as inter-
preted by the painter-miniaturists Girolamo da Cre-
mona and Liberale da Verona who were working in
Siena from 1467 to 1475. There are several authenticated
pictures by Matteo, among them three famous versions
of the *Massacre of the Innocents* painted between 1482 and
1491.

35 *The Crucifixion* 40.535

Fragment of a predella panel

Panel (poplar), 34 × 33 cm ($13\frac{3}{8}$ × 13 inches), including
added borders $1\frac{1}{2}$ inches wide, and a $\frac{3}{4}$-inch strip at top
of picture including the top of the cross, also a later
addition. Original painted surface: 29·8 × 31 cm ($11\frac{3}{4}$ ×
$12\frac{3}{16}$ inches).

COLLECTIONS: Monsieur Chaff, Paris (as Mantegna);
Baron Michel Lazzaroni, Paris and Rome(?), 1890s;
bought from the latter by John E. Fairfax Murray,
Florence; (Knoedler & Co., New York); James Parmelee,
Washington, 1929.
James Parmelee Collection, 1940.

Except for a crack across the center of the panel and
scattered retouchings throughout the picture, the panel
is in good condition. However, almost all the draperies
of the lower extremities of the figure of Mary reveal a
different crackle pattern, a color more opaque than in
the rest of the painting, and a change in the rhythm
of the design – all of which indicates a somewhat later
date for this area. The picture had been cleaned before its
acquisition by the Museum and has since been restored
by William Suhr in 1940 and 1950.

This was probably a horizontal panel in the center of a
predella. It is especially close in style to another predella
panel, *The Calling of SS. Andrew and Peter* (Fig. 35 a). It
is possible (despite the difference of $\frac{3}{4}$ inch in height) that
the two panels belonged to the same predella. Another
panel of approximately the same size as the *Calling of
SS. Andrew and Peter* is *Feast in the House of Levi* (Fig.
35 b), which also may have been part of the same ensemble.

Van Marle (1937, 358) dates the Cleveland *Crucifixion*
ca. 1479–1483, although it looks as if it could have been
done slightly earlier. Other *Crucifixions* by Matteo
with which this may be compared are predella panels at
Asciano (early); at Borgo San Sepolcro (Pinacoteca), ca.
1465; at Mells, England (from the S. Agostino *Massacre
of the Innocents* of 1482, see Pope-Hennessy, 1960); at
the M. H. de Young Memorial Museum, San Francisco,
(*The Samuel H. Kress Collection*, San Francisco, 1955, p.
42), said to have formed part of the predella to the
Massacre of 1491 at S. Maria dei Servi; and one, attributed to Matteo, at the Manchester Art Gallery in England.
E.F.G.

EXHIBITIONS: New York, M. Knoedler & Co., 1929: Loan
Exhibitions of Primitives.
LITERATURE: F. Mason Perkins in Thieme–Becker, XXIV (1930),
256 (listed as at Knoedler's); L. Venturi (1931), pl. 228; L. Venturi,
II (1933), pl. 297; Marialuisa Gengaro, "Per la Cronologia di
Matteo di Giovanni," *La Diana*, IX (1934), 182 (listed under
Works variously attributed to Matteo); Van Marle, XVI (1937),
342, 344, 358; Henry S. Francis, "The Bequest of James Parmelee:
The Department of Paintings" CMA *Bulletin*, XXVIII (1941), 16,
illus. p. 14; *Handbook* (1958), no. 403; John Pope-Hennessy, "A
Crucifixion by Matteo di Giovanni," *Burl. Mag.*, CII (1960), 63,
n. 1; *Handbook* (1966), p. 83; Berenson, *Pictures Renaiss.*, *Central
and North Italian Schools*, I (1968), 258.

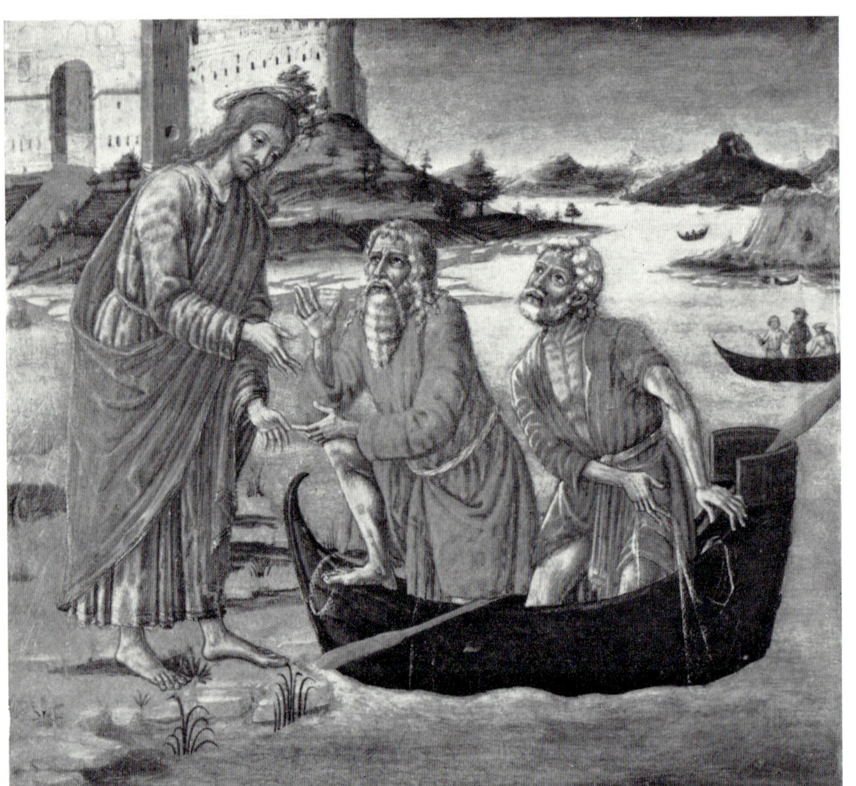

Figure 35 a.
The Calling of SS. Peter and Andrew.
28·9 × 32·4 cm ($11\frac{3}{8}$ × $12\frac{3}{4}$ inches).
Attributed to Matteo di Giovanni.
Sterling and Francine Clark Art
Institute, Williamstown, Mass., 931.

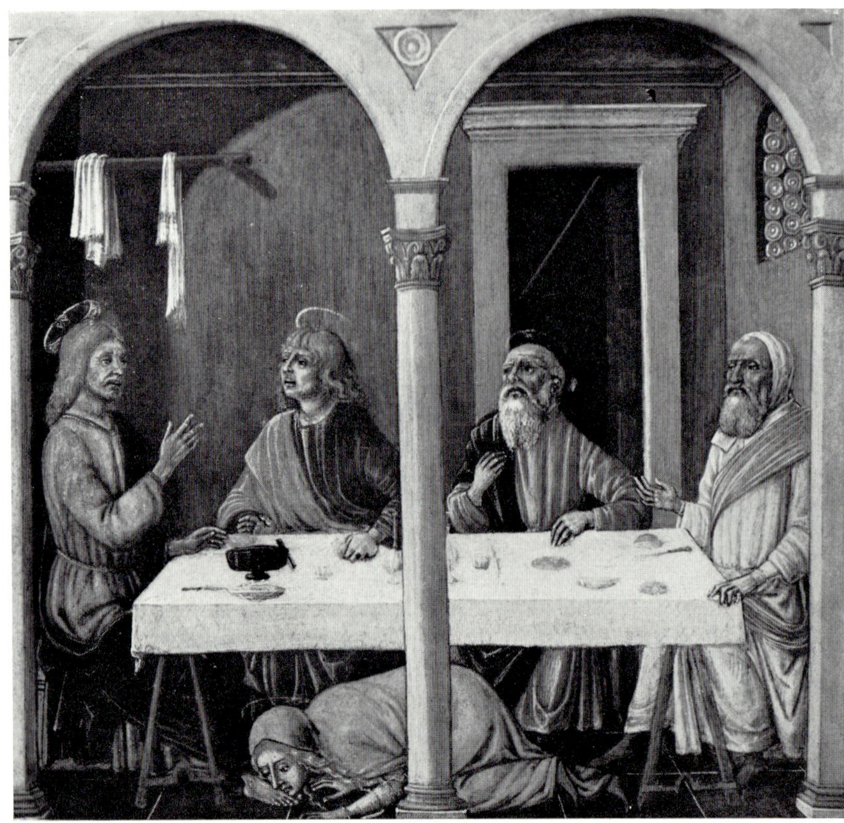

Figure 35 b.
Feast in the House of Levi.
28 × 30·5 cm (11 × 12 inches).
Matteo di Giovanni.
David M. Koetser Gallery, Zürich.

School of LIPPO MEMMI, Siena,
ca. 1317–1356

Lippo's first documented work, the signed *Maesta* of 1317 in the Palazzo del Popolo, San Gimignano, was painted in collaboration with his father and teacher, Memmo di Filipuccio. Some twelve other works are generally agreed to be by the latter. In 1324 Lippo became Simone Martini's brother-in-law. The two painters worked together in Siena, Orvieto, Pisa, and Assisi, and Simone's influence on Lippo was great. Lippo is last mentioned in 1347. According to Vasari he died twelve years after Simone Martini.

36 *Madonna and Child*   52.110

Panel (poplar), including molding, 71·3 × 44 cm (28$\frac{1}{16}$ × 17$\frac{5}{16}$ inches). Inside frame: 63 × 37·5 cm (24$\frac{13}{16}$ × 14$\frac{3}{4}$ inches).

COLLECTIONS: Richard von Kaufmann, Berlin; (sale: Cassirer and Helbing, Berlin and Munich, December 4, 1917, I, no. 7, illus. p. 22); August and Erich Lederer, Vienna.

Gift of Hanna Fund, 1952.

Inscribed on the scroll held in the Christ Child's hand [?]gosu via veritas et vita.

Several inches are missing from the bottom of the panel, which was probably the central panel from a polyptych. Both feet of the Child are abraded and the lower part of the scroll is repainted. A scratch through the Madonna's right eye, one on her forehead, as well as slight abrasions and blemishes on the Child's shirt and forehead (Fig. 36*a*) have been attenuated; dirty varnish was removed when the panel was cleaned by William Suhr in 1952. The gold of the background and tooling is slightly worn. On the back (Fig. 36*b*) are various dates, inscriptions, and a diamond-shaped design which according to Zeri (1965) are indications that this side of the panel was once decorated and intended to be free-standing.

Francis (1953) relates this panel to the *Madonna of the Palazzo Venezia* (now Galleria Nazionale, Palazzo Barberini, *Catalogue of the National Gallery, Barberini Palace, Rome*, 1964, no. 66, fig. 4) which has been variously attributed to Simone and Donato Martini, to Lippo Memmi, and to a follower of Simone designated as the Master of the Palazzo Venezia Madonna. In his œuvre are included works usually attributed to Memmi, others often ascribed to Barna's circle, and some (such as the probable laterals of the Palazzo Venezia *Madonna, St.*

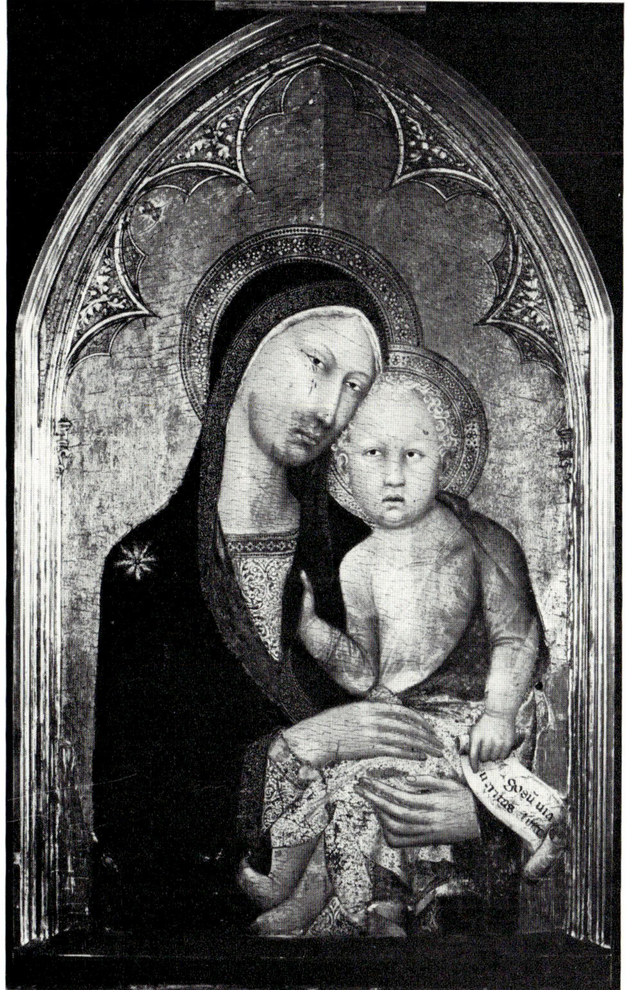

Figure 36*a*. Before restoration, partially cleaned.

Peter and *Mary Magdalen*, National Gallery, London nos. 4491, 4492) which have been given to Memmi, to Barna, and to their respective followers (see also Carlo Volpe, "Precisazioni sul 'Barna'e sul 'Maestro di Palazzo Venezia'," *Arte antica e moderna*, X, (1960), 149–158). Weigelt (1931) gave the Cleveland picture, together with a *Madonna* in Berlin (no. 1511), to the Master of the Lederer Madonna described as between the Palazzo Venezia Master and the Master of the Straus Madonna (or Pseudo-Barna). Zeri (orally, 1965) was also of the opinion that the Cleveland and Palazzo Venezia *Madonnas* were not by the same hand. However a workshop connection seems indicated by the fact that the same punch tool was used in the halo of the Christ Child in both the Cleveland and Palazzo Venezia paintings (Frinta, 1965). The same tool was used by

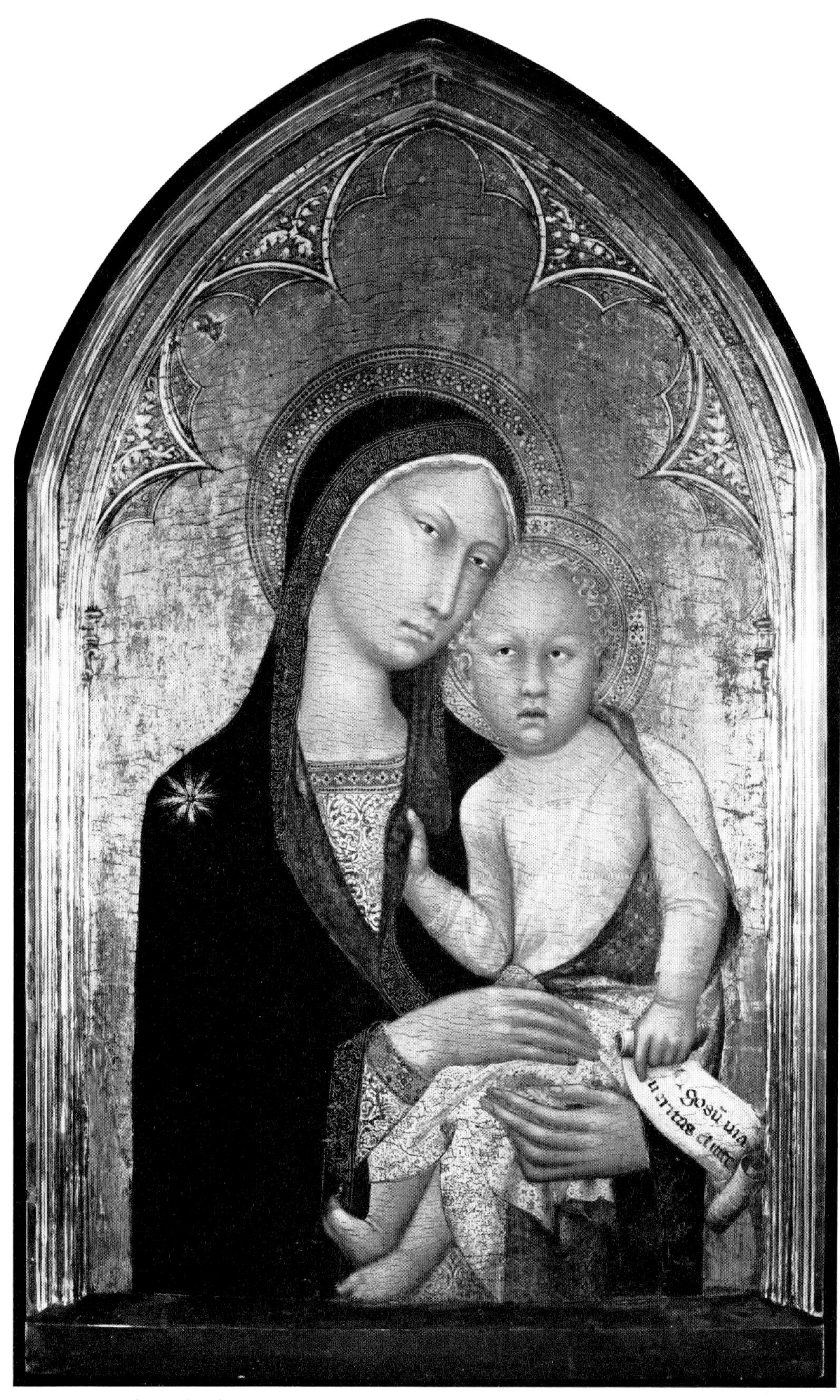

Figure 36. See also Colorplate XXI.

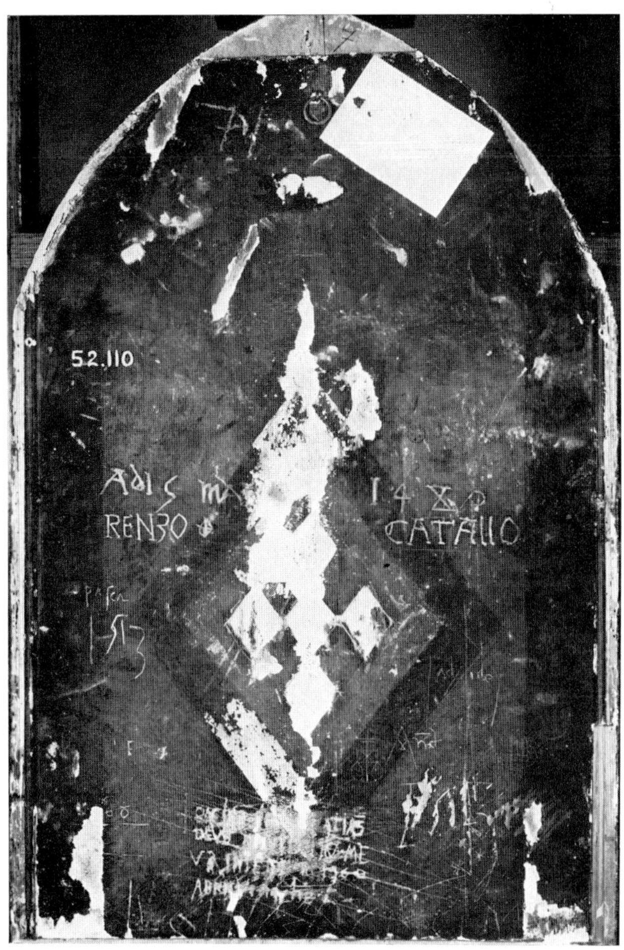

Figure 36 b. Back of panel.

many members of a shop and by related masters. Memmi used Simone's punch in most of his paintings.

Sandberg-Vavalà (1937) suggested that the Palazzo Venezia group, in view of similarities, especially in color, with Lippo's *Madonna* in the Lindenau Museum, Altenburg, might represent a phase of Lippo Memmi's activity. While the Cleveland picture agrees with the Palazzo Venezia group in the above respects it is closer in type and expression to Lippo's *Madonna and Child* in Berlin (no. 1067) of 1325–1330 (see Gertrude Coor, "Two Unknown Paintings by the Master of the Glorification of St. Thomas and Some Closely Related Works," *Pantheon*, XIX, 1961, pp. 126 ff.), and to the panels from the same polyptych which Coor attributes to Lippo Memmi and assistant. Although the Cleve-

land picture could be considered a transition between Lippo's ample and relaxed Madonnas, culminating in the melancholy Gardner Museum and Berlin examples and the Palazzo Venezia phase of ca. 1345–1356, its peculiar sophistication sets it apart. Our picture may belong to the same period as the *St. Peter* in the Parry collection, Highnam Court, which Weigelt (1931) assigned to the Master of St. Paul, Volpe (*op. cit.*) to the Master of the Palazzo Venezia Madonna, and Pietro Toesca (*Il Trecento*, Turin, 1951, p. 549) to Lippo Memmi. Hendrik W. van Os of the Institut voor Kunstgeschiedenis der Rijksuniversiteit, Groningen, The Netherlands (letters of October 19 and November 27, 1970), has suggested that this panel might be attributed to Naddo Ceccarelli whose work seems more naive and soft in treatment than the Cleveland picture. A note found by Van Os in the Berenson files made when the painting was still in the Kaufmann collection indicates he felt it dated from the 1350s and illustrated the late following of Simone Martini and Lippo Memmi.

E.F.G.

EXHIBITIONS: Vienna, Secession Building, 1924–1925; Meisterwerke italienischer Renaissance aus Privatbesitz, cat. no. 71; London, Royal Academy, Burlington House, 1930; Exhibit of Italian Art 1200–1900, cat. no. 30 (1931).

LITERATURE: (Attributed to Lippo Memmi in all unless otherwise noted.) F. Harck, "Quadri di Maestri Italiani in possesso di privati a Berlino," *Archivo storico dell'arte*, II (1889), 206; A. Venturi, V (1907), 655 (follower of Lippo), fig. 532; Salomon Reinach, *Répertoire de peintures du moyen âge et de la renaissance*, III (Paris, 1910), 378, fig. 1; Berenson, *Central Italian Painters...* (1908), p. 148; Crowe and Cavalcaselle, *History of Painting in Italy*, III (London, 1908), 79–80, n. 1 (School of Lippo); Van Marle, *Simone Martini et les peintres de son école* (Strasbourg, 1920), p. 190 (School of Lippo); Van Marle, II (1924), 274, n. 3; Louis Gielly, *Les Primitifs Sienois* (Paris, 1926), p. 111 ("Memmi — ?"); Kurt Weigelt in Thieme-Becker, XXIII (1929), 277 (close to the follower of Simone Martini, whom he later calls the Master of the Straus Madonna, who painted the *St. Agnes* in the Worcester Museum); Weigelt, "Minor Simonesque Masters," *Apollo*, XIV (1931), 13, fig. XII (as Master of the Madonna in the Lederer Collection); Berenson, *Pictures Renaiss.* (1932), p. 360; Evelyn Sandberg-Vavalà, "Some Partial Reconstructions – I," *Burl. Mag.*, LXXI (1937), 177, n. 6 (the Lederer Madonna...agrees with the Palazzo Venezia group in color though not altogether in form); Hans Vollmer in Thieme-Becker, XXXVII (1950), 194 (Meister der Lederer Madonna, ca. 1350); Henry S. Francis, "A Sienese Madonna and Child by Lippo Memmi," CMA *Bulletin*, XL (1953), 59–61, illus. p. 57; *Handbook* (1958), no. 392; Mojmír Frinta, "An Investigation of the Punched Decoration of Medieval Italian Paintings," *Art Bulletin*, XLVII (1965), 261, fig. 23; *Handbook* (1966), p. 54.

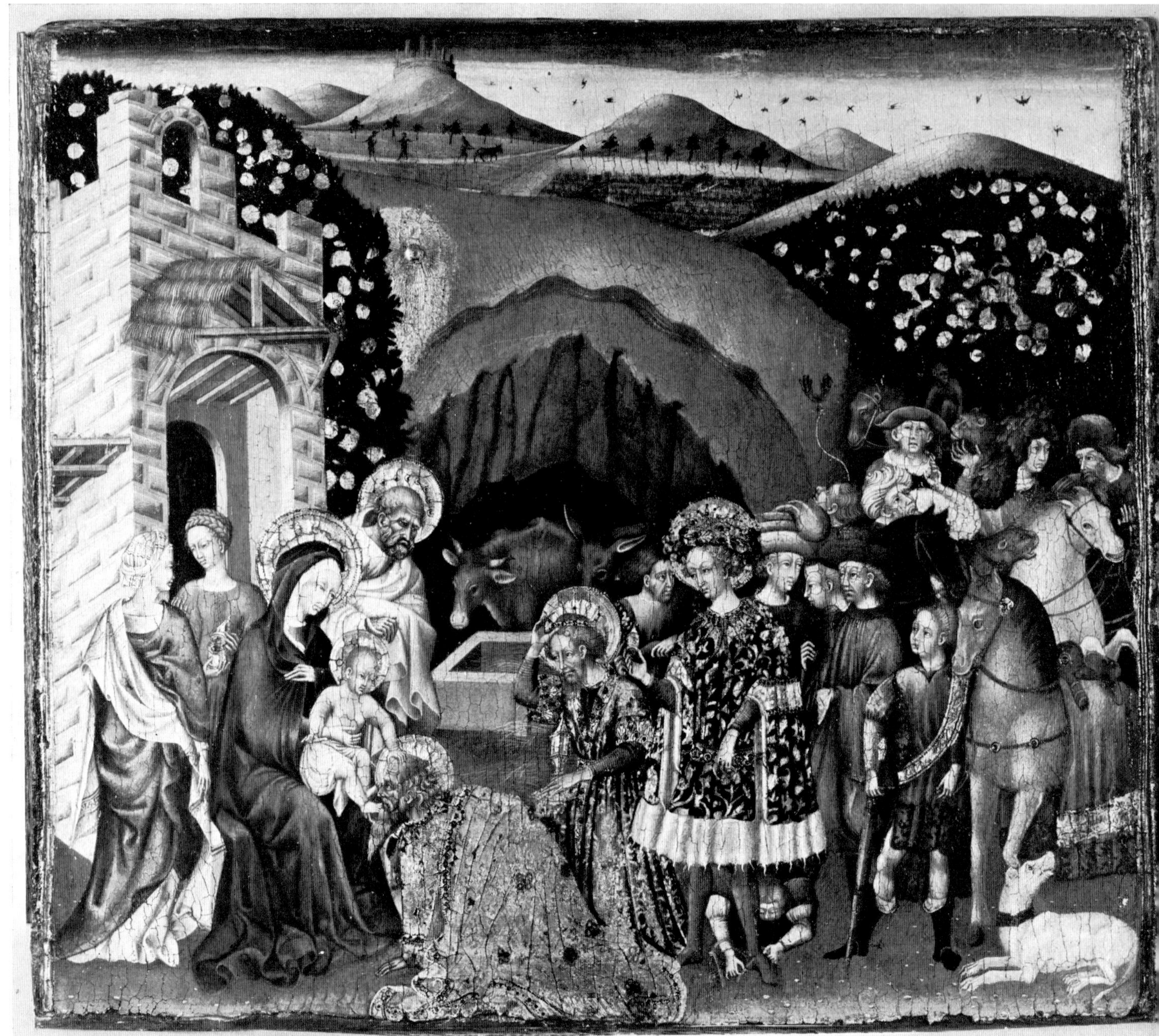

Figure 37. See also Colorplate XXII.

GIOVANNI DI PAOLO, Siena, ca. 1399–1482

Giovanni di Paolo di Grazia, called Boccanera, was also known as Giovanni dal Poggio after the district in Siena where he spent most of his life. Although his birth-date is often given as 1403, this date is not sufficiently supported by documentary evidence and a date of ca. 1399 seems more probable (see Peleo Bacci, *Documento e commenti per la storia dell'arte*, I, Florence, 1944, 65 ff.). He is mentioned as a painter in Siena from 1420; his first dated work was painted in 1426. His highly personal style, developed from the Sienese Gothic tradition of Sassetta and Taddeo di Bartoldo also shows the influence of Gentile da Fabriano, Fra Angelico, and Pisanello.

37 *Adoration of the Magi* 42.536

Panel (poplar), 39·7 × 46·2 cm (15⅝ × 18 3/16 inches).
Painted surface: 39·3 × 44·2 cm (15 7/16 × 17¾ inches).
COLLECTIONS: Mrs. Kerr (Miss Alice Hoffman), Baltimore (descendant of Thomas McKean, 1734–1817, one of the signers of the Declaration of Independence); (Arnold Seligmann, Rey & Co., through H. Sperling of F. Kleinberger & Co., New York).
Delia E. and L. E. Holden Funds, 1942.

Much of the foliage and the landscape background show scattered repairs, but otherwise this panel is in good condition.

It is one of five known parts of the predella from an altarpiece which has not been identified. The other four panels are: *The Annunciation* in the National Gallery (Fig. 37 a); *Nativity* (Pinacoteca Vaticana, Rome, no. 132); *Crucifixion* (Berlin-Dahlem Museum, no. 1112c); and *The Presentation in the Temple* (Metropolitan Museum of Art, Blumenthal Collection, 41.100.4). Except for the central *Crucifixion* all five predella panels have approximately the same measurements and the tooling

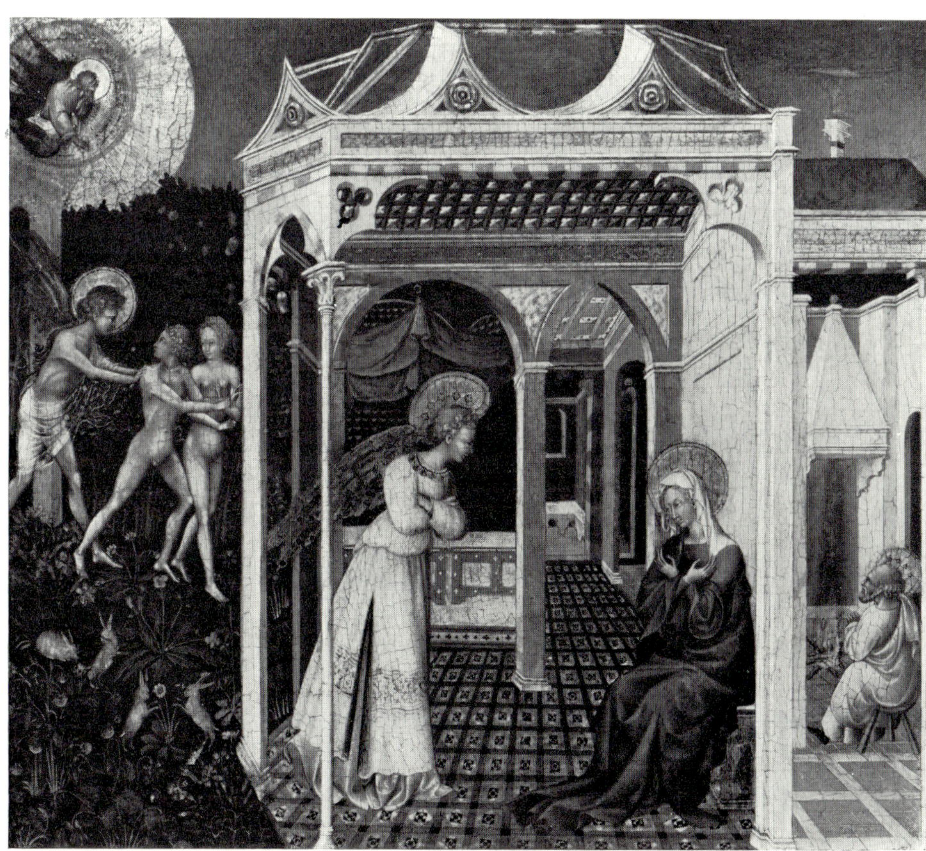

Figure 37 a. *The Annunciation.* 40 × 46 cm (15¾ × 18¼ inches). Giovanni di Paolo. National Gallery of Art, Washington, Samuel H. Kress Collection.

of the haloes in all of them is the same. Stylistically they show the influence of Gentile da Fabriano's *Adoration of the Magi* of 1423 in the Uffizi (Fig. 37*b*); the Cleveland painting reproduces part of its main panel, and the Vatican and Metropolitan pictures copy the corresponding parts of Gentile's predella panels in the Uffizi and the Louvre (no. 1278). John Pope-Hennessy (*Giovanni di Paolo*, London, 1937, p. 39) dated the then-known four panels ca. 1440–1445, and postulated the existence of a fifth panel, later identified by Francis (1942) as the Cleveland *Adoration* which is said to have appeared in America during the last quarter of the past century. Despite the difference in size there may be a connection with this panel and the vague reference in Van Marle (IX, 1927, 452), "if I remember rightly, a good many years ago I saw in Rome a large picture of the *Adoration of the Magi* copied by the hand of Giovanni di Paolo from Gentile's renowed panel . . . in the Uffizi; at least such was my impression at the time although . . . I was very sure of my own attribution and since then I have never again come across the picture."

E.F.G.

EXHIBITIONS: CMA, 1960: Paths of Abstract Art, cat. no. 4; CMA (1963), cat. no. 83, pp. 196, 213.

LITERATURE: Henry S. Francis, "An Adoration of the Magi by Giovanni di Paolo," CMA *Bulletin*, XXIX (1942), 166–168, illus. p. 162; Francis, "A New Giovanni di Paolo," *Art Quarterly*, V (1942), 313–322; Harry B. Wehle, "The Presentation in the Temple by Giovanni di Paolo," MMA *Bulletin*, n.s. III (1945), 185, 188; Cesare Brandi, *Giovanni di Paolo* (Florence, 1947), pp. 24, 73, n. 36, 120 (dates it 1436–1440); Brandi, *Quattrocentisti senesi* (Milan, 1951), p. 260, n. to pl. 134 (dates it ca. 1445); *Handbook* (1958), no. 393; *Handbook* (1966), p. 59; Berenson, *Pictures Renaiss., Central and North Italian Schools*, I (1968), 176; Hendrik W. van Os, *Sienese Paintings in Holland* (exh. cat.; Groningen, Museum voor Stad en Lande; Utrecht, Aartsbisschoppelijk Museum, 1969), mentioned in cat. no. 11 by Marjan Reinders in relation to a version by the School of Giovanni di Paolo in the Rijksmuseum Kröller–Müller, Otterlo, inv. no. 607-17.

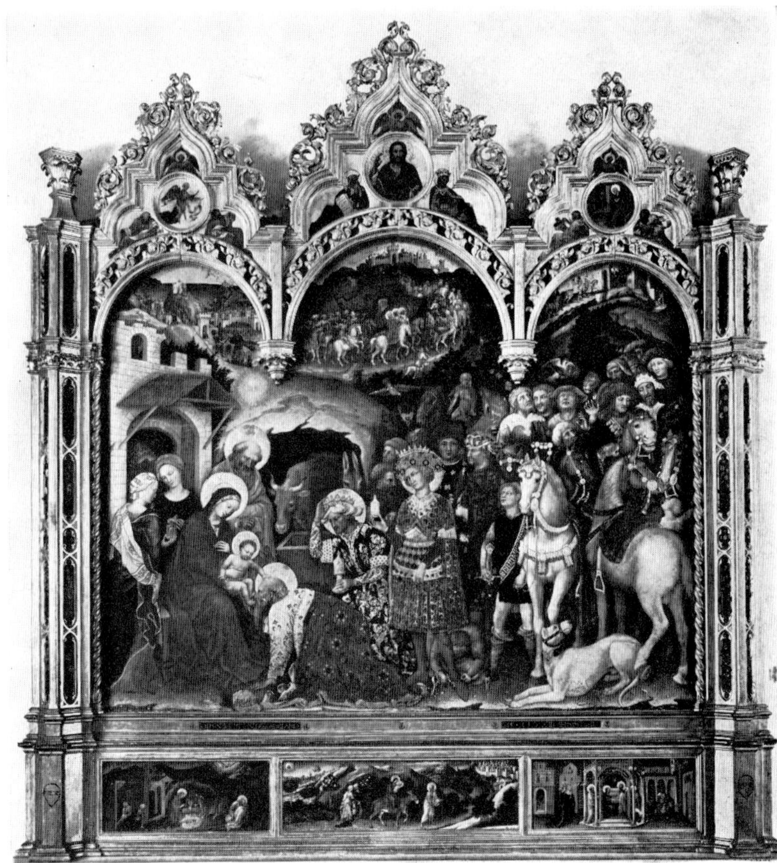

Figure 37*b*.
Adoration of the Magi.
300 × 282 cm (118⅛ × 111 inches).
Gentile da Fabriano, ca. 1370–1427.
Uffizi, Florence.

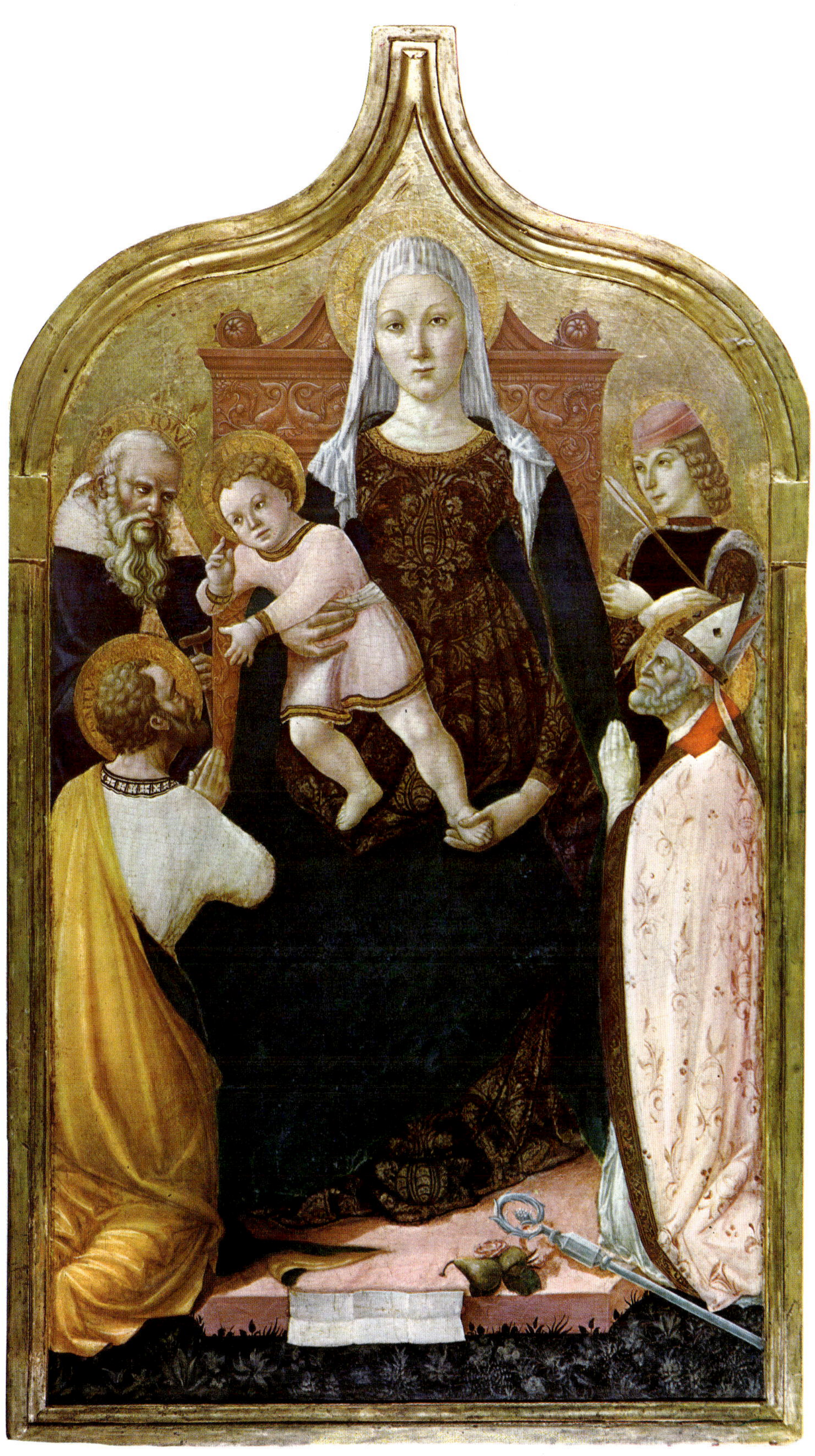

Plate XVII. *Madonna and Child with St. Anthony Abbot, St. Sebastian, St. Mark, and St. Severino,* Lorenzo d'Alessandro da Sanseverino (Painting 32).

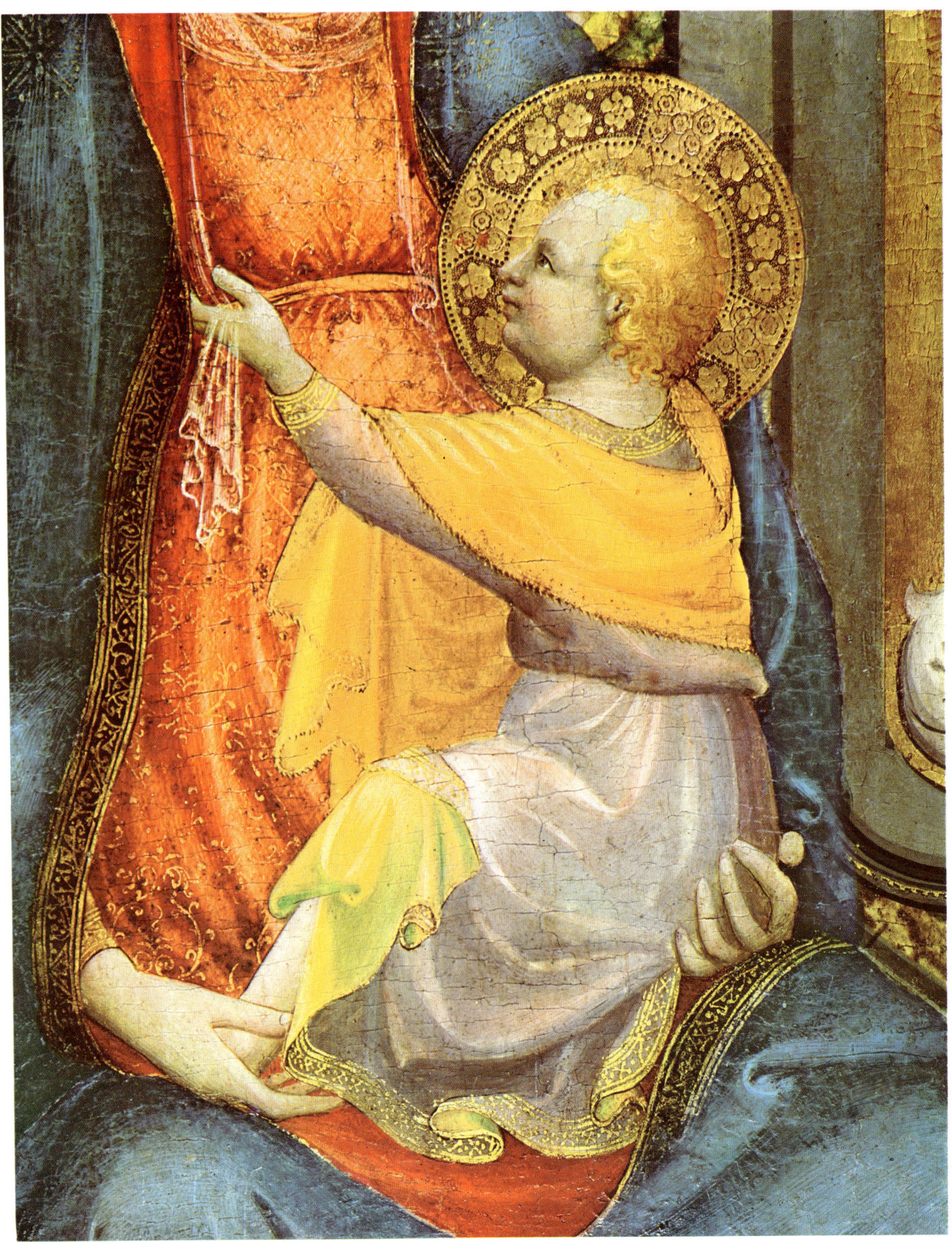

Plate XVIII. *Madonna and Child Enthroned*, Master of 1419 (detail of Painting 33).

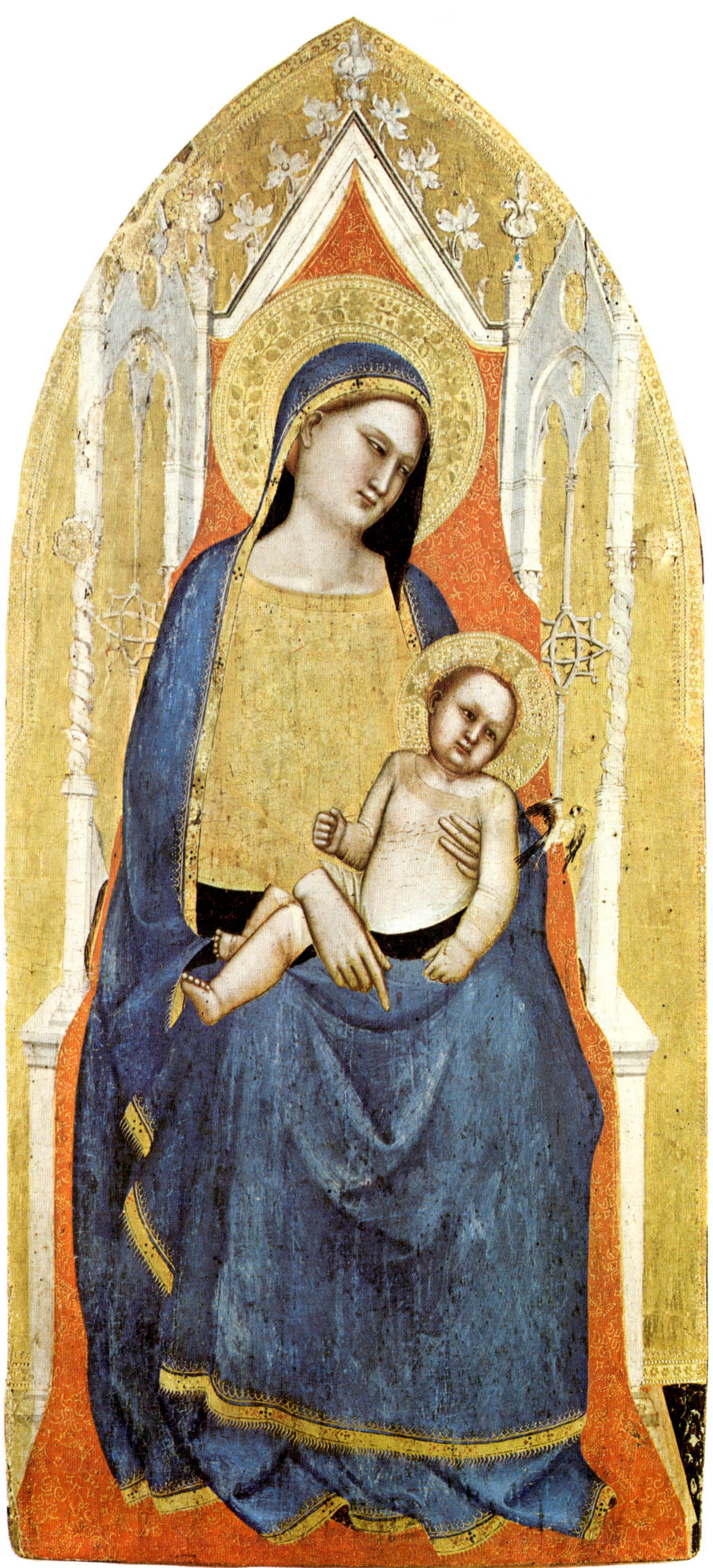

Plate XIX. *Madonna and Child Enthroned*, attributed to the Master of the San Lucchese Altarpiece (Painting 34).

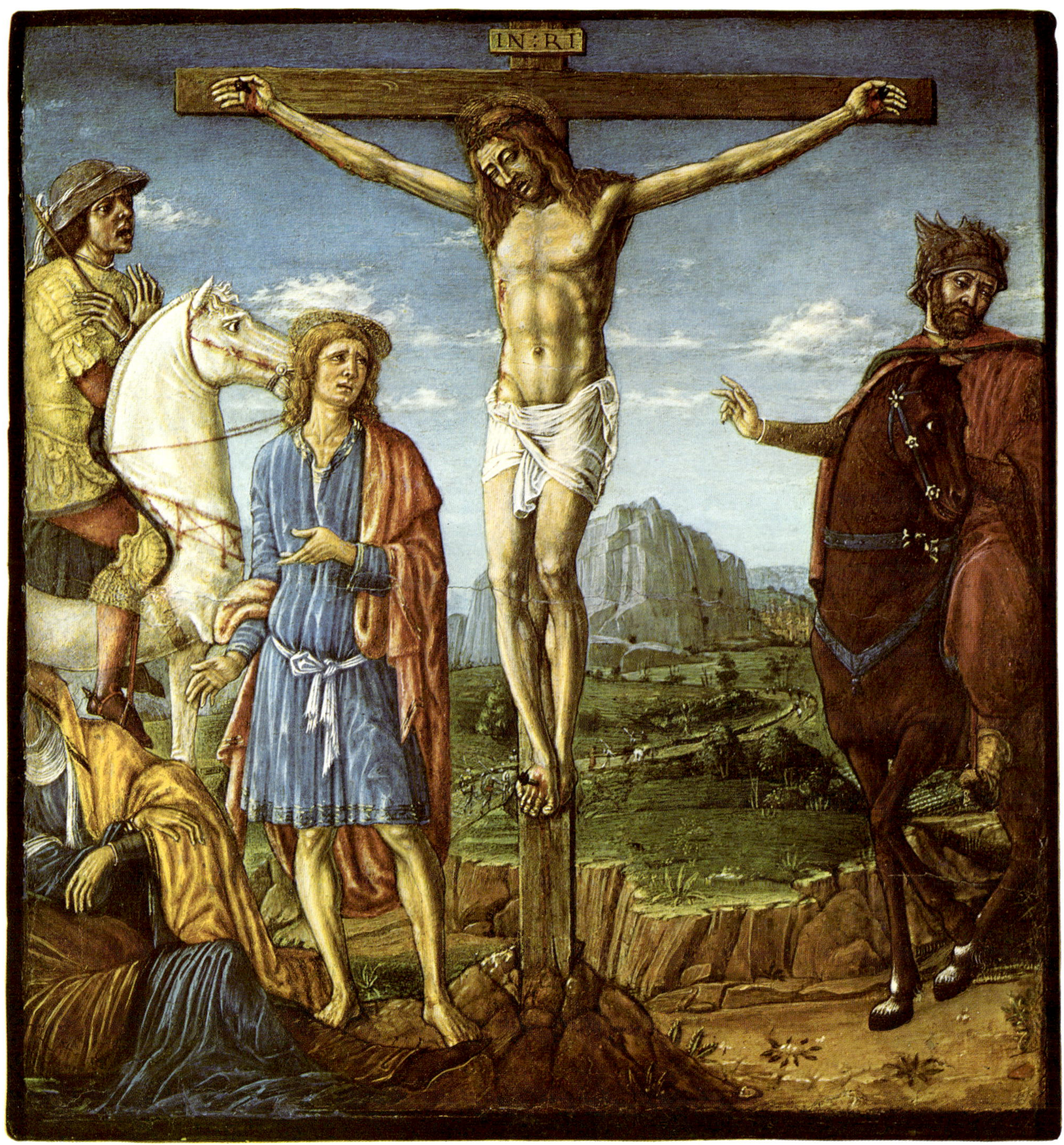

Plate xx. *The Crucifixion*, Matteo di Giovanni di Bartolo (Painting 35).

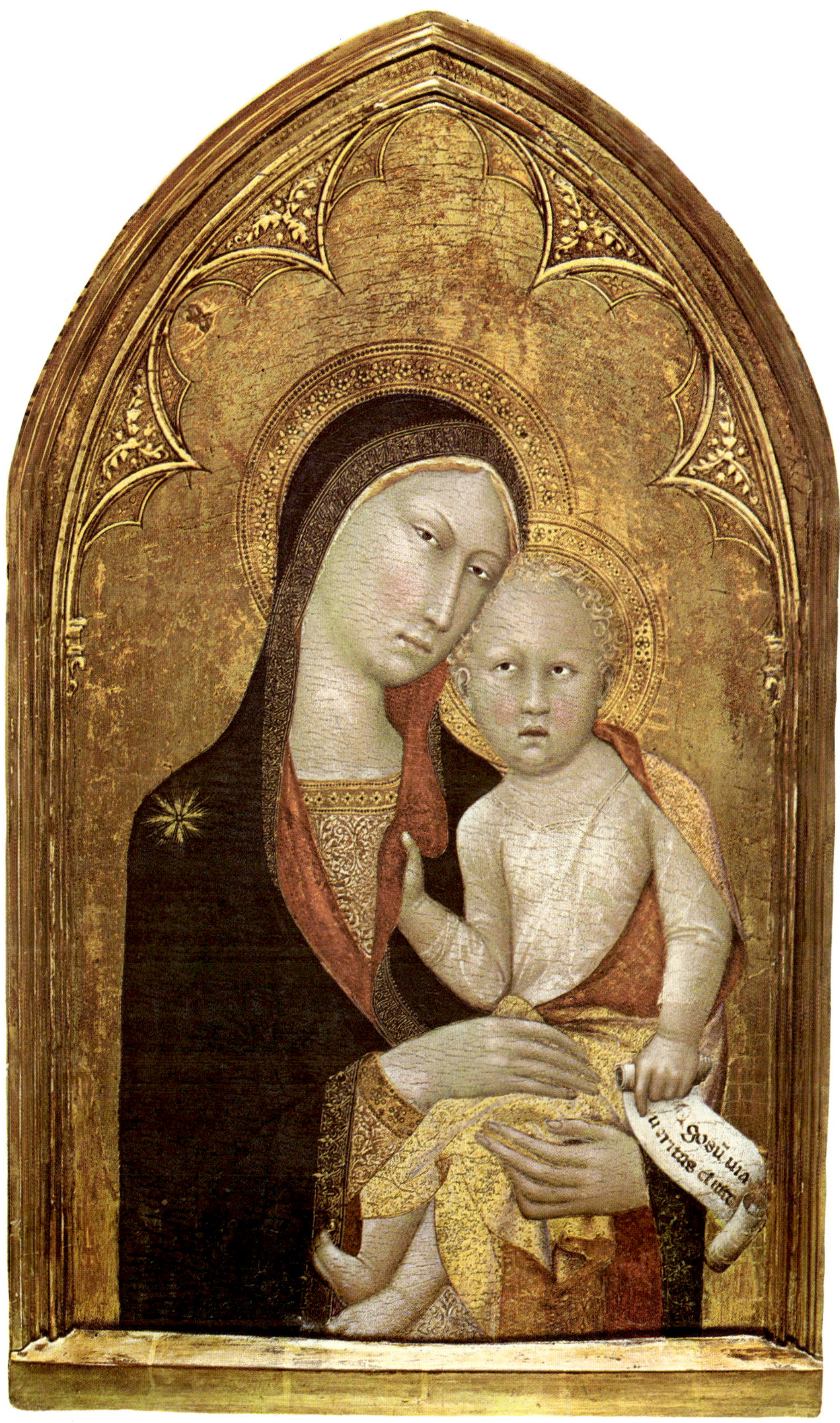

Plate XXI. *Madonna and Child*, School of Lippo Memmi (Painting 36).

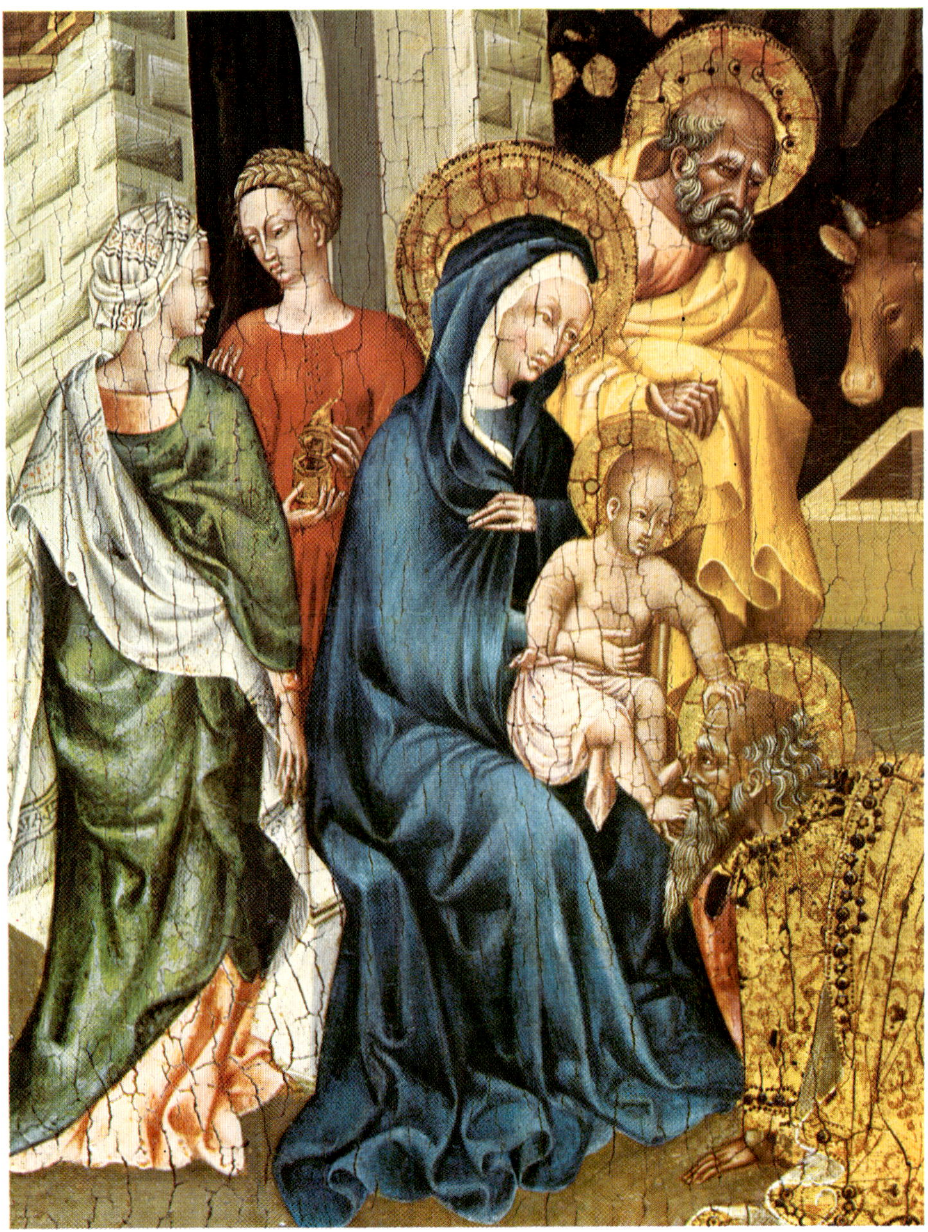

Plate XXII. *Adoration of the Magi*, Giovanni di Paolo (detail of Painting 37).

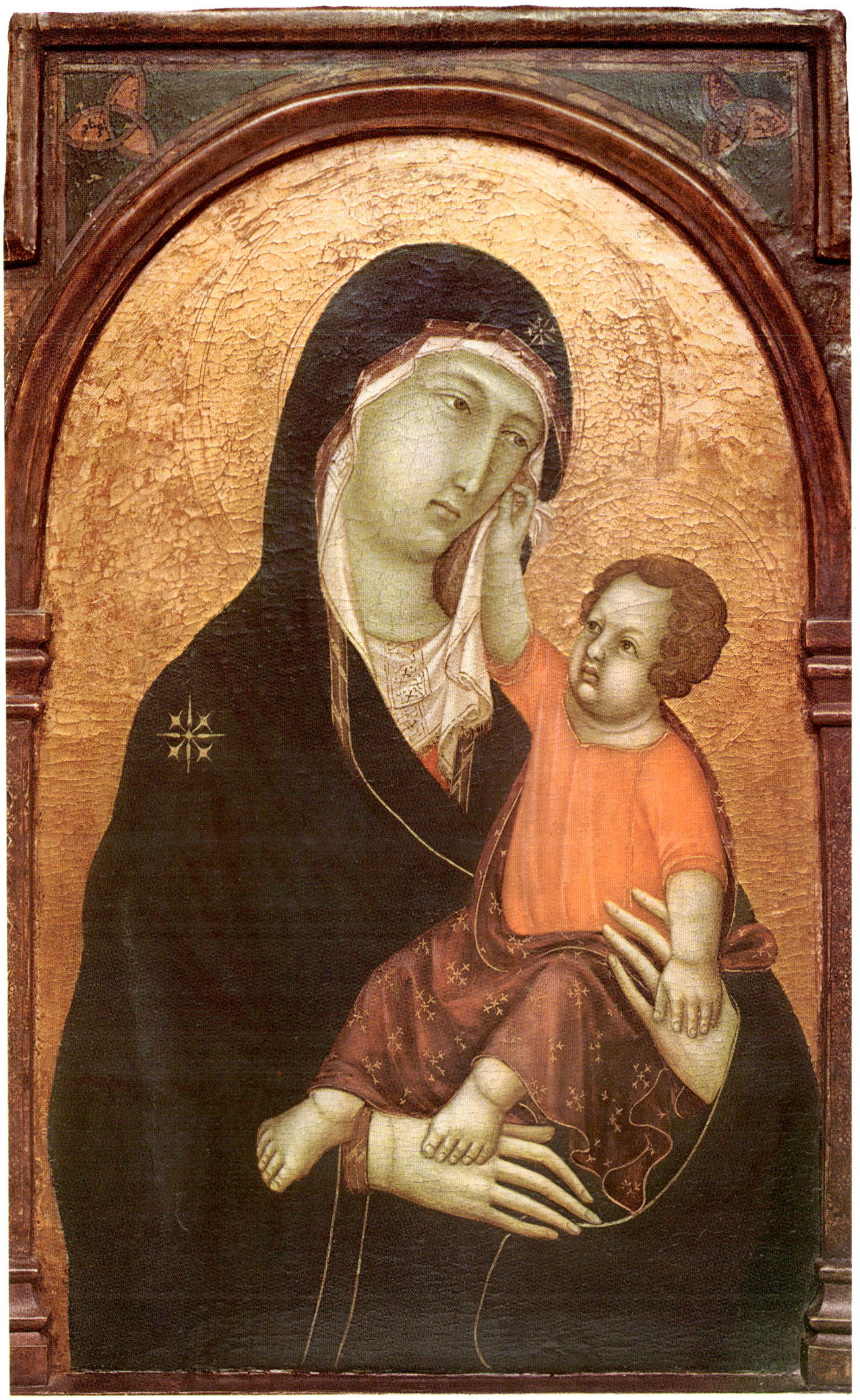

Plate XXIII. *Madonna and Child with St. Francis, St. John the Baptist, St. James the Great, and Mary Magdalen,* Ugolino di Nerio da Siena (center panel of Painting 46).

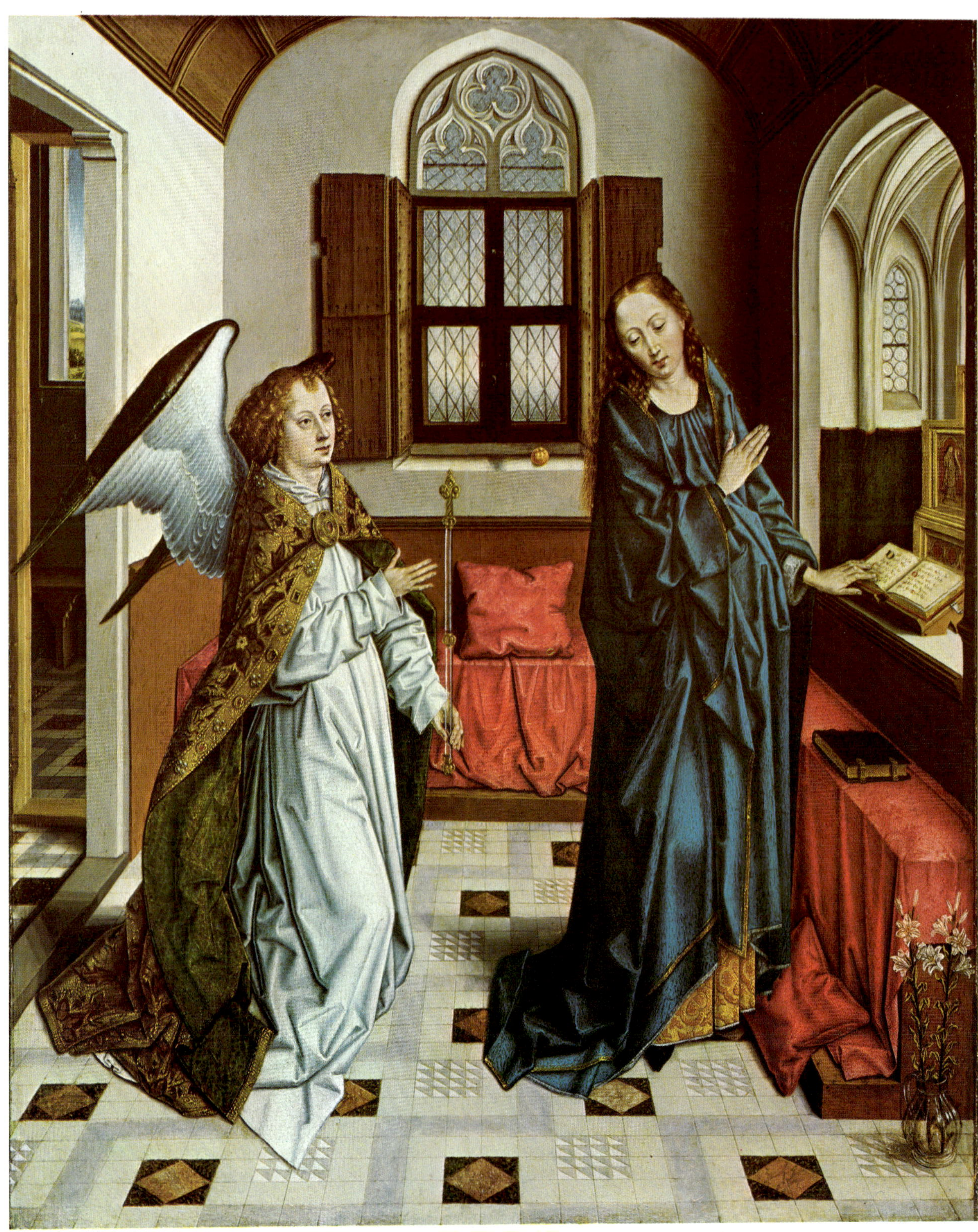

Plate XXIV. *The Annunciation*, Aelbrecht Bouts (Painting 50).

GIOVANNI DI PAOLO

38 A   *St. Catherine of Siena Invested*   66.2
        with the Dominican Habit

38 B   *St. Catherine of Siena and the Beggar*   66.3

Panels, Painting 38 A: 28·9 × 23 cm (11$\frac{3}{8}$ × 9$\frac{1}{16}$ inches).
Painting 38 B: 28·7 × 28·9 cm (11$\frac{5}{16}$ × 11$\frac{3}{8}$ inches).
PROVENANCE: The Church of the Hospital of S. Maria
della Scala, Siena; Altar of S. Christina in the cemetery
(Camposanto) of the Hospital; in the late eighteenth
century the panels were dismantled and hung in various
rooms of the Hospital proper (Carli, 1800–1810).
COLLECTIONS: Johann Anton Ramboux (sale: Cologne,
May 23, 1867, nos. 113, 115 with ten other parts of the
same altarpiece); Adolphe Stoclet, Brussels (with four
other episodes from the same series of the life of St.
Catherine); (Rudolf J. Heinemann).
Gift of the John Huntington Art and Polytechnic Trust,
1966.

Both panels are in good condition. The original panels
were thinned down, mounted on plywood and restored
ca. 1930. They were retransferred by William Suhr in
1965. Painting 38 A had losses around the four sides
of the panel, especially in the gilding of the background. Painting 38 B has two horizontal cracks above
the head of the standing St. Catherine and some losses
in the lower part of the kneeling Saint's robe. There is a
horizontal loss across the bottom edge of the panel.
Losses in both were gessoed and retouched with a yab
medium.

The Cleveland panels are two of the ten predella
panels depicting scenes from the life of St. Catherine of
Siena which belonged to Giovanni di Paolo's *Pizzicaiuoli* altarpiece, so-called because it was first commissioned by the guild of the *Pizzicaiuoli* [Pork-butchers]
in 1447 for their newly constructed chapel in the church
of the hospital of S. Maria della Scala. The central panel
of the altarpiece is the *Presentation in the Temple* (Siena,
Pinacoteca, no. 211) referred to in the documents as the
Purification of the Virgin Mary. The commission for the
altarpiece stipulated that it consist of the *Purification* with
figures and narrative scenes all to be completed by November 1449 (Bacci, 1944). Bossio in 1575 refers to its
predella (Brandi, 1933). This included, besides the two
Cleveland pictures, two panels in the Lehman collection,
New York; one in the Metropolitan Museum of Art
(Wehle, 1940, p. 89); one in the Detroit Institute of
Arts (Fig. 38 a); one (until 1957) in the Minneapolis
Institute of Art; one in the Museum Thyssen Borne-

misza, Lugano (Fig. 38 b); and two in a private collection in New York (Figs. 38 c, d). A wider panel, *The
Crucifixion* (Utrecht, Archiepiscopal Museum, 16 A) was
in the center of the predella. These panels are all the
same height but the St. Catherine episodes vary somewhat in width, five of them being square and the other
five slightly narrower. There were also three oblong
figures on each of the two pilasters flanking the main
panel, two of which are in the Archiepiscopal Museum,
Utrecht (nos. 564, 565), two in the Lehman collection,
New York, and two others which are recorded (Carli,
1800–1810) but whose whereabouts are unknown. All
known parts of the altarpiece except the *Presentation*
and the *Stigmatization of St. Catherine* (Lehman, New
York, acquired by William Wetmore Story in Rome
after 1849) were together in the Ramboux collection
where the St. Catherine scenes were attributed to Giovanni di Paolo but the others to Paolo di Neri and Sassetta. In the Ramboux catalogue it is stated that the nine
St. Catherine panels came from the Hospital of S. Maria
della Scala where they had formed the predella to the
Presentation (Ramboux, 1862; Pope-Hennessy, 1937, p.
131). Their association with the *Presentation* was once
doubted (Pope-Hennessy, 1937; Salinger 1942) but Carli's description of the various parts of the altarpiece
published by Brandi (1941, pp. 320–321) has since been
generally accepted as evidence that the association is indeed valid. Brandi's (see Fig. 38 e) reconstruction of the
altarpiece in which six of the St. Catherine panels flank
the central panel (the rest are in the predella) would have
been convincing had not the *Stigmatization* which he assumed to be of square shape turned out to be one of the
narrower panels. Coor suggested (1959, p. 85, n. 21) that
all the St. Catherine panels formed a one-zone predella
with the *Crucifixion* in the center and the first and last
panels projecting at the sides as in Taddeo di Bartoldo's
altarpiece in the cathedral of Montepulciano (1401) and
Fra Angelico's high altar for S. Marco. However, the
length of such an arrangement in proportion to the central panel (*The Presentation*) is greater than in the two
examples she cites. Coor also proposed that the narrative
scenes must follow the chronological sequence of episodes in the Blessed Raimondo of Capua's *Life of St.
Catherine* (ca. 1380). However, in her suggested sequence, no. 6 near the middle of the predella is *St. Catherine's Prayer for the Recovery of her Mother* (28 × 22·2 cm,
Lehman collection, New York). Its dexter edge (thick-
ness ca. 1$\frac{5}{8}$ inches) shows traces of a painted scene and its
sinister edge having originally been gilded would indi-

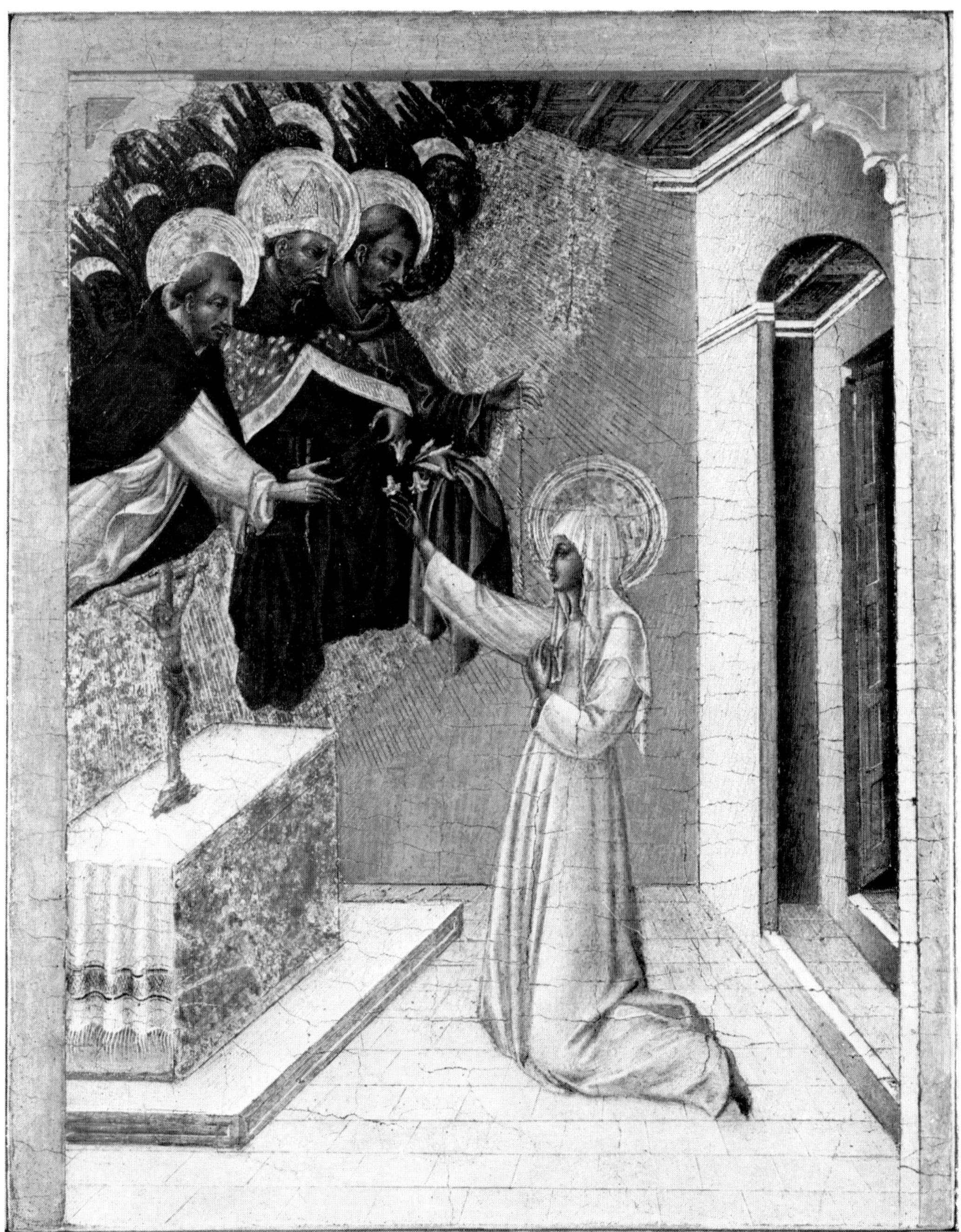

Figure 38 A.

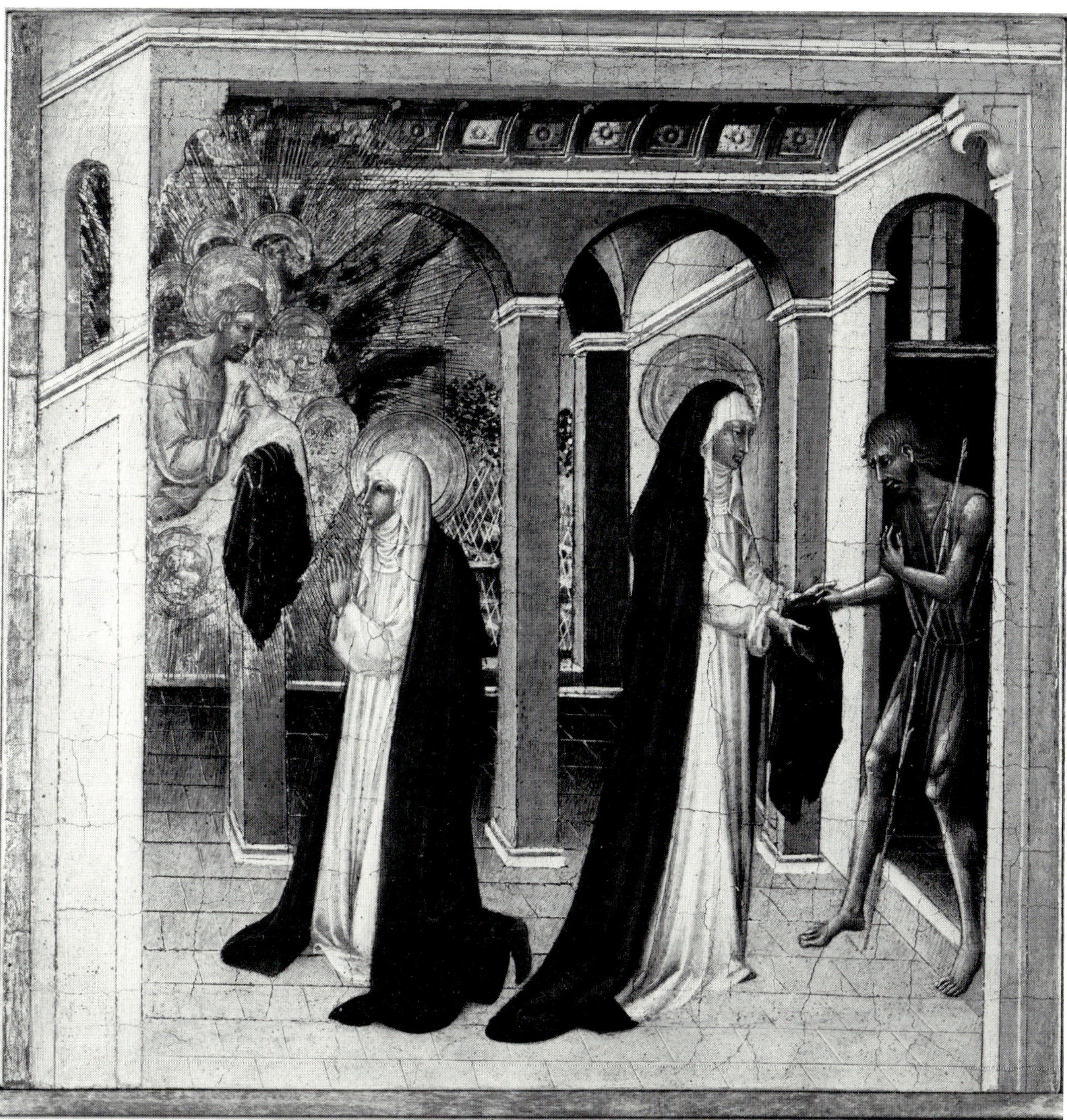

Figure 38 B.

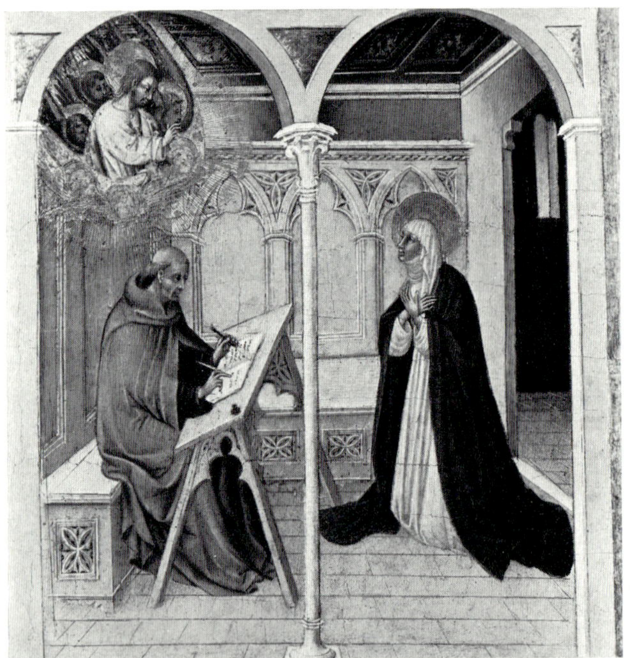

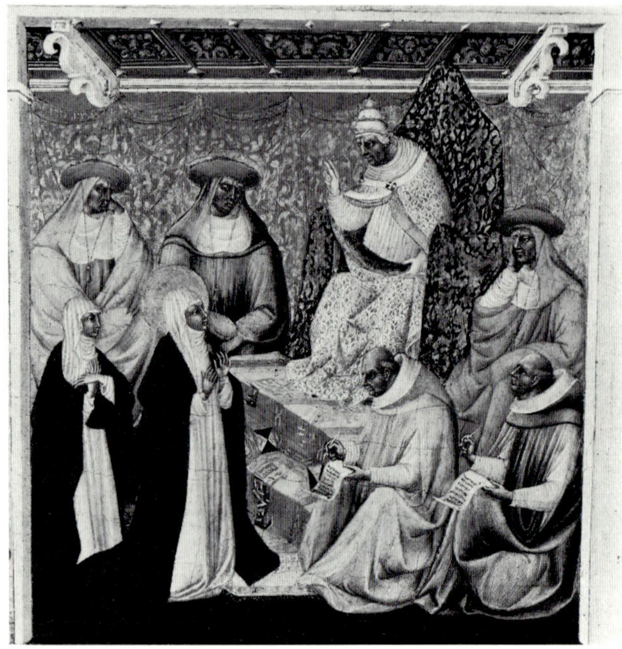

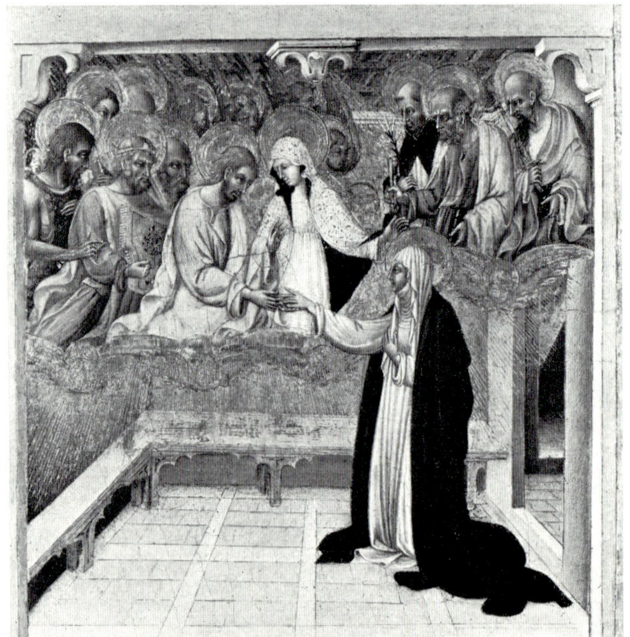

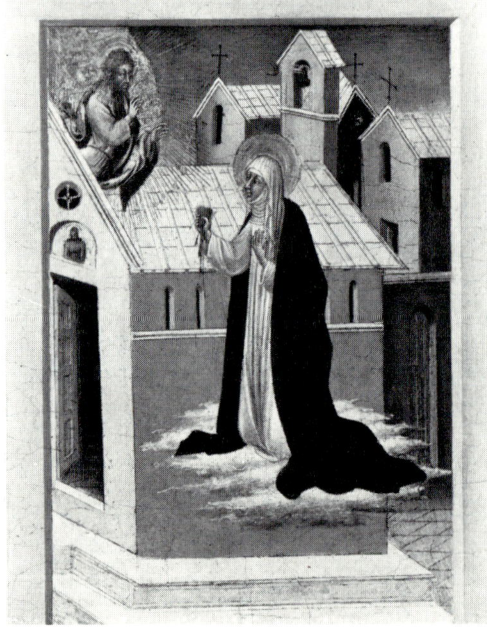

Figure 38 *a. St. Catherine of Siena Dictating the Dialogues.* 28·9 × 28·9 cm (11⅜ × 11⅜ inches). Giovanni di Paolo. Detroit Institute of Arts, 66.15.

Figure 38 *c. Mystic Marriage of St. Catherine.* 28·9 × 28·9 cm (11⅜ × 11⅜ inches). Giovanni di Paolo. Dr. and Mrs. Rudolf Heinemann, New York.

Figure 38 *b. St. Catherine before Pope Gregory XI.* 28·9 × 28·9 cm (11⅜ × 11⅜ inches). Giovanni di Paolo. Museum Thyssen-Bornemisza, Lugano.

Figure 38 *d. St. Catherine Gives Her Heart to Christ.* 28·9 × 22·6 cm (11⅜ × 8⅞ inches). Giovanni di Paolo. Dr. and Mrs. Rudolf Heinemann, New York.

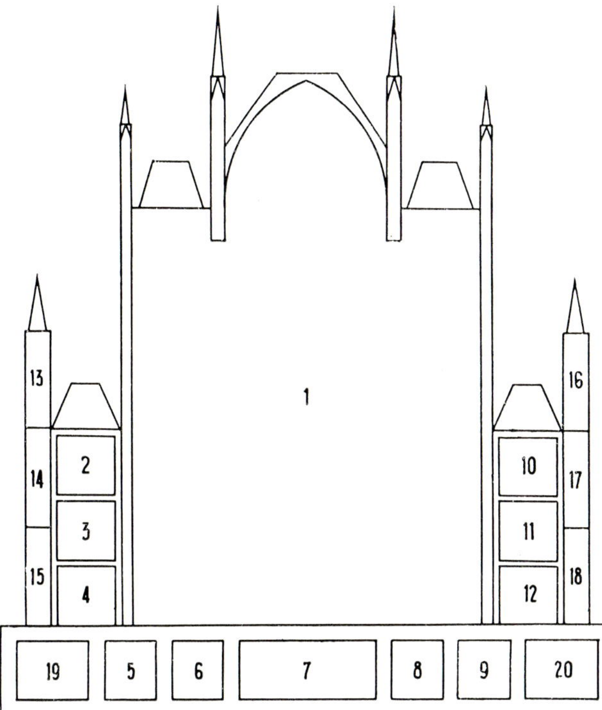

Figure 38*e*. Cesare Brandi's reconstruction of the *Pizzicaiuoli* Altar in S. Maria della Scala, Siena. (Courtesy of Casa Editrice, Felice le Monnier, Florence.)

1. *Presentation in the Temple*, Pinacoteca, Siena.

2. *St. Catherine of Siena and the Beggar*, Cleveland Museum of Art.

3. *Mystic Marriage of St. Catherine*, Heinemann collection, New York.

4. *St. Catherine Receiving the Stigmata* (lost).

5. *St. Catherine of Siena Invested with the Dominican Habit*, Cleveland Museum of Art.

6. *St. Catherine Gives Her Heart to Christ*, Heinemann collection.

7. *Crucifixion*, Archiepiscopal Museum, Utrecht.

8. *St. Catherine's Prayer for the Recovery of her Mother*, Lehman collection, New York.

9. *The Miraculous Communion of St. Catherine of Siena*, Metropolitan Museum of Art.

10. *St Catherine before Pope Gregory XI*, Museum Thyssen-Bornemisza, Lugano.

11. *St. Catherine of Sinea Dictating the Dialogues*, Detroit Institute of Arts.

12. *Death of St. Catherine* (formerly Minneapolis Institute of Art).

13. *St. Galgano* (lost).

14. *St. Catherine* (lost).

15. *Blessed Ambrogio Sansedoni*, Lehman collection.

16. *St. Martire* (lost).

17. *St. Bernardino* (lost).

18. *Blessed Andrea Gallerani*, Lehman collection.

19 and 20. Coats of arms of the Università and Guild of the *Pizzicaiuoli* and of the Hospital of S. Maria della Scala.

cate that this panel may have "projected beyond the setting of its neighboring panels," and perhaps adorned the base of a pilaster enframing the altarpiece (Salinger, 1942, p. 28) with the gilded edge possibly forming part of the outside edge. While a two-zone predella arrangement is conceivable – in which case the Lehman *Prayer* might have adorned a pilaster base (see Fernandez-Gimenez, 1967, fig. 7) – Zeri (unpublished manuscript for forthcoming MMA catalogue) concluded that eight of the St. Catherine panels formed the front of the predella (with the *Crucifixion*), the remaining two panels "decorating the sides of the predella itself along its thickness," with the Lehman panel "placed at the right end of the front of the predella." However, he feels the reconstruction of the main portions of the altarpiece remains problematic and he does not exclude the possibility of lost panels on either side of the *Presentation*. Van Os (1971) offers another reconstruction which puts the *Crucifixion* with the other ten panels flanking it across the bottom of the altarpiece. He proposes that the space needed to accommodate this arrangement is gained by placing two full-length figures of saints (one of them St. Catherine herself) on either side of the central *Presentation*.

Carli's dating of the altarpiece as a whole is (by implication of his text) ca. 1445–1450 and he associated the main panel with the style of Giovanni di Paolo by comparing it with the latter's *Coronation of the Virgin* in S. Andrea, dated 1445; but his equivocal comments on the style of the various parts are interesting in view of the subsequent controversy about their dating. Pope-Hennessy believes that the style of the St. Catherine panels is later than that of the central panel and that they were added to the altarpiece soon after 1461, the year of St. Catherine's canonization since she appears with the halo of a saint. Douglas (1938) and Brandi believe the St. Catherine panels to be earlier than 1461; Brandi (1941, 1947, 1951) argues for the iconographical probability of depicting Catherine of Siena with a saint's halo as early as 1447–1449, and believes these predella panels to be contemporary with the rest of the altarpiece, especially since the commission stipulated figures and narrative scenes. According to Kaftal (1952, pp. xxix–xxxii, who accepts Pope-Hennessy's dating for the panels), there was no consistent distinction in the representation of the saints from the blessed by their haloes (or otherwise) in the fifteenth century.

In the first panel St. Catherine receives from St. Dominic the habit of the order which she chose to join when the founders of three orders appeared to her in a vision (see Raymondus of Capua's *Life of St. Catherine* in Joannes Bollandus, *Acta Sanctorum*, Paris, 1866, Aprilis III, p. 875, no. 53). These have been identified as St. Dominic and St. Francis with (variously): St. Benedict (Kaftal, 1952, col. 236, 1); St. Augustine (Pope-Hennessy, 1937, p. 130), or St. Bonaventura (Mariano and Russoli, *Catalogue of the Berenson Collection*, Milan, 1962, pl. LII). In the second panel St. Catherine gives her cloak to a beggar, whereupon Christ appears to her carrying it and gives her instead an invisible coat which forever after protects her from the cold (see Bollandus, *op. cit.*, p. 896, nos. 135–138; Kaftal, 1952, col. 241, nos. 4, 5).

E.F.G.

EXHIBITIONS: CMA (1966), cat. no. 60, illus. (color).

LITERATURE: G. C. Carli, *Notizie de belle arti* (MS. of about 1800–1810 in the Biblioteca Comunale of Siena, cc. vii–20), pp. 86 ff.; Johann Anton Ramboux, *Katalog der Gemälde alter italienischer Meister (1221–1640) in der Sammlung des Conservators J. A. Ramboux* (Cologne, 1862), nos. 113, 115; Gaetano Milanesi, *Documenti per la storia dell'arte senese*, II (Siena, 1854), 241–242; Crowe and Cavalcaselle, *A New History...*, III (1866), 80, n. 6 (Giovanni's panels in the Ramboux collection, nos. 113–121, 123, 129); Berenson, *Pictures Renaiss.* (1932), p. 245; Cesare Brandi, *La Reggia Pinacoteca di Siena* (Rome, 1933), p. 96 (presentation and text from Bossio); John Pope-Hennessy, *Giovanni di Paolo* (London, 1937), pp. 130–135; R. Langton Douglas, Review of *Giovanni di Paolo*, by John Pope-Hennessy, *Burl. Mag.*, LXXII (1938), 43; Pope-Hennessy, "Letter: Giovanni di Paolo," *Burl. Mag.*, LXXII (1938), 95; Harry B. Wehle, *A Catalogue of Italian, Spanish and Byzantine Paintings* (New York, MMA, 1940), pp. 88–89; Brandi, "Giovanni di Paolo – II," *Le Arti*, II, fasc. V (1941), pl. CXXI, fig. 29, pl. CXXII, fig. 31, reconstruction, p. 323; Margaretta Salinger, "A New Panel in Giovanni di Paolo's St. Catherine Series," *MMA Bulletin*, n.s., I (1942), 26; Peleo Bacci, *Documenti i commenti per la storia dell'arte* (Florence, 1944), pp. 77–78; Brandi, *Giovanni di Paolo* (Florence, 1947), pp. 36–43; Pope-Hennessy, Review of *Giovanni di Paolo*, by Cesare Brandi, *Burl. Mag.*, LXXXIX (1947), 138–140 (suggests analysis...in the St. Catherine cycle of motifs from French miniature illumination); Brandi and Pope-Hennessy, "Letters: Giovanni di Paolo," *Burl. Mag.*, LXXXIX (1947), 196; George Kaftal, *St. Catherine in Tuscan Painting* (Oxford, 1949), pp. 36–37, figs. VIII, XV; Brandi, *Quattrocentisti senesi* (Milan, 1951), pp. 99–100, 201–206, n. 67, pls. 138, 143; Kaftal, *The Iconography of the Saints in Tuscan Painting* (Florence, 1952), col. 238, fig. 261 (dates them ca. 1463); Enzo Carli, *La Pittura senese* (Milan, 1955), p. 224 (says *Presentation* was originally surrounded by scenes from the life of St. Catherine); Gertrude Coor, "Quattrocento Gemälde aus der Sammlung Ramboux," *Wallraf-Richartz-Jahrbuch*, XXI (1959), 82–85; Coor, *Neroccio de' Landi* (Princeton, 1961), p. 23 (Painting 38A is the source for Neroccio's version of ca. 1468–1470, Berenson collection); *Handbook* (1966), p. 59; *Selected Works* (1966), p. 113; Elizabeth de Fernandez-Gimenez, "The Life of St. Catherine of Siena," *CMA Bulletin*, LIV (1967), 103–110, illus. pp. 104, 120 (color); Hendrik W. van Os, "Giovanni di Paolo's Pizzicaiuolo Altarpiece," *Art Bulletin*, LIII (1971), 289, 292, 302, figs. 1, 3.

BERNARDO PARENTINO (Parenzano; da Parenzo[?]), Padua, born ca. 1434–1437, died 1531

He was born at Parenzo d'Istria and died at the Convento degli Eremiti Augustiniani in Vicenza, where his epitaph calls him Bernardinus Parentinus Eremita Candidus. There are several authenticated works, including a signed *Christ between SS. Jerome and Augustine* in the Galleria Estense, Modena (no. 12), and frescoes of scenes from the life of St. Benedict (fragments of which survive) in the Cloisters of S. Giustina, Padua, which are recorded as having been signed and dated 1489–1494. Documents from the archives of this monastery confirm that the painter Bernardino, formerly called Master Johannis [Giovanni] of Parenzo, was in Venice for a time, became a resident of Padua, and worked for the monastery (Wazbinski, 1966, p. 10). He has been mistakenly referred to as Lorenzo (*Der Anonimo Morelliano*, Theodor Frimmel, Vienna, 1896, p. 12) which has caused some confusion among art historians. Tradition has it that Bernardo was also a writer of repute (Wazbinski, p. 10, n. 5). Some elements in his style suggest that he may have been trained as a miniaturist. The influence from Mantegna's contact with Venice, from Domenico Morone and the Veronese school, and the Ferrarese, are evident in his paintings to a degree that has resulted in some shifting attributions. According to Rutteri (1960–1961, p. 110) it is the older Parentino who probably influenced Morone.

39 *Procession of the Magi from Jerusalem* 16.790

Cassone panel

Panel (poplar), 47·3 × 53·7 cm (18⅝ × 21⅛ inches).
COLLECTIONS: James Jackson Jarves; Mrs. Liberty E. Holden, Cleveland, 1884.
Holden Collection, 1916.

Removal of very dark varnish in 1949 revealed the relatively good condition of the paint film, despite the worm-eaten and slightly warped state of the panel. Photographs show clearly the irregular additions at the top and sides of the painting which were revealed during cleaning. The upper corners and the losses at both sides were blended in and attenuated in dry color with damar varnish by Suhr. The back of the panel has an **L**-shaped groove in the upper right and indications of a tenon joint in a ¾-inch strip at the lower edge. What appears to be the remnant of a metal fastening is discernible in the top center.

M. L. Berenson (1907) was the first to ascribe to Parentino this painting which had formerly been attributed to Squarcione. Her attribution has been accepted in subsequent publications.

The irregularities at the top and sides of the panel suggest that the front of the cassone which it ornamented was decorated in pastille in a manner identical with a cassone front (Fig. 39 *a*) which is close in style to this panel (sale: American Art Association, New York, part II, April 16, 1926, no. 38, as Parentino). This type was common in Verona in the latter part of the fifteenth century. (For another example see the fragment reproduced in Schubring, *Cassone*, II, pl. CXLV, fig. 667 as circle of Domenico Morone.) According to Zeri (letter of March 8, 1966) the Cleveland and ex-Chiesa panels were

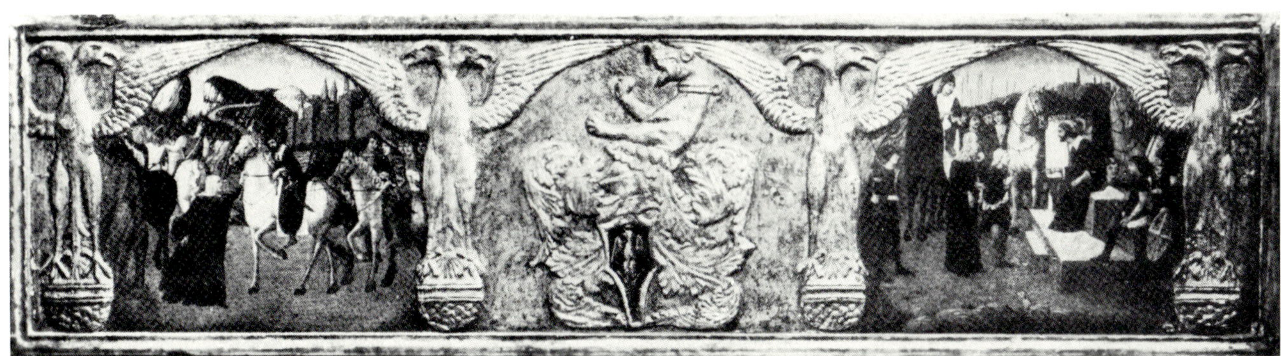

Figure 39 *a*. *Two Scenes from the Story of the Emperor Trajan*. Cassone front. Parentino. Formerly Achillito Chiesa collection; present whereabouts unknown.

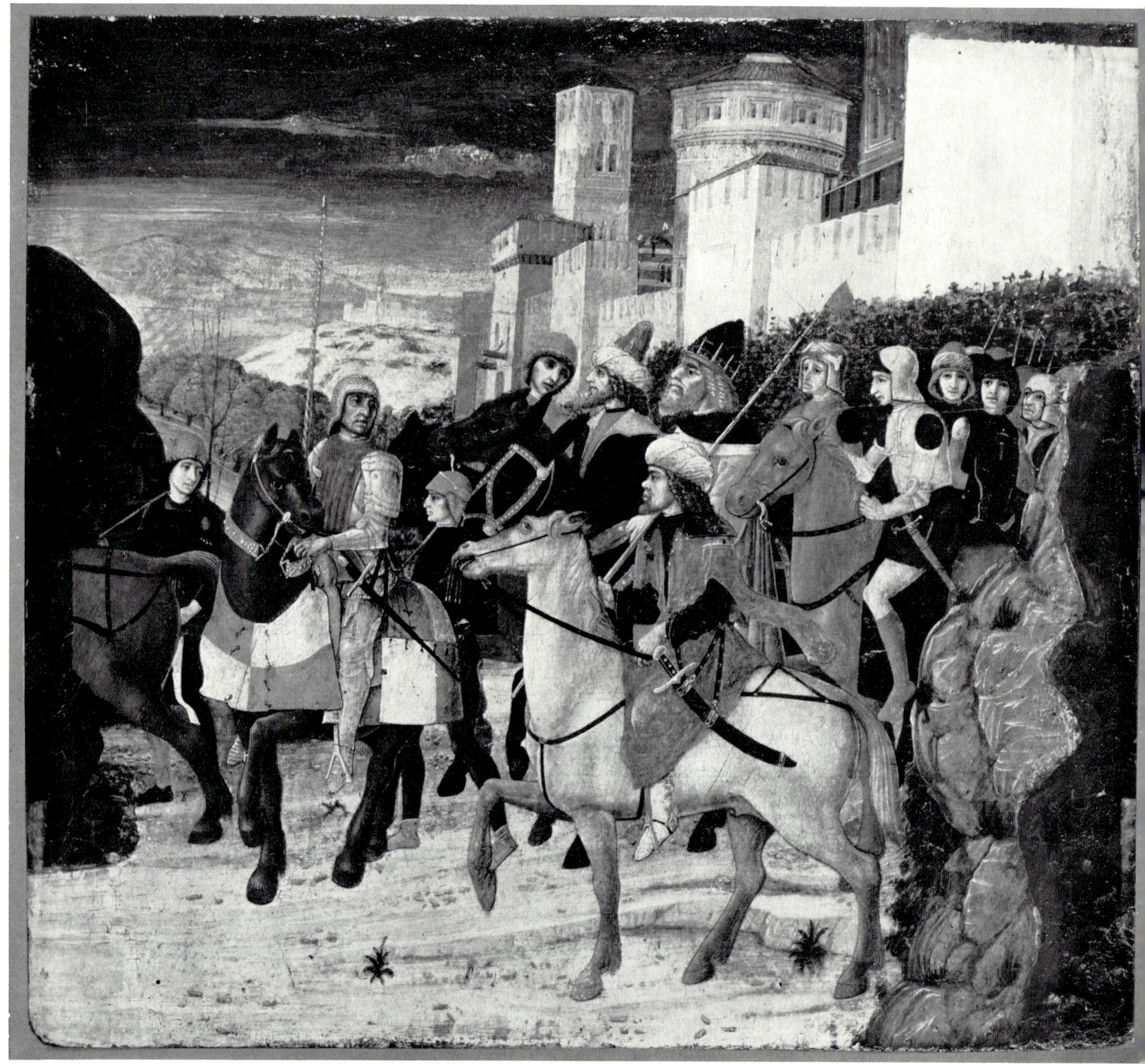

Figure 39.

112

apparently produced in the same circle and are Veronese, from the following of Domenico Morone, and have nothing in common with Parentino's particular style. It is true that the execution of our panel lacks Parentino's flickering touch and the complexity of his design, yet the Mantegnesque characteristics, with their suggestion of irony, are close in feeling to Parentino (cf., for example, the left-hand figure in his *Temptation of St. Anthony,* Wazbinski, 1966, pl. 35 with the foreground King in the Cleveland panel). Rutteri (1960–1961) finds that the figures in the CMA painting, which she considers an early work of Parentino, recall those in the *Battle Scene* in the Borromeo collection, Milan, which is generally attributed to Butinone. Without accepting the Borromeo panel as Parentino's, Wazbinski (1966) considers the Cleveland panel as probably by Parentino.

Formerly called *Darius Riding Out* (by Berenson) and *Procession from a Castle,* the subject of the Cleveland panel is clarified by comparison with the *Procession of the Magi* (Fig. 39*b*) in which a similarly attired group of Oriental personages, one of them riding a mule as in the Cleveland *Procession,* are depicted.

E.F.G.

EXHIBITIONS: Boston (1883), cat. no. 454; MMA (1912), cat. no. 21; CMA (1916), cat. no. 28; CMA (1936), cat. no. 100.
LITERATURE: Jarves (1884), no. 48 (as Squarcione); M. L. Berenson (1907), p. 3; Berenson, *North Italian Painters...* (1907), p. 277; A. Venturi, VII (1914), p. 290, no. 1; Rubinstein (1917), no. 29, pp. 29–30; Berenson, *Pictures Renaiss.* (1932), p. 429 (as *Darius Riding Out*); Maria Grazia Rutteri, "Contributo a Bernardo Parentino," *Acropoli,* I (1960–1961), 111–119; Zygmund Wazbinski, "Pour le premier portrait de Bernardo Parentino," *Saggi e memorie die storia dell'arte,* V (Florence, 1966), 19 (listed as probably by Parentino). Berenson, *Pictures Renaiss., Central and North Italian Schools,* I (1968), 318 (as Parentino).

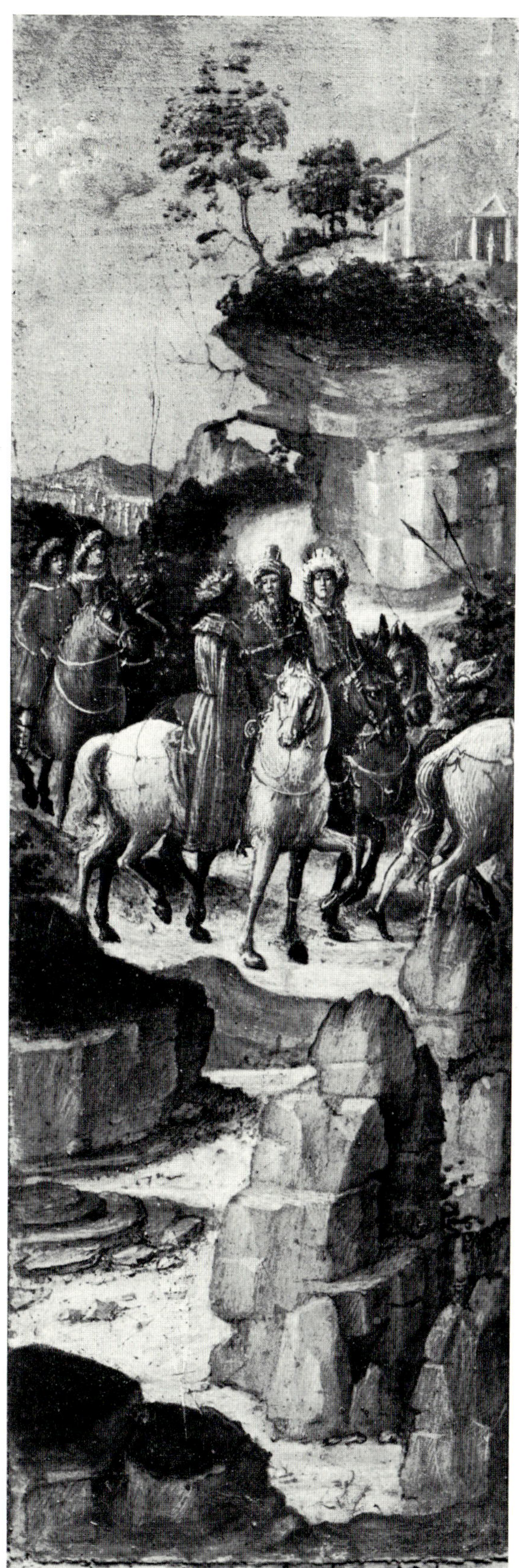

Figure 39*b*. *Procession of the Magi.*
32×10 cm ($12\frac{5}{8} \times 3\frac{15}{16}$ inches). Parentino.
Museo Civico, Vicenza, A. 187.

SANO DI PIETRO (Ansano di Pietro di Mencio), Siena, 1406–1481

Although enrolled in the painters' guild and recorded as assisting his supposed master Sassetta in 1428, no dated work by Sano is known before the polyptych of 1444 (Siena, Accademia, no. 246). Yet from that year until his death Sano's works are well documented. The lack of information about Sano's early career gave rise to the theory that the young Sano was identical with the Master of the Osservanza Triptych, a painter close to Sassetta first identified by Roberto Longhi ("Fatti di Masolino e di Masaccio," *Critica d'arte*, v, pt. 2, 1940, p. 188, n. 26) to whom was attributed the *Birth of the Virgin* (Asciano) and the Osservanza triptych of 1436 (both formerly ascribed to Sassetta). Enzo Carli (*Sassetta e il Maestro del Osservanza*, Milan, 1957) also attributes to him the *Legends of St. Anthony* which traditionally were given to Sassetta. The painter of these last panels is now generally thought to have been assisted by a second master whom Pope-Hennessy ("Rethinking Sassetta," *Burl. Mag.*, XCVIII, 1956, 364 ff.) called "Master B" and supposed him to be one Vico di Luca, but whom Carli (*op. cit.*) identified with Sano di Pietro, assisting the Master of Osservanza. The latter, if not identical with Sano, was at least largely responsible for his development. (For a résumé of the problem see Michel Laclotte, "Sassetta, le Maître de l'Observance, et Sano di Pietro. Un Probleme critique," *L'Information d'histoire de l'art*, v, 1960, 47 ff.) It is known that Sano was also in contact with Vecchietta and, in 1444 and subsequent years, with Giovanni di Paolo. Sano became an extremely prolific and popular painter of Madonnas and altarpieces. These later earned him a reputation for mediocrity which has seemed to some critics irreconcilable with a small number of superior works which they have therefore attributed to other painters (see Pope-Hennessy, 1939, Appendix A).

40 *Madonna and Child Adored by St. Mary Magdalen and St. Nicholas of Bari*   24.199

Panel (poplar), including original molding: $58 \times 27 \cdot 6$ cm ($22\frac{13}{16} \times 10\frac{7}{8}$ inches). Inside frame: $46 \cdot 2 \times 21 \cdot 5$ cm ($18\frac{3}{16} \times 8\frac{1}{2}$ inches).

COLLECTIONS: Federigo Ione, Siena (information from Federico Zeri, 1965); private collection, Florence; (Durlacher Bros., New York).

Gift of Mrs. B. P. Bole, Mr. and Mrs. Guerdon S. Holden, Mrs. Windsor T. White, and the Holden Fund, 1924.

The panel is in sound condition except for a split one inch left of center extending vertically up one-third of the panel. This was filled with wax by Suhr in 1951.

This painting is the central panel from a triptych. The tooling of haloes and borders is typical of Sano's workshop. Perkins (1925) who saw the panel in Florence in 1922 called it one of Sano's earliest works, influenced by Sassetta and comparable with the *Madonna of Humility*, S. Pietro (ex-church of S. Francesco) in Montalcino (Van Marle, 1927, p. 467, fig. 294). Van Marle and Salmi (1933) see in the Cleveland *Madonna* an early influence of Giovanni di Paolo. Pope-Hennessy (1939) mentions our panel in connection with the Montalcino and S. Severino (Pinacoteca no. 15) Madonnas which he accepts as by Sano di Pietro. Pico Cellini (orally, 1949) attributed the Cleveland *Madonna* to the Master of the Osservanza. Carli (letter of September 9, 1963) was undecided as to the authorship of the Cleveland panel (which he knew only from photographs) but tended to find in it a lively refinement uncharacteristic of the usually torpid Sano, and tentatively suggested that it could be a mature work (after 1436) of the Master of Osservanza momentarily influenced by Giovanni di Paolo. The Cleveland painting indeed has echoes of Giovanni di Paolo, as does Sano's *Crucifixion* of ca. 1447 (Fig. 40 a) with which the pinnacle of our panel is comparable (Fig. 40 b). Among other pictures usually attributed to Sano which would seem to argue for his authorship of this painting is *The Resurrection of Christ*, a fragment in the Wallraf-Richartz-Museum, Cologne (no. 729). Gertrude Coor ("Quattrocento-Gemälde aus der Sammlung Ramboux," *Wallraf-Richartz-Jahrbuch*, XXI, 1959, 80, fig. 30) called it Sano under the influence of the Osservanza Master in the 1440s. Carli ("A 'Resurrection' by the Master of the Osservanza," *Art Quarterly*, XXIII, 1960, 333 ff.) agreed and contrasted it with the similar subject in the Detroit Institute of Arts (60.61, cat. no. 1345) by

MADONNA AND CHILD ADORED BY SAINTS
SANO DI PIETRO
SIENESE SCHOOL, 1406-1481
GIFT OF MR. AND MRS. GUERDON S. HOLDEN,
MRS. B. P. BOLE AND MRS. WINDSOR T. WHITE
24.100

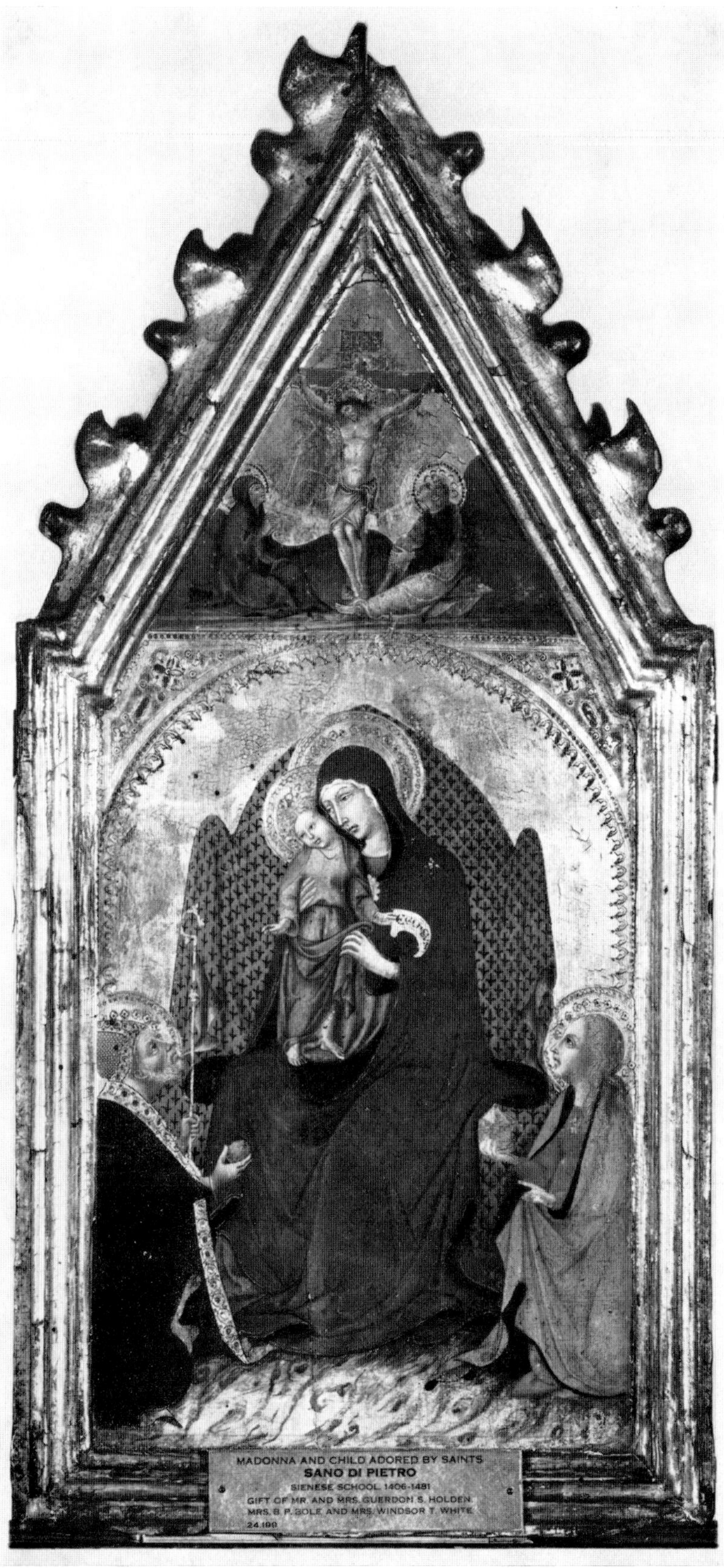

Figure 40.

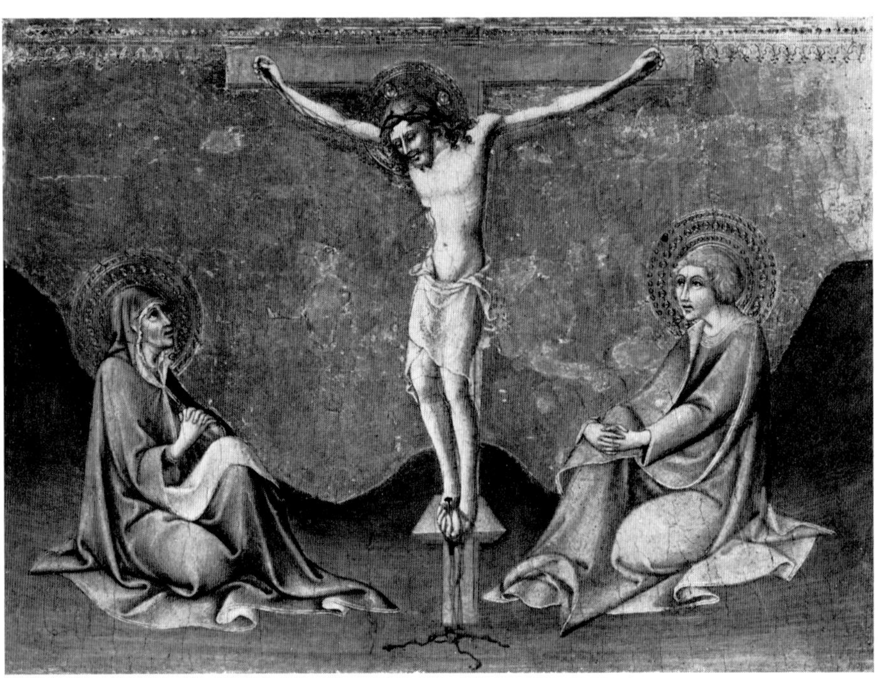

Figure 40 *a*. *The Crucifixion*. 23 × 33 cm ($9\frac{1}{4}$ × $12\frac{7}{8}$ inches). Sano di Pietro. National Gallery of Art, Washington, Samuel H. Kress Collection.

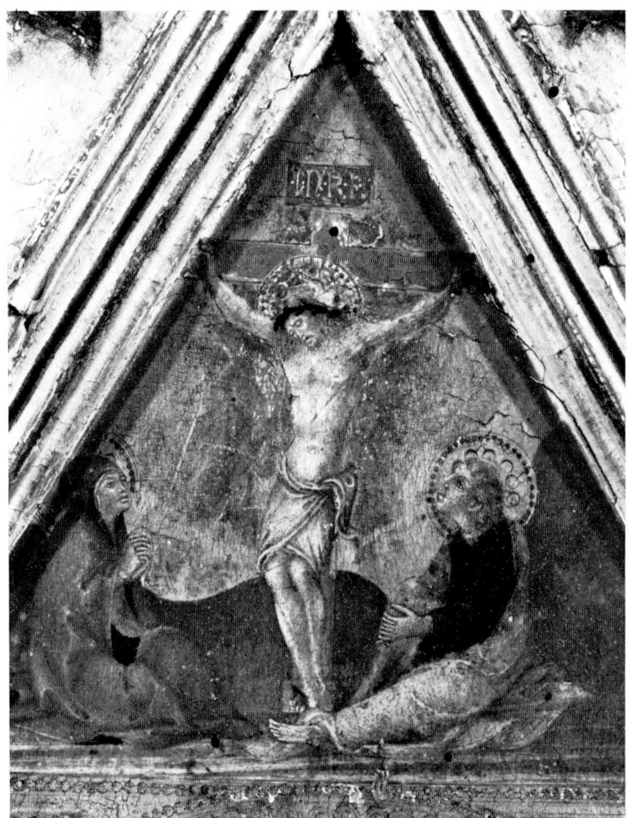

Figure 40 *b*. *Crucifixion*, pinnacle of Figure 40.

the Osservanza Master. The softer forms and tender sentiment which distinguish Sano's *Resurrection* from the more solid and classical figure in Detroit also distinguish the Cleveland *Madonna* from those attributed to the Osservanza Master. Since both the Cologne and Cleveland panels are rather exceptional for Sano, Pope-Hennessy attributed the Cologne *Resurrection* to his "Master 185," while the Cleveland *Madonna* was considered too subtle for Sano. However, the two panels are not only significantly comparable with each other, but with such authentic works as Sano's predella panels from the 1444 polyptych (cat. nos. 1128–1132, Louvre) and the predella panels of the *Life of the Virgin*, 1447–1451 (nos. 70 and 71, Altenburg, Lindenau Museum, and nos. 166 and 167, Vatican Museum).

E.F.G.

EXHIBITIONS: CMA (1936), cat. no. 101; CMA (1963), cat. no. 82.

LITERATURE: William M. Milliken, "A Sienese Painting by Sano di Pietro," CMA *Bulletin*, XI (1924), 75–77; F. Mason Perkins, "La Pittura alla mostra d'arte di Montalcino," *Rassegna d'arte senese*, XVIII (1925), pp. 65, 70, 71, n. 10; Van Marle, IX (1927), 469–470; Berenson, *Pictures Renaiss.* (1932), p. 498; Mario Salmi, "Dipinti senesi nella raccolta Chigi saracini," *La Diana*, VIII (1933), 81, 82; John Pope-Hennessy, *Sassetta* (London, 1939), pp. 187, 188, n. 7; Berenson, *Pictures Renaiss., Central and North Italian Schools*, I (1968), 374.

SANO DI PIETRO

of the Madonna's left hand, in the Child's hands, and parts of the Madonna's cloak and halo. The features, especially those of the Madonna, had been strengthened.

This panel is a characteristic work of Sano di Pietro and comparable with a panel once in the collection of A. K. Porter (Gaillard, pl. 38), and with another in a private collection which Van Marle (1927, fig. 304) dates ca. 1445.

41 *Madonna and Child*   44.56

Panel, including original molding, 30·4 × 28·8 cm (12 × 9 inches). Inside frame: 24 × 16·5 cm (9$\frac{7}{16}$ × 6$\frac{1}{2}$ inches).

COLLECTIONS: Mrs. B. B. Cleek; Henry White Cannon, Villa Doccia, Fiesole (given to Mr. Cannon before 1923 by Mrs. Cleek, who acquired it through Berenson).

Gift of Mrs. Henry White Cannon, 1944.

The original panel seems to have been reinforced by an oak backing covered with linen. The picture was cleaned by Joseph Alvarez in 1962. Aside from the visible filled losses at the right edge, past repairs were revealed under ultra-violet light between the faces of the Madonna and Child, in their necks, in the fingers

E.F.G.

EXHIBITIONS: CMA (1936), cat. no. 142.
LITERATURE: Emile Gaillard, *Sano di Pietro* (Chambery, 1923), p. 194; Van Marle, IX (1927), 528; Berenson, *Pictures Renaiss.* (1932), p. 499; Henry S. Francis, "Madonna and Child by Sano di Pietro," CMA *Bulletin*, XXXI (1944), 143-144; Berenson, *Pictures Renaiss., Central and North Italian Schools*, I (1968), 374.

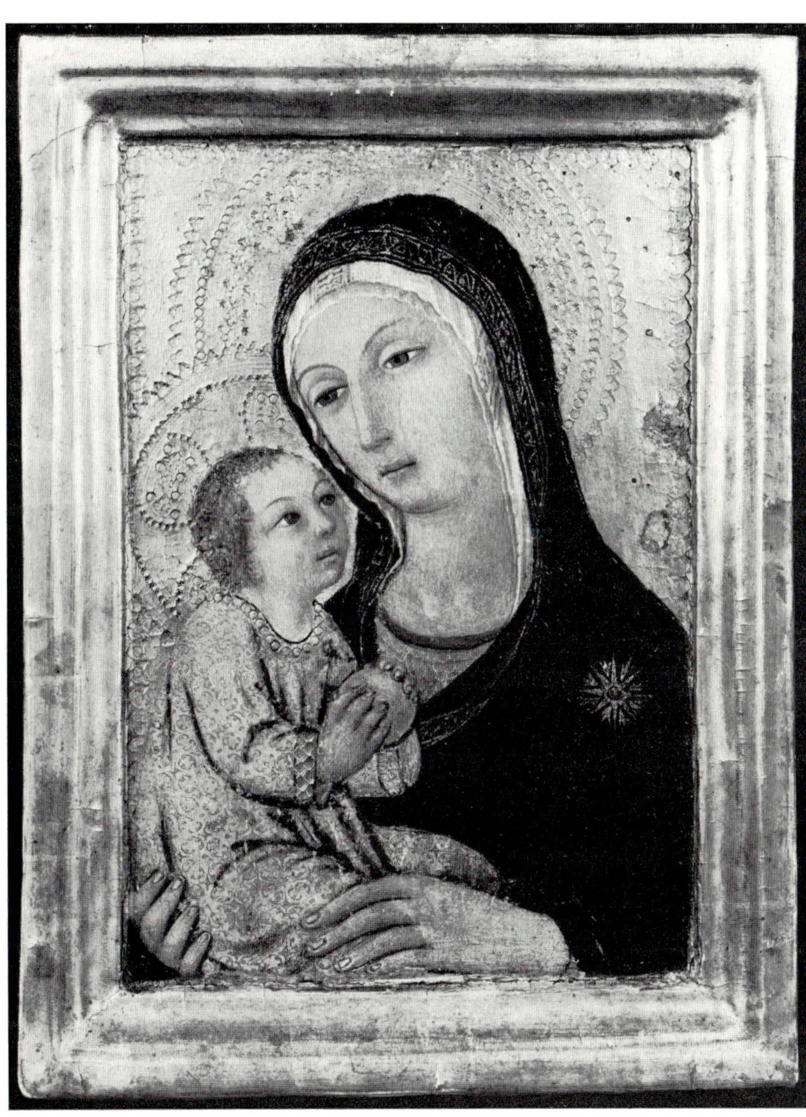

Figure 41.

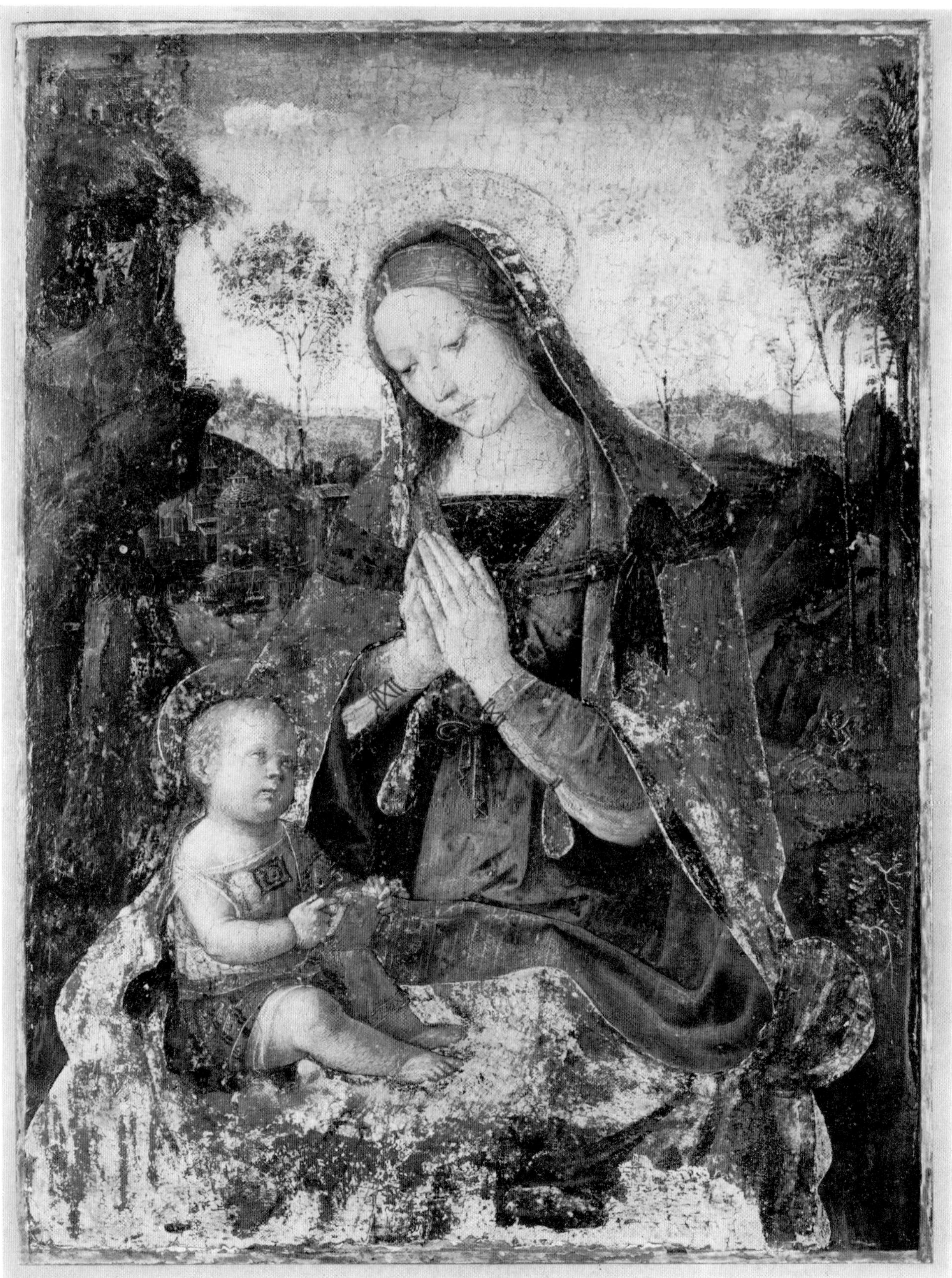

Figure 42.

118

PINTORICCHIO (Bernardino di Betto di
Biagio), School of Umbria, ca. 1454–1513

Pintoricchio was influenced by Fiorenzo di Lorenzo and
Perugino, whom he assisted with frescoes in the Sistine
Chapel. In 1481 he was inscribed in the painter's guild
of Perugia. He worked there, in Rome, Siena, and
Spello, becoming a favorite decorator of the Popes from
whom his most important works, the Borgia apartments
in the Vatican (for Alexander VI) and the Piccolomini
Library at Siena (for Pius III) were executed. Besides
these, there are numerous authentic wall and panel
paintings.

42 *Madonna and Child*   44.89

> Panel (walnut), 46·7 × 35 cm (18⅜ × 13¾ inches). Painted
> surface: 45·5 × 34 cm (17⅞ × 13⅜ inches).
> COLLECTIONS: (F. Kleinberger Galleries, Paris, New
> York, 1913–1915); Mrs. Dudley P. Allen (later Mrs.
> Francis F. Prentiss), Cleveland, 1915.
> Elisabeth Severance Prentiss Collection, 1944.

When this picture was seen by Berenson in 1913, he
described it as unfinished. "The Madonna's mantle instead of having the conventional blue has a beautiful
brownish tone.... This...which a miracle has spared
from the spoiling hand of the restorer is only the underpainting...it is more than probable that Pintoricchio
was at work on your Madonna when death took the
brush out of his hand...." It is indeed quite probable
that this painting was unfinished (and thus all the more
tempting to early restorers); by 1913 it must already
have been heavily retouched in oils, as the brown
mantle Berenson saw was ultimately removed, revealing a blue one. Before coming to the Museum, some-
time between 1942 and 1944, the picture was restored by
Pichetto (Fig. 42 a). Apparently at this time it was transferred and cradled. When examined by Suhr in 1944
blisters and cracks were developing in the center of the
picture which he attributed to the fact that too much
(¼ inch) of the original wood was retained for the mount-
ing on a new panel and to the heaviness of the cradle.
It was observed then that many of the folds on the brown
mantle looked new, as did much of the foliage. When a
partial cleaning was undertaken in 1960 the brown
mantle came off and much of the foliage and landscape at
left was obliterated. The uncharacteristic branches in the
foliage at the right (not cleaned) are probably not original. Although somewhat skinned and slightly damaged,

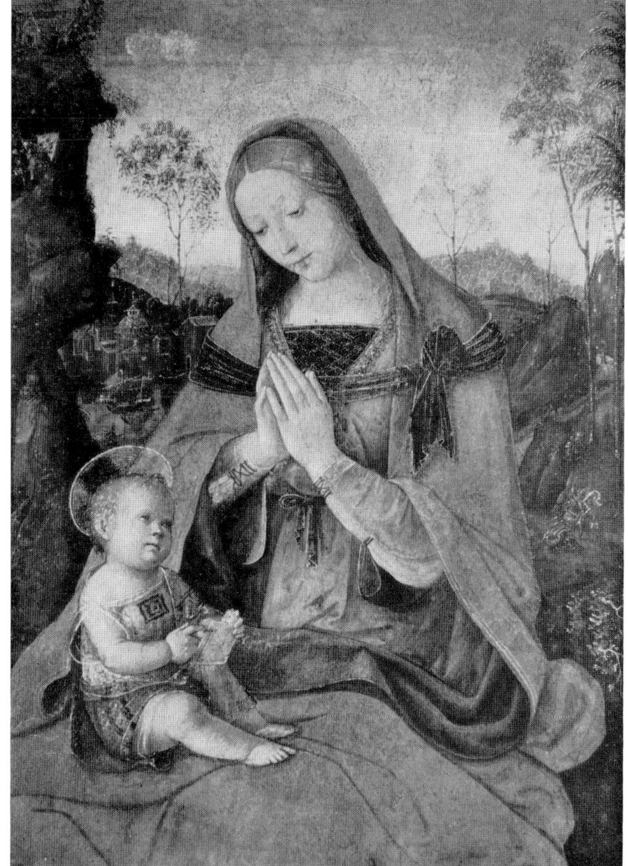

Figure 42 a. Before cleaning.

most of the flesh tones and the sky (except for a strip at
the top) had suffered little from retouching.

Even in its present sad and uncertain state, this remains an exceptionally lovely picture. Some idea of its
intrinsic merit emerges from seeing photographs before
and after cleaning and by comparison with the variant
by Pintoricchio and assistant in Honolulu (Fig. 42 b). In
the lower left of the Kress panel is St. Jerome with a lion,
of which perhaps faint shadows remain in the indeciph-
erable shapes in the Cleveland version. The Magi coming through the rocky pass at the upper left appear in
both paintings, but the landscape in the Cleveland painting is far more elaborate and refined in detail. At right
(uncleaned) St. George fights the dragon, two monks
pray, and horsemen gallop up the cliff-path.

Venturi (see William Suida, *The Samuel H. Kress Collection in the Honolulu Academy of Arts*, Honolulu, 1952,
p. 28) believed the Kress variant to be a work of the

artist's early maturity and contemporary with the *Madonna* in the cathedral of S. Severino. Carli (*Il Pintoricchio*, Milan, 1960, pl. 100, p. 56) includes it in a series of the Madonna with Child which he dates between the *Madonna* of S. Severino and the beautiful altarpiece of S. Maria dei Fossi (Perugia, Galleria) of ca. 1495. On the other hand, the Cleveland picture has been called a late work by Van Marle (1928) and Berenson (1932), and it does indeed match the delicacy of design and expression of the signed and dated *Way to Calvary* of 1513 in the Borromeo collection. However, in color, feeling, and type our picture coincides equally well with the subsidiary panels of the Perugia altarpiece, and the types of both Virgin and Child are so close to those in the predella panels of the *Annunciation* and the *Golden Legend* of that altarpiece that the Cleveland picture as well could be ca. 1496.

E.F.G.

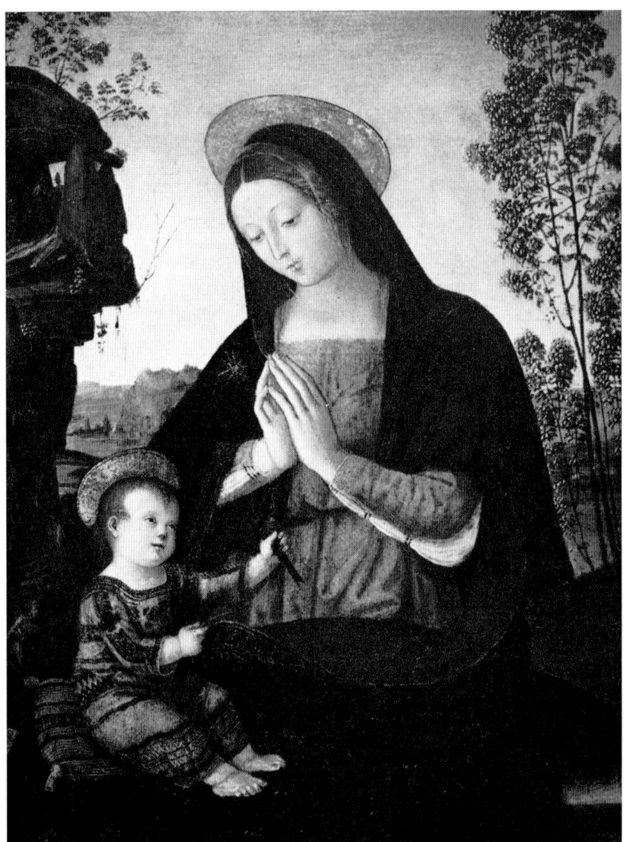

Figure 42 b. *Madonna Adoring the Child.*
45·4 × 34·5 cm ($17\frac{7}{8}$ × $13\frac{5}{8}$ inches).
Pintoricchio and Assistant. Honolulu Academy
of Arts, Samuel H. Kress Collection, 1.542.

EXHIBITIONS: Cambridge, Massachusetts, Fogg Art Museum, 1915: Loan exhibition of Italian paintings, no cat.
LITERATURE: G. E. Edgell, "The Loan Exhibition of Italian Paintings in the Fogg Museum, Cambridge," *Art and Archeology*, II (1915), pp. 18 and 20, fig. 8; Berenson, *Madonna and Child by Bernardino Biagio, called Il Pintoricchio* (Paris, New York, n.d.), illus.; *Collection of Medieval and Renaissance Paintings* (Cambridge, Mass., Fogg Art Museum, 1919), p. 166 (as "unfinished Madonna and Child by Pintoricchio, owned by Mrs. Frederick [sic] Allen of Cleveland"); Van Marle, XVI (1928), 284–285 (as from the last years of Pintoricchio's activity); Berenson, *Pictures Renaiss.* (1932), p. 459; Henry S. Francis, "Paintings in the Prentiss Bequest," CMA *Bulletin*, XXXI (1944), 87 (ca. 1500); *Prentiss Coll. Cat.* (1944), no. 11, pl. 1; René Gimpel, *Journal d'un collectionneur, marchand de tableaux* (Paris, 1963), p. 236; Berenson, *Pictures Renaiss., Central and North Italian Schools*, I (1968), 344 (as Pintoricchio).

SASSETTA (Stefano di Giovanni),
Siena, 1392(?)–1450

Sassetta was the son of Giovanni di Consolo of Cortona
and perhaps identical with the Stefano di Giovanni who
was baptized in Siena in 1392. His first documented
work, the Arte della Lana [Guild] altarpiece dates from
1423–1426. In 1428 Sassetta was inscribed in the Sienese
guild of painters and in 1430 he painted *The Madonna
of the Snow* (Contini Bonacossi collection) for the Duomo. The authorship of the panels depicting famous
legends of St. Anthony traditionally ascribed to Sassetta
is nowadays the subject of controversy. But other authenticated works exist, including the artist's most important commission, the St. Francis altarpiece of 1437–
1444. His last work, the decoration of the Porta Rom-
ana in Siena was interrupted by his death and completed
by Sano di Pietro.

43 *St. Francis before the Crucifix* 62.36

Panel (poplar), 81 × 40·2 cm ($31\frac{7}{8} \times 15\frac{7}{8}$ inches). Painted
surface (terminates in trefoil): 80 × 39·4 cm ($31\frac{1}{2} \times 15\frac{1}{2}$
inches).

PROVENANCE: Church of S. Francesco, Borgo San
Sepolcro, 1444–1472 (see Carli, 1951; Davies, 1961).

COLLECTIONS: Franciscan convent of Borgo San Sepolcro
(1752–ca. 1810); bought by Cavaliere Sergiuliani, Arezzo,
"who gave what may have been the whole altarpiece to
Canonico Giulio Anastasio Angelucci of Arezzo"
(Davies, 1961, p. 507). Carli (1951, p. 147) says, "before
passing from Sergiuliani to Canonico Angelucci, the
altarpiece had probably been stripped of its predella." If
this were the case, it is likely that any pinnacles, including
the Cleveland panel, would also have been separated from
the rest of the polyptych at the same time. This panel later
entered the collection of Prince Johann Georg of Saxony
(1869–1936). By 1950 when it was first published it was in
the collection of Gerhard Freiherr von Preuschen, Stuttgart
and Lugano, from whom it was acquired by the Paul
Drey Gallery, New York.

Mr. and Mrs. William H. Marlatt Fund, 1962.

All sides of the panel, except for the uppermost lobe
of the trefoil, have been slightly cut down. There are
horizontal dowel grooves extending inward from the
lower right and left sides of the back of the panel. The
condition of the back indicates this panel was sawed
off from a thicker piece and possibly could have been
painted on both sides. The missing part according to
Carli (1951) might have been *Christ Blessing*. The condition of the paint is generally satisfactory; however,
much of the gold has worn off. Traces suggest that
perhaps originally blood emerged from the wound in
the side of Christ, but this has been rubbed away along
with the gold background. Past repainting includes the
top of Christ's head, the blood on the cross, and the
strengthening of folds in the robe of St. Francis.

It is most probable that *St. Francis before the Crucifix*
formed the apex of the reverse side of Sassetta's high
altar for the church of S. Francesco in Borgo San Sepolcro. This altarpiece was commissioned in 1437 and paid
for in three installments while Sassetta was painting it in
Siena. By June 15, 1444, Sassetta had received full pay-
ment for the work whose installation at Borgo San Sepolcro he had supervised. According to Carli's (1951) and
Davies' (1961) reconstructions (supported by the des-
criptions in Ettore Romagnoli's MS. *Biografia cronologica
de' bellartisti senesi*, IV, p. 432, in the Biblioteca Comunale, Siena) the altarpiece was a pentaptych, painted
on both sides, arranged as follows:

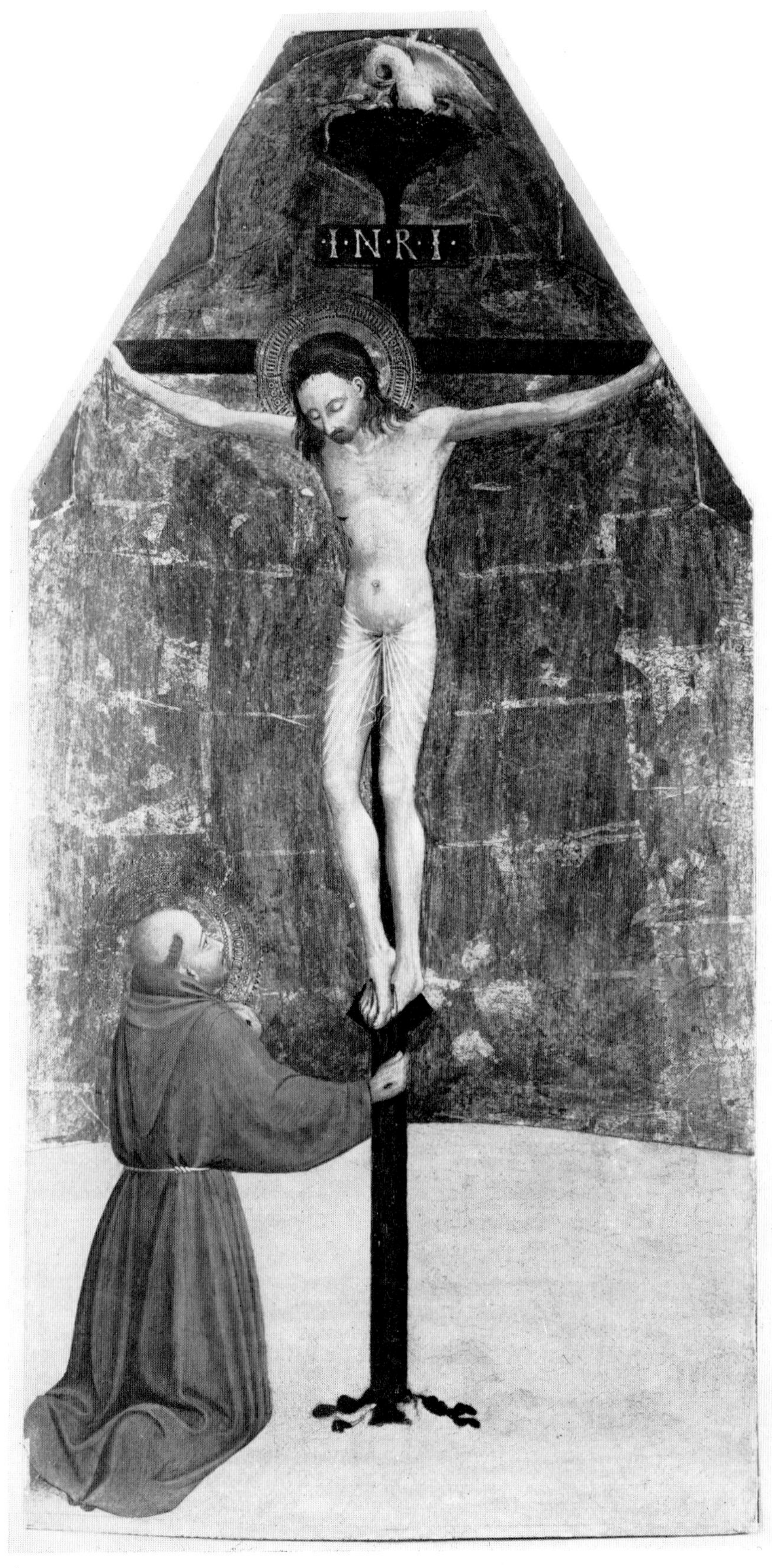

Figure 43.

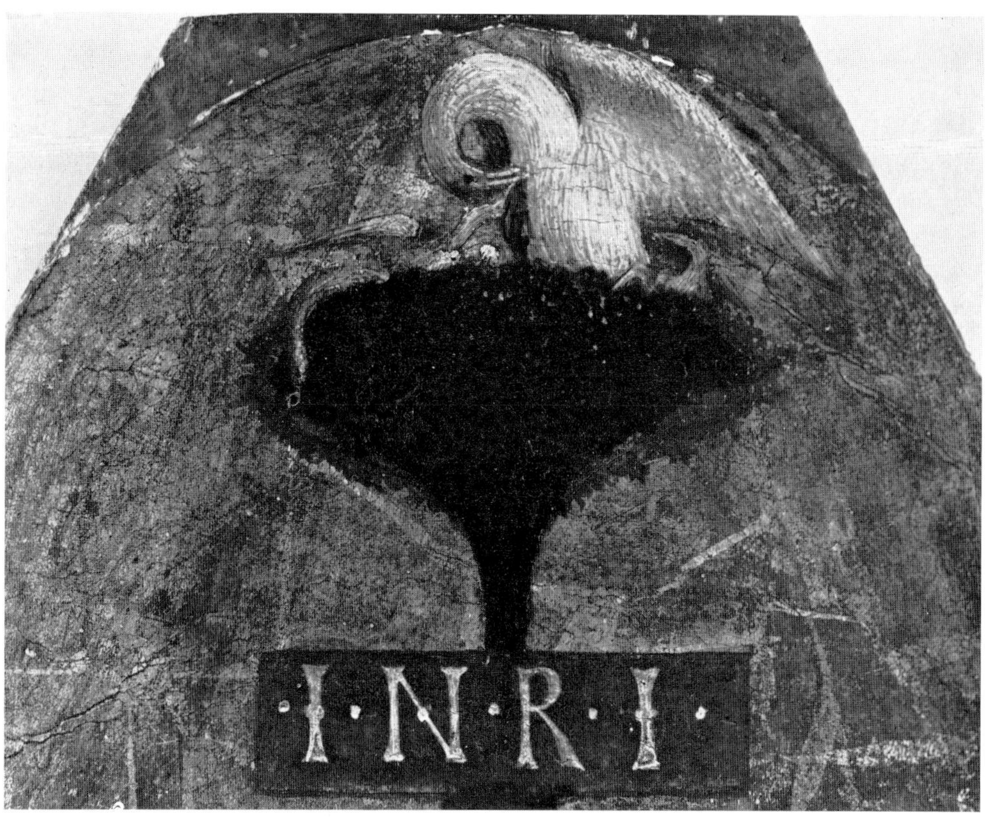

Figures 43 *a*, *b*. Details.

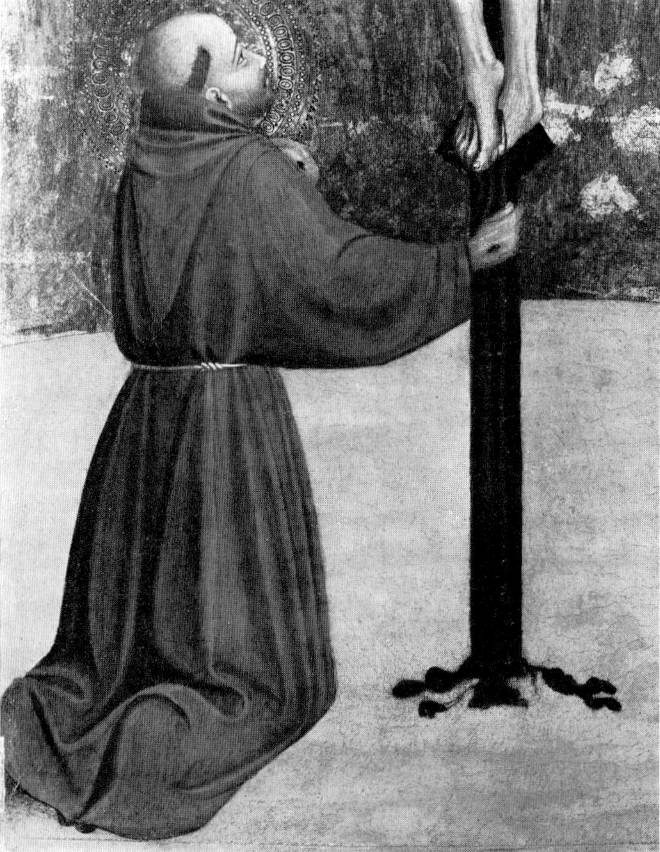

Obverse. Center. *Madonna and Angels* (Louvre), flanked by [dexter] *St. Anthony of Padua* (Louvre), *Blessed Ranieri Rasini* (Harvard University Center for Renaissance Culture, Villa I Tatti, Settignano), [sinister] *St. John the Baptist* (I Tatti), and *St. John the Evangelist* (Louvre). The supposedly missing side of our panel would have surmounted the central *Madonna and Angels*. Predella panels depicting episodes from the lives of the saints flanking the Virgin probably belonged to this side of the altarpiece. Four pictures of the legends of Blessed Ranieri (Davies, 1961, pp. 510–511, n. 23) are recorded, but only two are known to exist today, *A Cardinal's Vision of the Blessed Ranieri* (formerly Staatliche Museen, Berlin–Dahlem, no. 1945) and *The Deliverance of Ninety Paupers from the Prisons of Florence by the Intervention of the Blessed Ranieri* (private collection).

Reverse. Center, *St. Francis in Ecstasy* (I Tatti) flanked by eight scenes from his life, arranged in two zones; in the upper the sky is gold, in the lower it is blue. Seven of these scenes are in the National Gallery, London (Davies, 1961, pp. 502 ff.). The eighth, the *Marriage of St. Francis with Poverty*, is at the Musée Condé, Chantilly.

Zeri ("Tre argomenti umbri," *Bollettino d'arte*, XLVIII, 1963, pp. 38, 41, 44, n. 17) has further identified the following pinnacles and pilaster panels as having belonged to the Borgo San Sepolcro altarpiece: *St. Lawrence* and *St. Stephen* (Pushkin Museum, Moscow, nos. 1494, 1495); *St. Christopher* (the late F. Mason Perkins collection, Assisi); *St. John the Evangelist* (Cini collection, Venice); *Bishop St. [Augustine?]* (Wildenstein, New York). Michel Laclotte ("Sassetta, le Maître de L'Observance et Sano di Pietro, un problème critique," *L'Information d'histoire de l'art*, V, 1960, pp. 52 ff.) suggests that Sassetta's three scenes from the *Passion* at the Detroit Institute of Arts might have belonged to a predella from the reverse side of the polyptych. He says that their style and dimensions (approximating those of the Berlin predella panel) would support this hypothesis which, however, is weakened by the difference in the design of Christ's halo, and on the whole seems implausible. The tooling of the haloes in the Cleveland panel is, to be sure, different from those in the other panels belonging to the St. Francis altarpiece. This has made Gronau (1950) doubtful of its connection with the said altarpiece, despite the fact that there is some variation in the halo designs among the other known parts of the complex. The Cleveland panel was first identified as part of Sassetta's high altar for the church of S. Francesco by Robert

Oertel (*Frühe italienische Tafelmalerei*, exh. cat.; Stuttgart, Württembergische Staatsgalerie, 1950, no. 94). Longhi (1950) agreed and thought that it was the pinnacle above the *St. Francis in Ecstasy*. This reconstruction was followed by Davies (1961) and Carli (1951) but not by Bauch (1950) who, unaware of the Louvre Madonna, thought the narrative scenes formed the reverse of *St. Francis in Ecstasy* and that the Cleveland panel was above the narrative scenes. Certainly Longhi's idea of its position is convincing, for the large St. Francis "floats . . . in mystical simulation of the Crucifixion" (Pope-Hennessy, *Sassetta*, London, 1939, p. 102) which he is contemplating in the pinnacle above. As Bauch (1950, p. 105) points out, the representation of the already stigmatized St. Francis alone before the Crucifix is an iconographical rarity.

E.F.G.

EXHIBITIONS: Stuttgart, Württembergische Staatsgalerie, 1950: Frühe italienische Tafelmalerei veranstaltet vom Stuttgarter Galerieverein, cat. no. 94; Zürich, Kunsthaus, 1956: Unbekannte Schönheit, bedeutende Werke aus 5 Jahrhunderten, cat. no. 227, pl. 1; Stuttgart, Württembergische Staatsgalerie, 1958–1959: Meisterwerke aus badisch-württembergischem Privatbesitz, cat. no. 175, pl. 66; CMA, November 1962: Year in Review, cat. no. 97, illus.; CMA (1963), cat. no. 81, illus. p. 197.
LITERATURE: Kurt Bauch, "Christus am Kreuz und der heilige Franziskus," *Sonderdruck aus der Festschrift zum 60. Geburtstag von C. G. Heise* (Berlin, 1950), pp. 103–112, reconstruction illus. pp. 104 and 112; Roberto Longhi, "Primitivi italiani a Stoccarda," *Paragone*, I (1950), 47–48; Hans Dietrich Gronau, "Early Italian Paintings at Stuttgart," *Burl., Mag.*, XCII (1950), 322, fig. 22; Enzo Carli, "Sassetta's Borgo San Sepolcro Altarpiece," *Burl. Mag.*, XCIII (1951), 147, 151 reconstruction, figs. A–B; Carli, *La Pintura senese* (Milan, 1955), p. 196; Carli, *Sassetta e il Maestro dell'Osservanza* (Milan, 1957), p. 56; Martin Davies, *The Earlier Italian Schools* (London, National Gallery, 1961), p. 511, n. 24; Nicky Mariano and Franco Russoli, *La Raccolta Berenson* (Milan, 1961), pl. XL; Henry S. Francis, "Sassetta – Crucifixion with St. Francis," *CMA Bulletin*, L (1963), 46–49, illus. pp. 47, 48; *Handbook* (1966), p. 58; Berenson, *Pictures Renaiss., Central and North Italian Schools*, I (1968), 384 (titled *St. Francis Worshipping Christ on the Cross*).

School of JACOPO DEL SELLAIO, Florence,
ca. 1441–1493

A Florentine painter who, according to Vasari, was in
the workshop of Fra Filippo Lippi. He was a member
of the Compagnia di S. Luca in Florence in 1472. There
are three more or less authenticated works of the artist,
an *Annunciation* of ca. 1473 in S. Lucia dei Magnoli which
may be by Jacopo del Sellaio or Filippo di Giuliano with
whom he had a workshop in 1473 and in 1480–1481; a
Pietà at Berlin from S. Frediano, Florence, of ca. 1483;
and a *Crucifixion*, traditionally assigned to the artist by
Vasari, now in another church dedicated to S. Frediano
in Florence.

44 *The Entry of Tarquinius Priscus*   42.646
    into Rome

Cassone panel

Transferred from panel to canvas, 41 × 165·4 cm (16½ ×
65⅛ inches).

COLLECTIONS: Friedrich Lippmann, Berlin; (sale:
Rudolph Lepke, Berlin, November 26–27, 1912, cat. no.
33, pl. 2); Guillaume, Cologne; John L. Severance,
Cleveland, by 1922.

John L. Severance Collection, 1942.

This cassone was transferred from panel to canvas, probably in the nineteenth century. There is considerable
repaint, particularly in the sky, and the painting is covered with thick yellowed varnish.

Tarquinius Priscus, the fifth legendary King of Rome
(616–578 B.C.), is making his entry into Rome. At the
extreme left the prophetess, Tanaquil, the wife of Tarquinius, is kneeling upon a lofty place as if foreseeing the
future glory of her husband. The central portion is taken
up by a triumphal chariot, upon which Tarquinius and
Tanaquil sit, attended by an array of numerous attendants and courtiers, while the Roman eagle hovers pre-
cariously over Tarquin's head. At the right, Rome is
represented with the cortege again approaching the city
gate with the eagle perched upon the head of Tarquin
himself. According to the story from Livy i. 34–41, as
Tarquinius was about to enter the city, the eagle flew
down, seized his helmet, and after flying to a great
height with it, replaced it on his head. This was regarded
as an omen that Tarquinius would rise to great power in
Rome.

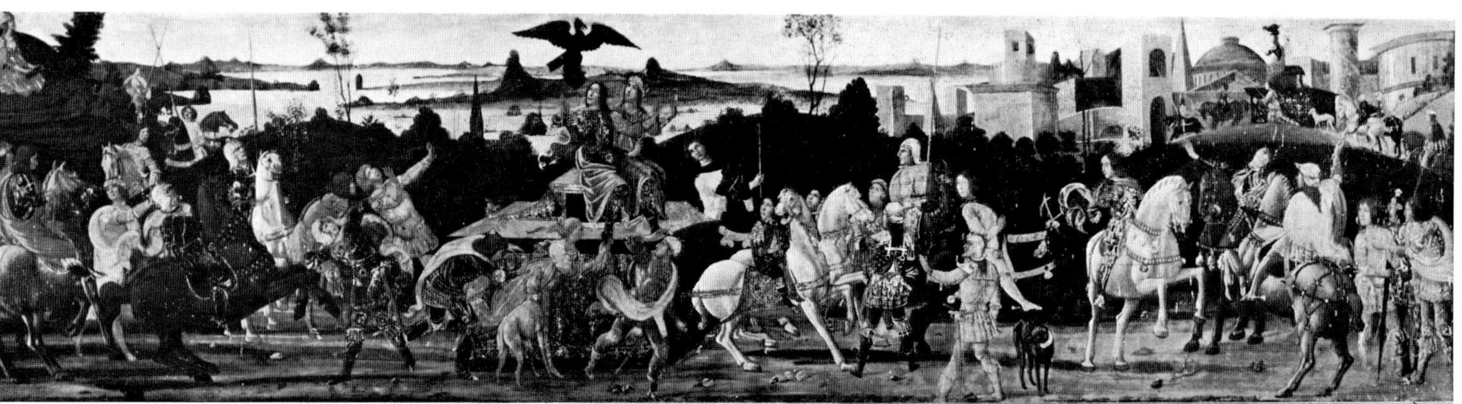

Figure 44.

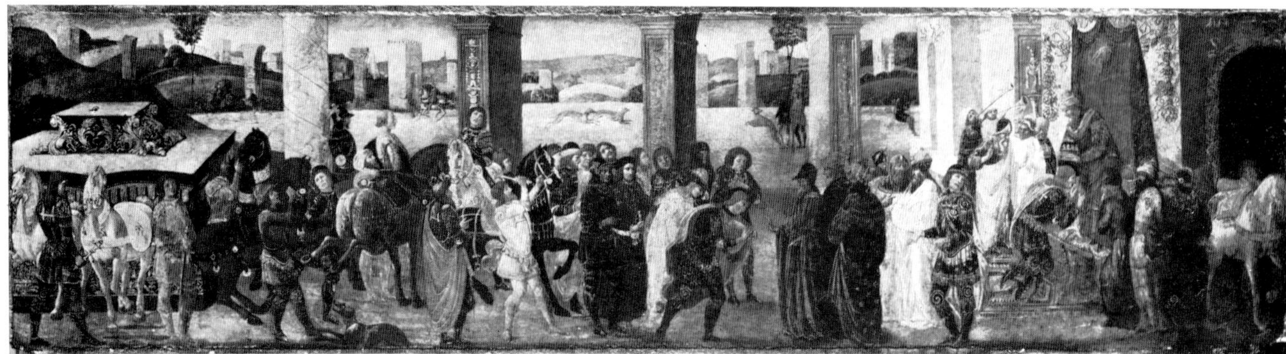

Figure 44 a. *David Meeting the Men of Judah at Hebron*. Cassone panel, 41·6 × 166·1 cm (16⅜ × 65⅜ inches). Attributed to Sellaio. National Galleries of Scotland, Edinburgh, 1538.

This cassone has been given to Jacopo del Sellaio by Schubring (1915), Borenius (1926), Van Marle (1931), and Berenson (1963). It would seem to date ca. 1480–1490 and follows closely in the tradition of Jacopo del Sellaio. Borenius noted the stylistic similarity of the Cleveland panel to a cassone in the National Galleries of Scotland, Edinburgh (Fig. 44 a). Federico Zeri (letter of February 25, 1969, from Hugh Brigstocke, Asst. Keeper, National Galleries of Scotland) has suggested it is possibly a companion piece to ours, both stylistically and physically, although there has not been a definite identification of the scene represented in the Edinburgh cassone.

N.C.W.

EXHIBITIONS: CMA, 1922: Special Exhibition of Renaissance Art (see Milliken, "Special Exhibition..."); CMA (1936), cat. no. 146; CMA, 1942: Exhibition of the John L. Severance Collection, cat. no. 15.

LITERATURE: Paul Schubring, *Cassoni* (Leipzig, 1915), I, 307, no. 368; II, pl. LXXXVI; William M. Milliken, "Special Exhibition of Renaissance Art in Gallery II," CMA *Bulletin*, IX (1922), 56, illus. p. 54; Tancred Borenius, "Italian Cassone Paintings," *Apollo*, III (1926), 135; Van Marle, XII (1931), 405, 410, n. 1; Henry S. Francis, "Bequest of John L. Severance: Department of Paintings," CMA *Bulletin*, XXXIX (1942), 132–133; Berenson, *Pictures Renaiss., Florentine School*, I (London, 1963), 197.

GIOVANNI DI FRANCESCO TOSCANI
(Master of the Griggs Crucifixion), Florence, born ca. 1370–1380, died 1430

The Master of the Griggs Crucifixion was so-called after a picture by an anonymous painter given by Maitland F. Griggs to The Metropolitan Museum of Art. A number of works have been attributed to this master (see Richard Offner, "The Mostra del Tesoro di Firenze Sacra - II," *Burl. Mag.*, LXIII, 1933, 173, n. 17; Roberto Longhi, "Fatti di Masolino e di Masaccio," *Critica d'arte*, V, 1940, 185, n. 22) but more recently Luciano Bellosi ("Il Maestro della Crocifissione Griggs: Giovanni Toscani," *Paragone*, XVII, 1966, 44- 58) identified the Master of the Griggs Crucifixion and Giovanni di Francesco Toscani as the same artist.

He was born about 1370, became a member of the Guild of St. Luke in 1424, and died in Florence in 1430. Various works by Toscani are recorded in his tax returns of 1427 and those of his widow, Mona Nicolosa, of 1430 and 1433. Bellosi brought together a study of his works, many of which were attributed to others or were difficult to distinguish from the style of Arcangelo di Cola and Rossello di Jacopo Franchi. An overpainted *Pietà* in the Ardinghelli Chapel in S. Trinita in Florence and a hard-to-distinguish fresco above the entrance arch of the chapel (Bellosi, pls. 20–25) are documented works by Toscani which were erroneously listed by Vasari (1906 ed., II, 19 ff.) as the work of Lorenzo Monaco which confused the problem. Among other works, including the CMA cassone panel, which Bellosi also attributed to Toscani are the *Adoration of the Magi* (New York, Schaeffer Galleries), *The Presentation at the Temple* and *Christ among the Doctors* (Philadelphia, Johnson Collection), *St. Francis Receiving the Stigmata* and *The Miracle of St. Nicholas* (Florence, Accademia), a *Madonna of Humility* (formerly Florence, Gallery Bellini), and an altarpiece with a predella (formerly in the Nevin collection; Schloss Crottorf, Altenkirchen).

45   *The Race of the Palio in the Streets*   16.801
of Florence

Cassone panel

Panel (poplar), 42 × 139.3 cm ($16\frac{9}{16}$ × $54\frac{7}{8}$ inches).
COLLECTIONS: Marchese Alamano Bartolini-Salimbeni, 1741; Pitti family, Florence, 1798; James Jackson Jarves; Mrs. Liberty E. Holden, Cleveland, 1884.
Holden Collection, 1916.

Unfortunately, the rondels containing the coats of arms and the Virtues which appear at either end of the Bargello example (Fig. 45 a) have been sawed off the ends of the Cleveland panel, and the rest of the original chest is lost. The triangular surface of stucco and gilded decoration in the four corners of the rectangular panel are not original and probably supplanted the original fleur-de-lis decoration of the Bargello piece in the nineteenth century. The original poplar panel was made up of two separate horizontal pieces which split apart at the join for the entire length and have been repaired with considerable repaint along the point of separation. There are large areas of repaint but the exact degree throughout is difficult to determine. There is evidence of some surface damage with gougings and deep scratches. The panel was cleaned by William Suhr in 1935.

The cassone panel of *The Race of the Palio* and its companion in the Bargello in Florence, *The Procession of the Palii* (Fig. 45 a), were probably on the marriage chests made for the wedding of Tommaso di Giovanni di Berto Fini and Giacoma di Filippo Aldobrandini. The coats of arms of these two Florentine families appear between the two rondels of the Virtues at each end of the Bargello cassone. De Nicola (1918) states that the Florentine geneaologists give 1417 or 1418 as the year of their marriage and that this is the only known wedding between the two families which coincides stylistically with the painting. He also points out the important and indisputable fact that the Bargello cassone must have been executed before 1429 because of the isolation of the porphyry columns in front of the Baptistery in Florence which were not built into the sides of the doorway until that date. The scenes on these chests represent the most popular feast day in the city of Florence, that of St. John the Baptist. The procession before the race, starting at the Piazza della Signoria and ending at the piazza in front of the Baptistery and Duomo (as seen on the Bargello cassone), took place the day before. For an accurate account of the procession see the description of one of the earlier chroniclers at the beginning of the fifteenth

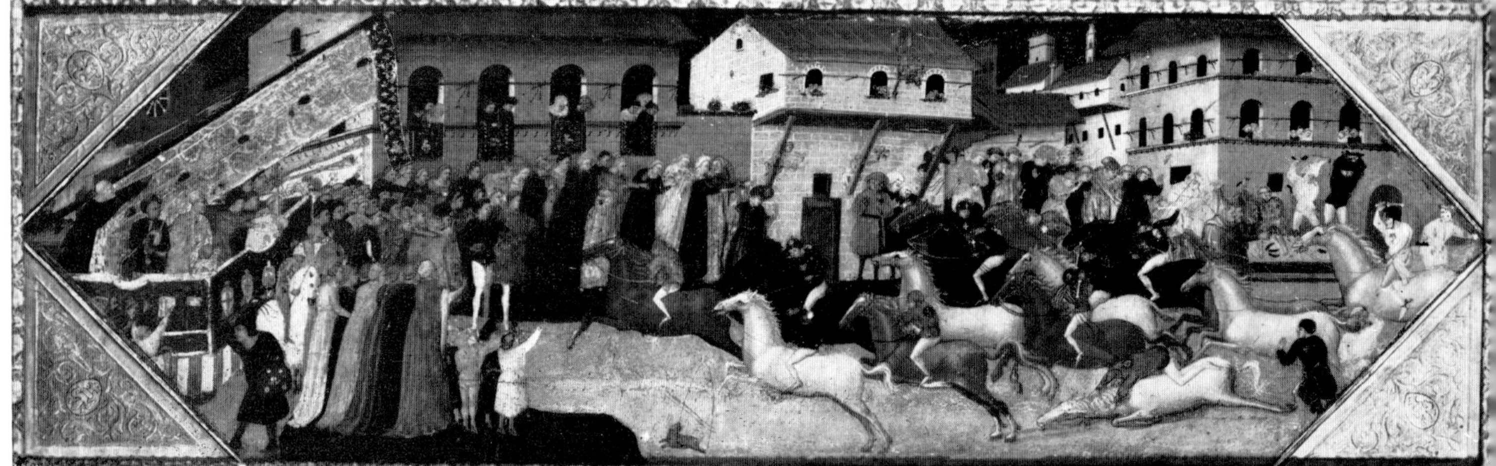

Figure 45.

century, Goro Dati (*Istoria di Firenze*, Florence, 1735, pp. 84–89) quoted by De Nicola. The *palii* (banners) of the territories subservient to Florence were borne by men on horseback as offerings. The last gilded *palio* to enter the cathedral in the Bargello cassone can be seen at the left in the Cleveland panel as it is about to be presented to the winner of the race. Collobi (1949) suggests that this scene takes place in the Piazza di S. Croce. The virtually contemporary account of the scene by Goro Dati (*op. cit.*) is as follows: "Afterwards at the sound of three strokes of the great bell of the Palace of the Signoria, the racers, prepared to start, set out to run, and on the tower one sees the devices of the boys, which are there, who this one and that one are (there having come from all the confines of Italy the finest Barbary racers of the world), and the one who is first to reach the palio wins it, which is carried on a triumphal car with four wheels adorned by four carved lions . . . ."

This panel first appeared in the literature in 1741 when it was in the collection of the Marchese Alamano Bartolini-Salimbeni. The author, Cav. Andrea da Varrazzano, illustrates a line drawing after the Museum panel (Fig. 45 *b*) formerly in the collection of the Società Colombaria in Florence, and now lost. Although the drawing follows the painting quite closely, it extends the action into the four triangular corners (now covered with nineteenth-century gilded plaster decorations), and thereby shows more clearly the four-wheeled triumphal platform from which the *palio* is extended. However, it includes fewer figures in the crowds in the center of the panel, and the drawing may possibly have been cut

slightly at the right as the painting in the Museum panel extends beyond including another figure.

This cassone was described in the *Osservatore fiorentino* (1798) as Florentine school, and belonged to the Pitti family in Florence. Jarves (1884) attributes it to "some scholar of Gaddo Gaddi, A.D. 1239–1312." The general attribution of Florentine School has been given to the *Race of the Palio* by Rankin (1906; 1908), Burroughs (Exh: 1912), and Rubinstein (1917) who date it loosely fifteenth century. Van Marle (1927) again calls both of them Florentine school, first half of the fifteenth century, and Schubring (1923) agrees, mentioning that the CMA panel which he dates ca. 1420 is a companion piece to the Bargello cassone which he dates ca. 1400 (see also *Cassoni*, I, 1915, no. 24). M. L. Berenson (1907) was first to suggest the school of Paolo Uccello, an opinion agreed upon by Crowe and Cavalcaselle (1911) and by Mather (1915; 1920; 1923). This attribution would seem to be impossible, as the CMA cassone is a Gothic painting of the International Style with attenuated-figure style and a naive, picturesque perspective. The action of the horses in the Cleveland panel is lively and decorative, but the general handling of detail is rough and not sophisticated and the work of a minor artist. The name of Rossello di Jacopo Franchi and his workshop was first suggested by De Nicola (1918) as the master of these cassoni. This opinion has been seconded by Antal (1947), by Collobi (1949), and Berenson (*Pictures Renaiss., Florentine School*, 1963, p. 193) who listed the Bargello piece under this name. Mario Salmi has given the Bargello piece to the Master of the Griggs Crucifixion, and Robert Oertel (*Frühe italienische Malerei in Altenburg*, Ber-

128

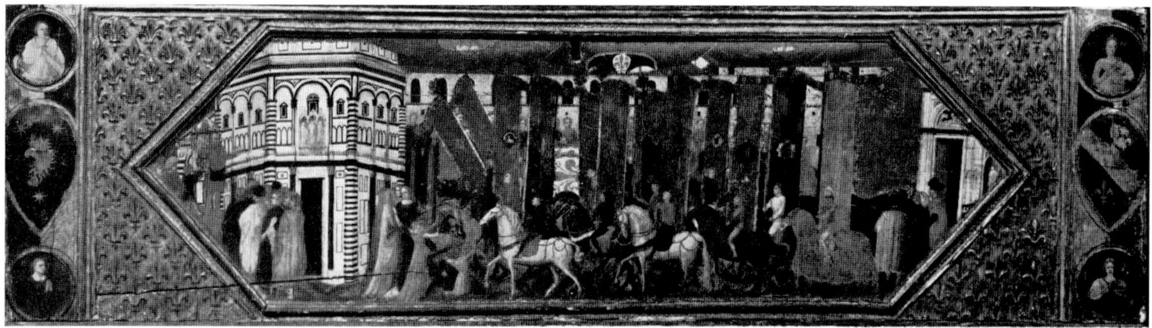

Figure 45*a*. *The Procession of the Palii*. Cassone front. Attributed to Toscani. Museo Nazionale (Bargello), Florence.

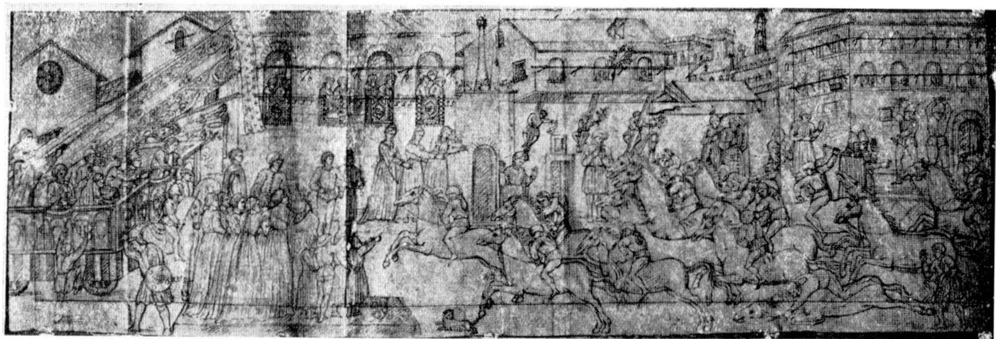

Figure 45*b*. *The Race of the Palii*, drawing of a cassone front.
Cav. Andrea da Varrazzano. Formerly Società Colombaria, Florence (now lost).

lin, 1961, pl. 52*a,b*), attributed it to the Maestro del Bambino Vispo on the basis of its similarity to the oriental battle-scene cassone in the Altenburg Gallery whose attribution is debatable and is of a far more sophisticated design than the Cleveland cassone. Bellosi (1966) has published the two cassoni as the late work (1428–1429) of the painter Giovanni di Francesco Toscani, an artist whom he identifies with the Master of the Griggs Crucifixion. The early date of 1417–1418 offered by De Nicola (1918) for reasons of genealogy is dismissed by Bellosi as impossible because he feels that the special composition could not predate the Masaccio frescoes in the Brancacci Chapel but the *a posteriori* date of 1429 cannot be questioned. The authorship of a number of cassoni of this period as well as their condition is a very complex problem; however, Bellosi offers a convincing argument with documents for considering these cassoni as the late work of Giovanni Toscani, and Everett Fahy (orally, 1970) has confirmed this opinion in regard to our panel.   N.C.W.

EXHIBITIONS: Boston (1883), cat. no. 409; MMA (1912), cat. no. 8; CMA (1916), cat. no. 17; CMA (1936), cat. no. 88; Florence, Palazzo Strozzi, 1949: Lorenzo il Magnifico e le arti, cat. no. 2; CMA (1963), cat. no. 78, illus. p. 183; CMA (1971), cat. no. 4.

LITERATURE: Cav. Andrea da Varrazzano, "Atti della Società Colombaria," *Sunto di materie proposte dal Tarpato* (Biblioteca della Società Colombaria), IX (1741), 362–363; *Osservatore fiorentino*, III (1798); Jarves (1884), cat. no. 6; William Rankin, "Cassone Fronts in American Collections," *Burl. Mag.*, IX (1906), 288; M. L. Berenson (1907), 2; Rankin, "Cassone Fronts and Salvers in American Collections – VII," *Burl. Mag.*, XIII (1908), 381; Crowe and Cavalcaselle, *History of Painting in Italy*, IV (1911), 122; Frank J. Mather, "Bride-Chests of Renaissance Italy," *Arts & Decoration*, VI (1915), 75; Rubinstein (1917), cat. no. 17, illus.; "The Bartolini-Salimbeni Race of the Palio," *Burl. Mag.*, XXXII (1918), 245; Giacomo De Nicola, "Notes on the Museo Nazionale of Florence – VII: Two Florentine Cassoni," *Burl. Mag.*, XXXII (1918), 218–226; Mather, "Three Florentine Furniture Panels: The *Medici Desco*, the *Stibbert Trajan*, and the *Horse Race* of the Holden Collection," *Art in America*, VIII (1920), 154–159, illus. p. 157; Mather (1923), p. 128, fig. 85; Paul Schubring, *Cassoni*, Suppl. (Leipzig, 1923), no. 904, pl. V; Van Marle, IX (1927), 100, fig. 64; Van Marle, *Iconographie de l'art profane au moyen âge et à la renaissance*, I (The Hague, 1931), 138–139, fig. 121; Frederick Antal, *Florentine Painting and its Social Background* (London, 1947), p. 363, pl. 154A; Licia Ragghianti Collobi, *Lorenzo il Magnifico e le arti: Mostra d'arte figurativa antica* (exh. cat.; Florence, Palazzo Strozzi, 1949), pp. 18–20, pl. 2; Denys Sutton, *The Art of Painting in Florence and Siena from 1250–1500* (exh. cat.; London, Wildenstein & Co., 1965), p. xxiv; Luciano Bellosi, "Il Maestro della Crocifissione Griggs: Giovanni Toscani," *Paragone*, n.s. XVII (1966), 53, pl. 30A; Charles L. Mee, *Lorenzo de'Medici and the Renaissance* (New York, 1969), illus. pp. 36–37 (color).

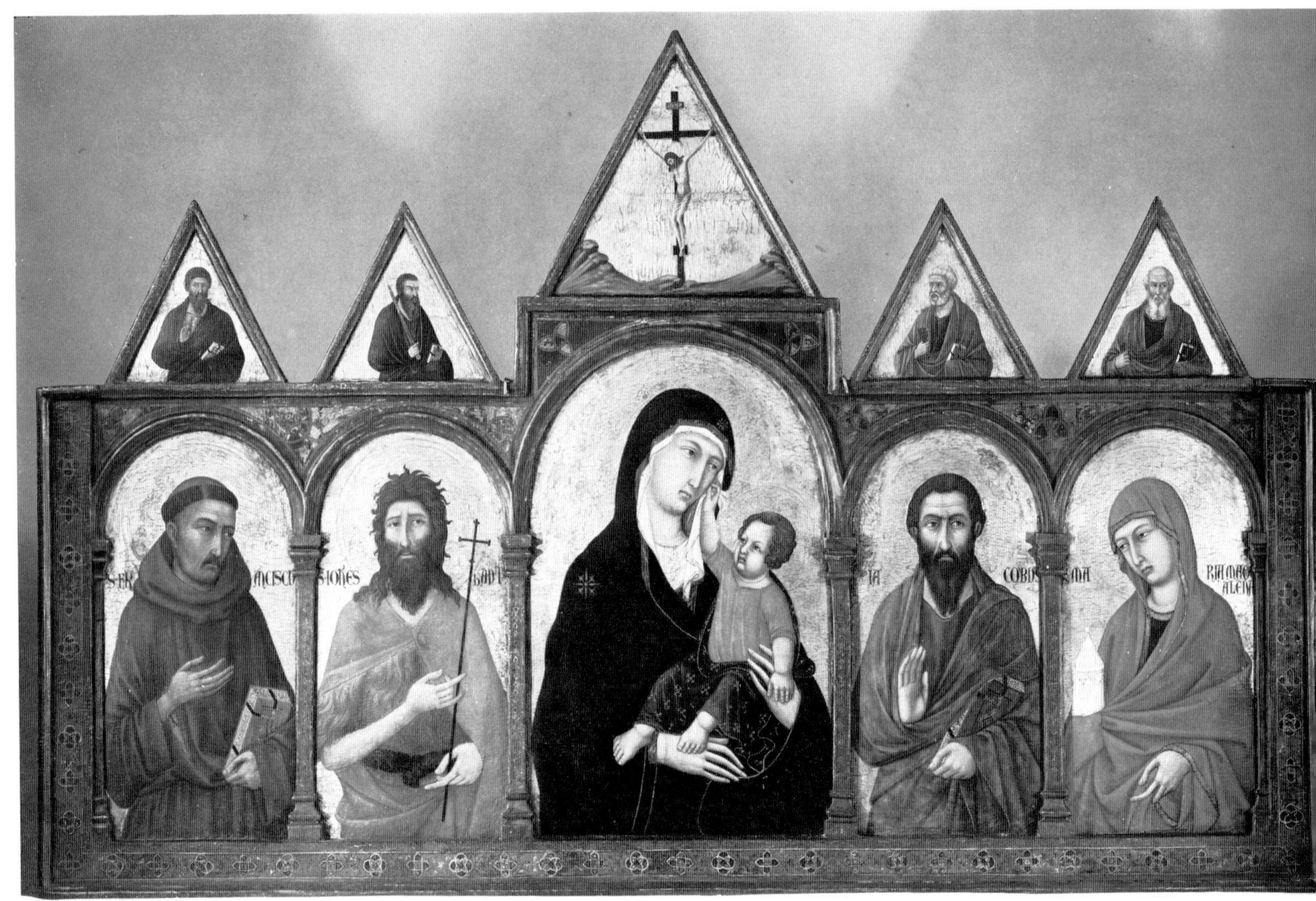

Figure 46. See also Colorplate XXIII.

UGOLINO DI NERIO DA SIENA, Siena,
active ca. 1305–1310, died ca. 1339–1349

The artist is referred to in Sienese documents of 1317,
1325, and 1327 (see Peleo Bacci, *Dipinti inediti e scono-
sciuti di Pietro Lorenzetti, Bernardo Daddi, etc. in Siena e
nel contado*, Siena, 1939, pp. 142–144). Vasari gives his
death date as 1339 in the 1550 edition of the *Lives* and
as 1349 in subsequent editions. He was the pupil of his
father, Nerio di Ugolino. Ugolino's two brothers were
also painters and possibly collaborated with him. Only
Ugolino's work is known, however, and only the signed
polyptych, now dispersed, which he painted for the
high altar of S. Croce in Florence is authenticated (see
Martin Davies, *The Early Italian Schools*, London, National Gallery, 1961, pp. 533–537). This and the works
generally attributed to him are so close to Duccio that
Ugolino is presumed to have been that master's most
gifted associate and to have been working for him
when Duccio was painting his *Maesta* of 1308–1311.

46 *Madonna and Child with St. Francis,*　61.40
St. John the Baptist, St. James the
Great, and Mary Magdalen

Polyptych

Dexter pinnacles: *St. Bartholomew, St. Paul*
Center pinnacle: *Crucifixion*
Sinister pinnacles: *St. Peter, St. John the*
　Evangelist(?)

Panel (poplar), over-all, including molding, 122·5 × 192·5
cm (48$\frac{1}{4}$ × 75$\frac{3}{4}$ inches). Painted surface of main panels:
St. Francis – 58·3 × 28·7 cm (22$\frac{15}{16}$ × 11$\frac{3}{8}$ inches); *St. John* –
58·3 × 29·5 cm (22$\frac{15}{16}$ × 11$\frac{9}{16}$ inches); *Madonna and Child* –
70 × 46·4 cm (27$\frac{9}{16}$ × 18$\frac{1}{4}$ inches); *St. James* – 58·1 × 29·1
cm (22$\frac{7}{8}$ × 11$\frac{7}{16}$ inches); *Mary Magdalen* – 58·3 × 29·4 cm
(22$\frac{15}{16}$ × 11$\frac{1}{2}$ inches). Pinnacles: *St. Bartholomew* – 21·6 ×
24·1 cm (8$\frac{1}{2}$ × 9$\frac{1}{2}$ inches); *St. Paul* – 21·6 × 23·5 cm (8$\frac{1}{2}$ ×
9$\frac{1}{4}$ inches); *Crucifixion* – 33·6 × 38 cm (13$\frac{1}{4}$ × 14$\frac{15}{16}$ inches);
St. Peter – 21·6 × 23·9 cm (8$\frac{1}{2}$ × 9$\frac{3}{8}$ inches); *St. John* –
21·6 × 22 cm (8$\frac{1}{2}$ × 8$\frac{5}{8}$ inches).

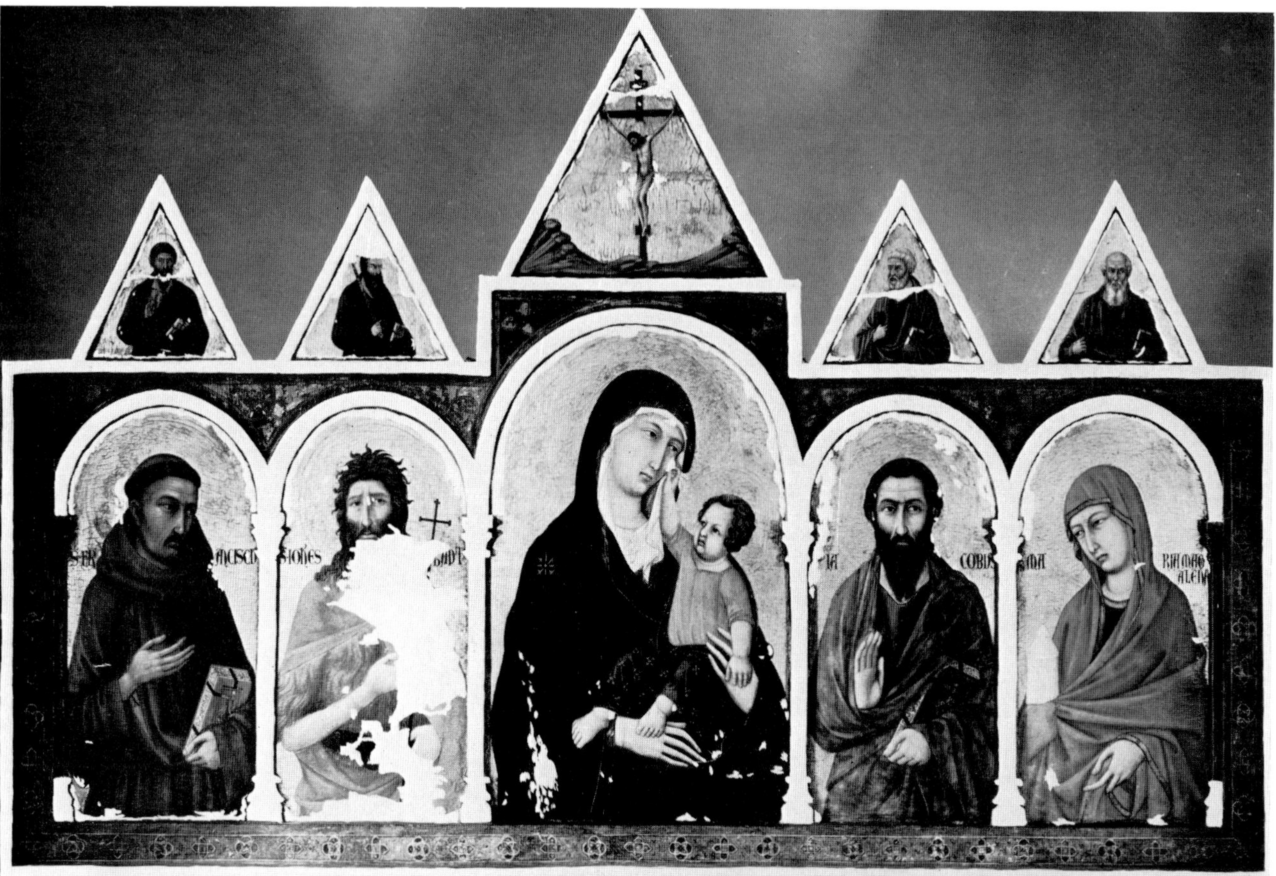

Figure *46a*. Before restoration.

COLLECTIONS: Private collection; (Frederick Mont, New York).

Purchase, Leonard C. Hanna Jr. Bequest, 1961.

The major restoration of this altarpiece and its original frame are shown in the restoration photograph (Fig. 46a). The new parts of the frame and the repaired losses in the panels are indicated in white. The altarpiece had been dismembered into three parts and covered with wax to protect and hold detached paint particles. Therefore, William Suhr who treated it in 1961 had to work in wax to join and reinforce the panels. The juncture is indicated by visible cracks in the gesso and paint, as is the filled vertical crack in the panel of the Madonna. All the panels are heavily worm-eaten. The arches framing the main parts had nineteenth-century gilding which was removed and replaced with bole.

Using as her point of departure the S. Croce altarpiece of ca. 1321–1325 and Duccio's *Maesta* of 1308–1311, Coor-Achenbach developed a chronology of Ugolino's work extending from ca. 1305–1310 to ca. 1325–1330 (see Gertrude Coor-Achenbach, "Contributions to the Study of Ugolino di Nerio's Art," *The Art Bulletin*, XXXVII, 1955, 153 ff.). She assigns the present altarpiece to the third period of Ugolino's activity, ca. 1315–1320, and believes all of it, excepting possibly the ornament on the frame, to be by Ugolino (letters of May 12, 1960 and January 15, 1961). However, Pope-Hennessy (1962, p. 12) believes the Cleveland polyptych may not be entirely by Ugolino and is somewhat later than his large heptaptych in the Sterling and Francine Clark Art Institute which seems closer to the S. Croce panels and datable between 1317 and 1321. The resemblance of the Magdalen and St. John the Baptist in the Cleveland picture to the same representations in the altarpiece attributed to Duccio and collaborators, ca. 1315, in the Accademia, Siena (no. 47), would suggest Ugolino's collaboration in the latter work at a time near to that of his execution of the Cleveland painting, whose central panel is also very like Ugolino's *Madonna and Child* of the same period, ex-Tadini-Buoninsegni collection (Cesare Brandi, *Duccio*, Florence, 1951, pl. 117).

Although the St. Francis in the Cleveland panel is similar in pose to a later figure in the Barber Institute of Art, Birmingham, they are in clear stylistic contrast and we cannot accept Pope-Hennessy's dating in the 1320s for the former based on a resemblance to the late work at Birmingham. A rare feature of the present polyptych is the solitary *Crucifixion* replacing the more

usual (for that time) *Christ Blessing* as the crowning pinnacle of the altarpiece. This has also been used as an argument for a later dating of the Cleveland altarpiece (Pope-Hennessy, 1962, p. 15, n. 18), but it does not seem convincing enough to outweigh those in favor of the earlier date of ca. 1315–1317.

E.F.G.

EXHIBITIONS: CMA, November 1961: The Year in Review, cat. no. 71, illus.

LITERATURE: Henry S. Francis, "An Altarpiece by Ugolino da Siena," CMA *Bulletin*, XLVIII (1961), 194–205, illus. pp. 204, 205 (color); Malcolm Vaughan, "The Connoisseur in America," *The Connoisseur*, CXLIX (1962), 276 (erroneously confuses the CMA panel with the S. Croce altarpiece); John Pope-Hennessy, "Heptatych Ugolino da Siena," *Sterling and Francine Clark Art Institute, Exhibit Twenty* (1962), pp. 12–13, n. 18; Francis, "An Altarpiece by Ugolino da Siena" (reprint), *The Connoisseur*, CLI (1962), 128–134; *Handbook* (1966), p. 54; *Selected Works* (1966), p. 100.

ANONYMOUS ITALIAN MASTER,
School of Milan, ca. 1480–1500

47   *Adoration of the Shepherds*   16.781

Panel (poplar), 35·9 × 34·5 cm (14$\frac{1}{8}$ × 13$\frac{9}{16}$ inches). Painted surface: 34·2 × 33 cm (13$\frac{1}{2}$ × 13 inches).
COLLECTIONS: James Jackson Jarves; Mrs. Liberty E. Holden, Cleveland, 1884.
Holden Collection, 1916.

Annotated (falsely) on *cartellino* on lower right: MASO-LINUS. The letters have been tampered with, but the *cartellino* is original.

The panel has suffered from abrasions and some old restorations are evident in the faces and hands, sky, landscape, the yellow garment of Joseph, and the blue mantle of the Madonna on which the left inner contour shows an alteration of design. The face of the Madonna and the building behind her seem to be in good condition, although the strange perspective of the projecting roof is disturbing and may be the result of restoration. On the other hand it may result from the carelessness of a young painter and is reminiscent in this respect of the very early Luini. The picture was cleaned and the losses attenuated by Suhr in 1951.

This panel was considered an early work of Agostino da Lodi (Pseudo-Boccaccino) by M. L. Berenson (1907), Suida (1956), and B. Berenson (1907; 1932) although in 1949 (unpublished notation) he suggested that it might be a late Butinone. The connection with Butinone has also been remarked by Zeri (letter of April 4, 1966) who notes (with M. L. Berenson) as well an association with the early Bramantino – for example, compare the shepherds in the Cologne *Bacchus and Philemon*. Neither Zeri, Offner, Stechow (orally), Nicodemi, nor Mather consider the attribution to Agostino da Lodi at all convincing. Giorgio Nicodemi (letter of August 13, 1940) of the Castello Sforzesco found it closer to a follower of Borgognone. Offner (on photograph mount in Frick Art Reference Library, New York) assigned it to the Milanese School. Mather (letter of May 17, 1921) thought its color Piedmontese and on the basis of the letters in the *cartellino* suggested Massone "in a Foppesque phase" as its author. The echoes of Foppa and Borgognone certainly imply a Lombard origin for this picture, and the more immediate relation to Butinone and his probable pupil Bramantino, with their Veneto-Ferrarese reminiscences, suggest that it may be the work of

a painter of Butinone's circle, which included the latter's contemporary Bernardo Zenale. (Both collaborated on works in Treviglio and Milan, but Zenale was a more progressive painter, and more susceptible to Leonardo da Vinci's influence.) An adaptation of color combinations and of types (as in the Christ Child and the face of the younger shepherd) from Zenale's works, as well as the drawing of the borders of the Virgin's mantle, seems to point especially to some contact of the painter of the Cleveland panel with Zenale. (For a group of works attributed to Zenale, some of which have some bearing on the Cleveland picture, see Maria Louisa Ferrari "Lo Pseudo-Civerchio e Lo Zenale," *Paragone*, XI, 1960, no. 127, 34 ff.; and "Ritorno a Bernardo Zenale," *Paragone*, XIV, 1963, no. 157, 14 ff.) This panel may have been part of a predella or tabernacle made of small pictures, such as Butinone's in the Castello Sforzesco, Milan (*Guida al Castello Sforzesco ed ai suoi musei*, Milan, 1957, pl. XLVI).

E.F.G.

EXHIBITIONS: Boston (1883), cat. no. 410; CMA (1916), cat. no. 5 ("Pseudo-Boccaccino"); CMA (1936), cat. no. 102.
LITERATURE: Jarves (1884), cat. no. 44 (as Masolino da Panicale); M. L. Berenson (1907), p. 4; Berenson, *North Italian Painters...* (1907), p. 169; Rubinstein (1917), no. 5; Berenson, *Pictures Renaiss.* (1932), p. 89; William Suida, "Pitture lombarde del rinascimento – I: Lo Pseudo-Boccaccino," *Arte lombarda*, II (1956), 90, fig. 4 (cropped photo); Berenson, *Pictures Renaiss., Central and North Italian Schools*, I (1968), 173 (as Giovanni Agostino da Lodi, "Pseudo-Boccaccino").

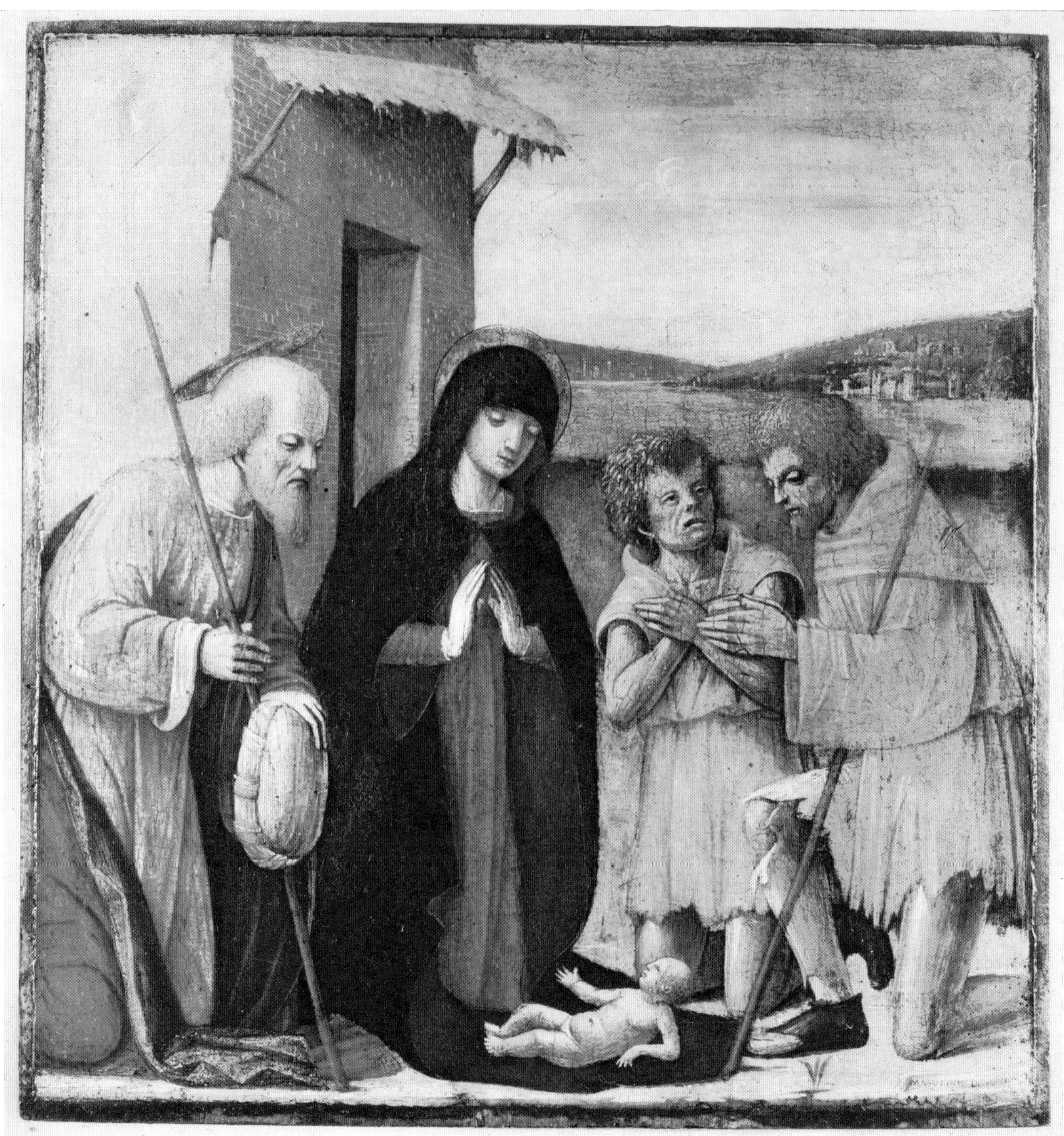

Figure 47.

ANONYMOUS ITALIAN MASTER,
Siena, ca. 1315

48 A, B   *Two Angels*   62.257, 62.258

Pinnacles from a polyptych

Panels, each, 31 × 23 cm (13 × 9 inches).
COLLECTIONS: Count della Gherardesca, Florence;
(Annesley Gore, London); Mrs. Albert S. Ingalls,
Cleveland, by 1935.
Bequest of Jane Taft Ingalls, 1962.

On the back of each panel stamped in purple with an
Italian custom stamp: 23 Aprile, 1930.

The condition of the painted surfaces is good. The
original edge of the paint is visible on all three sides
of both panels and the original bevelled edges are on
the backs. The gold leaf is in good condition and there
is only minor retouching on the edge of the hair of the
angel in Painting 48 A which has been reinforced; the
edges of the wings of the angel in Painting 48 B have
been refilled and repainted.

One of the most perplexing problems in Sienese painting is the attribution of the paintings of the numerous
close followers of Duccio. Zeri (letter of February 18,
1966) has suggested Segna di Bonaventura as the painter
of the Museum's angel pinnacles. Segna's name is recorded in documents between 1298 and 1326. Among
the many paintings attributed to him, there are four
signed works in existence (see Peleo Bacci, *Fonti e commenti per la storia dell'arte senese*, Siena, 1944, pp. 3 ff.;
Enzo Carli, "Archivistica e critica d'arte," *Emporium*,
XCIX, 1944, 58–59).

Segna had two painter sons, Francesco and Niccolò,
who signed a *Crucifix* in the Ducciesque tradition in the
Accademia in Siena which is dated 1345. There is a
close stylistic similarity in the treatment of the hair and
highlighted facial features of the *Maesta*-type *Enthroned
Madonna and Angels* of Segna in the Collegiata at Castig-
lione Fiorentino as well as a similar lack of vitality but
with the typical gentleness of Segna's work. These pinnacles with two others and a *Redeemer* probably made
up the top register of a polyptych. Zeri (letter, *op. cit.*)
suggested that the central pinnacle might be *Christ Blessing* (Fig. 48 a) which is presently called a work by an
artist close to Duccio of about 1320. This suggestion is
further substantiated by a photograph in the Kunsthistorisches Institut in Florence of the angel pinnacles
and the Raleigh *Christ Blessing* when they were still in

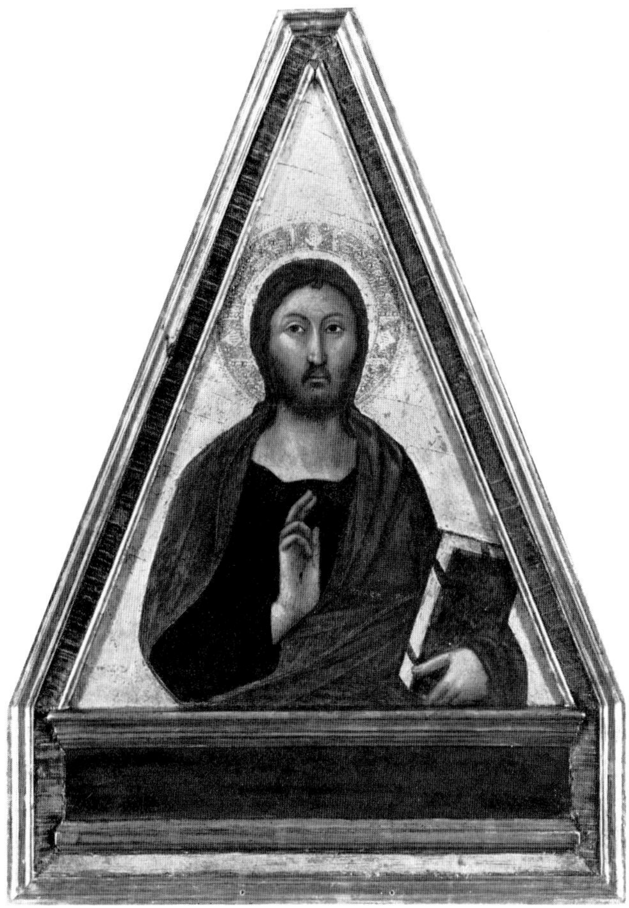

Figure 48 a. *Christ Blessing*.
45·4 × 36·2 cm (17$\frac{7}{8}$ × 14$\frac{1}{4}$ inches).
Follower of Duccio, ca. 1320, Siena.
North Carolina Museum of Art, Raleigh,
Samuel H. Kress Collection, K 219.

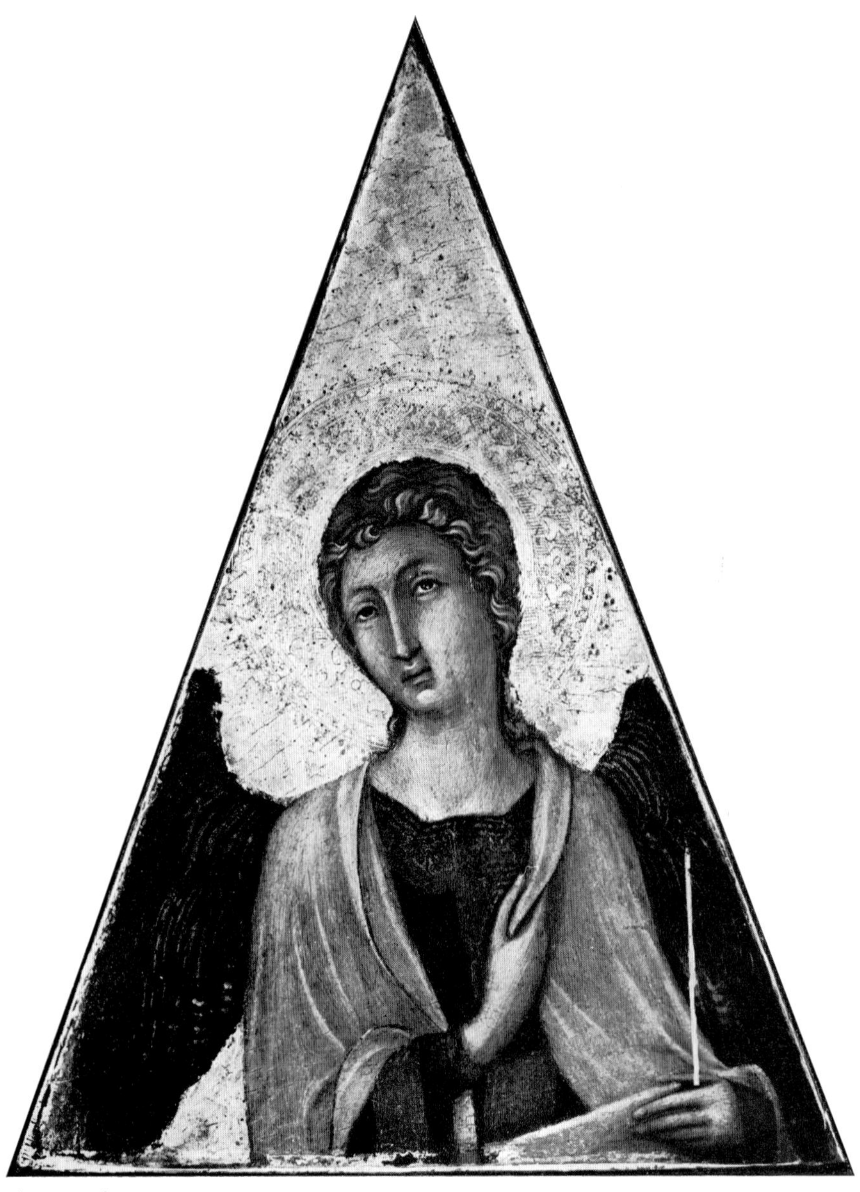

Figure 48 A.

the Gherardesca collection. At that time, before cleaning, they were framed alike and according to Ulrich Middeldorf (letter of July 29, 1966), obviously formed an ensemble. Zeri also suggested the very interesting possibility that this dismembered polyptych might have included the *St. Margaret Holding the Cross*, now in the Kress Collection of the Portland Museum of Art, Oregon (*Handbook of the Samuel H. Kress Collection of Paintings of the Renaissance*, The Portland Art Museum, 1952, no. 9, illus. p. 29 as Sienese painter ca. 1330, close follower of Segna di Bonaventura) and the half-length figure of *St. Lucy* in the Szépmüvészeti Múzeum in Budapest (Gabriel von Térey, *Die Gemälde-Galerie des Museums*

für Künste in Budapest, Berlin, 1916, no. 31, illus. p. 29, as the work of Segna's son, Niccolò Segna di Bonaventura). Van Os (1972) suggested the Museum's *Angels* can be attributed to Niccolò Segna di Bonaventura.

Considering other isolated angels related to the Museum's in varying degrees, five angel pinnacles of this period have been published by Cesare Brandi (*Duccio*, Florence, 1951, p. 145, pls. 104–106): (1) formerly in the collection of Mrs. William H. Hill (incorrectly listed as owned by Wellesley College); (2) in the Philadelphia Museum of Art, Johnson Collection; (3) in the Stoclet collection; (4, 5) two formerly in the Loeser collection, Florence. None of these retains its original shape and

136

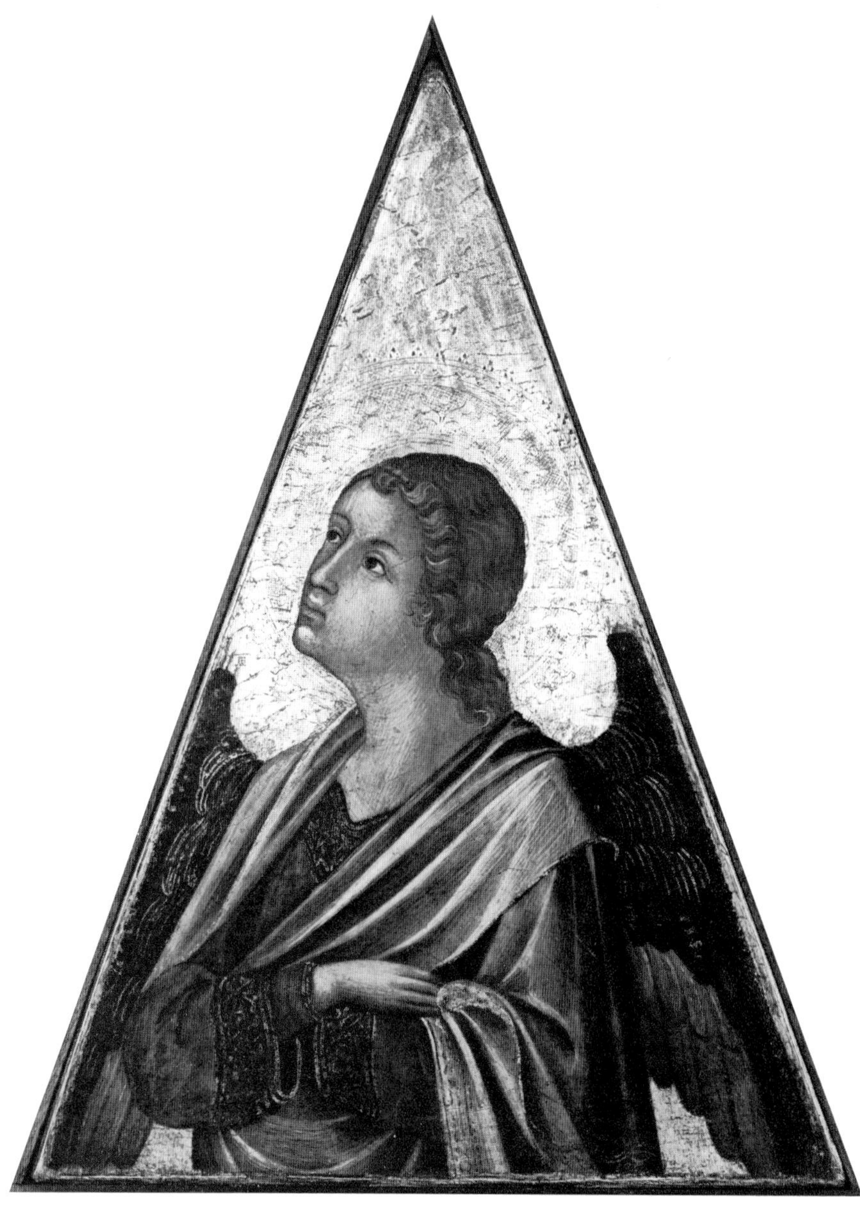

Figure 48 B.

Brandi suggested they might have been the terminals of the Duccio *Maesta*. Another group of four angels with a *Redeemer*, which was formerly in the Ramboux collection and the Wallraf-Richartz-Museum in Cologne, is closely related to the above group and is given to the workshop of the Badia a Isola Master, so-called because of an altarpiece in the church at Badia a Isola near Monteriggioni and considered one of Duccio's oldest and finest followers (see Gertrude Coor-Achenbach, "A Dispersed Polyptych by the Badia a Isola Master," *Art Bulletin*, XXIV, 1952, 312, fig. 6). Two angel pinnacles (33 × 24 cm) of about the same size as the Museum's are listed in the *Catalogo generale*, Mostra dell'antica arta senese (Siena, 1904, pp. 301–302, nos. 12, 15) as Maniere di Duccio, owned by the Fratelli Pannilini, S. Giovan d'Asso (present whereabouts unknown).

N.C.W.

EXHIBITIONS: CMA (1936), cat. nos. 125–126; CMA, November 1962: Year in Review, cat. no. 110, illus.
LITERATURE: Berenson, *Pictures, Renaiss., Central and North Italian Schools*, I (1968), 119 (as Duccio follower); Hendrik W. van Os, "Possible Additions to the Œuvre of Niccolò di Segna," CMA *Bulletin*, LIX (1972), pp. 78–83.

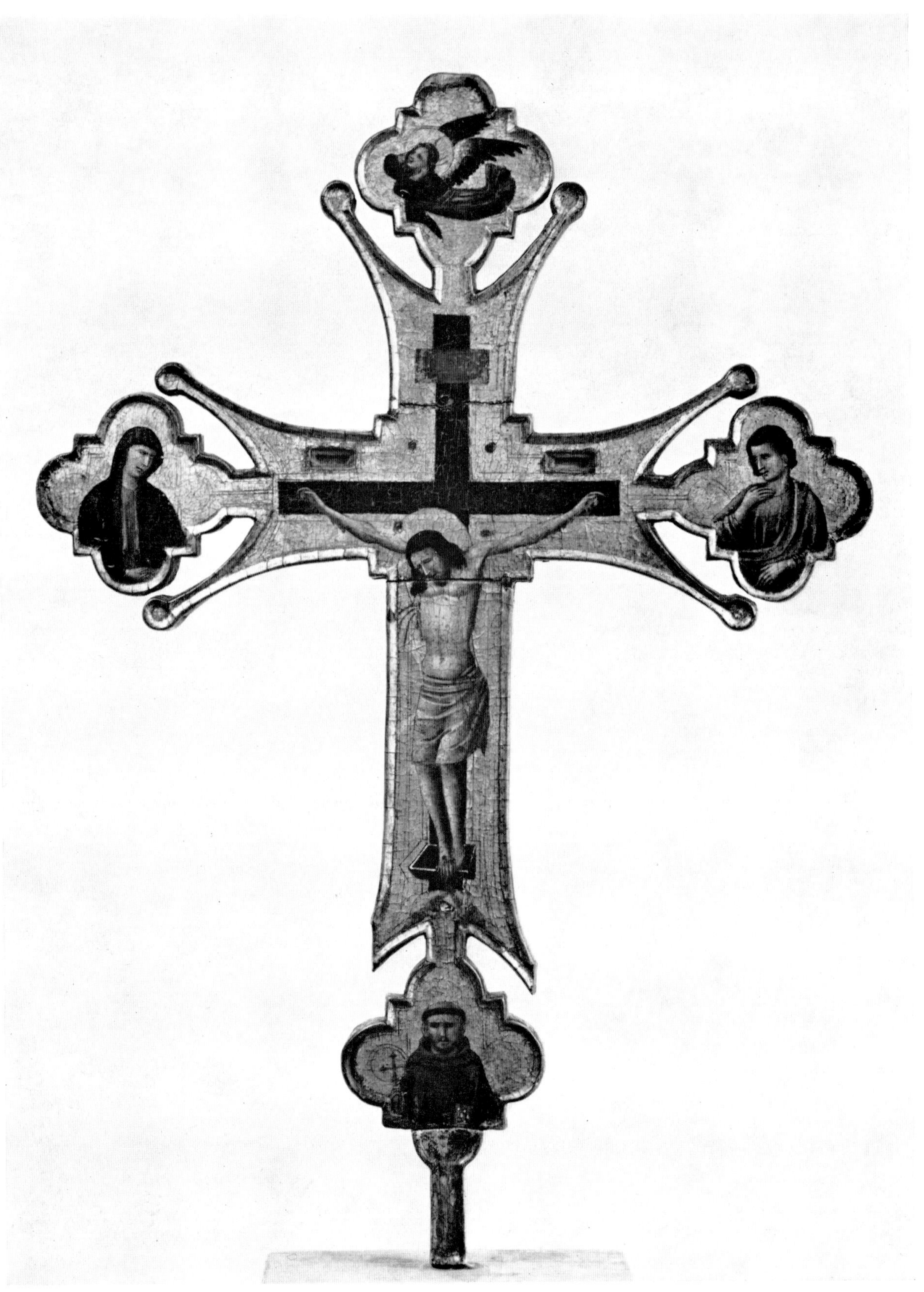

Figure 49.

ANONYMOUS ITALIAN MASTER,
Venice, fourteenth century

49 *Crucifixion*   43.280

Double-faced processional cross

Obverse. Center: Christ on the Cross
Top terminal: Angel
Bottom terminal: St. Francis
Dexter terminal: Virgin Mary
Sinister terminal: St. John

Reverse. Center: Christ on the Cross
Top terminal: Angel
Bottom terminal: St. Clare
Dexter terminal: Virgin Mary
Sinister terminal: St. John

Canvas attached to poplar, over-all, 61·3 × 44·2 × 2·6 cm
($24\frac{1}{8}$ × $17\frac{3}{8}$ × 1 inches).
COLLECTIONS: Charles A. Loeser, Florence; (Adolphe
Loewi, Los Angeles, California).
Purchase from the J. H. Wade Fund, 1943.

This crucifix has horizontal fractures in both arms of
the cross on the obverse side and vertical fractures on
the reverse side. There are minor retouchings particularly in the angels in the upper finials. Unexplainable
incised double-lines border all the figures and the cross.
They are mechanically executed except for the irregular
cutting around the Virgin on the reverse side.

This processional cross has been called Venetian school
of the mid-fourteenth century (Zeri, letter of August 17,
1956); Florentine, fourteenth and fifteenth century;
Umbrian, fourteenth century; and given to Jacopo del
Casentino (see Literature). The shape and iconography
follow a tradition of medieval painting, sculpture, and
metalwork found in the Veneto. The angels in the
upper finials are also characteristic of this area and are not
found on Florentine crosses of the Trecento. The painting style shows a strong influence of Giotto, a tradition
firmly entrenched in the Veneto, and the cross should
date about 1370; the elaborate shape is close to the
crucifix in the Correr Museum in Venice (n. 1891, see
Giovanni Mariacher, *Il Museo Correr di Venezia*, Venice,
1959, 137–138), and the Cleveland example probably
had similar nodules in the presently plugged holes of the
three terminals. Other similar elaborate portable Venetian crosses may be found in S. Maria in Trivio in Rome;
Yale University Gallery (1943.258), New Haven, Conn.;

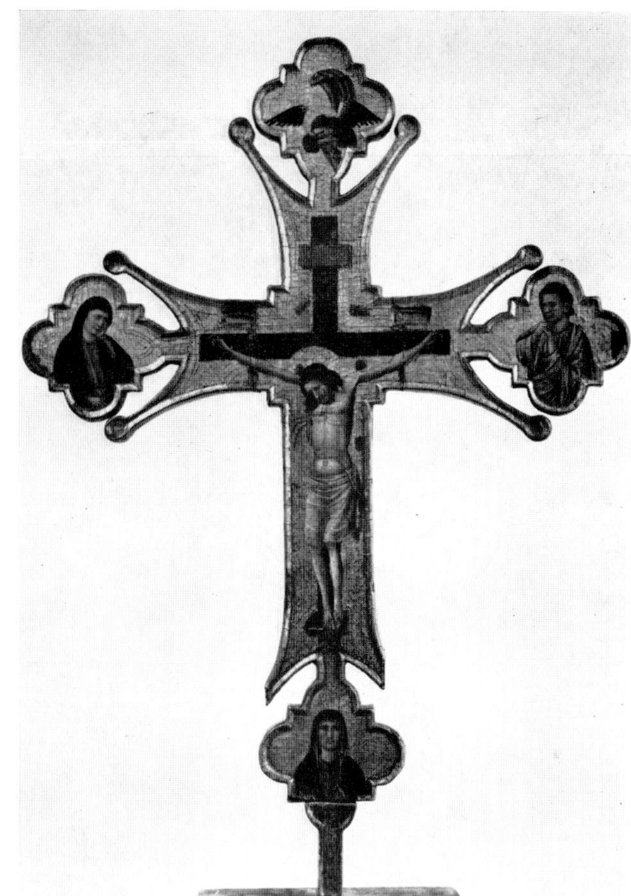

Figure 49a. Reverse.

the church of S. Pantaleone and the church of S. Bene-
detto in Venice (see Mariacher, "Croci dipinte vene-
ziene del '300," *Scritti di storia dell'arte in onore di Lionello
Venturi*, I, Rome, 1956, 101–120).

N.C.W.

EXHIBITIONS: None.
LITERATURE: Henry S. Francis, "A Fifteenth-century Florentine
Processional Cross," CMA *Bulletin*, XXXII (1945), 3–5, illus. p. 1;
Offner, *Corpus*, sect. III, Vol. VI (1956), 166–167, n. 1 (as Umbrian,
fourteenth century); Francis, "Sassetta: Crucifixion with St.
Francis," CMA *Bulletin*, L (1963), 46, fig. 1; Berenson, *Pictures
Renaiss., Florentine School*, I (1963), 101 (as Jacopo del Casentino);
Handbook (1966), p. 58; Berenson, *Pictures Renaiss., Central and
North Italian Schools*, I (1968), 356 (as Riminese Trecento); Miklòs
Boskovits, "Un pittore 'espressionista' del trecento umbro,"
Storia e Arte in Umbria Nell'eta' Comunale (Perugia, 1968),
pp. 126–127, figs. 11, 12; Charles Seymour, Jr., *Early Italian
Paintings in the Yale University Art Gallery* (New Haven, London,
1970), p. 101.

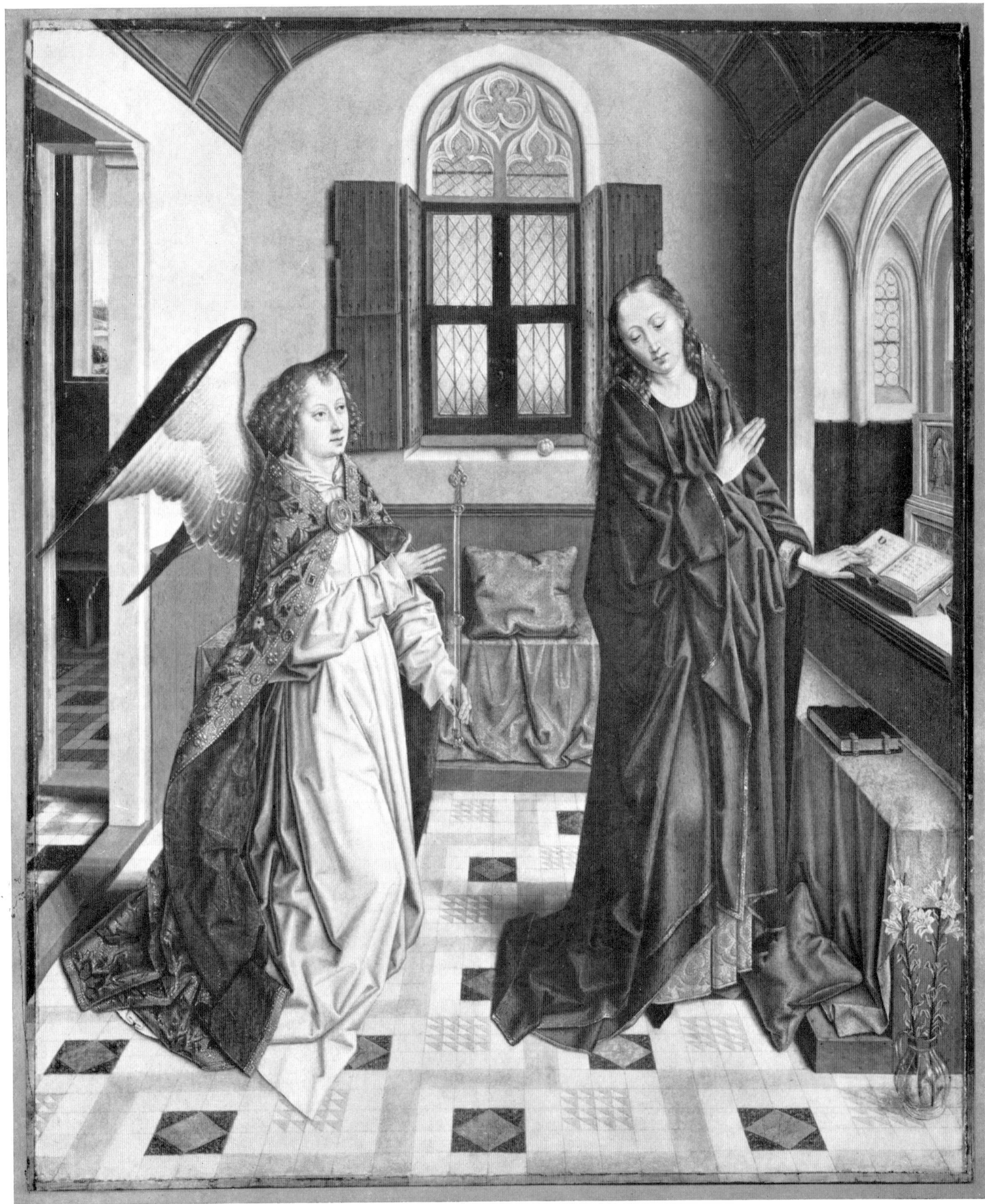

Figure 50. See also Colorplate XXIV.

AELBRECHT BOUTS, Louvain,
born ca. 1452–1455, died 1549

He was probably born in Haarlem whence his father
Dieric Bouts moved to Louvain ca. 1456–1457. He was
mentioned in Louvain between 1473 and 1476, and as a
painter from 1479 until 1549. Bouts was a pupil and
imitator of his father, his œuvre has been assembled
around the authenticated *Assumption of Mary* in the
Brussels Museum.

50   *The Annunciation*   42.635

> Panel (oak), 50·2 × 41·5 cm (19¾ × 16⅜ inches).
> COLLECTIONS: Graf Sierstorpff, Driburg, Westphalia;
> (sale: Rudolph Lepke, Berlin, April 19, 1887, no. 106, as
> Jan van Eyck); Eugen Schweitzer, Berlin, before 1912;
> (M. Knoedler, New York); John L. Severance, Cleveland,
> 1915.
> John L. Severance Collection, 1942.

This well-preserved panel (Schöne, 1938, no. 84 *a*), painted ca. 1480, is an adaptation of a lost work by Dieric
Bouts, of which Aelbrecht painted another signed version, now in the Munich Alte Pinakothek (Schöne,
1938, no. 84 *b*). The composition of the much larger
Munich version, contrary to Friedländer (1925), is not
entirely identical with the present painting, but is apparently closer to Dieric Bouts. Note the two roundels
with highly original representations of typological
parallels of the *Annunciation*, the *Temptation of Eve*, and
the *Fleece of Gideon*, as well as the more elaborate landscape view and greater emphasis on depth, which are
not found in the present panel. A painting in Berlin
(Schöne, 1938, no. 85) is a free version in reverse of the
Cleveland panel by Bouts himself, while the crude picture once in the Augustinermuseum in Freiburg im
Breisgau and now in a private collection in South Germany (*Meisterwerke aus badenwürttembergischem Privatbesitz*, exh. cat.; Staatsgalerie Stuttgart, 1958–1959, no.
19) is a slightly varied copy of the Cleveland panel by a
different hand. The theory that the picture preserves a
composition by Dieric Bouts is supported by its unusual
iconography (vaulted niche with house altar) which re-
curs in a few works datable between 1467 and the pre-
sumable date of the present panel (Schöne, 1938).

W.S.

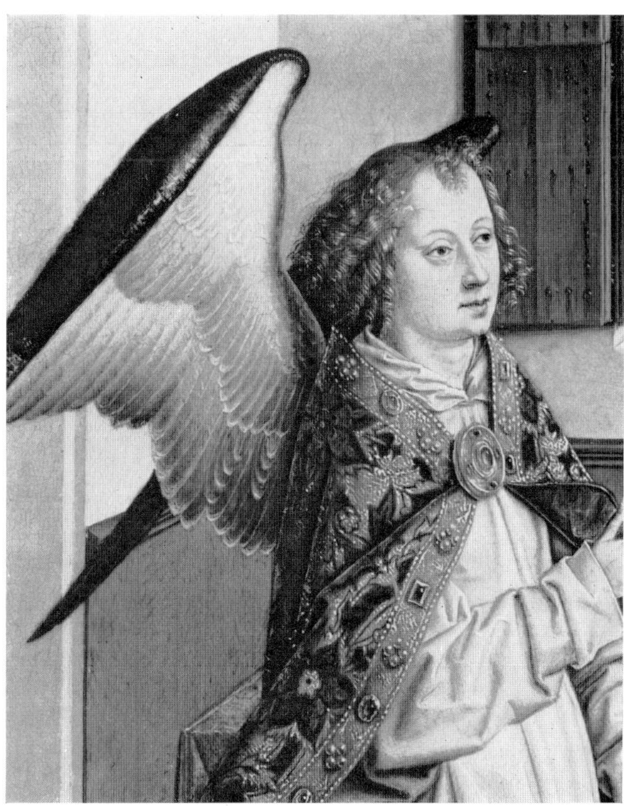

Figure 50 *a*. Detail of the Angel of Annunciation.

EXHIBITIONS: Cleveland, Gage Gallery, 1915: Old and Modern
Masters in the Knoedler Gallery; CMA (1931); New York,
World's Fair, 1939: Masterpieces of Art, cat. no. 23; CMA, 1940:
Masterpieces of Art from the New York and San Francisco
World's Fairs, cat. no. 1; Bruges, Musée Groeninge, 1960: Le
siècle des primitifs flamands, cat. no. 32; Detroit, Institute of Arts,
1960: Flanders in the Fifteenth Century, cat. no. 28.

LITERATURE: Friedländer, *Altniederl. Mal.*, III (1925), 66, 115, no.
44 *a*; David M. Robb, "The Iconography of the Annunciation in
the Fourteenth and Fifteenth Centuries," *Art Bulletin*, XVIII (1936),
513, n. 91; Wolfgang Schöne, *Dieric Bouts und seine Schule* (Berlin,
Leipzig, 1938), pp. 148, 149, 191 (no. 84 *a*), pl. 54 *b*; Henry S.
Francis, *Catalogue of the John L. Severance Collection* (CMA, 1942),
pp. 10, 21, pl. 1; *Handbook* (1958), no. 438; *Handbook* (1966), p.
69; Friedländer, *Early Netherl. Paintg.*, III (1968), 39, 65, pl. 60, fig.
44 *a*.

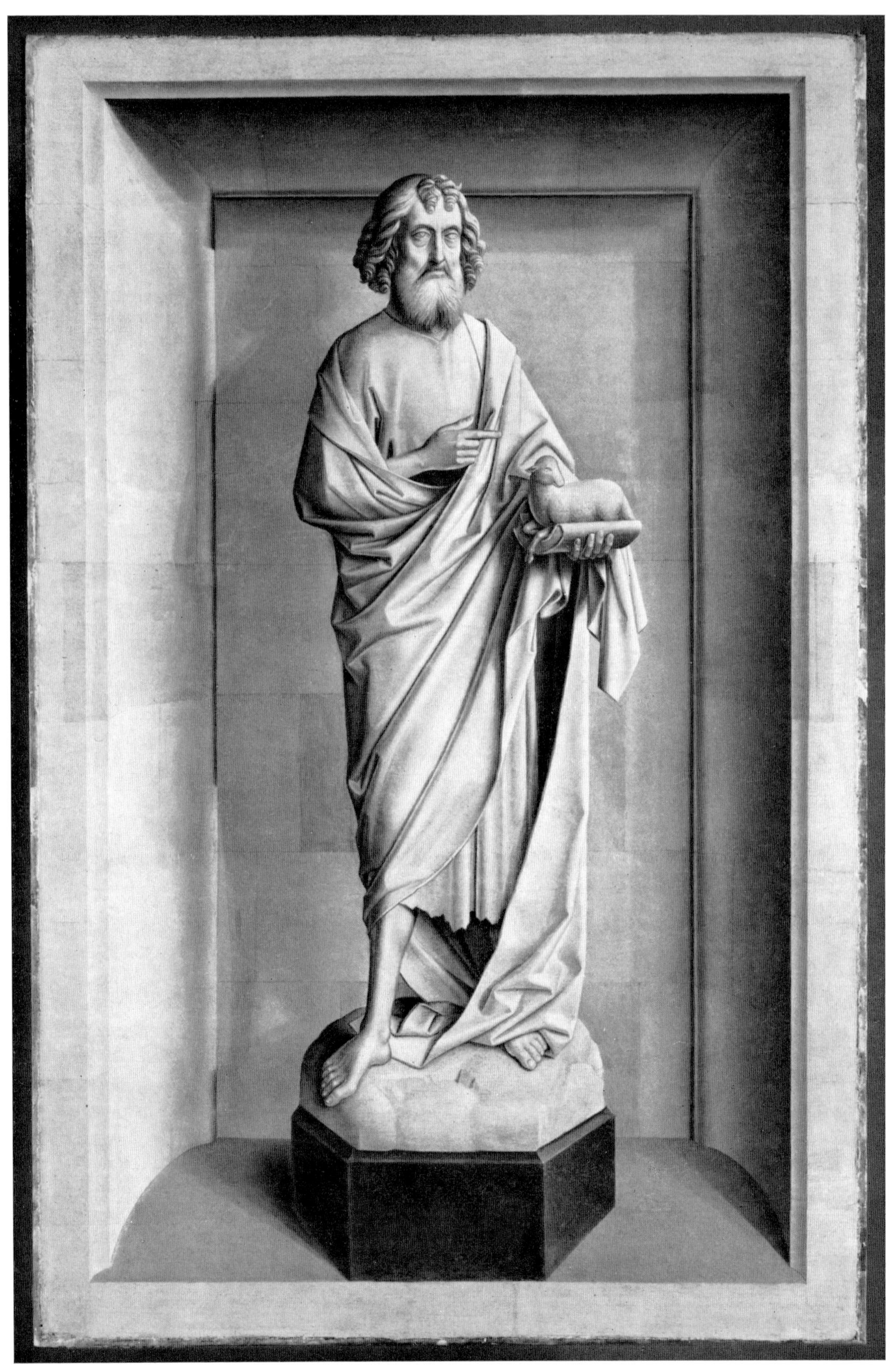

Figure 51.

DIERIC BOUTS, Louvain, ca. 1415–1475

Born in Haarlem ca. 1415, he was married at Louvain in or before 1448 but not mentioned there as a painter before 1457. He was possibly active in Haarlem once more between 1448 and 1457, and after that, in Louvain until his death in 1475.

51 *St. John the Baptist* 51.354

Grisaille panel

Panel (oak), 106 × 68·5 cm (41¾ × 27 inches). Painted surface: 102·8 × 65·5 cm (40½ × 24¾ inches).
PROVENANCE: St. Laurentius Church, Cologne (pulled down in 1818).
COLLECTIONS: Rector Fochem, Cologne (probably from 1818 to 1822 when the obverse of the panel was acquired for the Munich Pinakothek); Heinrich Wilhelm Campe, 1770–1862, Cologne; (sale: C. G. Boerner, Leipzig, September 24, 1827, no. 132, as Hemmeling [Memling], bought by "Beck in Dessau"); Duke of Anhalt-Dessau, Wörlitz, 1864 (as Memling); (J. Goudstikker, Amsterdam, 1928, cat. no. 34, no. 5, illus.); Baron Thyssen-Bornemisza, Castle Rohoncz, Lugano, 1930; (Rosenberg & Stiebel, New York).
Purchase, Leonard C. Hanna Jr. Bequest, 1951.

The painting is well preserved, with pentimento on the outline of the garment near the right knee.

The panel belonged to an altarpiece painted for the St. Laurentius church in Cologne. It formed the reverse of the *Arrest of Christ*, now in the Alte Pinakothek in Munich (Fig. 51 *a*), not of the *Resurrection* as erroneously stated by Friedländer (1925). Contrary to a statement by Voll (1906), the *Arrest of Christ* is almost exactly the same size as the Cleveland panel. Once part of the same altarpiece, two other panels now in Munich are the *Resurrection* (obverse) and *St. John the Evangelist*, grisaille (reverse) (Figs. 51 *b, c*).

Most writers consider Dieric Bouts the author of this group of panels. Voll (1906; 1923) suggested Ouwater, Ernst Heidrich (*Alt-niederländische Malerei*, Jena, 1910, fig. 61) a follower of Ouwater, without finding much support. Schöne (1938) has constructed the *Meister der Münchener Gefangennahme* [Master of the Munich Arrest of Christ] but his theory has not found universal acceptance. The painting must antedate 1464 because in that year the Cologne Master of the Lyversberg Passion made use of the composition on its obverse in his *Arrest of Christ* now in the Wallraf-Richartz-Museum in Cologne (no. 144). However, the same subject in Koerbecke's Marienfeld altarpiece of ca. 1453–1456 is not clearly based on the Bouts model and cannot be used as has been suggested (*Westfälische Maler der Spätgotik, 1400–1490*, exh. cat.; Münster, 1952, no. 59) for dating the latter before 1456.

W.S.

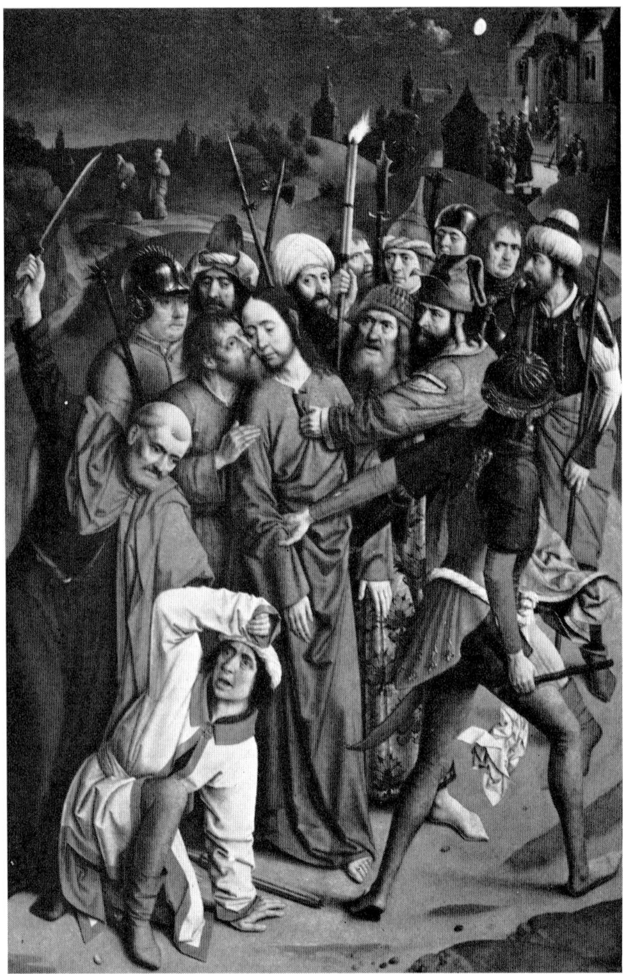

Figure 51 *a. Arrest of Christ.*
104 × 67 cm (40$\frac{15}{16}$ × 26$\frac{3}{8}$ inches).
Bouts. Alte Pinakothek, Munich, 990.

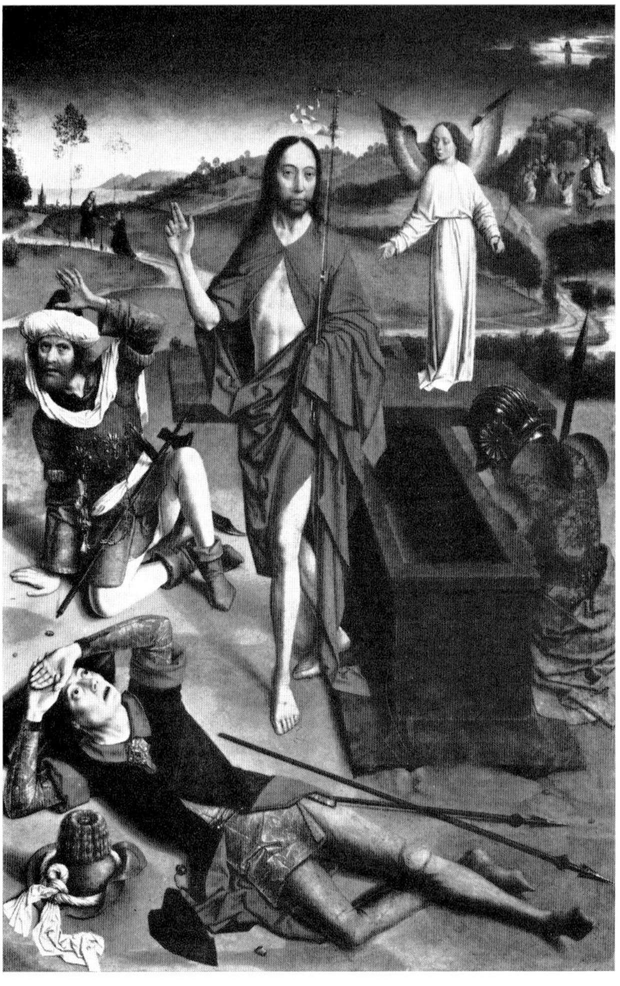

Figure 51 *b. Resurrection of Christ.*
105 × 68 cm (41$\frac{5}{16}$ × 26$\frac{3}{4}$ inches).
Bouts. Alte Pinakothek, Munich, WAF 74.

144

EXHIBITIONS: Bruges, Hôtel Gruuthuse, 1902: Primitifs flamands et art ancien, cat. no. 219; Amsterdam, 1928: Nouvelles
acquisitions de la Collection Goudstikker, cat. no. 34; Munich,
Neue Pinakothek, 1930: Sammlung Schloss Rohoncz, cat. no. 37.
LITERATURE: Gustav Parthey, *Deutscher Bildersaal*, II (Berlin,
1863–1864), 18 (as Memling); Ludwig Scheibler, *Die hervorragend-
sten anonymen Meister und Werke der Kölner Malerschule von 1460
bis 1500* (Bonn, 1880), p. 19 (as Bouts); Paul Heiland, *Dirk Bouts
und die Hauptwerke seiner Schule* (Strassburg, 1902), pp. 73–74;
Karl Voll, *Die altniederländische Malerei von Jan van Eyck bis
Memling* (1st ed.; Leipzig, 1906), p. 164; Arnold Goffin, *Thiery
Bouts* (Brussels, 1907), p. 100; Eduard Firmenich-Richartz, *Die
Brüder Boisserée*, I (Jena, 1916), 457; Martin Conway, *The Van
Eycks and Their Followers* (New York, 1921), p. 165; Voll, *Die
altniederländische Malerei von Jan van Eyck bis Memling* (2nd ed.;
Leipzig, 1923), p. 156; Winkler (1924), p. 92; Friedländer,
Altniederl. Mal. (1925), III, 109, no. 20; XIV (1937), p. 90; Hippo-
lyte Fierens-Gevaert and Paul Fierens, *Histoire de la peinture
flamande des origines à la fin du XVe siècle: La maturité de l'art
flamand* (Paris, Brussels, 1929), p. 12; Franz Dülberg, *Nieder-
ländische Malerei der Spätgotik und Renaissance* (Wildpark-Potsdam,
1929), p. 70; Ludwig Baldass, "Die Entwicklung des Dirk Bouts,"
Jahrbuch der kunsthistorischen Sammlungen in Wien, n.s. VI (1932), 88;
Paul Clemen, *Die Kunstdenkmäler der Rheinprovinz, Köln II, 3:
Ergänzungsband: Die Ehemaligen Kirchen*...(Düsseldorf, 1937),
p. 60; Wolfgang Schöne, *Dieric Bouts und seine Schule* (Berlin,
Leipzig, 1938), p. 163, no. 45 a; Henry S. Francis, "Two Dutch
Fifteenth-century Panels," CMA *Bulletin*, XXXIX (1952), 3–6, illus.
p. 9; Egbert Haverkamp Begemann, "Een aanwinst bij een
aanwinst," *Bulletin Museum Boymans*, IV (Rotterdam, 1953), 9, 11;
Panofsky (1953), p. 495, n. 324.4; *Dieric Bouts* (exh. cat.; Brussels,
Palais des Beaux-Arts, Delft, Museum Prinsenhof, 1957–1958),
pp. 28, 32; *Handbook* (1958), no. 437; *Handbook* (1966), p. 70;
Friedländer, *Early Netherl. Paintg.*, III (1968), 21, pl. 34.

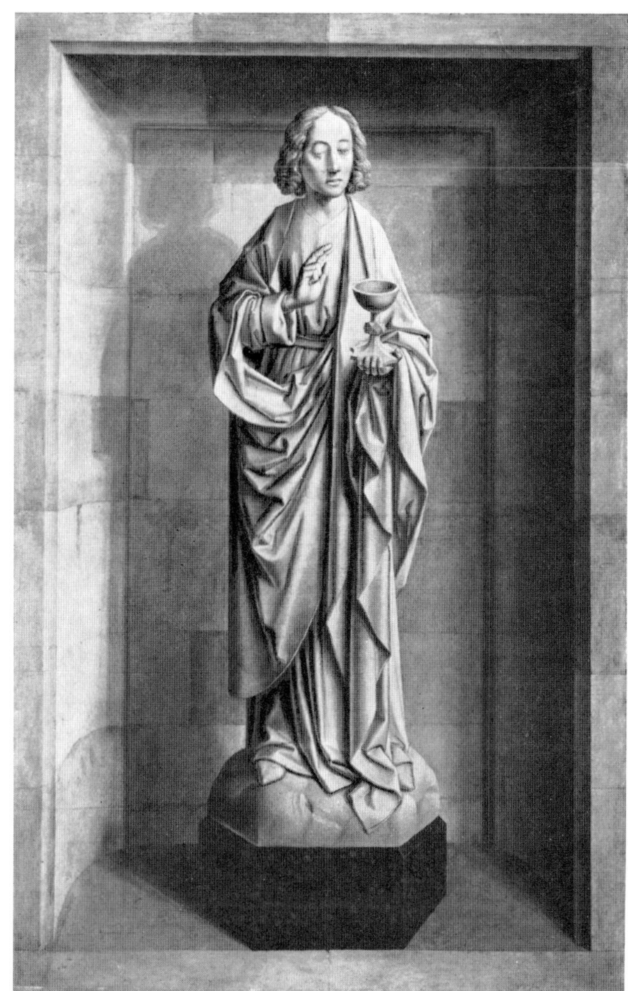

Figure 51 c. *St. John the Evangelist.*
Grisaille panel, 105 × 68 cm $\left(41\frac{5}{16} \times 26\frac{3}{4}\right.$ inches).
Bouts. Bayerische Staatsgemäldesammlungen, Munich.

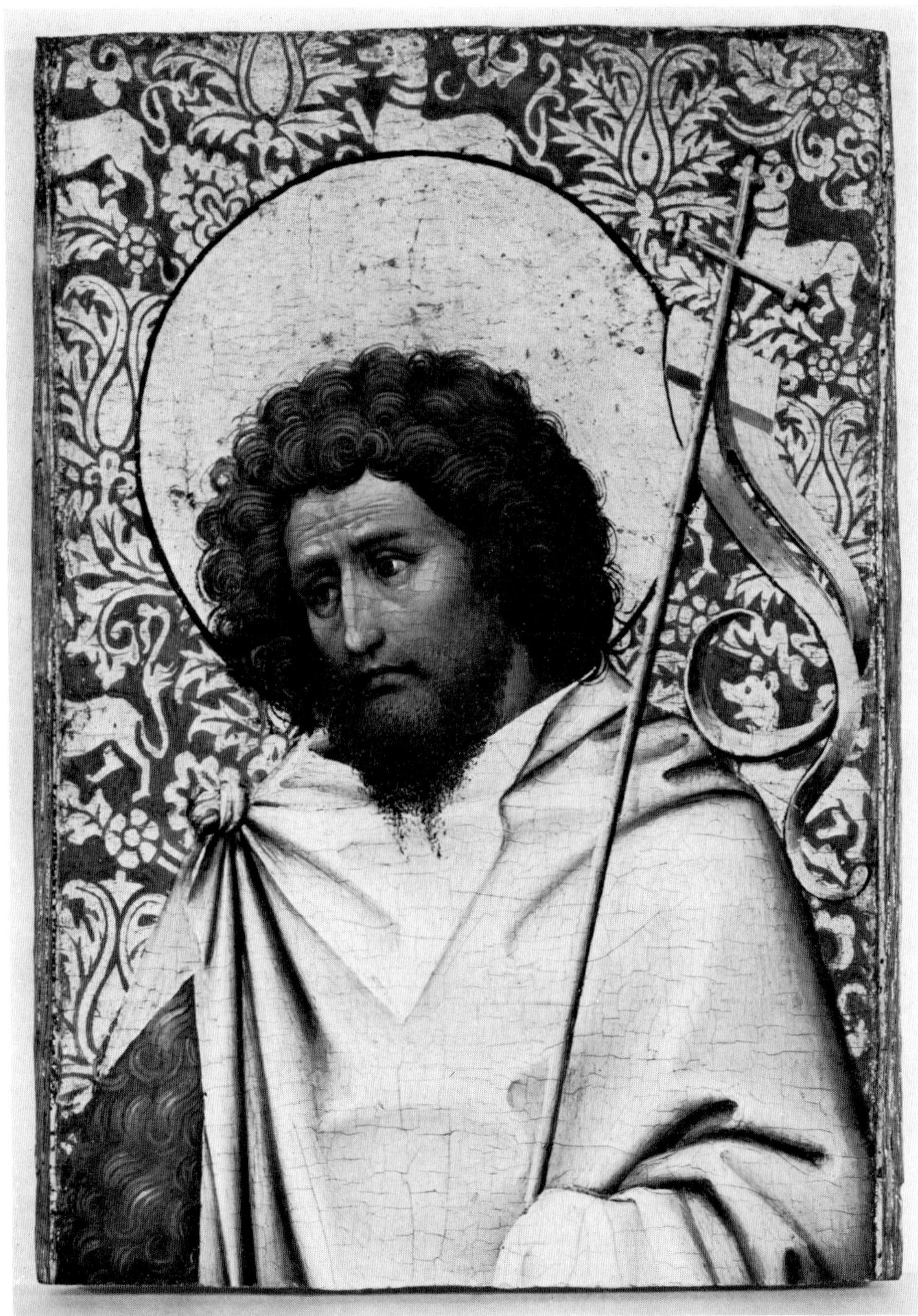

Figure 52. See also Colorplate xxv.

ROBERT CAMPIN (Master of Flémalle),
Tournai, ca. 1375–1444

Being close in style to Roger van der Weyden he was
long considered his follower until a document of 1427
in Tournai disclosed his name as the teacher of Roger
(as well as of Jacques Daret) to whom an important
group of works has since been ascribed, distinct in style
from either pupil and synonymous with that of the
Master of Flémalle. The latter's name was derived from
the alleged provenance (Abbey of Flémalle) of an altarpiece, of which three panels are in the Städelsches
Kunstinstitut in Frankfurt. Some of the most outstanding among Campin's works now firmly attributed to him are the *Annunciation* (often referred to as the
Mérode altarpiece) in the Cloisters in New York, the
Dijon *Nativity*, and the wings of the Werl altarpiece in
the Prado – Campin's only dated work (1438). Despite
the fact that Campin was listed as master painter in
Tournai as early as 1406 and granted the Freedom of the
City in 1410, an honor reserved to men of high standing,
no work of his has as yet been found datable before 1410.
(For the earliest discussion on the identity of this master
see Georges Hulin de Loo, "An Authentic Work by
Jacques Daret, Painted in 1434," *Burl. Mag.*, XV, 1909,
203–208.)

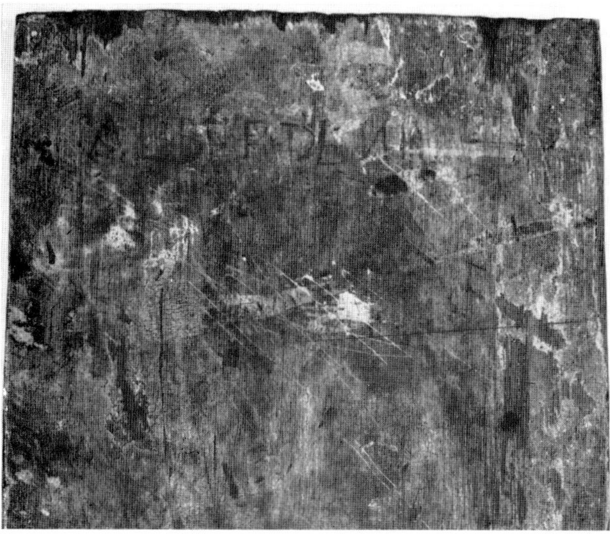

Figure 52 *a*. Back of panel (upper half).

52 *St. John the Baptist*   66.238

> Panel (oak), 17·2 × 37·7 cm (6$\frac{13}{16}$ × 14$\frac{13}{16}$ inches).
> COLLECTIONS: Ducs de Clermont-Tonnerre;
> Nettancourt-Vaubecourt family, Château Choiseul; Le Molt,
> Bourbonne-les-Bains; (sale: Christie's, London, June 26,
> 1964, no. 44, as Master of the School of Cologne);
> (Thomas P. Grange, London).
> Gift of the John Huntington Art and Polytechnic Trust,
> 1966.

On the back of the panel on worn-down yellowish
gesso ground a faint inscription appears (Fig. 52 *a*).

The panel and painted surface are in excellent condition with the upper and two lateral painted edges
intact; the bottom of the panel has been crudely cut
reducing the figure of the saint to less than half its size.
Assuming it was originally painted in full length, and
basing the panel's proportion on that of the full-length
figure of *St. Veronica* in Frankfurt, the original height
would have measured ca. 42·5 cm (Fig. 52 *b*). The nar-
row width of the panel (17·2 cm) in relationship to its
assumed height suggests that *St. John the Baptist* may
once have been part of a small triptych, and presumably

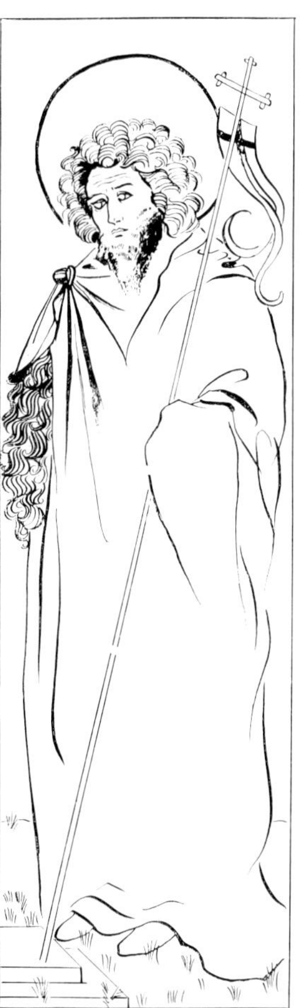

Figure 52 *b*. Reconstruction of the figure
of St. John the Baptist.

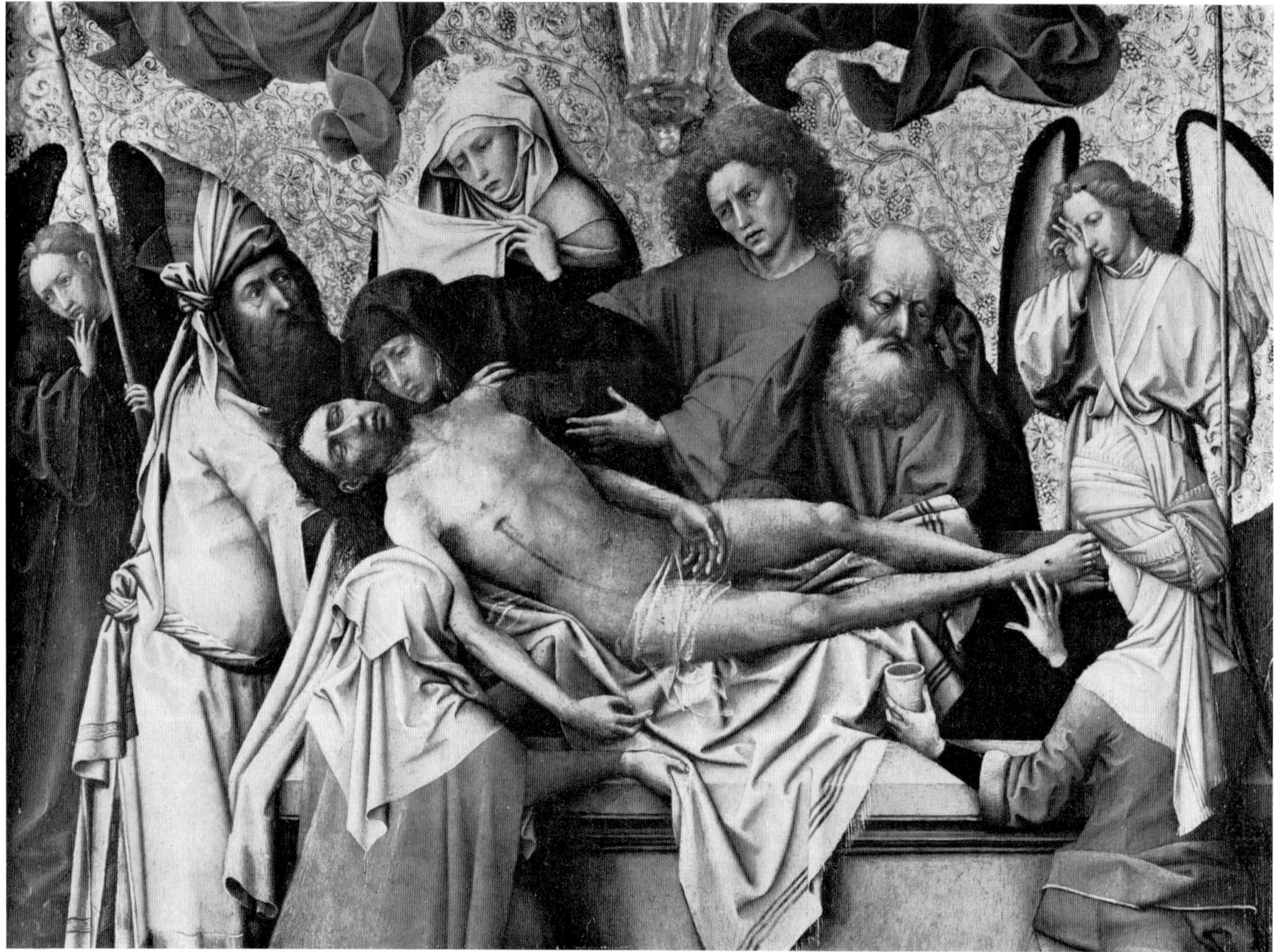

Figure 52c. *Entombment* (detail of central panel of a triptych). Central panel, 60 × 48·9 cm (25⅝ × 19¼ inches). Campin. Count Antoine Seilern, London.

the sinister wing of it, since the saint is turned towards his right (as are the dogs in the textile pattern).

The Cleveland panel was first attributed to Robert Campin by Friedrich Winkler in 1964 and published for the first time by Pieper (1966), after Winkler's death. Pieper convincingly assigns the picture to Campin's early period, pointing to its close stylistic relationship with the *Entombment* triptych in the Seilern collection (Fig. 52c) which has been dated anywhere from 1410 to 1420. Van Gelder (1967, 2–3), dating the Seilern triptych ca. 1410–1415, agrees with Pieper's early date maintaining that it was by no means the work of a beginner and that it must have been preceded by other works, now lost except for the Cleveland fragment. Pieper, too, considers it possible that the latter may have preceded the Seilern *Entombment*, pointing to the similarity which exists between the Cleveland St. John and that of St.

John the Evangelist in the *Entombment* such as the deep-set eyes, long noses, the pronounced modeling of their cheekbones, the wrinkles drawn in separate lines on their foreheads, and above all the thick wig-like hair enframing their thin faces. One should further compare St. John of the Cleveland panel with the mourning angel in the Seilern picture and note the similarity in the strong highlights along their high-ridged noses, painted, it appears, with one stroke from the tip of a loaded brush. All the Seilern figures share this feature, including Christ in the sinister panel of the *Resurrection*. He, too, has the hair of his beard dabbed on with a fine-pointed brush and his face is similar in type to the Cleveland *St. John*. Both carry the thin cross-staff with a split banner (a red cross on white, symbolic of triumph over death). In Campin's later and only other known full-length depiction of this saint (in the dexter wing of the Werl

148

altar) he carries the more usual attributes of book and lamb.

An early date for the panel is further supported by Campin's strong dependence on illuminated manuscripts immediately preceding this panel in date. The untooled gold nimbus outlined in black set against a foil of a boldly patterned textile does not appear again in any of his firmly attributed works. The Cleveland figure recalls the single full-length saints, with untooled gold and black-outlined haloes standing in front of heraldic hangings such as those in the *Boucicaut Hours* (cf., *St. John the Baptist*, *St. John the Evangelist*, and *St. Peter Martyr*, Millard Meiss, *French Painting in the Time of Jean de Berry, The Boucicaut Master*, London, 1967, figs. 3, 4, and 15 respectively, dating from ca. 1405–1408). Campin's figure not only shares their general stance, inclined heads, and downward glances but also their meditative and preoccupied expression, particularly the *St. Peter Martyr* and the figure of *St. James Major* (Meiss, fig. 6). This "worried" expression may be rooted in an earlier depiction of a bearded, seated figure of Saturn, his tragic face inclined in grief, who appears as the symbol of wisdom and sorrow in a manuscript of ca. 1403 (from southwest of Bruges), copied from a medieval astrological treatise (see Panofsky, 1953, I, 106–107, II, pl. 64).

The green on gold textile pattern in the background, its repeats and shapes being treated with artistic freedom, offers no direct clue to the panel's exact date. However, the pattern of prancing dog combined with floral and stylized pomegranate forms is similar to that of numerous brocaded silks from Italy of around 1400; Bruges was an important trading post for these brocaded silks (J. Heinrich Schmidt, "Die Seidenstoffe in den Gemälden des Konrad von Soest und seiner Schule," *Westfalen*, XXIII, 1938, 195).

The figure of St. John is detached from its flat background, as are most of the figures in the Seilern triptych, by a strong contour shadow along the saint's sinister shoulder and arm. The subtle shading of mauve and blackish-purple playing over the saint's white garment, and describing its creases and tubular folds, reveals Campin's intimate knowledge of Claus Sluter's sculpture before and after it was polychromed (a task which fell to him as well as to many of his fellow painters; Campin polychromed the Annunciation group in the St. Magdalen church in Tournai completed by Jean Delemer in 1428). The Cleveland panel anticipates Campin's later grisaille figures. The first ones painted were

his two saints on the reverse of the *Marriage of the Virgin* in the Prado — also considered an early work by most scholars — which offers the earliest extant example of the striking duality in Campin's style, combining an almost hard realism with a tenderness in sentiment climaxing in his *Trinity* in Frankfurt (Städelsches Kunstinstitut).

A.T.L.

EXHIBITIONS: CMA, 1966: Golden Anniversary Acquisitions, cat. no. 58, illus. p. 179 (color).

LITERATURE: Paul Pieper, "Eine Tafel von Robert Campin," *Pantheon*, XXIV (1966), 279–282, illus. opp. p. 279 (color); *Handbook* (1966), p. 66; Alfred Stange, "Vier südflandrische Marientafeln – ein Beitrag zur Genese der niederländischen Malerei," *Alte und Moderne Kunst*, XI (1966), 19, fig. 23; J. G. van Gelder, "An Early Work by Robert Campin," *Oud Holland*, LXXXII (1967), 3, 10, figs. 12, 13; Friedländer, *Early Netherl. Paintg.*, II (1967), 92, pl. 141; Antoine Seilern, *Corrigenda & Addenda to the Catalogue of Paintings & Drawings at 56 Princes Gate London SW 7* (London, 1971), pp. 16, 17, n. 4; Martin Davies, *Rogier van der Weyden* (London, 1972), p. 247, fig. 157.

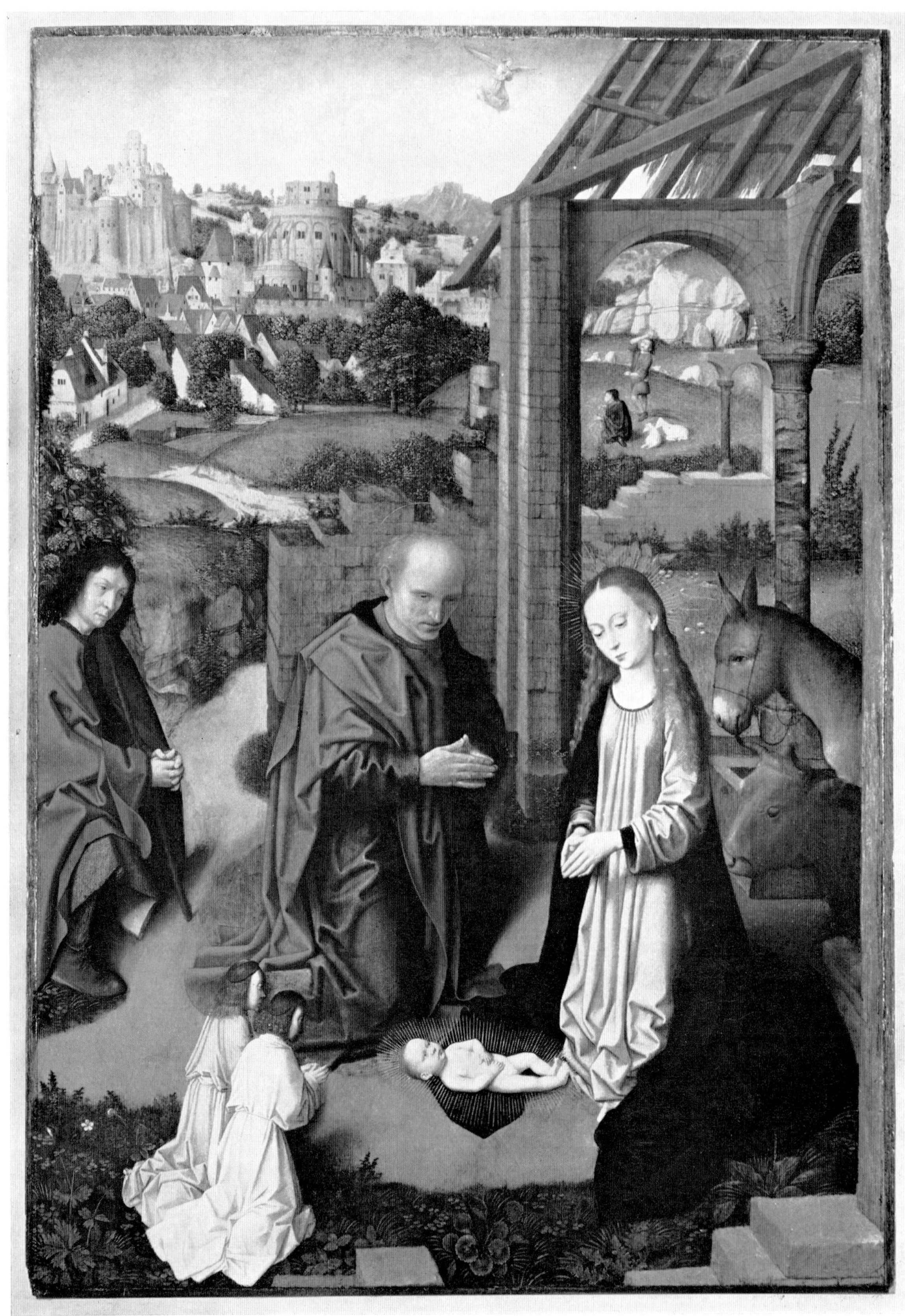

Figure 53. See also Colorplate XXVI.

GERARD DAVID, Bruges, ca. 1460–1523

Born in Oudewater (near Gouda) ca. 1460, David probably trained in Haarlem. Admitted (as a foreigner) to
the painters' guild at Bruges in 1484, he was active there
until his death in 1523. He was also inscribed in the
painters' guild at Antwerp, 1515.

53   *The Nativity*   58.320

> Panel (oak), 85·2 × 59·7 cm ($33\frac{9}{16} × 23\frac{1}{2}$ inches).
> Painted surface: 83·2 × 57·5 cm ($32\frac{3}{4} × 22\frac{5}{8}$ inches).
>
> COLLECTIONS: Private collection in Russia, nineteenth
> century; Richard von Kaufmann, Berlin, 1898; (sale:
> Cassirer and Helbing, Berlin, December 4, 1917, no.
> 78); Walter von Pannwitz, Berlin; Frau C. von Pannwitz,
> Hartekamp near Haarlem; (Rosenberg & Stiebel, New
> York).
>
> Purchase, Leonard C. Hanna Jr. Bequest, 1958.

The painting is well preserved with the exception of
the head of Joseph, which may have been a donor's
portrait at an earlier date and has since suffered from
repainting. X-ray investigation has revealed some important pentimenti: (1) a second shepherd was originally
placed to the right of the remaining one, on the same
level, turning to his companion; (2) the right hand of
Joseph appeared originally in exactly the same attitude
as in the Budapest version (Fig. 53 *b*), almost at the level
of Mary's neck; (3) the two main towers in the background were originally almost identical with those in
the Budapest version; (4) changes in the drapery under
the Christ Child suggest that He was originally lying in
a basket (Fig. 53 *c*). There is no trace of the bearded head
of Joseph which Von Bodenhausen (1905) claimed to
have seen under the present surface; but he was probably right in assuming that the whole figure of Joseph
was shifted farther to the foreground than it was before,
presumably in connection with the greater emphasis on
the donor portrait. However, David himself seems to
have been responsible for this, since the elimination of
the original right hand of Joseph (the left probably held
the candle as in the Budapest version) and of the second
shepherd would have been the logical result.

The Cleveland picture in its present state can rather
confidently be placed fourth in a series of six representations of the subject: (1) the very Geertgen-like panel
in the Budapest Museum (no. 1336, Friedländer, 1928,
pl. LXXIX); (2) the Friedsam panel in the Metropolitan
Museum (no. 32.100.40, Friedländer, 1928, pl. LXVII);
the miniature in the Escorial prayerbook of 1486 (Wolf-

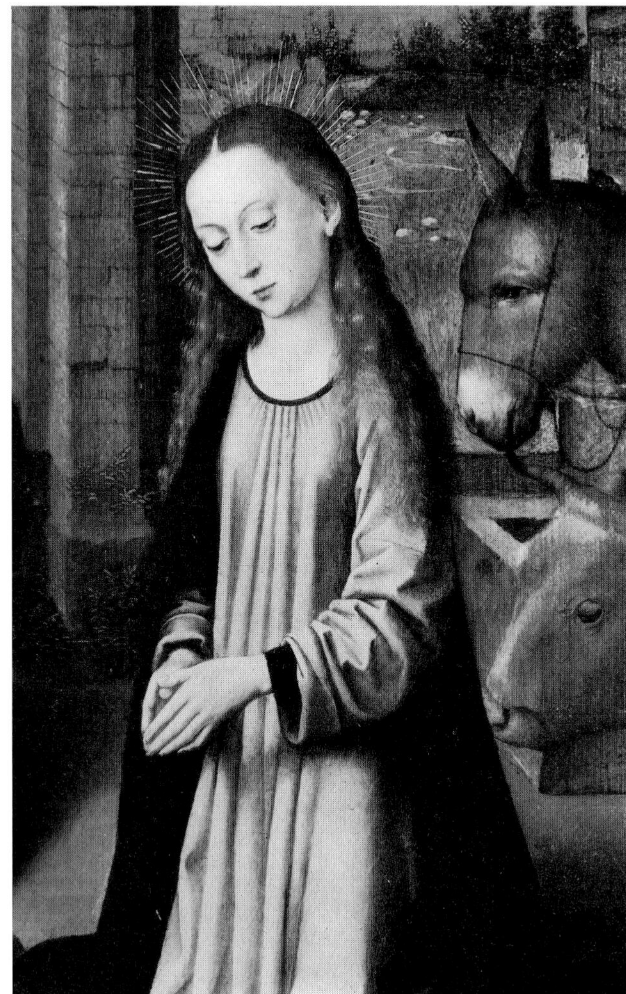

Figure 53 *a*. Detail.

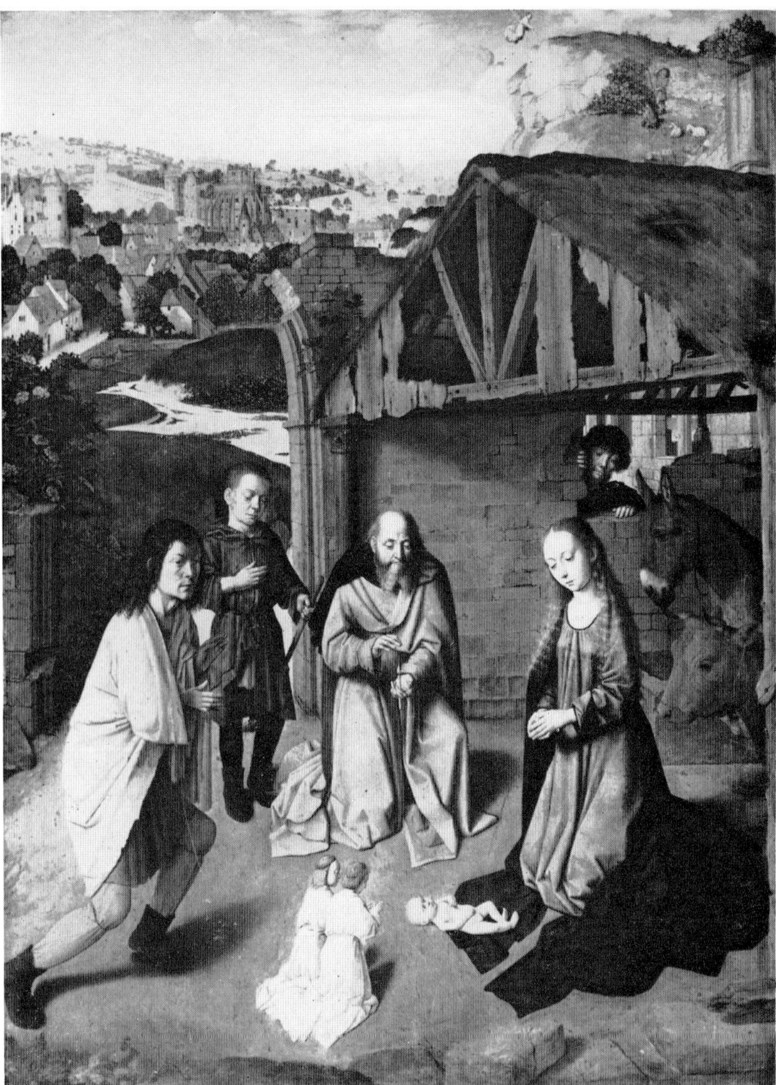

Figure 53 *b*.
The Nativity.
76·5 × 56 cm
($30\frac{1}{8} \times 22\frac{1}{16}$ inches).
David.
Budapest Museum of Fine Arts, 1336.

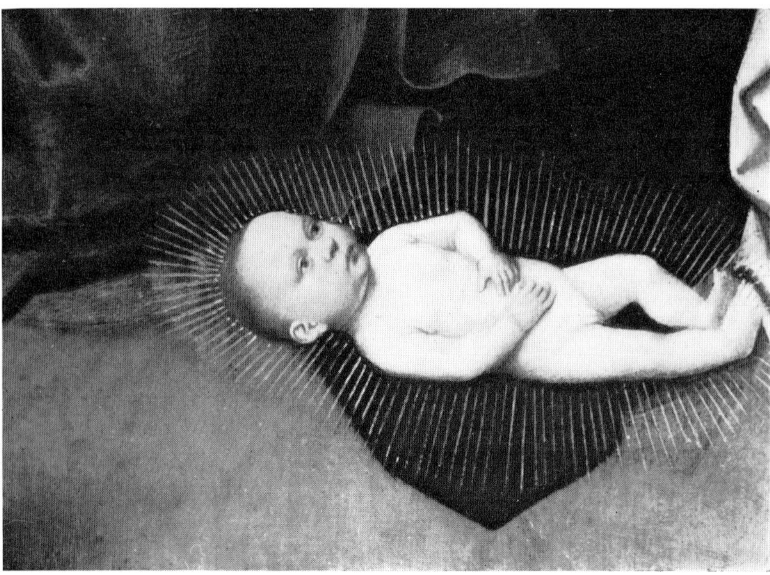

Figure 53 *c*. Detail.

gang Schöne, *Jahrbuch der preussischen Kunstsammlungen*, LVIII, 1937, 170); (4) the Cleveland panel; (5) the miniature in the Isabella Breviary in the British Museum usually dated ca. 1490–1495; (6) the Bache picture in the Metropolitan Museum (no. L 44.23.20). This places the present panel at ca. 1490, about six years after David settled in Bruges; the Geertgen-like Mary of the early works has been replaced with a Roger–Memling type. Sulzberger (1955) proposed that the shepherd is a self-portrait of the artist.

W.S.

EXHIBITIONS: Berlin, Kunstgeschichtliche Gesellschaft, 1898: Kunstwerke des Mittelalters und der Renaissance aus Berliner Privatbesitz, cat. no. 56; Rotterdam, Museum Boymans, 1939–1940: Schilderijen, beeldhouwerken en teekeningen uit particuliere verzamelingen in Nederland, cat. no. 12; The Hague, 1945: Nederlandsche kunst van de XVe en XVIe eeuw, cat. no. 45; Bruges, Musée Communal, 1949: Gerard David, cat. no. 6; Detroit Institute of Arts, 1960: Flanders in the Fifteenth Century, cat. no. 47; CMA, 1973: Dutch Art and Life in the 17th Century, no cat.

LITERATURE: Eberhard Freiherr von Bodenhausen, *Gerard David und seine Schule* (Munich, 1905), p. 93, pl. 3; Hippolyte Fierens-Gevaert, *Les primitifs flamands* (Brussels, 1909), I, 144; Martin Conway, *The Van Eycks and Their Followers* (New York, 1921), p. 278; Winkler (1924), p. 92; Max J. Friedländer, *Die Kunstsammlung von Pannwitz, I: Gemälde* (Munich, 1926), no. 15; Friedländer, *Altniederl. Mal.*, VI (1928), 88, 90, 147, no. 178; Fierens-Gevaert and Paul Fierens, *Histoire de la peinture flamande des origines à la fin du XVe siècle: La maturité de l'art flamand* (Paris, Brussels, 1929), p. 80; Ludwig Baldass, "Gerard David als Landschaftsmaler," *Jahrbuch der kunsthistorischen Sammlungen in Wien*, X (1936), 93; K. G. Boon, *Gerard David* (Amsterdam, 1938), p. 8; Martin Davies, *Early Netherlandish Schools* (London, National Gallery, 1945), p. 29 (1955), p. 33; Harry B. Wehle and Margaretta Salinger, *A Catalogue of Early Flemish, Dutch and German Paintings* (New York, MMA, 1947), p. 90; Suzanne Sulzberger, "Autoportraits de Gerard David," *Bulletin Musées Royaux des Beaux-Arts*, III (Brussels, 1955), 176–178; Henry S. Francis, "The Nativity by Gerard David," CMA *Bulletin*, XLV (1958), 225–236, illus. pp. 225 (color detail), 226, 231; Jaffé, *Apollo* (1963), 461, 467; *Handbook* (1966), p. 69; *Selected Works* (1966), p. 131; Charles D. Cuttler, *Northern Painting from Pucelle to Bruegel: Fourteenth, Fifteenth and Sixteenth Centuries* (New York, Chicago, etc., 1968), p. 191, fig. 239; Zsusza Urbach, Review of *Northern Painting from Pucelle to Bruegel: Fourteenth, Fifteenth and Sixteenth Centuries* by Charles D. Cuttler, *Acta Historiae Artium*, XVII (1971), 135; Friedländer, *Early Netherl. Paintg.*, VI, Pt. II (1971), 85, 86, 93, 103, no. 178, pl. 190.

GEERTGEN TOT SINT JANS, Haarlem,
ca. 1460–late 1480s

He was perhaps a pupil of Aelbert Ouwater in Haarlem
and possibly identical with the Gheerkin de Hollandere
inscribed (1475–1476) in the illuminators' guild in Bruges. Active in Haarlem in the 1480s, particularly for the
Knights of St. John (hence his name), he died at the age
of about twenty-eight.

54 *The Adoration of the Magi* 51.353

Panel (oak), 29·2 × 18·7 cm ($11\frac{1}{2} \times 7\frac{5}{16}$ inches).
COLLECTIONS: Private collection, England; (Rosenberg &
Stiebel, New York).
Purchase, Leonard C. Hanna Jr. Bequest, 1951.

The panel has been cut on all sides but the left. The face
of Mary has suffered abrasion. The black king is a later
addition. The original composition can be reconstructed
as extending a little to the top and bottom and to the
right, where the original black king must have been
standing.

As already pointed out by Friedländer (1950), this is a
late work of the master. Figures and architecture are
more cogently related to the picture plane than in Geertgen's other representations of the same subject, from
which this work also differs by virtue of its strong emphasis on ox and ass.

W.S.

EXHIBITIONS: CMA, 1973: Dutch Art and Life in the 17th
Century, no cat.
LITERATURE: Max J. Friedländer, "Eine bisher unbekannte
Epiphanie von Geertgen," *Maanblad voor Beeldende Kunsten*, XXVI
(1950), 10–12, illus. p. 11; Henry S. Francis, "Two Dutch Fifteenth-
century Panels," CMA *Bulletin*, XXXIX (1952), 5, 6, illus. pp. 1, 19;
Panofsky, I (1953), 494, n. 3244; Friedländer, *Early Netherlandish
Painting from Van Eyck to Bruegel* (London, 1956), p. 53, n. 5,
p. 420, pl. 141; *Handbook* (1958), no. 435; J. E. Snyder, "The
Early Haarlem School of Painting: II, Geertgen tot Sint Jans," *Art
Bulletin*, XLII (1960), 121; Friedrich Winkler, *Das Werk des Hugo
van der Goes* (Berlin, 1964), p. 20, n. 1; Johan Quirijn van Regteren
Altena, "Wanneer verbleet Geertgen tot Sint Jans in Vlaanderen?"
Oud Holland, LXXXI (1966), p. 80, fig. 7; *Handbook* (1966), p. 68;
K. G. Boon, *Geertgen tot Sint Jans* (Amsterdam, 1967), p. 9,
pl. IV (color); Charles D. Cuttler, *Northern Painting from Pucelle to
Bruegel: Fourteenth, Fifteenth and Sixteenth Centuries* (New York,
Chicago, etc., 1968), p. 162, fig. 201; Friedländer, *Early Netherl.
Paintg.*, V (1969), 91, 94, 109, pl. 121.

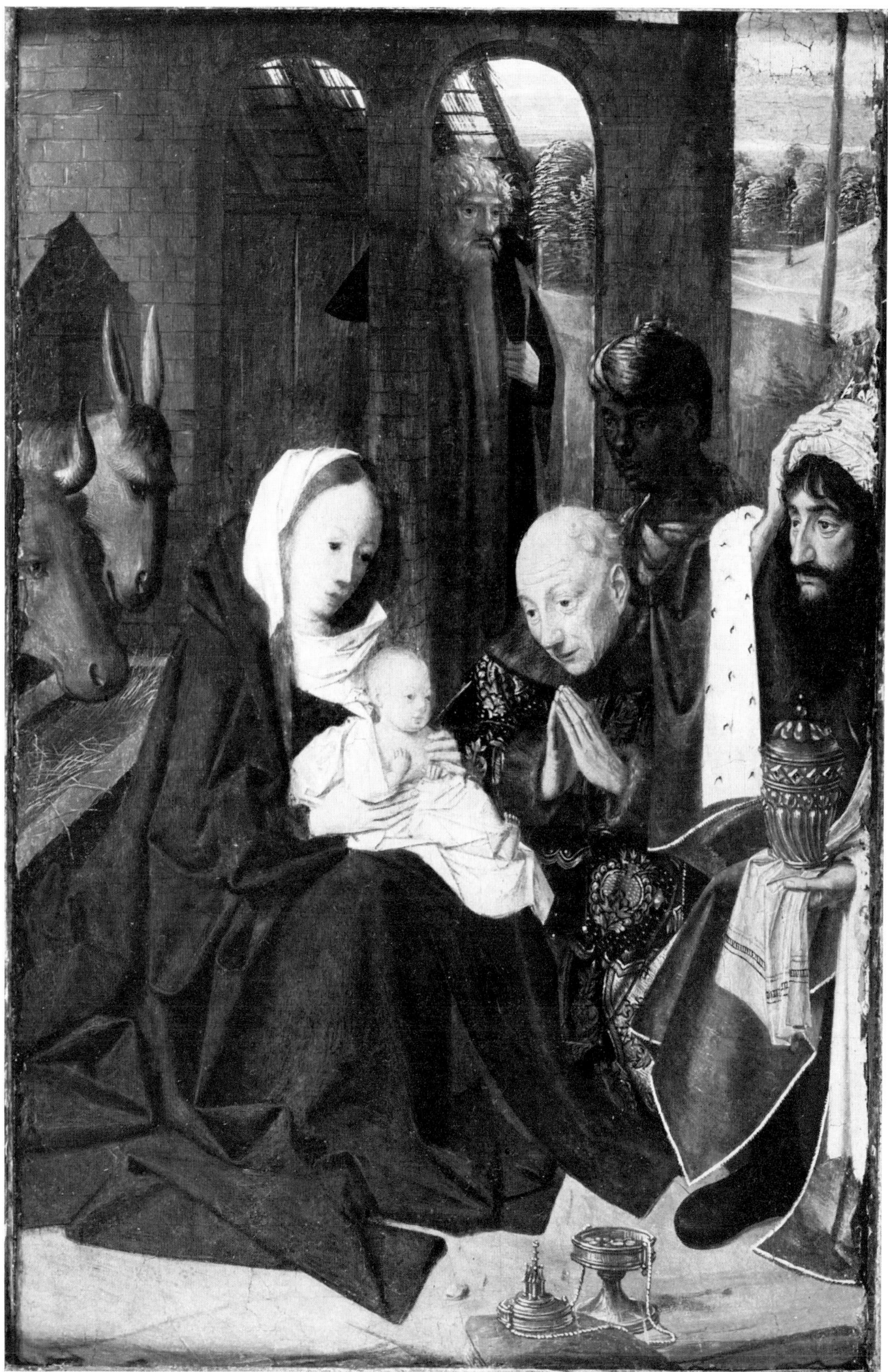

Figure 54. See also Colorplate XXVII.

Follower of HANS MEMLING, Bruges, ca.
1440–1494

Hans Memling was born in Seligenstadt (Main) ca.
1440. Probably by 1459 he was in the workshop of
Roger van der Weyden at Brussels. First mentioned at
Bruges in 1466, he was active there until his death in
1494.

55 *Madonna and Child* 34.29

Panel (oak), $33 \cdot 2 \times 23 \cdot 8$ cm ($13\frac{1}{16} \times 9\frac{3}{8}$ inches).
Painted surface: $31 \cdot 3 \times 21 \cdot 4$ cm ($12\frac{5}{16} \times 8\frac{7}{16}$ inches).
COLLECTIONS: Private collection, Spain; (Grete Ring,
London); (Arnold Seligmann, Rey & Co., New York).
Delia E. and L. E. Holden Funds, 1934.

The panel is well preserved except for the (renewed?)
clouds and reinforced diadem of Mary.

The picture, hitherto given to Memling himself, belongs to a group with the Madonna suckling the Child
which ultimately derives from Roger and his circle
(Friedländer, 1924, II, pl. LXXIV; Musée Royal des Beaux
Arts de Belgique, *Catalogue de la peinture ancienne*, Brussels, 1922, nos. 650, 667). Numerous features and general
stylistic aspects have been taken from Memling. The
Christ Child is nearly identical with that of the Granada
panel (Friedländer, 1928, VI, no. 55, pl. XXXII); the hands
of the Madonna go back to the same work but are translated into the style of a later phase of Memling's art.
Similar adaptations were made by the Master of the
Lucy Legend and the Master of the Ursula Legend
(Colin Eisler, *Les Primitifs Flamands: New England Museums*, IV, Brussels, 1961, nos. 74, 77, and no. 76 for the
Christ Child); but the Cleveland panel is closer to Memling and probably comes from his workshop proper,
dating about 1485–1490.

W.S.

EXHIBITIONS: The Toledo Museum of Art, Ohio, 1935: French
and Flemish Primitives, cat. no. 26; CMA (1936), cat. no. 204;
The Worcester Art Museum, Mass., Philadelphia Museum of Art,
1939: Flemish Paintings, cat. no. 24 (as Memling in all).
LITERATURE: Henry S. Francis, "A Madonna and Child by Hans
Memling," CMA *Bulletin*, XXI (1934), 139–144, illus. p. 137;
Friedländer, *Altniederl. Mal.*, XIV (1937), 103; *Handbook* (1958),
no. 433; *Handbook* (1966), p. 69; Friedländer, *Early Netherl. Paintg.*,
VI, Pt. II (1971), p. 109, pl. 231, supp. 226.

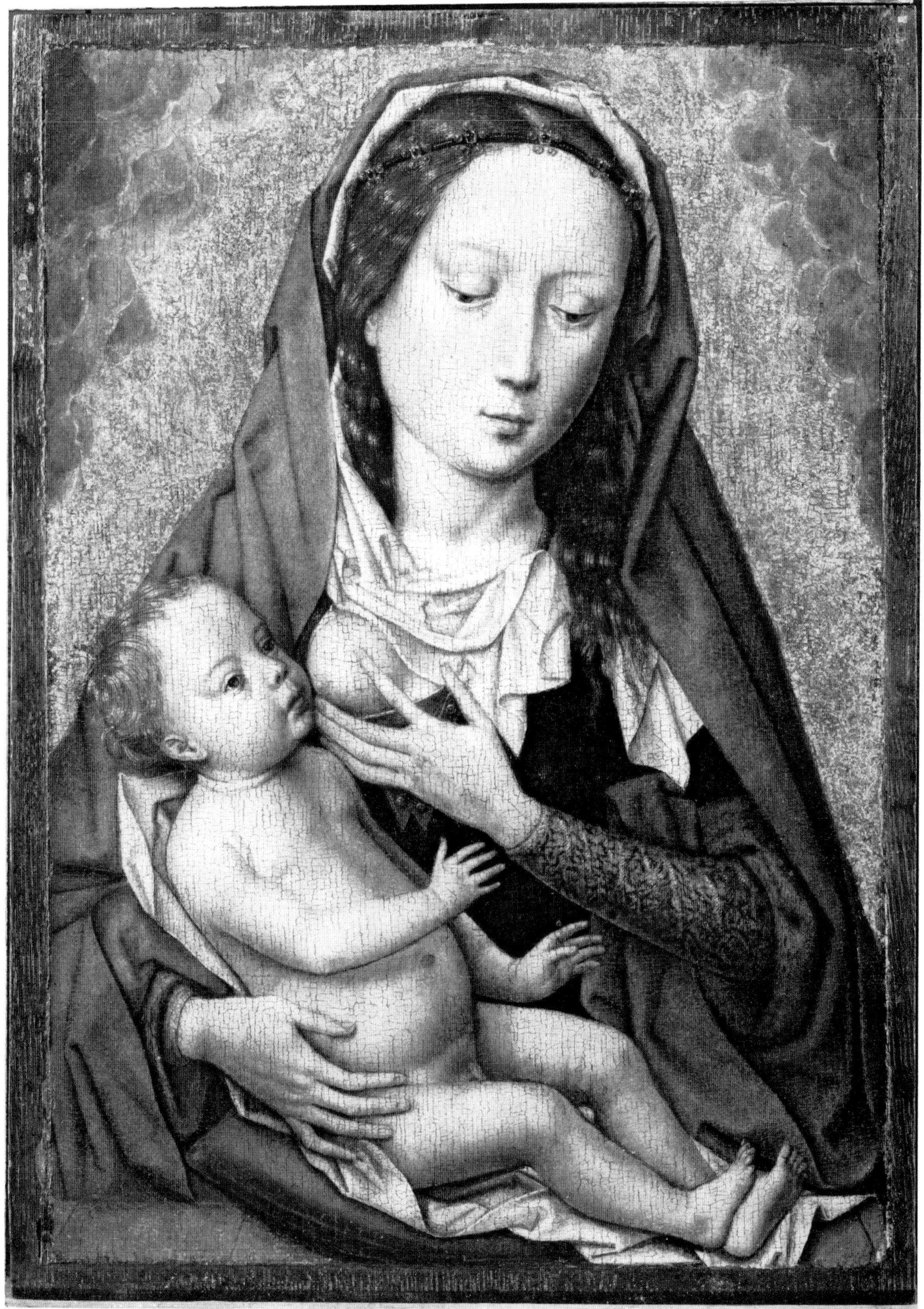

Figure 55.

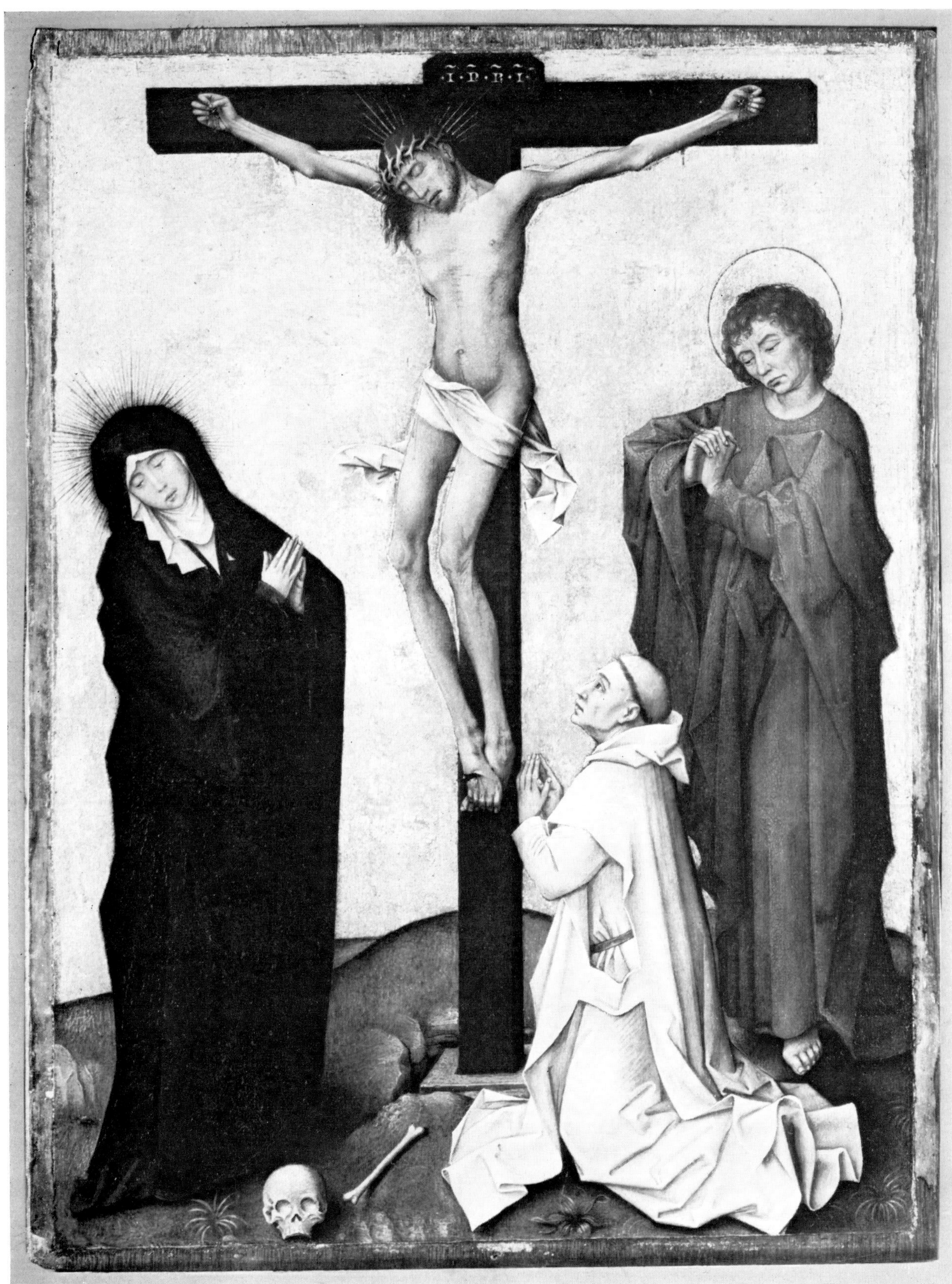

Figure 56.

ANONYMOUS MASTER, Netherlands(?),
ca. 1470

56 The Crucifixion   31.449

> Panel (oak), 38·4 × 29·2 cm (15⅜ × 11½ inches).
> Painted surface: 37·1 × 27·3 cm (14⅝ × 10¾ inches).
> COLLECTIONS: Private collection, Lower Rhine; (A. S.
> Drey, Munich, New York).
> Delia E. and L. E. Holden Funds, 1931.

The painting is well preserved.

The three holy figures and the upper outline of the
ground are an exact replica of the so-called "Sforza
Triptych," painted ca. 1460 in the workshop of Roger
van der Weyden (Fig. 56a). The donor (probably a
Carthusian monk) has been added, the skull (with
added bone) rearranged, and the landscape replaced
with a gold ground. A certain stylizing tendency suggests the possibility of a French origin for the panel; this
opinion is shared by Sterling (orally, 1961) who thinks
of Burgundy (Dijon, Carthusian monastery?).

                                          W.S.

EXHIBITIONS: CMA (1931); CMA (1936), cat. no. 201.
LITERATURE: Jules Destrée, *Roger de la Pasture van der Weyden*,
I (Paris, Brussels, 1930), 108; Henry S. Francis, "A Flemish Panel
of the Crucifixion," CMA *Bulletin*, XIX (1932), 3–7, illus. p. 1;
Handbook (1958), no. 434; *Handbook* (1966), p. 68.

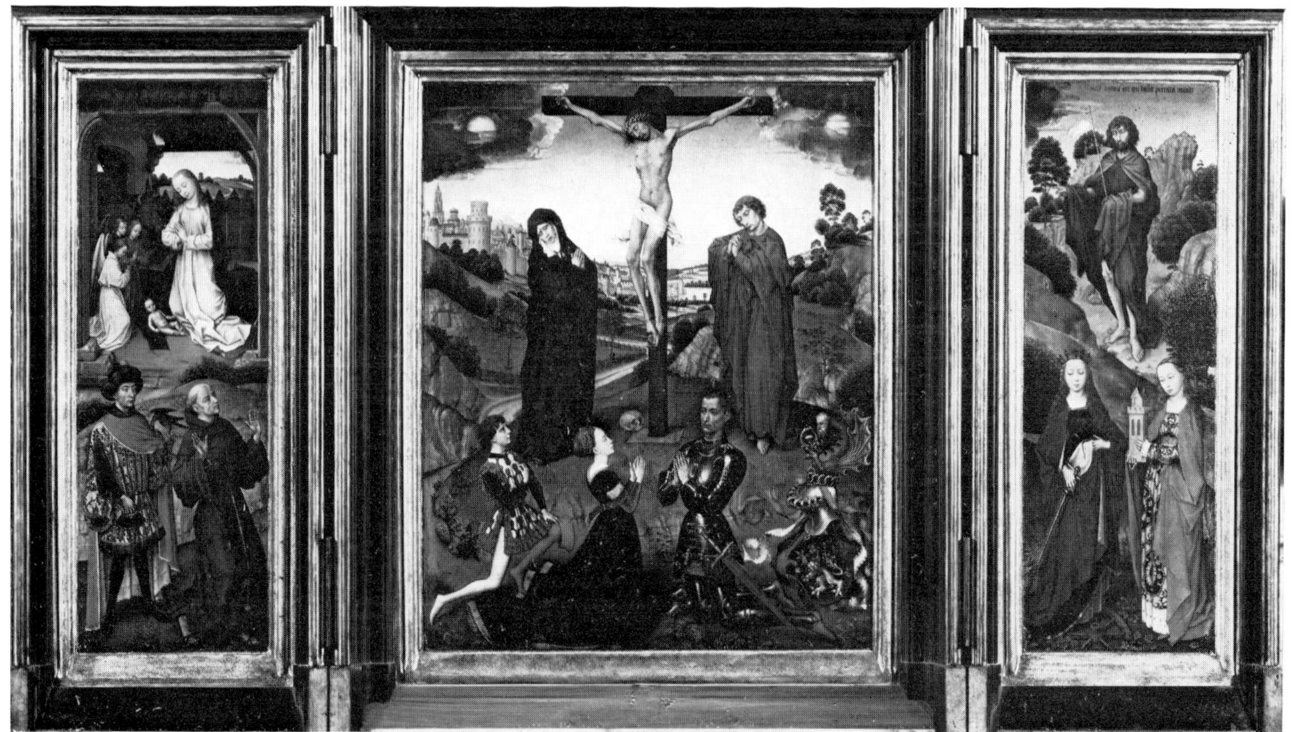

Figure 56a. *Crucifixion*. Central panel, 53·5 × 45·5 cm (21 1/16 × 17 15/16 inches); each wing,
54 × 19 cm (21¼ × 7½ inches). Workshop of Roger van der Weyden.
Musées Royaux des Beaux-Arts de Belgique, Brussels.

ANONYMOUS MASTER, Netherlands(?),
ca. 1480

57 *Portrait of a Lady* 62.259

Panel (oak), 31·7 × 22·7 cm ($12\frac{9}{16}$ × 9 inches).
Painted surface: 30·3 × 21·3 cm ($11\frac{15}{16}$ × $8\frac{3}{8}$ inches).
COLLECTIONS: Comte Bissaccio, Chartres; A. Berg,
Portland, Oregon; (F. Kleinberger Galleries, New York,
1927); Jane Taft Ingalls, Cleveland.
Bequest of Jane Taft Ingalls, 1962.

The painting is well preserved, but the pattern of the
background has been reinforced.

No other pictures by the same hand have so far become known. The attributions to the Maître de Moulins
(Exh: 1927) and Jean Perréal (Goldblatt, 1949) are out
of the question, and the possibility of a French origin is
slight. The face bespeaks the vicinity of Memling; the
hands suggest a survival or revival of features found in
portraits of the Master of Flémalle (Friedrich Winkler'
letter of June 8, 1963). The unusual background (green
star-pattern with white highlights and red and black
stripes on gold) has no exact parallels in known Flemish
and French paintings. The possibility of an origin on the
Lower Rhine (first suggested by Julius Held, orally)
must be kept in mind, but no convincing parallels have
as yet been traced. The rosary roundels show a standing
saint (right) and a standing woman praying (Annunciation?) before an altar with another figure (left) in imitation of enamel work (Fig. 57a).

W.S.

EXHIBITIONS: New York, F. Kleinberger Galleries, 1927:
French Primitives and Objects of Art, no. 36 (as Maître de Moulins).
LITERATURE: R. R. Tatlock, "An American Exhibition of French
Primitives," *Burl. Mag.*, LI (1927), 194 (as Maître de Moulins);
Maurice H. Goldblatt, "Jean Perréal, Thirty Portraits Identified,
I," *The Connoisseur*, CXXIII (1949), 9 (as Perréal); *Handbook* (1966),
p. 73.

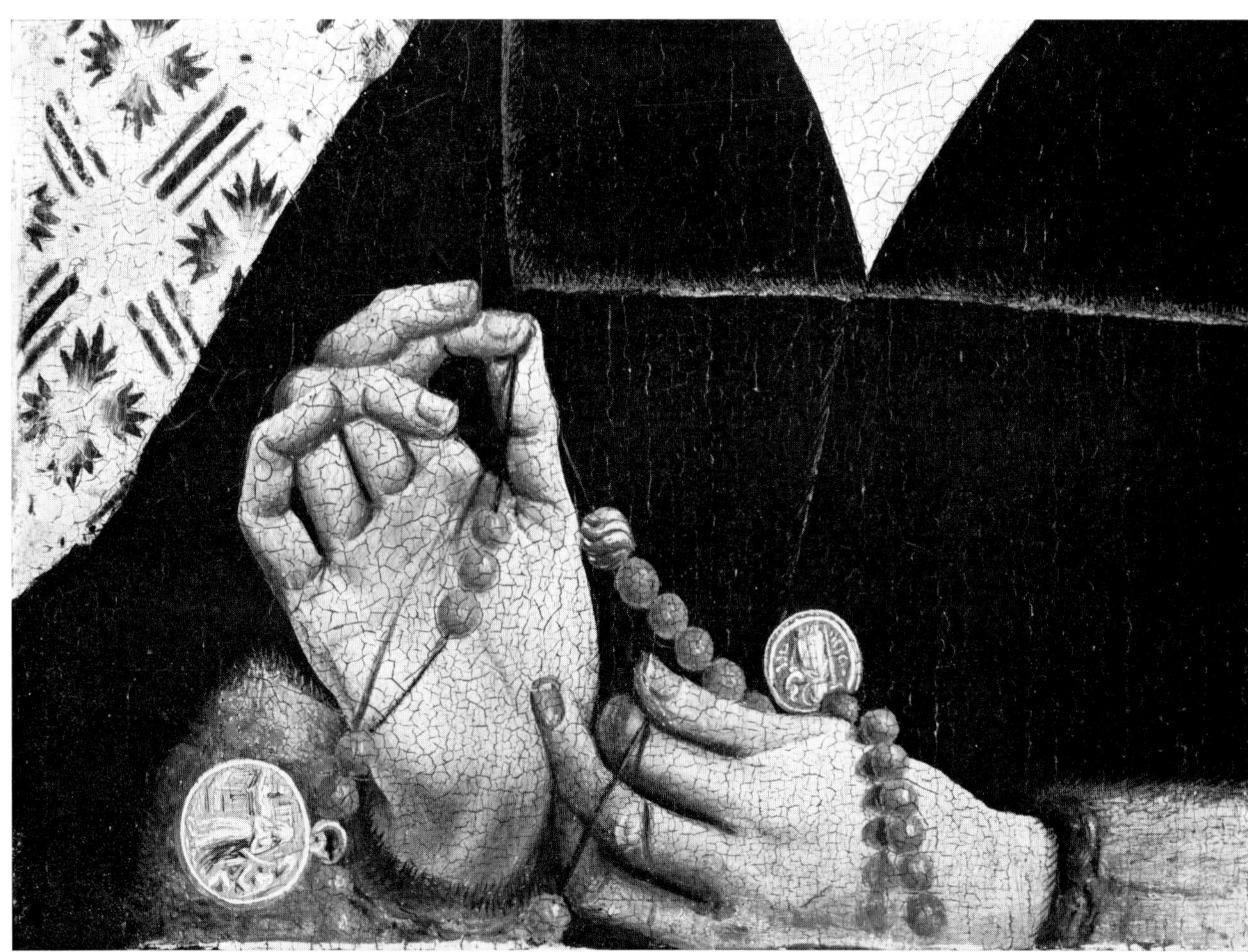

Figure 57a. Detail.

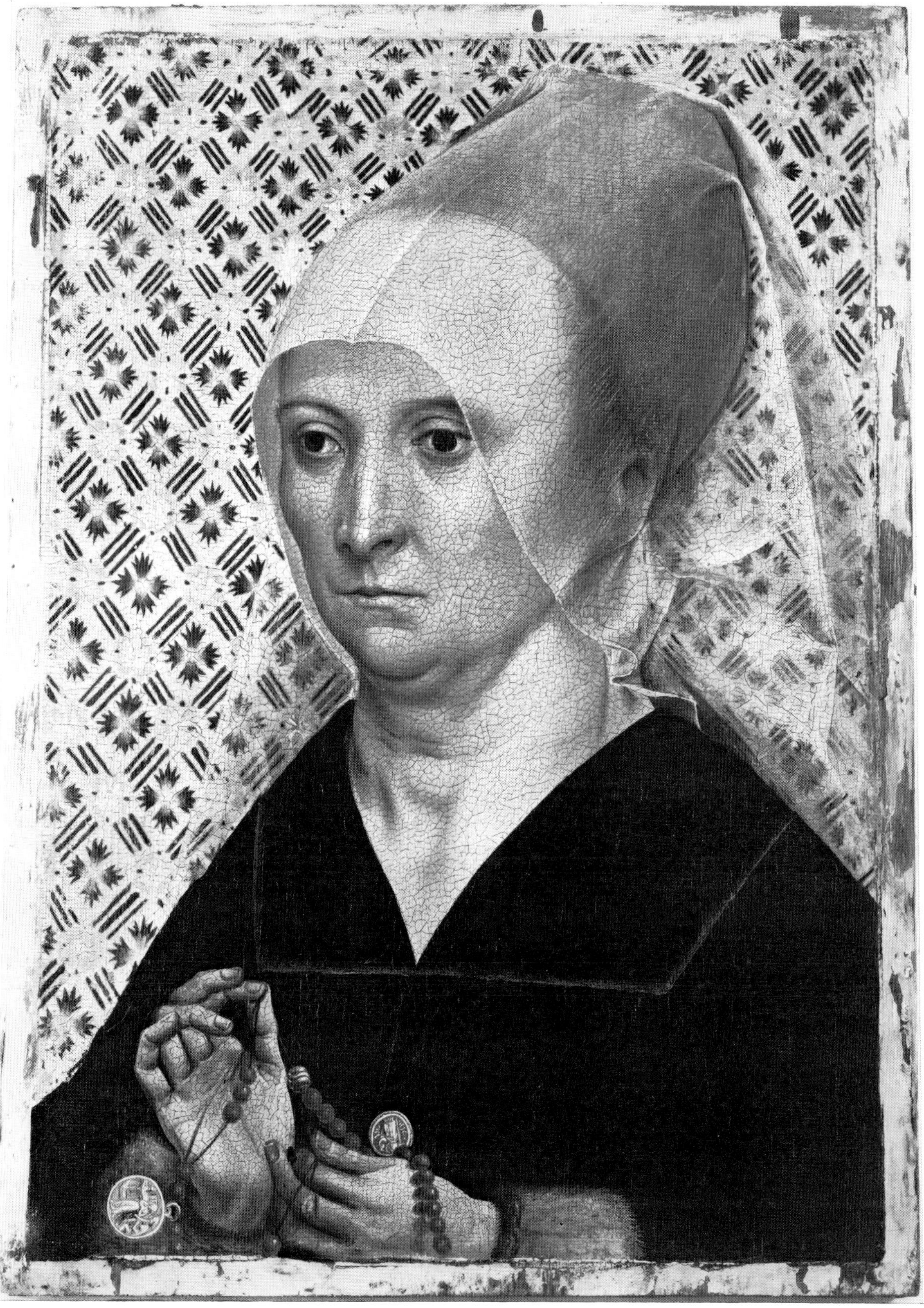

Figure 57.

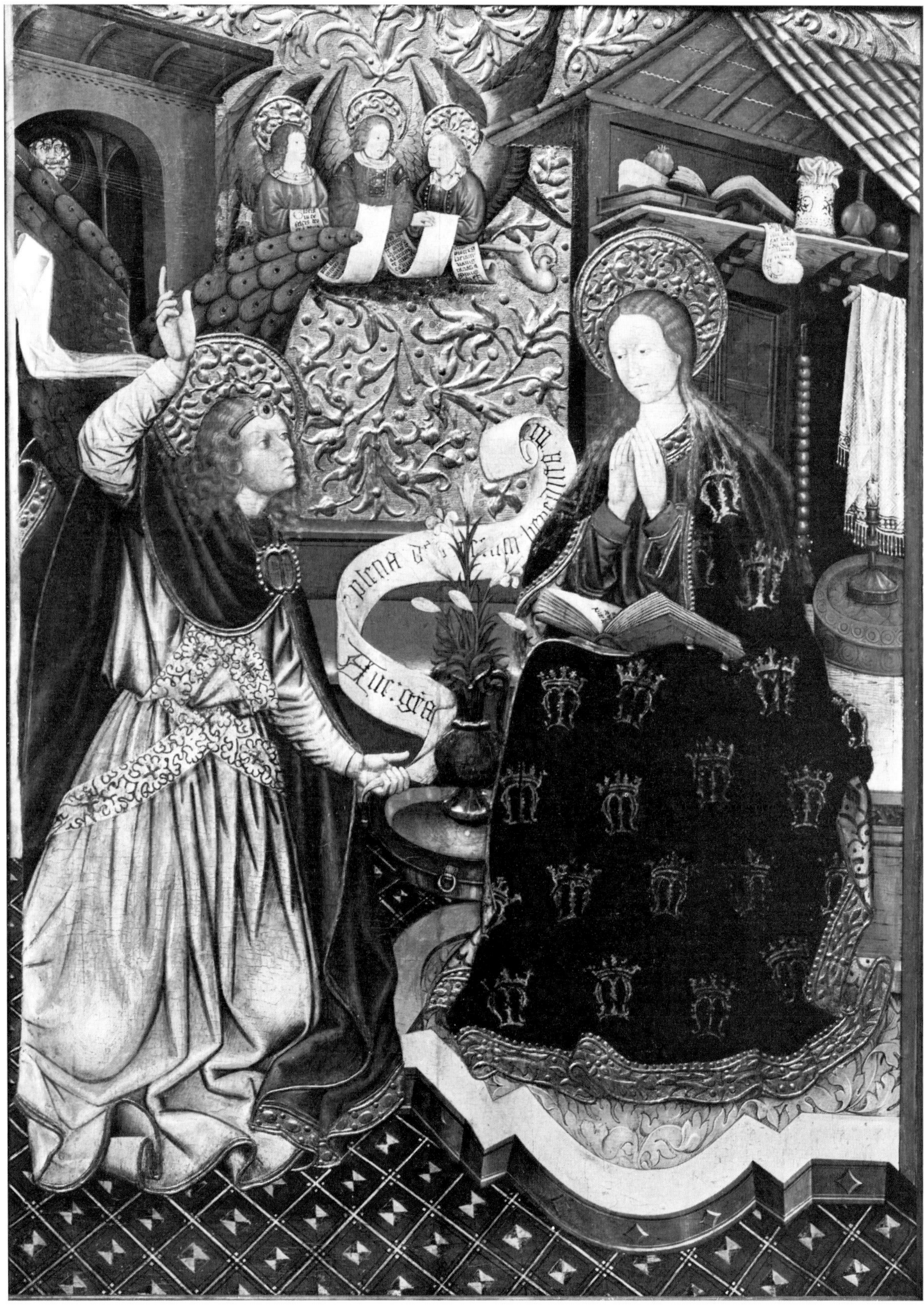

Figure 58.

162

JAIME FERRER II, Lérida, active mid-fifteenth century

A Catalan painter active in Lérida and Alcover (near Tarragona) in the middle of the fifteenth century, Ferrer is closely connected and now almost universally identified with Post's Master of Verdú (altarpiece of ca. 1434, now in Vich) and Master of the Pahería, Lérida (altarpiece of 1439, actually commissioned to Ferrer and Pedro Teixidor). He painted the altarpiece at Alcover in 1457.

58   *The Annunciation to the Virgin*   53.660

Companion piece of Painting 59

Panel (fir), 172·7 × 124·4 cm (68 × 49 inches).
COLLECTIONS: Frank Hadley Ginn, Cleveland, 1953. Gift of Francis Ginn, Marian Ginn Jones, Barbara Ginn Griesinger, and Alexander Ginn in Memory of Frank Hadley Ginn and Cornelia Root Ginn, 1953.

Both this panel and its companion piece appear to be reasonably well preserved (in spite of Post's remarks, 1938, p. 536).

Works of approximately the same period of Ferrer's activity are the Alcover altarpiece, 1457, and the *St. Julian* at Aspa (J. Gudiol Ricart, "Pintura gótica," *Ars hispaniae*, IX, Madrid, 1955, 112, fig. 82); the gold floral pattern is near-identical in these three works. The crowned M on Mary's garb appears to be identical with that on the *Dormition* (Fig. 58a) ex-Muntadas collection, Barcelona, which Post (1938, p. 532) had called Ferrer (?). Recently Joan Ainaud (letter of December 19, 1972, from M. Blanch of MAS) gave it to García de Benabarre.

W.S.

EXHIBITIONS: Toledo Museum of Art, Ohio, 1941: Spanish Painting, no. 18 (from the Powell-Jones collection, Gates Mills).
LITERATURE: Chandler R. Post, *A History of Spanish Painting*, VII (Cambridge, Mass., 1938), 536–539, fig. 197; Juan Antonio Gaya Nuño, *La pintura española fuera de España* (Madrid, 1958), p. 146, no. 740; *Handbook* (1958), no. 406; *Handbook* (1966), p. 73.

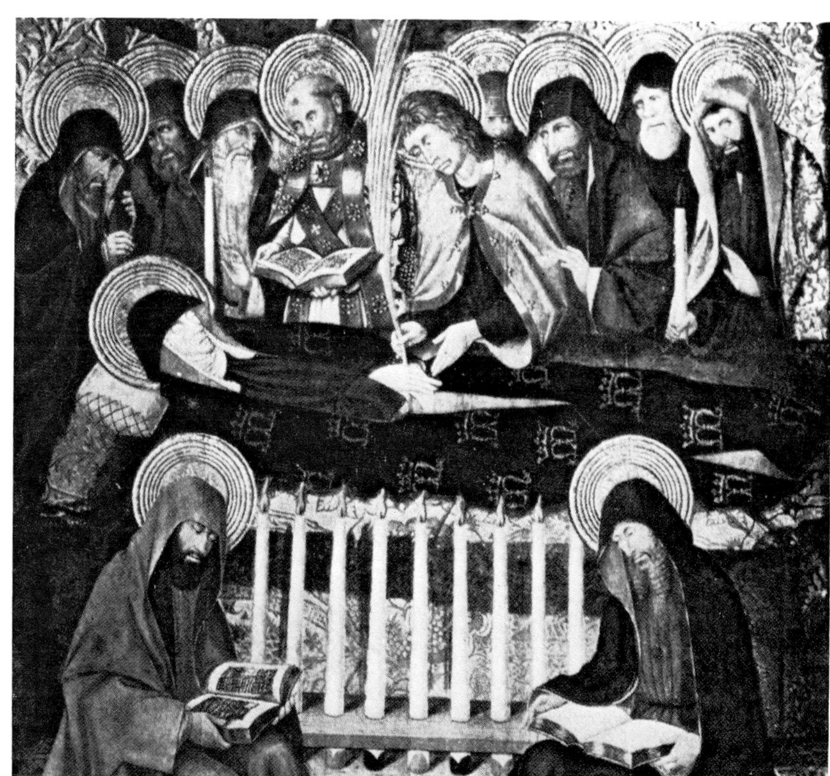

Figure 58a. *Dormition* (detail). Ferrer (?). Museo de Arte de Cataluña.

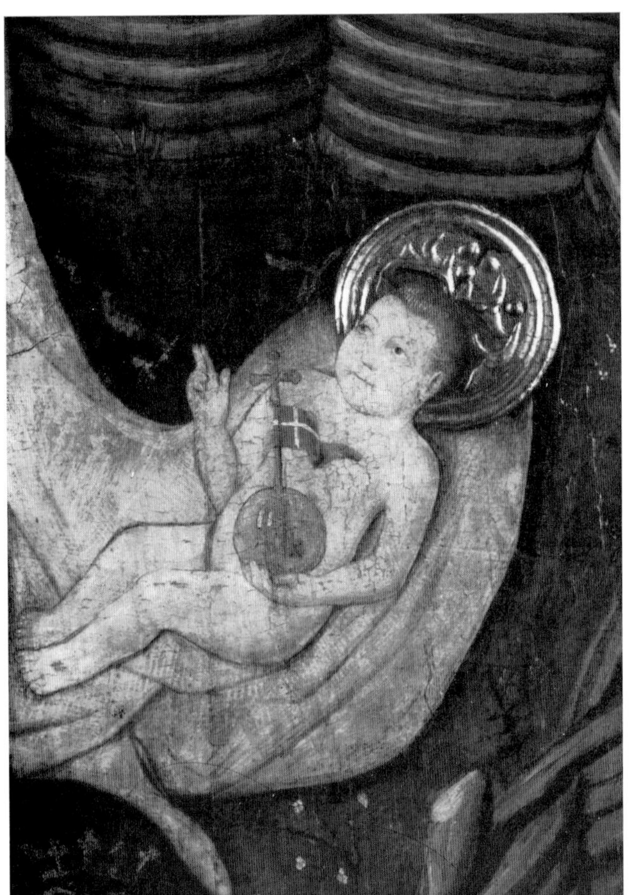

JAIME FERRER II

59 *The Nativity* 53.661

Companion piece of Painting 58

Panel (fir), 172 × 124·7 cm (67¾ × 49⅛ inches).

EXHIBITIONS: None.
LITERATURE: Chandler R. Post, *A History of Spanish Painting*, VII (Cambridge, Mass., 1938), 536–539, fig. 197; Juan Antonio Gaya Nuño, *La pintura española fuera de España* (Madrid, 1958), p. 146, no. 741.

Figures 59*a, b, c.* Details.

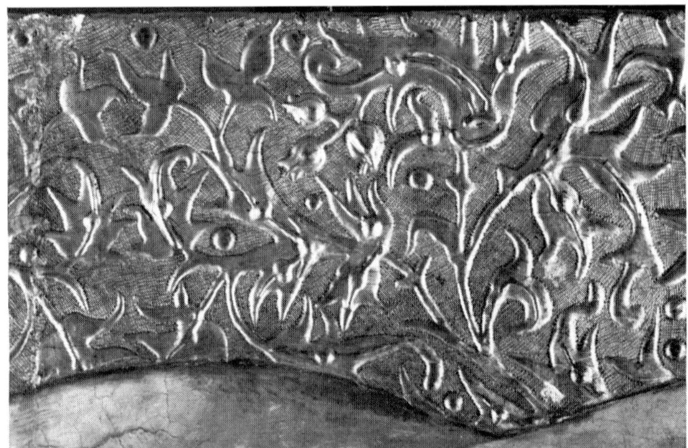

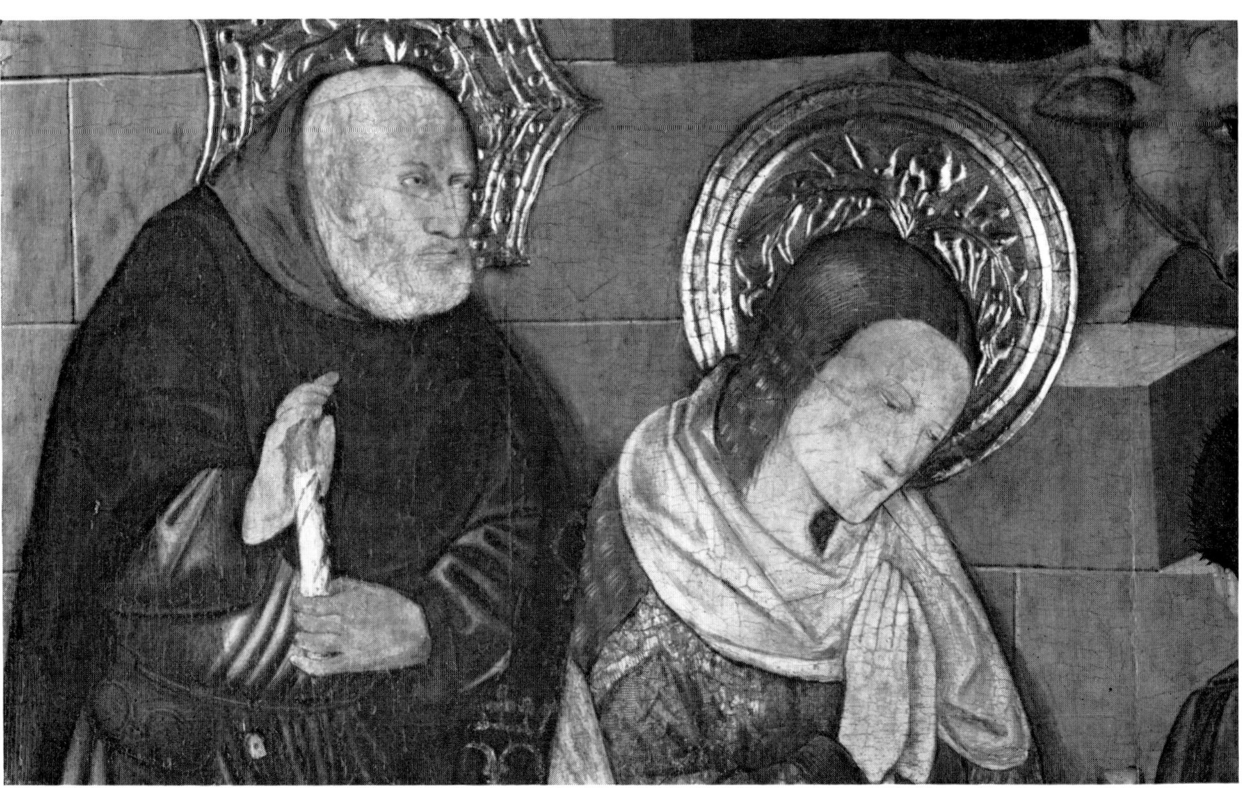

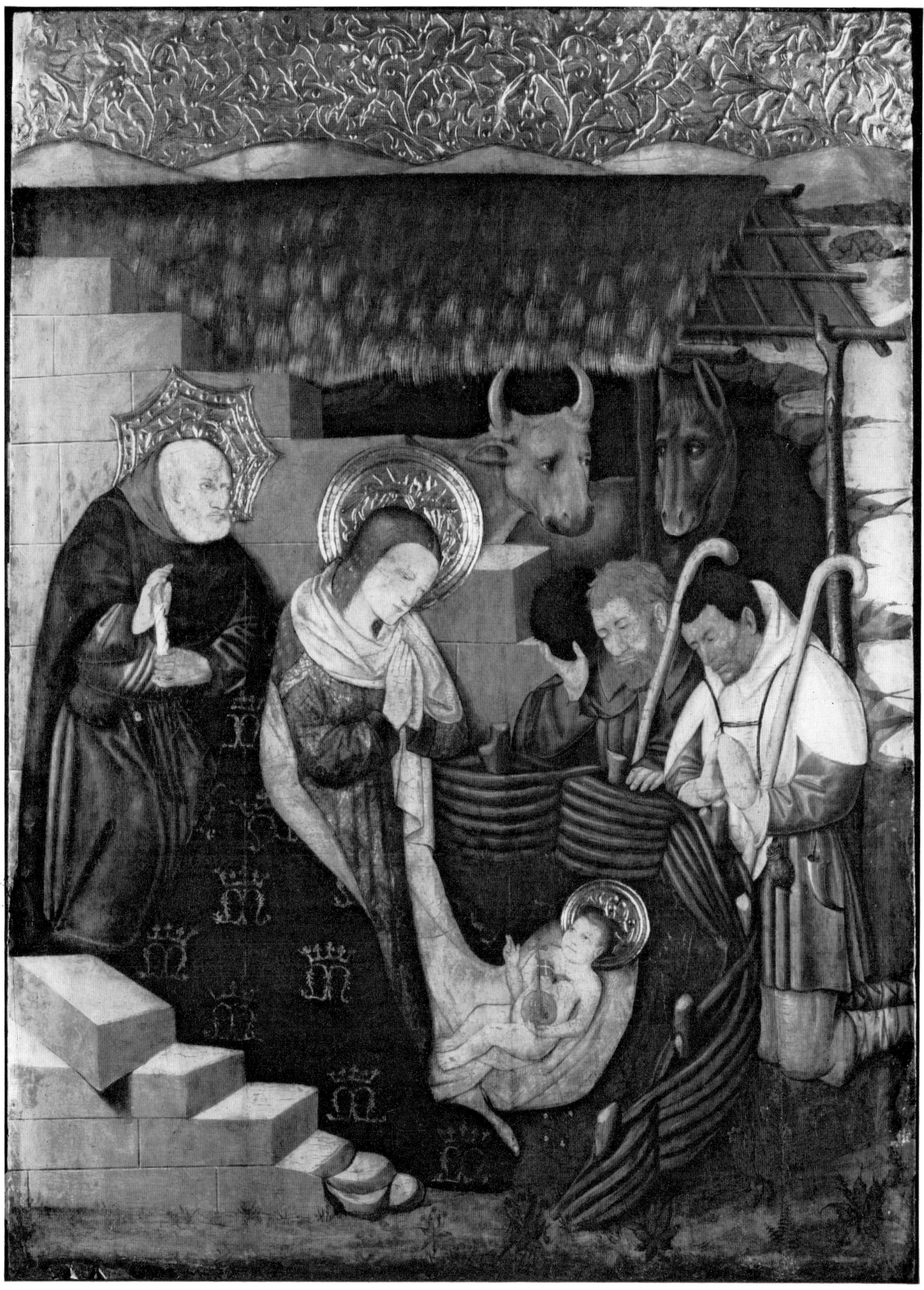

Figure 59.

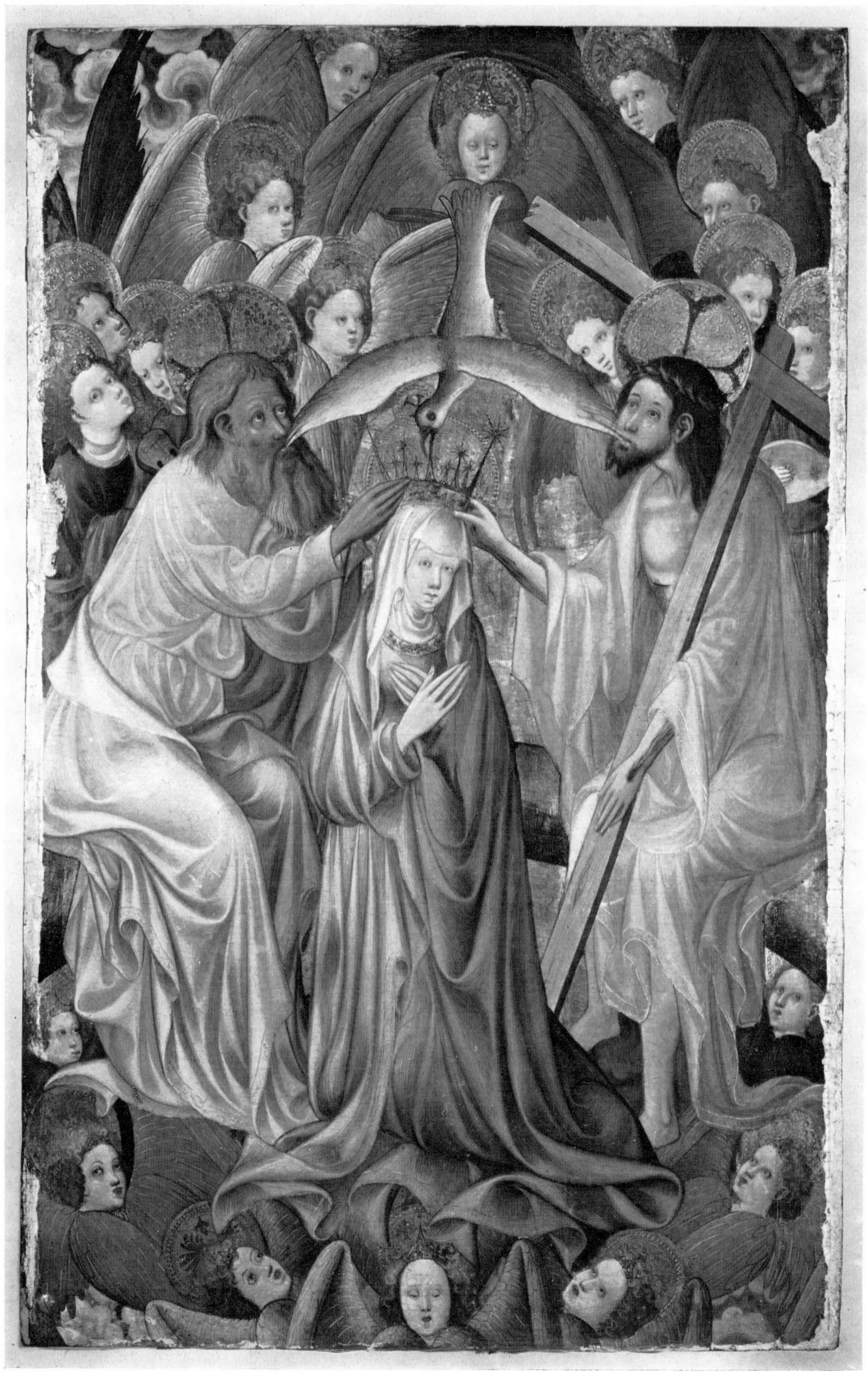

Figure 60. See also Colorplate XXVIII.

THE RUBIELOS MASTER, Valencia, active
ca. 1400–1410

The painter was named for an altarpiece he did for the
church at Rubielos-de-Mora, Teruel. He was active in
collaboration with, or in the workshop of, Pedro Nicolau-de-Albentosa in and around Valencia, ca. 1400–
1410. He is sometimes also called the Master of Burgo
de Osma for the altarpiece of which the Cleveland panel
probably formed a part.

60   *The Coronation of the Virgin*   47.208

>   Panel (fir), 144·6 × 91·4 cm (56$\frac{15}{16}$ × 36 inches).
>   COLLECTIONS: Conde del Asalto, Madrid; Heirs of
>   Conde del Asalto (Post mentions the painting as in their
>   collection in 1929); (Joseph Brummer, New York, by
>   1938).
>   Gift of Hanna Fund, 1947.

There are retouchings in the faces and elsewhere.

Very probably from a large polyptych made for the
cathedral at Burgo de Osma (Soria) to which the following also belonged: the *Dormition of the Virgin*, formerly
in the Lucas-Moreno collection in Paris; the *Virgin and
Child with Angels* in the Louvre (Fig. 60a); two panels
with saints in the Perpignan Museum (formerly in the
Louvre); two other panels with saints and two with
the *Annunciation to Joachim* and *Annunciation to St. Anne*
(Fig. 60b), still in the cathedral of Burgo de Osma. Saralegui (1955) recognizes the hand of Nicolau-de-Albentosa himself in parts of the present panel. Post (letter of
September 29, 1955) considers it possible that the Rubielos Master is identical with Jaime Mateu, mentioned
in Valencia between 1402 and 1449. This is an early example of the Coronation of Mary with the Trinity
(Denny, 1963).

W.S.

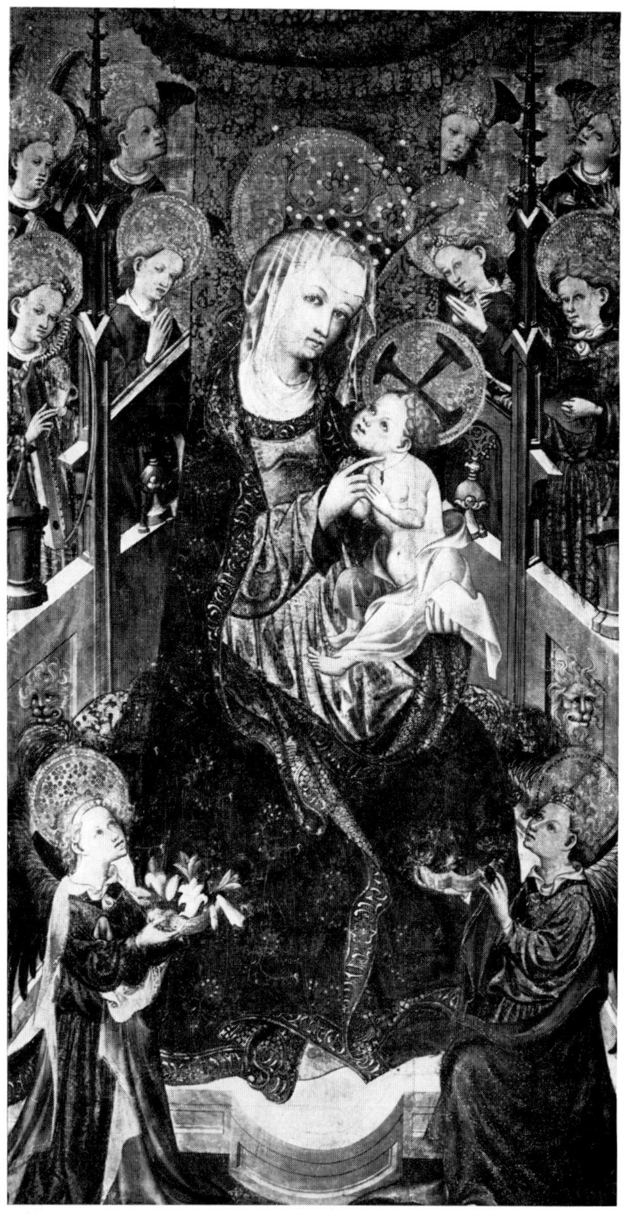

Figure 60a. *Virgin and Child with Angels.*
1·71 × 92 cm (67$\frac{5}{16}$ × 36$\frac{3}{16}$ inches).
The Rubielos Master. Louvre, R.F. 1579.

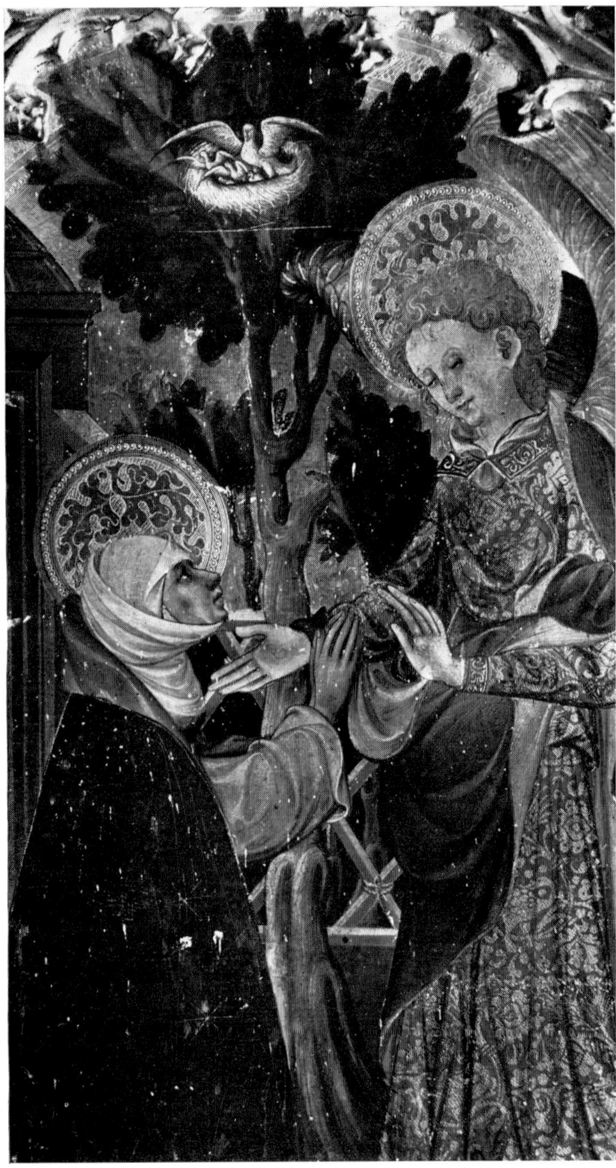

Figure 60b. *Annunciation to St. Anne*
(detail of altarpiece).
Attributed to the Rubielos Master.
Cathedral of Burgo de Osma (Soria).

EXHIBITIONS: CMA (1963), cat. no. 105, illus. (color).

LITERATURE: August Liebmann Mayer, *Geschichte der spanischen Malerei* (Leipzig, 1922), p. 34 (circle of Lorenzo Zaragoza); Chandler R. Post, *A History of Spanish Painting* (Cambridge, Mass.) III (1930), 30, 32; VI (1935), 579; VII (1938), 788–790; IX (1947), 759; X (1950), 310; Leandro de Saralegui, "Pedro Nicolau," *Bolletin de la sociedad española de excursiones*, XLI (1933), 166, n. 1; XLIX (1941), 96–97; L (1942), 116–117; Henry S. Francis, "Coronation of the Virgin by Pedro Nicolau-de-Albentosa or a Close Follower," CMA *Bulletin*, XXXV (1948), 192–198, illus. pp. 194–195 (color); Saralegui, "Miscelanea de remembranzas vicentinas," *Archivo de arte valenciano*, XXVI (1955), 18–20, fig. 9; José Gudiol Ricart, "Pintura gótica," *Ars hispaniae*, IX (Madrid, 1955), 149; Juan Antonio Gaya Nuño, *La pintura española fuera de España* (Madrid, 1958), p. 258, no. 2040; *Handbook* (1958), no. 397; *Trésors de la peinture espagnole: Eglises et musées de France* (exh. cat.; Paris, Musée des arts decoratifs, 1963), p. 91; Don Denny, "The Trinity in Enguerrand Quarton's Coronation of the Virgin," *Art Bulletin*, XLV (1963), 51; Jaffé, *Apollo* (1963), 467, illus. p. 459 (color); *Handbook* (1966), p. 65; Santiago Alcolea, *Il gotico internazionale in Spagna* ("I Maestri del colore," no. 226; Milan, 1966), pp. 5, 7, pl. IX (as Pedro Nicolau); Charles D. Cuttler, *Northern Painting from Pucelle to Bruegel: Fourteenth, Fifteenth and Sixteenth Centuries* (New York, Chicago, etc., 1968), p. 242, fig. 300.

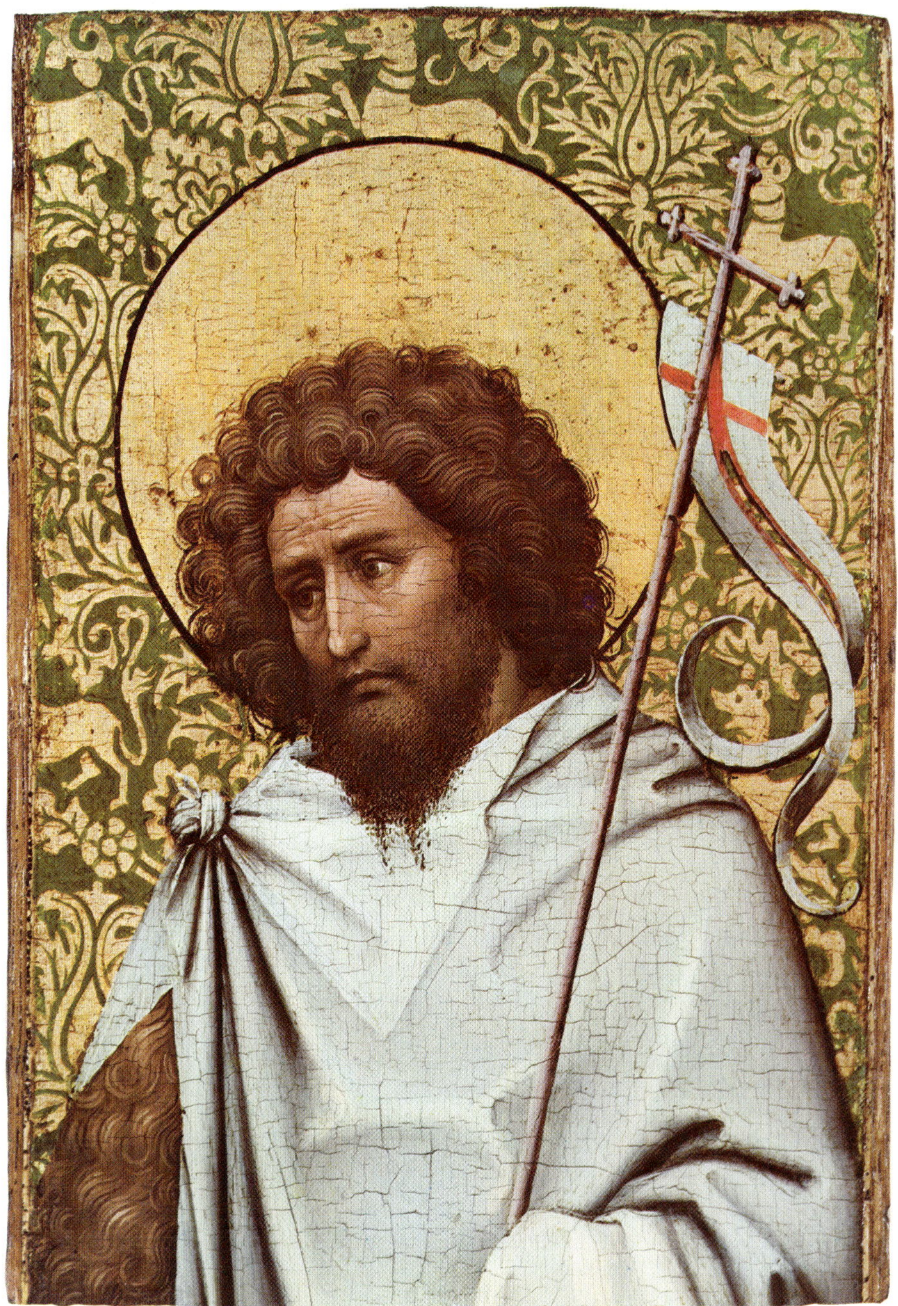

Plate xxv. *St. John the Baptist*, Robert Campin (Master of Flémalle) (Painting 52).

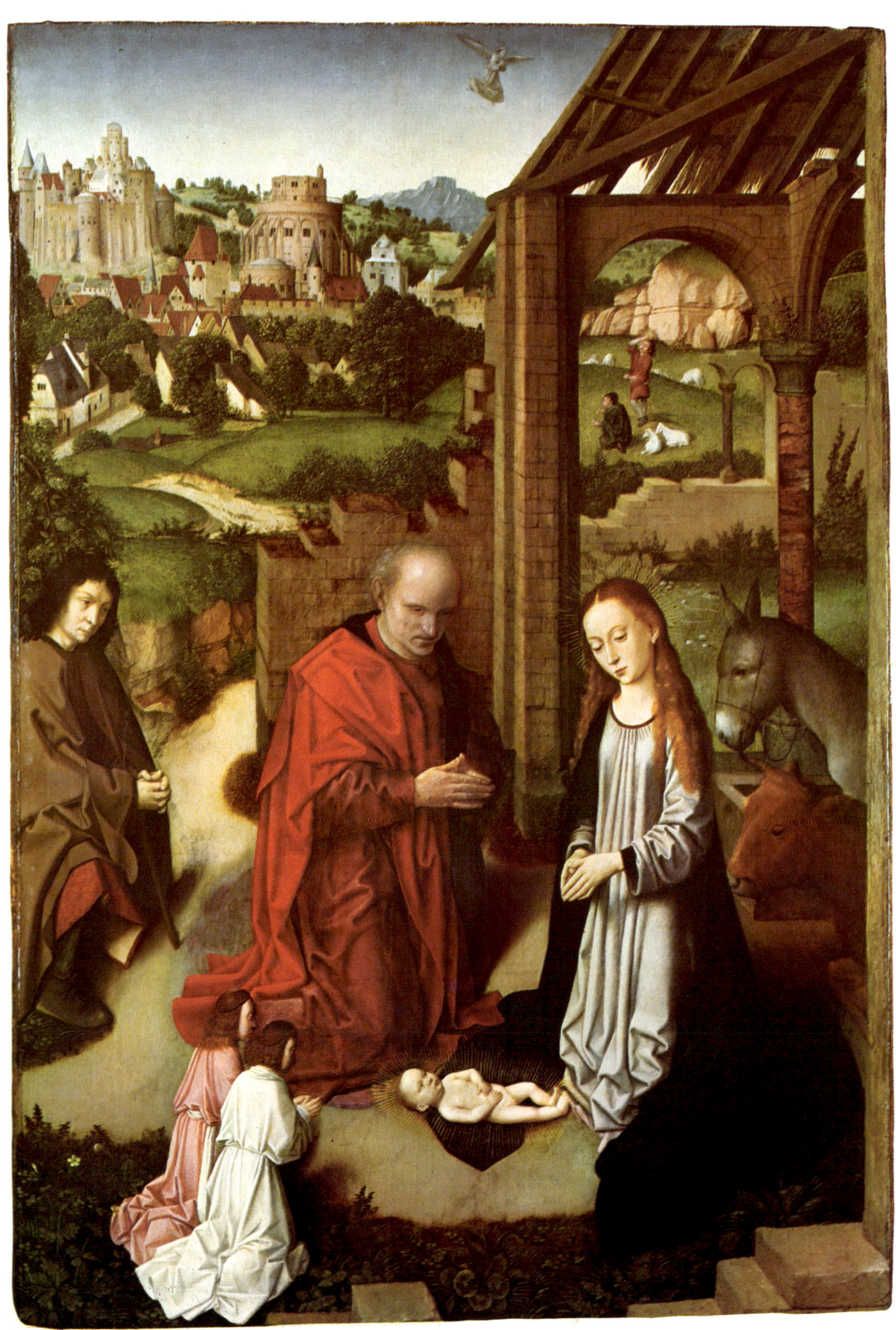

Plate XXVI. *The Nativity*, Gerard David (Painting 53).

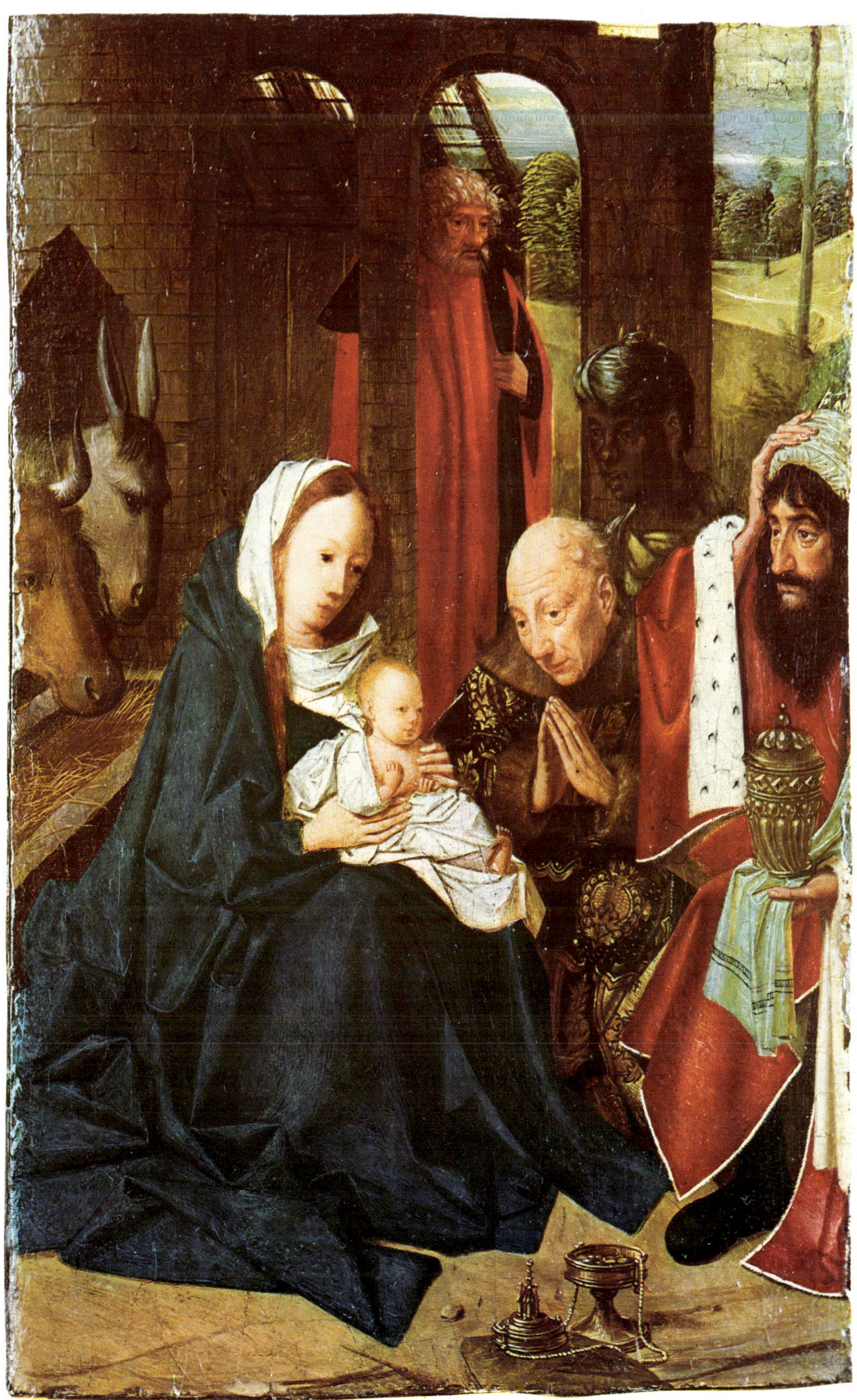

Plate XXVII. *The Adoration of the Magi*, Geertgen tot Sint Jans (Painting 54).

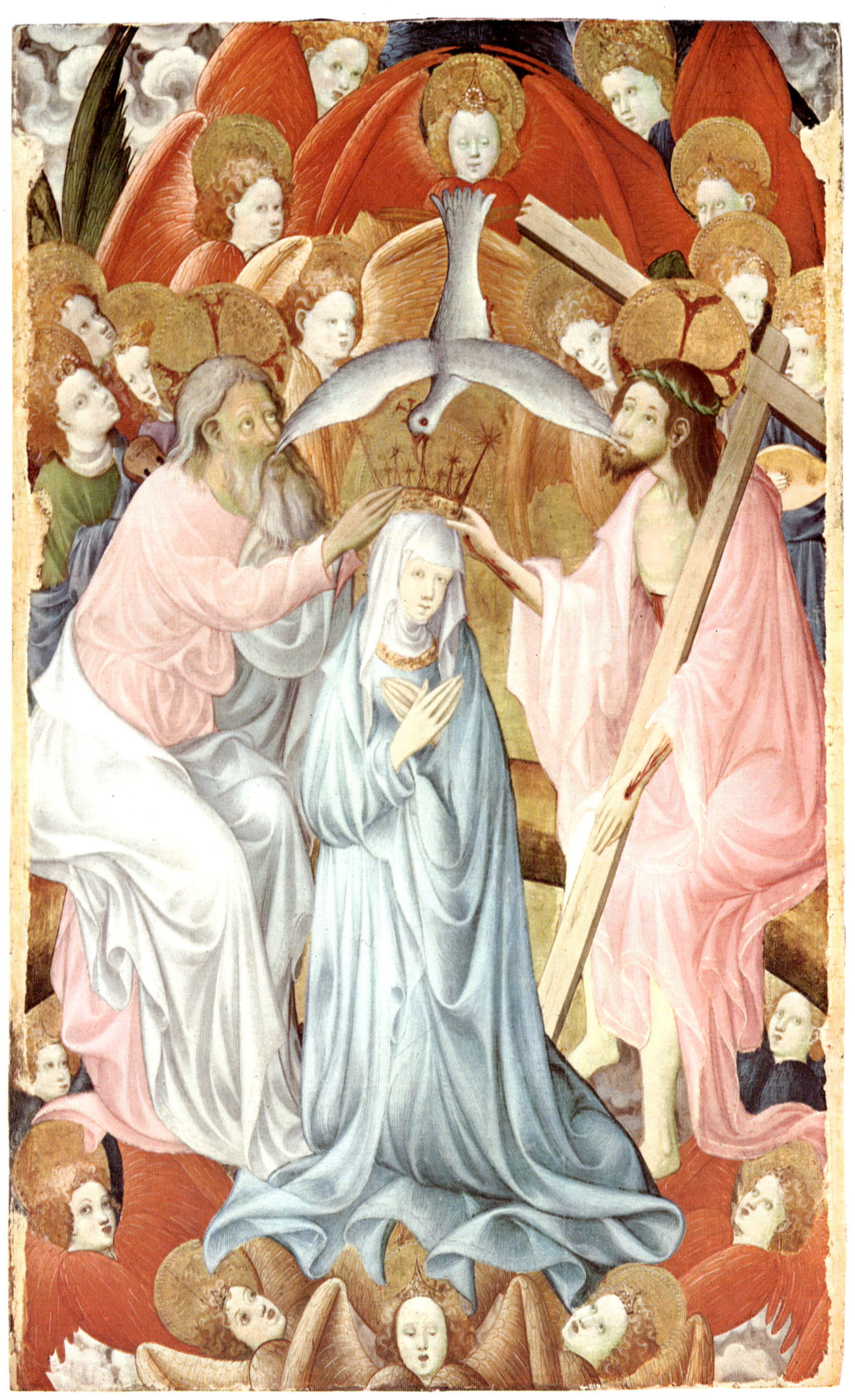

Plate XXVIII. *The Coronation of the Virgin*, The Rubielos Master (Painting 60).

ANONYMOUS MASTER, Spain(?), ca. 1420

61 *A Bishop Saint with Donor*   27.197

Panel (fir), 178 × 117·2 cm (70 × 46⅛ inches).
Painted surface: 171·5 × 107 cm (67½ × 42⅛ inches).
COLLECTIONS: M. G. de Chastenet, Toulouse, 1858;
(Wildenstein & Co., Paris); (Durlacher Bros., New York).
Gift of the Friends of The Cleveland Museum of Art,
1927.

The face of the Saint has suffered losses and "soft" retouching; it was originally more crisply handled. The
same is true of the donor (Fig. 61 *a*). There are many
other restored areas.

Contrary to Sarthou (1927), the provenance of the
panel from the east coast of Spain cannot be proved,
and it was in fact in Toulouse by 1858; but his and Post's
attribution to a Spanish rather than a French painter
must be very seriously considered (so also Sterling,
1941). Post (1930) attributed it to the School of Valencia
and later (1935) proposed the name of Lorenzo Zaragoza
(who, however, is last heard of in 1402). There is a distinct relationship, particularly in color, to Valencian
works, including those of the Rubielos or Burgo de
Osma Master (see Painting 60); a similar whimsical (and
un-French) throne occurs in this master's Louvre *Virgin
and Child* (Fig. 60 *a*). For other examples with heavy
embossing and other Spanish features see Post (1930).
The original shape of the face of the bishop (see the reproduction in Sarthou, 1927) fits a Spanish provenance.
The saint does not seem to represent St. Louis of Toulouse; the figure lacks the fleur-de-lis on the cope and
the Franciscan habit under the vestment (Post, 1930).
The clasp shows an angel swinging a censer. The fact
that the type of the picture is akin to that of the St.
Nicholas panel in the Nikolaikapelle, Soest, attributed
to Conrad von Soest (Fritz, 1950; Pieper, 1964) brings
up the question whether St. Nicholas could have been
represented here as well. However, unless the face of the
saint is even more drastically restored than is now apparent, his youth speaks against identification. In any case,
the painter may well have been inspired by Simone
Martini's *Enthroned St. Louis* in Naples, Museo Nazionale.   W.S.

EXHIBITIONS: Toulouse, Musée des Augustins, 1858: Exposition
d'antiquités, d'objets d'art et de peinture ancienne, cat. no. 9;
CMA (1936), cat. no. 127, illus. pl. XLI; CMA (1963), cat. no. 20,
illus. as Southern France, Toulouse(?), ca. 1425.

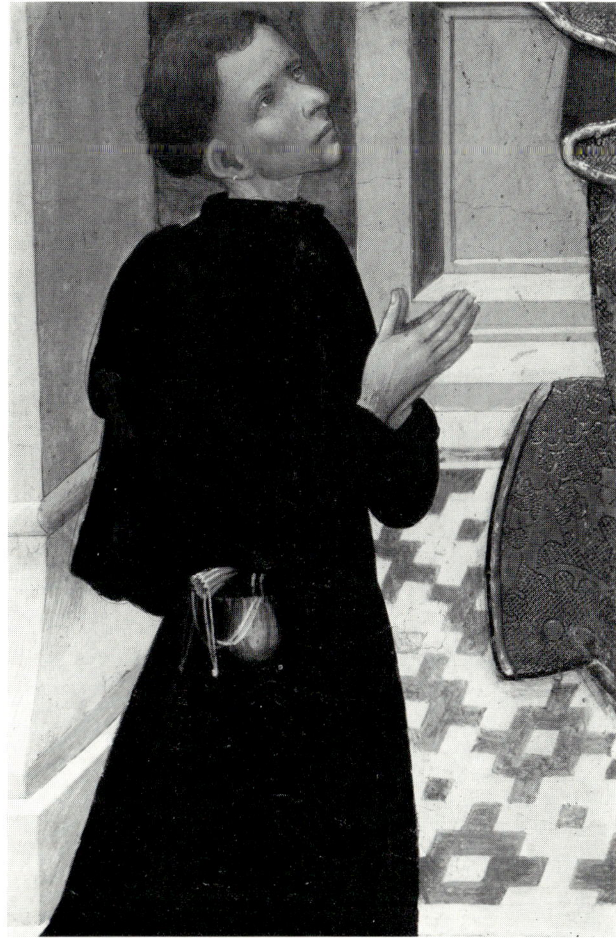

Figure 61 *a*. Detail.

LITERATURE: Carlos Sarthou y Carreras, "Els tresors de l'art
retrospectiu en els estats de l'antiga corona d'Aragó," *Butlletí
excursionista de Catalunya*, XXXVII (1927), 49, pl. X; William M.
Milliken, "A Sainted Bishop," CMA *Bulletin*, XV (1928), 79–82,
illus. p. 77; Chandler R. Post, *A History of Spanish Painting*, III
(Cambridge, Mass., 1930), 53, 54, fig. 267; IV (1933), 590; VI
(1935), 579; Hans Tietze, *Meisterwerke europäischer Malerei in
Amerika* (Vienna, 1935), p. 243 (Southern French); Germain Bazin,
La peinture française des origines au XVI siècle (Paris, 1937), pl. 28
(Southern French, ca. 1410); Charles Sterling, *La peinture française:
Les peintres du moyen âge* (Paris, 1941), Rép. B, p. 16, no. 22
(Spanish); Ring (1949), p. 198, no. 56 (attributed to the School of
Southern France, about 1410–1420); Rolf Fritz, *Conrad von Soest
und sein Kreis* (exh. cat.; Dortmund, Schloss Cappenberg, Museum
für Kunst und Kulturgeschichte, 1950), no. 35; Juan Antonio
Gaya Nuño, *La pintura española fuera de España* (Madrid, 1958),
p. 91, no. 54 (School of Valencia); *Handbook* (1958), no. 396;
Paul Pieper, *Westfälische Malerei des 14. Jahrhunderts*, (exh. cat.;
Münster, Landesmuseum, 1964), p. 86; Robert Mesuret, "Les
primitifs du Languedoc," *Gaz. des B.-A.*, LXV (1965), 2, 11, no. 31
(Languedoc); *Handbook* (1966), p. 63.

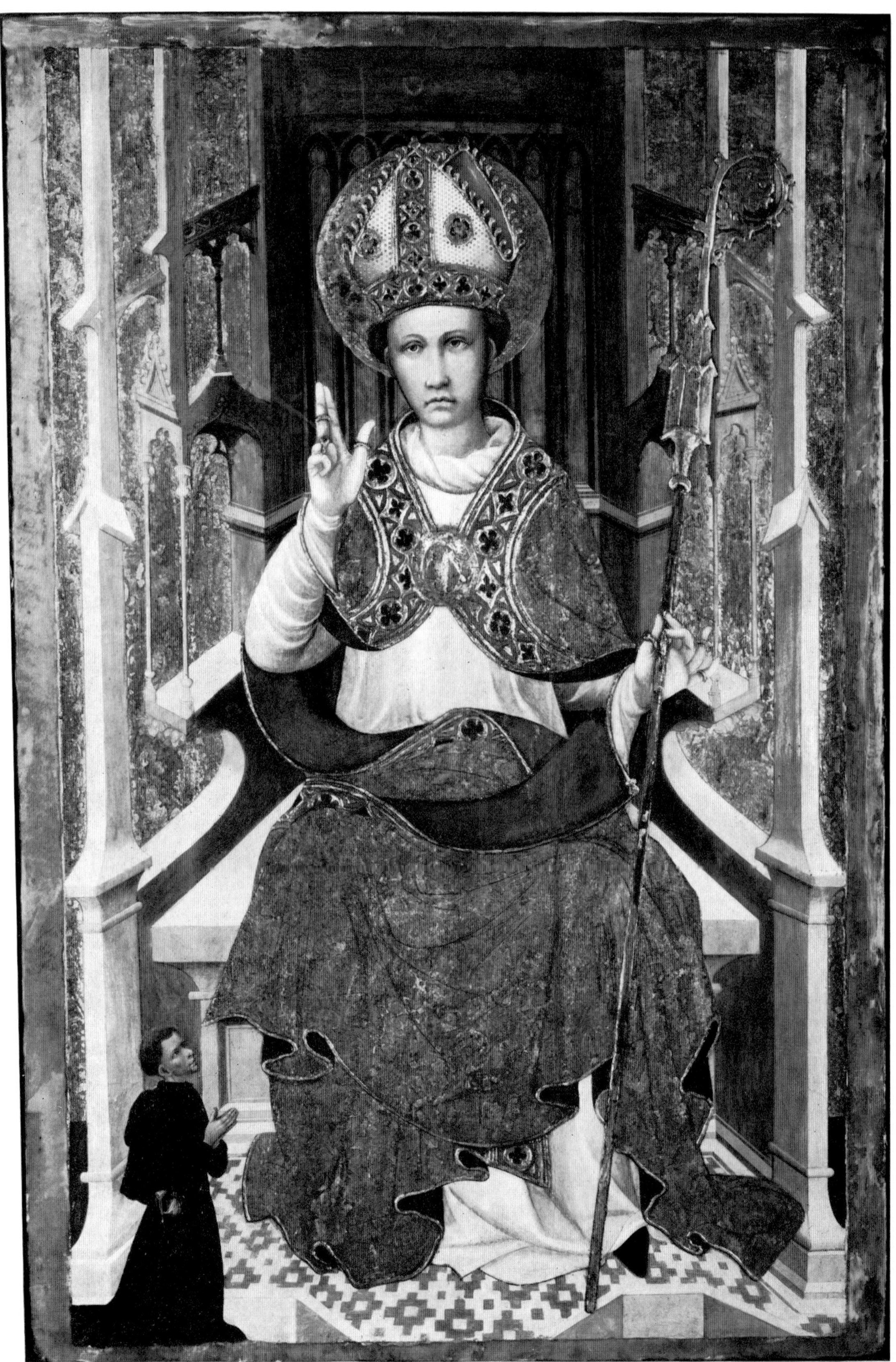

Figure 61.

APPENDICES AND INDEX

Appendix I. Colorplates

Appendix II: Cleveland Paintings, Alphabetically by Artist

Photograph Credits